Quality Engineering Series

Volume 6

TAGUCHI METHODS™: CASE STUDIES FROM THE U.S. AND EUROPE

Taguchi Methods™ *Case Studies from the U.S. and Europe* is part of a seven-volume Quality Engineering Series that the American Supplier Institute (ASI), Inc., Dearborn, Michigan, is publishing in conjunction with the Japanese Standards Association (JSA), Tokyo, Japan. ASI is publishing the English editions of the series. JSA is publishing the Japanese editions, including a translation of *Taguchi Methods Case Studies from the U.S. and Europe*. The other volumes in the series are:

Volume 1:
Taguchi Methods: Research and Development

Volume 2:
Taguchi Methods: On-Line Production

Volume 3:
Taguchi Methods: Signal-to-Noise Ratio for Quality Evaluation

Volume 4:
Taguchi Methods: Design of Experiments

Volume 5:
Taguchi Methods: Case Studies from Japan

Volume 7:
Taguchi Methods: Case Studies in Measurement from Japan

Quality Engineering Series

Volume 6

T A G U C H I   M E T H O D S

Case Studies from the U.S. and Europe

Dr. Genichi Taguchi
Publication Committee Chairman

Yuin Wu
Principal Editor

Japanese Standards Association

ASI Press

© 1989 by the American Supplier Institute, Inc. All rights reserved.

Published by the ASI Press, an ASI company, in conjunction with the Japanese Standards Association, Tokyo, Japan. Printed in the United States of America.

This publication may not be reproduced, stored in a retrieval system, or transmitted in whole or part, in any form or by any means, electronic, mechanical, photocopying, recording, or otherwise, without the written permission of the American Supplier Institute, Inc., P.O. Box 567, Dearborn, Michigan 48121-0567.

Library of Congress Cataloging-in-Publication Data

Quality engineering series / Genichi Taguchi, publication committee
   chairman; Yuin Wu, principal editor.
          p. cm.
   Includes bibliographical references.
   Contents: -- v. 6. Taguchi methods case studies from the U.S. and Europe.
     ISBN 0-941243-09-5 (v. 6)
     ISBN 0-941243-11-7 (set)
     1.   Taguchi methods (Quality control)   I. Taguchi, Gen 'ichi, 1924-
. II. Wu, Yuin.
TS156.Q3627 1989
658.5'62--dc20   89-17614
                                                                              CIP

To

JOHN P. KENNEDY
Founder and first Director of the ASI Press

A good friend of Dr. Taguchi
and
a dedicated advocate of his methods

and

EIZABURO NISHIBORI
Advisor, Japanese Standards Association

A great leader in quality control,
an adventurer,
and
long-time mentor to Dr. Taguchi

CONTENTS

ABOUT THE SERIES xi

QUALITY ENGINEERING SERIES PUBLICATION COMMITTEE xiii

PREFACE xv

INTRODUCTION 1

PART 1: MECHANICAL—PROCESS

1. PARAMETER DESIGN FOR A HEAT-STAKING PROCESS:
   ADHESION OF RUBBER GASKET/BODY ASSEMBLY 13
   Diane M. Byrne and Ronald L. Dow
   Ann Arbor Assembly Corp.

2. SHEET-MOLDED COMPOUND PROCESS IMPROVEMENT 31
   P.I. Hsieh and D.E. Goldwin
   Chrysler Motors Engineering

3. INSTRUMENT PANEL PROCESS DEVELOPMENT 41
   Coloman G. Adam
   Davidson Instrument Panel—Textron

4. THERMOPLASTIC EXTRUSION PROCESS IMPROVEMENT:
   AN APPLICATION OF DYNAMIC CHARACTERISTICS 57
   Joseph F. Dick
   Flex Technologies, Inc.

5. FACTORS AFFECTING SOLVENT-BONDED CONNECTOR DURABILITY:
   OPTIMIZATION OF THE STRENGTH OF AN EMISSION CONTROL
   HARNESS ASSEMBLY 73
   Jim Quinlan
   Flex Technologies, Inc.

6. OPTIMIZATION OF THE STRENGTH OF DIESEL INJECTION 91
   Steve Crisp
   Lucas Girling Ltd.

7. CRUISE CONTROL VACUUM VALVE IMPROVEMENT STUDY 107
   Engineering Staff
   Malco Montgomeryville

8. Optimization of a Hot-Stamping Process 127
   Steve Sykes and William Ross
   Kenkor Division, North American Reiss

9. Automatic Wave Soldering of Electronic Printed
   Circuit Assemblies 135
   Robert A. Miller
   Body and Assembly, Ford Motor Co.
   Charles A. Phaneuf, and Joseph F. Rypl
   Electrical Division, Wickes Manufacturing Co.

Part 2: Mechanical—Product

10. Experiment to Optimize the Design Parameters of an
    Elastomeric Connector and Tubing Assembly 151
    Engineering Staff
    Baylock Manufacturing Corp.

11. An Experiment to Reduce Post-Extrusion
    Shrinkage of a Speedometer Cable Casing 161
    Jim Quinlan and Engineering Staff
    Flex Technologies, Inc.

12. Robust Design of a Disk-Brake System: An Analytical
    Simulation Study Using Taguchi Methods 175
    Edward Lumsdaine and John C. Cherng
    University of Michigan—Dearborn, School of Engineering

Part 3: Electrical—Process

13. Computer Response-Time Optimization Using Orthogonal
    Array Experiments 203
    T.W. Pao, M.S. Phadke, and C.S. Sherrerd
    AT&T Bell Laboratories

14. Process Optimization and Gold Usage Reduction Utilizing
    Taguchi Methods 219
    Michael G. White
    Military/Aerospace Division, ITT Cannon

15. Photo-Receptor Optimization via Taguchi Methods 235
    Dr. H. Heil, Dr. B. Hofmann, N. Schmidt, and J. Segain
    ITT Passive Components

16. STRIP-FORCE EXPERIMENT USING TAGUCHI METHODS 247
    D. Bernstein and M. Koulopoulos
    Automotive Division, ITT Suprenant

17. OPTIMIZATION OF BOND STRENGTH AND CONTACT
    USING TAGUCHI METHODS 259
    Dr. Pirrung
    ITT SWF

18. PROCESS DEVELOPMENT OF A PARALLEL GAP BONDER 267
    Eric Schild and Tim Pishko
    Texas Instruments, Inc.

PART 4: ELECTRICAL—PRODUCT

19. IMPROVEMENT OF THE DESIGN OF A POWER SUPPLY CIRCUIT 283
    Joe Conticchio
    ITT Avionics

20. AN EXPERIMENT TO MINIMIZE VARIATION IN POT CORE
    TRANSFORMER PROCESSING 299
    Gerard Pfaff
    ITT Electron Technology

21. SABRE (EMD) DISK-DRIVE THERMAL PERFORMANCE IMPROVEMENT 311
    Neal F. Gunderson
    Magnetic Peripherals, Inc.

22. COLD-START NOISE REDUCTION FOR HYDRAULIC ROLLER TAPPETS 335
    Joseph Vihtelic and Robert Roos
    Hy-Lift Division, SPX Corp.

APPENDIX: KEY DATES 351
GLOSSARY A: KEY TERMS 353
GLOSSARY B: KEY SYMBOLS 360
INDEX 361

ABOUT THE SERIES ...

Taguchi Methods, as Dr. Genichi Taguchi's Quality Engineering methodology is called in the United States, is an engineering approach to quality control that is currently generating much attention in North American and European countries. Taguchi Methods has a long history in Japan, where related research has been accumulated. In order to systematically present the various aspects of Taguchi Methods, the American Supplier Institute (ASI), Dearborn, Michigan, and the Japanese Standards Association (JSA), Tokyo, Japan, the primary promoters of Taguchi Methods in the United States and Japan, respectively, are collaborating on the publication of a comprehensive, seven-volume "Quality Engineering Series."

In August 1987, ASI and JSA established a Quality Engineering Series Publication Committee that consists of both American and Japanese quality control professionals. During the Publication Committee's discussion about what structure the series should take, it was suggested that actual application examples be published as soon as possible, because users of Taguchi Methods have requested such examples, which will help them understand and master Taguchi Methods. Hence, four volumes of the seven-volume "Quality Engineering Series" summarize the basic methods and approaches of Taguchi Methods, and the remaining three volumes contain application examples from several different fields. The series itself is a global endeavor, in that both English and Japanese editions are being prepared and published.

Although the series title, "Quality Engineering Series," is not necessarily a new one, the title was selected so as to separate the subject matter from traditional quality control and design techniques and to emphasize that this is *quality design engineering*, which offers a new and efficient engineering technology of quality design for improved productivity.

We sincerely hope that the books in this series will help enhance readers' understanding of Taguchi Methods and promote the application of the methodology. Your questions and comments will be greatly appreciated.

QUALITY ENGINEERING SERIES
PUBLICATION COMMITTEE

Quality Engineering Series Publication Committee

Committee Chairman
Dr. Genichi Taguchi
Senior Technical Consultant, Japanese Standards Association

Executive Secretary
Hiroshi Yano
Director, Mechanical Metrology Department
National Research Laboratory of Metrology
Ministry of International Trade and Industry

Committee Members
Masanobu Kawamura
Executive Director, Japanese Standards Association

John P. Kennedy
Publisher Emeritus, American Supplier Institute, Inc.

Shozo Konishi
Semiconductor Division
Hitachi Co., Ltd.

Shin Taguchi
Vice President, American Supplier Institute, Inc.

Yuin Wu
Vice Chairman, American Supplier Institute, Inc.

Shogo Yamamoto
Executive Director, TQC Promotion Center
Hamanako Denso Co., Ltd.

Yoshiko Yokoyama
Technical Consultant, Japanese Standards Association

MASATAKA YOSHIZAWA
Section Manager, New Xerox Movement Office
Fuji-Xerox Co., Ltd.

Editorial Advisors

EDMUND M. CARPENTER
President, ITT Corp.

HIROSHI HAMADA
President, Ricoh Co., Ltd.

WAYLAND R. HICKS
President, Xerox Business Products and Systems
Executive Vice President, Xerox Corp.

HAJIME KARATSU
Professor, Tokai University

KOHJI KOBAYASHI
Chairman Emeritus, NEC Corporation

YOHTARO KOBAYASHI
President, Fuji-Xerox Co., Ltd.

EIZABURO NISHIBORI
Advisor, Japanese Standards Association

NORIO OHGA
President, Sony Corporation

KUNIO OHWADA
President, Nachi Fujikoshi Corporation

AKIO TANII
President, Matsushita Electric Industrial Co., Ltd.

Preface

Western methods of design of experiments were adapted in Japan to meet the needs of corporate technical research. This began near the end of World War II with the use of Latin Squares in experiments to optimize the yield of penicillin and continued with the work of Dr. Genichi Taguchi. Taguchi Methods™ represent the culmination of this development.

Taguchi Methods are relatively new to the West. They were introduced in the United States in the early 1980s. A major vehicle for their dissemination has been the annual Taguchi Methods Symposium, sponsored by the American Supplier Institute since 1984. Today they are employed by a number of companies in North America, the United Kingdom, and continental Europe, as well as some Asian countries, and the ranks are growing.

Taguchi Methods are a way of thinking and a method for efficiently designing and utilizing small-scale experiments in the laboratory to find reliable designs for large-scale production and the marketplace. They differ significantly from traditional Western design of experiments in objectives, philosophy, and methodology.

A key feature of the implementation of these methods in the West has been a confusion with the objectives and methods of classical design of experiments. Many Western researchers believed that the use of an orthogonal array constitutes a Taguchi experiment. Orthogonal arrays were often used under the name of fractional factorials in classically designed experiments. Orthogonal arrays are used in traditional DOE and in Taguchi experiments, but their role and their application is very different.

Perhaps the greatest difference between the Taguchi approach and traditional DOE is that in a Taguchi experiment, orthogonal arrays are used to assure the reproducibility of parameter effects downstream. By selecting quality characteristics that have additivity, interactive effects can be avoided. Orthogonal arrays are used to prove that interactions are insignificant.

Since the objectives of the two approaches are different, the steps in designing and analyzing an experiment are different (i.e., selection of orthogonal arrays, assignment of factors, data analysis). Another major difference is that in a Taguchi study, various types of Signal-to-Noise Ratios are used as an index of quality. A part of Dr. Taguchi's unique and effective philosophy is that increasing the signal is as important as reducing variability. Nobody has provided industrial research with a comparably important idea.

Not all studies reflect this confusion, and understanding is growing. The case studies in this volume were selected from the past six Taguchi symposia (1984–1988). They represent some of the applications of Taguchi methodology in the West during the decade of the 80s. Unfortunately, for proprietary reasons, we were forced to exclude many, very good case studies.

The case studies in this volume are intended to provide practitioners with examples of applications and points of departure for future experimental efforts. The major methodological points of each case study are highlighted in a question and answer discussion of the study prepared by Shin Taguchi and myself.

The diffusion of Taguchi Methods in the West will continue. At the time of the first symposium, in 1984, an estimated 150 Western engineers were actively involved in their use. By 1990, several thousand will have been trained in these methods.

Most of the studies in North America and Europe have, so far, dealt with the improvement of manufacturing processes. While such applications are extremely useful, they may not represent the most productive application of the methodology for long term corporate technical development.

Dr. Taguchi feels that the best place to apply such studies is in research and development, at the product design stage. Design optimization at this stage is maximally cost effective. In addition, the selection of good quality characteristics for avoiding interactions and the efficient reduction of variability at this stage serves as the basis for the development of new corporate technology and technical capability.

Robust design using dynamic characteristics and simulation studies are rapidly becoming the most efficient means for developing new products and processes. Dynamic characteristics more closely reflect engineering intent and simulation can provide for a more thorough and efficient study.

The majority of studies in the West have used non-dynamic characteristics. While such studies will continue to be important, I would like to see an increase in research using simulation and dynamic characteristics at the product design stage, as well as applications in the evaluation and improvement of measurement systems. These will represent the wave of the future in the improvement of product and process quality.

YUIN WU

Introduction

*Shin Taguchi,
American Supplier Institute, Inc.*

The case studies in this volume represent some of the many applications of Taguchi Methods in the West during the 1980s. Included are studies from companies in the United States, the United Kingdom and West Germany. They are studies in parameter design, the most important stage of Dr. Taguchi's system for quality improvement.

Parameter design is the stage of product design at which improvement in quality and reduction in cost can be made most effectively. The Japanese spend 40% of their development efforts at this stage. In the early 1980s, it was estimated that U.S. engineers spent only 2% of design activity on parameter design. As these case studies show, this has already begun to change.

Taguchi has addressed the need for methods of design that can bring products to production relatively defect-free. In the West, his system has initiated a reexamination of the basis for evaluating and improving quality, and brought fresh insight into the nature of the design and production process.

Parameter design is but one part of Taguchi's overall system for measuring, improving and maintaining quality. In reviewing the studies in this volume the reader should be aware of the basis and the scope of the Taguchi approach. The following is a brief overview of Taguchi's system of Quality Engineering with respect to the three main issues regarding product quality.

Shin Taguchi is Vice President of Product Development of the American Supplier Institute, Inc., Dearborn, Michigan.

Three Issues Regarding Quality

Dr. Genichi Taguchi's approach to product and process design has created renewed interest in industrial experimentation. It has solved many of the problems of applying classical experimentation to industrial situations by redefining the assumptions about and methods for dealing with quality, cost, and the objectives of design and experimentation. Called Quality Engineering, the Taguchi approach emphasizes the efficient application of engineering knowledge, rather than advanced statistical techniques.

Taguchi Methods provide a complete system for improving and maintaining product and process quality, at the lowest cost, in the shortest development time. They redefine and address the three fundamental issues regarding product quality:
1. How to evaluate quality
2. How to efficiently improve quality and cost
3. How to cost-effectively monitor and maintain quality.

1. How to Evaluate Quality

A company is in business to make a profit. Its products must be competitive with those of other companies to maintain the financial health of the company. A simple equation for determining profit can be given by:

$$\text{Profit} = \text{Sales} - \text{Cost}$$

Profits are increased by increasing sales while decreasing costs. Quality improvement is the most effective way of achieving a simultaneous sales increase and cost reduction. This may seem paradoxical. Our first reaction is that an increase in quality means an automatic cost increase.

Cost and quality are linked in the way in which customers evaluate products. The way in which we evaluate quality must take this relationship into account and allow us to continuously improve product quality. A company improves quality in order to remain competitive. We must be able to evaluate quality in a way that reflects corporate objectives.

Most Western companies use the following types of measures as indicators of product quality: Number of defects, % defective, number of failures, probability of failure, scrap/rework cost, process capability indices, warranty and service information, competitive analyses, etc. However, these indicators are artifacts that detect poor quality after the fact. These measures are cost related and tell us that action is needed, but from a technical standpoint, they are poor indices for assessing and

INTRODUCTION

improving quality. A useful evaluator of quality must satisfy the following criteria:

- **It can be used in upstream quality improvement.**

  Many of the usual measures of quality rely on post-production figures, available only after the product has been designed and manufactured. By that time it is too late to improve quality. We must be able to evaluate quality in upstream stages—in research and development, product and process design and material selection.

- **It must appropriately express customer and engineering objectives.**

  Our measure of quality must truly express the quality of the product/process in terms of engineering intent and customer response to product function.

- **It must express the relationship between cost and quality.**

  It must be able to evaluate quality in terms of ideal product function and include the effect of costs that arise because products fail to function as expected in the hands of the customer. These costs affect market share and long term profit.

Taguchi has proposed two evaluators of quality that effectively meet these criteria. These are the *Quality Loss Function* and the *Signal-to-Noise Ratio*.

Every product, process or service has a specific function and an ideal performance target. This represents the engineering intent of the product to which customers will respond. Quality Engineering focuses on reducing variability around the ideal function. The smaller the variability, the higher the quality.

> Both the Loss Function and the Signal-to-Noise
> Ratio are measures of this variability.

The Quality Loss Function (QLF) converts this variability into monetary terms that represent an estimate of the costs a customer incurs when a product fails to function as intended. These costs can include scrap/rework costs, the cost of replacing a failed product, time and money spent for repair, etc. These are factors that affect market share. Taguchi calls these costs Loss (i.e., Loss to Society). The QLF provides a quantitative estimate of this Loss.

The QLF thus evaluates quality in terms of ideal product function and customer response. As we will see, it can be used in the earliest stages of product planning and development, as well as in production. Because it evaluates quality in monetary terms, it is a tool for engineering management planning i.e., for finding the balance between cost and quality that can increase profit. Improving quality cost effectively reduces Loss. In management terms: *The objective of Quality Improvement is to reduce the loss.*

The Signal-to-Noise (S/N) Ratio also measures variability around target performance. It is a measure of the stability or reliability of performance in the face of those uncontrollable factors that a product will encounter on the factory floor and when used by the customer. The S/N gives the design engineer a reliable upstream estimate of how a product will function at downstream stages. It evaluates quality in terms of decibels (dB) and serves as an ideal characteristic for measuring quality improvement in engineering terms. In engineering terms: *The objective of Quality Improvement is to increase the S/N.*

The QLF and the S/N are related measures. They are both measures of variability around the target value. The S/N can easily be converted into the QLF and thus quality improvement can be evaluated in monetary terms. Engineering objectives can be expressed in terms that are relevant to management, and this facilitates communication and the achievement of company objectives.

2. How to Efficiently Improve Quality and Cost (Off-Line Quality Control)

Quality Engineering uses designed experiments to improve product and process quality. The objectives of experimentation in Quality Engineering are significantly different from those of traditional Design of Experiments.

Traditional experimentation developed in the context of scientific research—to meet the objectives of the scientist. The scientist seeks to discover and describe natural law. In general, he is not constrained by the realities of cost and time. Precision and completeness of explanation are more important than cost and delivery time. His is a more open ended activity.

The objective of the corporate engineer is to achieve ideal product function—to reduce variability around a target value at the lowest cost, in the shortest development time. In learning to do this he accumulates technical know-how for his company. He needs methods that allow him to efficiently acquire technical information for improving quality while reducing cost. The engineer's activity is constrained by cost, time and resources.

There are many ways in which one can get a product to function ideally, some more expensive and time consuming than others. Good

Introduction

engineering achieves quality cost effectively, delivering the product to market before the competition. The job of the engineer is to specify product/process nominal values, their tolerances, grades of materials, components, etc., in such a way that cost and quality can be optimized. And he must do this as quickly and efficiently as possible. *The engineer must design products that reduce loss.*

Since the objectives of the two approaches to research are different, the techniques and steps in designing and analyzing an experiment are different. While Taguchi Methods uses many of the methods of traditional Design of Experiments, the application of these techniques and the philosophy that underlies them were developed to be used by engineers to fit the realities of industrial design and production.

Three Stages in Product/Process Development

Taguchi Methods for Quality Engineering are a system for achieving corporate engineering objectives, i.e., for reducing loss and improving profit. Off-line (design stage) quality improvement includes the following stages:

- Stage 1 - System Design
- Stage 2 - Parameter Design
- Stage 3 - Tolerance Design

System Design is the conceptual design stage in which scientific and engineering expertise is applied to develop new and original technologies. New systems that have an intended function under normal operating conditions are developed. The original conceptual design of the Video Cassette Recorder (VCR) was developed in the United States.

Quality Engineering techniques do not focus on this stage. Since it is not possible to study all potential systems, Taguchi suggests that engineers compare one to three systems by applying Parameter and Tolerance Design to select the optimal system. This can be repeated through a number of steps in the development of a product.

Parameter Design is the stage at which a system is optimized (quality improved at least cost). Numerous variables can affect system function. They need to be categorized from an engineering point of view. Some will be controllable (Control Factors). The engineer is free to set the values of these variables. Others will be uncontrollable or too expensive to control (Noise Factors). These are the downstream variables that cause functional variation.

The goal of Parameter Design is not to find and remove these causes of variation (i.e., to discover cause and effect relationships), but to find that combination of control factor settings that allow the system to achieve its ideal function and remain insensitive to the effects of those variables that we cannot control. This allows us to develop designs with high performance, stability and reliability.

This stability of performance in the face of noise factors is called *robustness*. Improving robustness allows the engineer to improve quality without increasing cost. It allows him to design products that are highly reliable under a wide range of conditions, using inexpensive materials and parts.

The S/N Ratio evaluates the robustness of selected control factor levels. *The objective of experimentation in parameter design is to reduce loss by increasing robustness.*

Once variability of function is reduced, other measures for reducing cost can be implemented. This increases the ability of a company to apply technology to compete economically (corporate technological capability).

Tolerance Design is the stage at which variability can be further reduced by tightening tolerances. This requires the upgrading of the materials, parts and sub-components of the system and increases cost. Tolerance design attempts to further reduce variability by controlling noise factors. But it does this rationally. Rather than a costly upgrade of everything, it uses designed experiments and analysis of variance to find the impact of each factor on variability. The QLF is applied to evaluate the impact of factors with respect to cost, and a trade-off between cost and quality is found. Only those tolerances that can be economically tightened are upgraded.

The Most Important Task of the Quality Engineer

In evaluating and improving quality, the selection of quality characteristics that properly reflect the engineering function of a product or process is the most important, and perhaps the most difficult task of the quality engineer. To evaluate robustness or improve existing product performance, what should we measure to accurately express the data and allow us to efficiently reduce variability?

Characteristics such as yield, number of defects, percent defective, probability of failure, product life, categorical sensory evaluation, etc., are often used. Such characteristics do relate to economics and are needed to monitor and confirm the quality of products and processes. However, such characteristics do not directly express engineering function. They are often quite removed from the fundamental physics of product function and involve numerous extraneous interactions. Their use can compromise the efficiency and reliability of experimentation.

For the upstream evaluation and improvement of products and processes we need characteristics that accurately reflect engineering intent—those that are close to the basic energy transfer of the system and can be used to express performance, reliability and durability.

For example, a painting process may produce various types of defects such as voids or sags. Rather than counting the number of such defects, or measuring yield as an output characteristic, a better strategy would be to use paint thickness, measured in microns, as our quality characteristic. Our objective would be to both reduce the variability of the paint thickness and improve the adjustability of the thickness.

A characteristic such as paint thickness more closely represents the actual energy transfer of the painting process. It allows us to better study variability of energy transfer without as many intervening variables (i.e., interactions between control factors). The use of data such as occurrence of defects or yield for reducing variability in the system is an inefficient strategy. It is poor engineering. The selection of the best quality characteristic to express product/process function is case dependent and depends upon the engineer's knowledge of the particular field of technology.

3. How to Cost-Effectively Monitor and Maintain Quality (On-Line Quality Control)

Even after quality has been improved and costs reduced using off-line methods, sources of variability still remain at the production level. These include variability in materials and purchased components, tool wear, machine fatigue, the drifting of process parameters, measurement error, etc. To maintain the benefits of off-line improvements, these sources of process variability must be controlled.

Dr.Taguchi has developed a system of on-line quality control methods that utilize the QLF. It allows manufacturing engineers to design process control systems that minimize Loss by monitoring the balance between cost and quality.

An on-line reduction in variability comes from inspection, the measurement and adjustment of of equipment and process parameter levels, etc. These procedures have associated costs. Taguchi's on-line system takes these costs into account to determine how often a product characteristic or a process parameter should be measured and adjusted and what the optimal adjustment limits should be. This allows for economically informed decisions regarding production control measures to optimize process control systems.

This is quite different from the strategy of Shewhart control charting. Feedback and feed-forward control, for example, are very important in flexible manufacturing and the design of automated processes. Automated control systems can become expensive if not optimized.

Feedback control measures a product or process parameter every n units and adjusts the process closer to the target using an adjustment factor. It thus compensates for the effects of variation rather than trying to remove the causes of variation. The frequency of measurement and the control limits are optimized as a function of the costs of measurement, adjustment and scrap/rework, the capability of the process, and manufacturing tolerances.

How often to measure and what the control limits should be are determined by Dr. Taguchi's on-line methods. Taguchi's on-line system includes methods for product control, prediction and correction, diagnosis and adjustment and preventive maintenance.

What to measure, what to adjust, how much to adjust, how to improve adjustability and how to improve measurement are dealt with through off-line methods. By the application of off-line and on-line methods, control can be improved, monitored and maintained on the basis of an optimal balance between cost and quality.

A System for Improving Quality and Profit

The demands of today's competitive marketplace often require companies to engage in the small quantity production of many different types of products. With development and delivery time shortened, products must be relatively defect free from the start of production. The arena for the improvement and maintenance of product quality has shifted from the production department to the design department.

Dr. Taguchi has redefined the basic issues regarding cost and quality to fit the realities of industrial design and production. His system of Quality Engineering provides relevant indices for evaluating and improving quality, off-line methods for the efficient design of low-cost, robust products, and cost-driven, on-line methods for maintaining improved quality in production. It is an overall system for improving quality and profit and providing key insights into the nature of the design and production process.

TAGUCHI HAS REDEFINED THE FUNDAMENTAL ISSUES REGARDING QUALITY

1. How to evaluate quality
   - Quality Loss Function
   - Signal-to-Noise Ratio
2. How to efficiently improve quality and cost
   (Off-Line Quality Characteristics)
   - Design of Experiments
   - Three stages in product/process development
     Stage 1–System Design
     Stage 2–Parameter Design
     Stage 3–Tolerance Design
   - Selection of Characteristics
   - Use of the Signal-to-Noise Ratio in Parameter Design
   - Use of the Loss Function in Tolerance Design
3. How to cost-effectively monitor and maintain quality
   (On-Line Quality Control)
   - Use of the Loss Function and Cost Function in On-Line Quality Control
   - Methods of On-Line Quality Control
     Feedback Control
       (On product characteristics)
       (On process parameters)
     Feed-Forward Control
     Diagnosis and Adjustment
     Preventive Maintenance
     Product Control
     Inspection

Since their introduction to the West in the early 1980s, Taguchi Methods have been employed by companies in the United States, Canada, Mexico, Great Britain, Australia and Continental Europe. Thousands of engineers have participated in the the evolution of these methods and their implementation and development will continue as companies develop their own engineering training programs.

The studies in this volume cover both product and process design for the development and improvement of mechanical and electrical products and processes. So far, most applications in the West have been to process and product improvement. Fifteen of the twenty-two included case studies deal with design for the improvement of manufacturing processes.

In the future, more companies will be applying these methods for research in product development. This is the area in which the most benefit can be derived, both in terms of profit and the development of corporate technical capability.

The majority of the case studies report on hardware experiments utilizing non-dynamic characteristics. Notable exceptions are the study by Joseph Dick of Flex Technologies, "Dynamic Extrusion Analysis," which uses a dynamic characteristic to improve the quality of a plastics extrusion process, and "Design of a Disk Brake System Using Taguchi Methods," by Edward Lumsdane and John Cherng, of the University of Michigan, Dearborn, which is an analytical computer simulation study.

Studies using dynamic characteristics and computer simulation are the most effective methods for designing robust products and processes. Dynamic characteristics are excellent indicators of engineering intent, and simulation allows us to expand the scope and increase the efficiency of a study. The emphasis on robust design using dynamic characteristics and computer simulation will greatly increase during the 1990s as the evolution of Taguchi Methods continues.

Part 1:
Mechanical —Process

1. Parameter Design for a Heat-Staking Process: Adhesion of Rubber Gasket/Body Assembly

Diane M. Byrne and Ronald L. Dow,
Ann Arbor Assembly Corp.

An experiment was conducted to find a combination of levels for the controllable factors that would produce good adhesion during the assembly of rubber gaskets to the body portion of automobile hood hinges, in the presence of a specified production. Coded attributes data was used and proved to be effective for improving the process in this case. Using the existing optimal combination as determined through the experiment, good adhesions are now achieved more consistently than in the past. An annual cost savings of $18,000 should be realized in the reduction of scrap and rework, and the total annual savings is probably in excess of $50,000, as estimated by the Quality Loss Function.

1. Introduction — The Heat Staking Process

Originally, in the attachment of rubber gaskets to the body portion of automobile hood hinges, the rubber gasket was glued to the hinge with a contact adhesive. This soon proved to be undesirable for a number of reasons: the excess glue interfered with the welding of the hinge to the vehicle; production was inefficient, and the fumes from the glue were noxious. In response to these problems, a heat-staking process was developed.

A spot-welding machine was modified to heat the body portion of the hinge. The gasket is placed onto the subassembly, which is then placed onto a fixture. The welder must generate sufficient heat in the metal and provide adequate pressure to ensure adhesion of the gasket.

Alternate means of attaching the gasket to the hinge are also under study, and the results of this study will aid in this evaluation.

From the *Fifth Symposium on Taguchi Methods*™, pp. 13–30, Copyright © 1987, American Supplier Institute, Inc., Dearborn, Michigan.

2. OBJECTIVE OF THE EXPERIMENT

The objective of the experiment is to optimize the heat-staking process so that good adhesion of the gasket to the hinge can be consistently achieved. The adhesion is considered good when both sides of the gasket are securely attached to the hinge and no melting of the gasket occurs (see Figure 1).

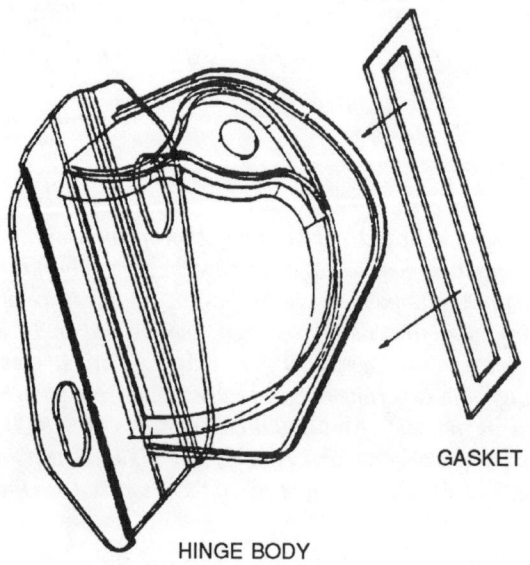

Figure 1. Gasket and Body Portion of Hood Hinge

3. SELECTION OF A QUALITY CHARACTERISTIC FOR ADHESION

Much thought was given to the selection of the quality characteristic to be evaluated and optimized. Measuring pull-off force was ruled out since a sensitive measuring device needed for this application was not readily available in the plant; and, it was thought that pull-off force would not adequately reflect the goodness of the adhesion with the additional constraints of 1) adhering to both sides and 2) no melting.

It became clear that the only obtainable measure of the adhesion would be some type of classified attributes data. The desired condition is when both sides of the gasket are adhered to the hinge without melting. Defects, however, can occur in both directions of this nominal condition. No adhesion occurs when too little energy is present, while melting (the other extreme) occurs when too much energy is present.

One approach applied was to classify the defects into two categories and analyze them separately. The number of insufficient adhesions was counted and the goal was to bring that number to zero. Then the number of melting instances was counted and, again, the target was zero. The standard smaller-the-better Signal-to-Noise (S/N) Ratio was used in each analysis.

The analysis just described did not work well in this case, however, since the total number of a particular type defect was zero for many of the test conditions (especially for the insufficient adhesion defect).

It was finally decided to use the five classifications given in Table 1, where the classes are ordered to reflect the energy of the process. The intent was to perform 1) an accumulation analysis to highlight significant factors and 2) some additional analysis, using a coding scheme, to aid in the selection of factor levels.

The coding scheme used for the second analysis is also given in Table 1. An assembly that was judged to have good adhesion (adhesion on both sides with no melting) was given a zero. This is the target. Assemblies judged to have insufficient adhesion were given a –2 or –8 (too little energy) and those judged to be over-adhered or melted (too much energy) were given a 2 or 8 as described in the table. The particular numerical assignment for the classifications, although somewhat arbitrary, is an attempt to represent a cost relationship among the classifications, and is also thought to reflect the energy of the process. Using this coding scheme, the intent was then to achieve a target of zero with minimum variation.

Table 1. Classifications/Coding Scheme

ENERGY		
	8	Gasket melted
	2	Gasket slightly melted
	0	TARGET: Adhesion both sides and no melting
	–2	Adhesion one side only
	–8	No Adhesion

4. Control and Noise Factors

A brainstorming session revealed that six controllable factors and three noise factors were thought to affect adhesion. The factors and levels are given in Table 2.

5. Experimental Layout

The controllable factors were assigned to the first six columns of the L_{18} orthogonal array and the noise factors were placed in an L_4 outer array. Thus, the experiment required a total of 18 x 4 = 72 test combinations. At each combination, eight assemblies were produced and evaluated. The entire experiment, then, involved 575 assemblies. The experimental layout can be seen in Table 3, and the data for test condition #8 (as an example) is given in Table 4.

Table 2. Factors

Controllable Factors	Levels		
A. Tip Surface	I	II	
B. % Heat	60	75	90
C. Weld Time (cycles)	30	45	60
D. Squeeze Time (cycles)	60	90	120
E. Off Time (cycles)	10	30	50
F. Hold Time (cycles)	30	45	60
Noise Factors	**Levels**		
G. Frequency of spraying fixture with silicone	Just Sprayed	20 Min.	
H. Cleanliness of parts	Clean	Dirty	
I. Lot	I	II	

Table 3. Experimental Layout

							L_4	G	H	I
								1	1	1
								1	2	2
								2	1	2
								2	2	1
L_{18}	A	B	C	D	E	F				
1	1	1	1	1	1	1
2	1	1	2	2	2	2
3	1	1	3	3	3	3
4	1	2	1	1	2	2
5	1	2	2	2	3	3
6	1	2	3	3	1	1
7	1	3	1	2	1	3
8	1	3	2	3	2	1
9	1	3	3	1	3	2
10	2	1	1	3	3	2
11	2	1	2	1	1	3
12	2	1	3	2	2	1
13	2	2	1	2	3	1
14	2	2	2	3	1	2
15	2	2	3	1	2	3
16	2	3	1	3	2	3
17	2	3	2	1	3	1
18	2	3	3	2	1	2

Table 4. Data From Test Condition #8 of Inner Array

Outer Array Condition	1	2	0	2	8	2	2	2	0
	2	8	2	2	0	2	0	2	0
	3	2	8	2	8	2	0	0	2
	4	2	0	8	2	2	2	0	8

6. ACCUMULATION ANALYSIS AND THE S/N RATIO

The first analysis performed was an accumulation analysis using the five classifications. The analysis of variance (ANOVA) table (see Table 5) and the graphs (see Figure 2) from the accumulation analysis show that factors A, B, and C have the strongest impact on the adhesion.

Table 5. ANOVA Table (Accumulation Analysis)

SOURCE	df	S	V
A	5	232.395	46.479
B	10	170.521	17.052
C	10	115.712	11.571
D	[10]	33.268	3.327
E	[10]	10.275	1.028
F	[10]	58.124	5.812
$A \times B$	[10]	66.022	6.602
(e)	(2850)	2361.372	0.829

Since the classifications are ordered to reflect the energy of the process and the desired classification is the middle classification, the characteristic is really a nominal-the-best characteristic, even though actual variables data was not used. Because of this, a second analysis was performed in order to provide some additional information and to aid in the selection of the factor levels.

The purpose of converting the classified attributes data to variable data through coding was to facilitate a nominal-the-best analysis where the objective is to achieve a desired target value (in this case, zero) with minimum variation. While this strategy was developed for actual variables data, the hope was that the same strategy would at least provide indications of significant factors and optimal levels for this case where the data set includes only five (somewhat arbitrary) numerical values.

The analysis involved two steps:

A. S/N Ratio analysis was performed to find the factors affecting variation.
B. An analysis was performed on the raw data to find the factors that affect the mean.

Parameter Design for a Heat-Staking Process

The factors that were found to affect variation were controlled to minimize variation. One factor, which did not affect variation, was found to affect the mean, and was used to adjust the mean to the target.

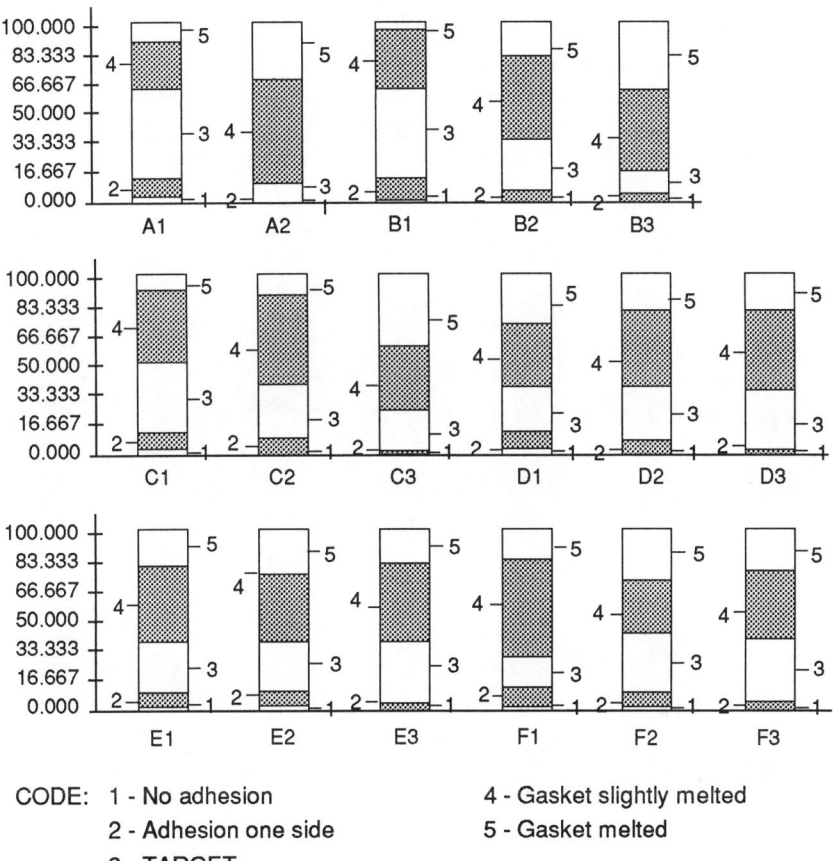

CODE: 1 - No adhesion
        2 - Adhesion one side
        3 - TARGET
        4 - Gasket slightly melted
        5 - Gasket melted

Figure 2. Graphs of Factor Effects (Accumulation Analysis)

A. S/N Ratio Analysis

The S/N Ratio that was used is as follows:

$$S/N = -10 \log V_e \qquad (1.1)$$

For each of the 18 test conditions of the controllable factors, a corresponding S/N Ratio was computed. They are shown in Table 6.

For example the S/N Ratio for the number 8 condition is calculated as:

T = Total of data from No. 8 = $2 + 0 + 2 + 8 + \ldots + 8$
= 82

V_e = Variance of data from No. 8
$$= \frac{1}{31}\left(2^2 + 0^2 + 2^2 + 8^2 + \ldots + 8^2 - \frac{T^2}{32}\right)$$
= 7.8024

S/N = $-10 \log 7.8024$
= -8.9 dB

Table 6. S/N Ratios

	A	B	C	D	E	F	S/N
1	1	1	1	1	1	1	−6.2
2	1	1	2	2	2	2	−4.1
3	1	1	3	3	3	3	4.5
4	1	2	1	1	2	2	−8.0
5	1	2	2	2	3	3	−5.7
6	1	2	3	3	1	1	−10.8
7	1	3	1	2	1	3	−4.5
8	1	3	2	3	2	1	−8.9
9	1	3	3	1	3	2	−10.7
10	2	1	1	3	3	2	−4.5
11	2	1	2	1	1	3	−6.4
12	2	1	3	2	2	1	−7.7
13	2	2	1	2	3	1	−5.0
14	2	2	2	3	1	2	−7.7
15	2	2	3	1	2	3	−9.4
16	2	3	1	3	2	3	−9.6
17	2	3	2	1	3	1	−10.0
18	2	3	3	2	1	2	−5.0

An ANOVA table and a response table (averages) were constructed from the column of S/N Ratios. These are given in Tables 7 and 8, respectively. These tables indicate that factor B has a strong influence on variation and that factors D, E, and F may possibly affect variation. The main effects show that the optimal levels for these factors (in order to reduce variation) are:

$$B_1 \ D_2 \ E_3 \ F_3$$

since these are the levels corresponding to the highest average S/N Ratios.

Table 7. ANOVA Table (S/N)

SOURCE	df	S	V
A	[1]	6.688	6.688
B	2	60.837	30.419
C	[2]	2.248	1.124
D	2	31.089	15.545
E	2	22.839	11.420
F	2	25.719	12.860
$A \times B$	2	22.098	11.049
(e)	(7)	(55.663)	(7.952)
TOTAL	17	218.245	12.838

Table 8. Response Table (S/N)

	A	B	C	D	E	F
1	−6.0	−4.1	−6.3	−8.4	−6.8	−8.1
2	−7.3	−7.8	−7.1	−5.3	−8.0	−6.7
3		−8.1	−6.5	−6.2	−5.2	−5.2
Difference:	1.3	4.0	0.8	3.1	2.8	2.9

The $A \times B$ interaction shown in Figure 3 suggests that factor A may also be important with regard to variation. Its preferred level is A_1 providing B_1 is used.

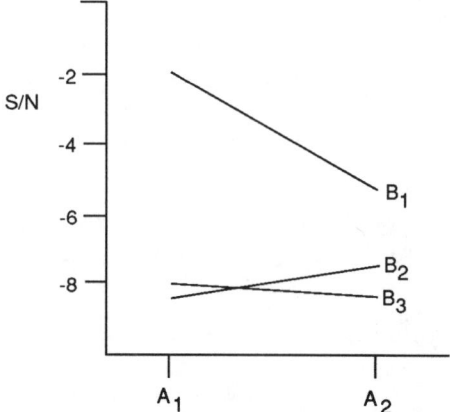

Figure 3. $A \times B$ Interaction

B. Analysis of Raw Data

Similarly, an ANOVA table and a response table were constructed from the raw data (see Tables 9 and 10). This analysis indicates that factors A, B, and C affect the mean. Since factor C did not appear to affect variation and does affect the mean, it could serve as a signal factor to adjust the mean to the target.

Table 9. ANOVA Table (Raw Data)

SOURCE	df	S	V
A	1	1040.063	1040.063
B	2	1116.375	558.188
C	2	826.292	413.146
D	[2]	12.125	6.063
E	[2]	10.125	5.063
F	[2]	15.500	7.750
$A \times B$	[2]	25.792	12.896
(e)	(570)	(3440.708)	(6.036)
TOTAL	575	6423.438	11.171

Table 10. Response Table (Raw Data)

	A	B	C	D	E	F
1	1.0	0.7	1.2	2.6	2.5	2.1
2	3.7	2.3	1.8	2.3	2.5	2.5
3		4.1	4.0	2.2	2.2	2.4
Difference:	2.7	3.4	2.8	0.4	0.3	0.4

Recall that the accumulation analysis identified factors A, B, and C to be important with respect to adhesion. The additional information provided by the nominal-the-best analysis is that these three factors all seem to affect the mean, and that factors A and B also appear to affect variation. This information was useful in selecting factor levels. Levels for factors A and B were selected to minimize variation, while factor C was used to shift the mean to the target. In addition, the S/N Ratio analysis suggested that factors D, E, and F may have some mild effect on variation.

7. Estimation and Confirmation Experiment

The first confirmation experiment was run using the following conditions:

A_1 = Tip surface — I
B_1 = % heat — 60
C_2 = Weld time — 45
D_2 = Squeeze time — 90
E_3 = Off time — 50
F_3 = Hold time — 60

where all the levels were selected to reduce variation, except for factor C. Factor C is the signal factor to be used for adjusting the mean to the target. The C_2 level was selected for the first confirmation run based on the prediction of the mean. The predictions for the levels of C, while at $A_1 B_1$, are given on the following page:

$$\hat{\mu} \text{ at } C_1 = \overline{A}_1 + \overline{B}_1 + \overline{C}_1 - 2\overline{T} \tag{1.2}$$
$$= 1.0 + 0.7 + 1.2 - 2(2.36) = -1.8$$

$$\hat{\mu} \text{ at } C_2 = \overline{A}_1 + \overline{B}_1 + \overline{C}_2 - 2\overline{T} \tag{1.3}$$
$$= 1.0 + 0.7 + 1.8 - 2(2.36) = -1.2$$

$$\hat{\mu} \text{ at } C_3 = \overline{A}_1 + \overline{B}_1 + \overline{C}_3 - 2\overline{T} \tag{1.4}$$
$$= 1.0 + 0.7 + 4.0 - 2(2.36) = 1.0$$

The results of the first confirmation experiment is given in Table 11. Sixteen data were obtained from each of the four test conditions of the L_4 outer orthogonal array that was used in the original experiment. Little variation is present in the 64 data. The average of all the data is $\bar{y} = 0.125$. The fact that the actual mean does not agree closely with the predicted value (–1.2) is not terribly alarming considering that the raw data is not true variables data. The predictions, like the ANOVA tables and the response tables, should be regarded as mere indicators in this application.

Table 11. Data From First Confirmation Experiment: $A_1 B_1 C_2 D_2 E_3 F_3$

Outer Array Condition																
1	0	0	0	0	0	0	0	0	0	0	0	0	2	0	0
2	0	0	0	0	0	0	0	0	0	0	0	0	0	0	0
3	0	0	0	0	0	0	2	0	0	0	0	0	0	0	0
4	0	2	0	0	0	0	0	0	0	0	0	2	0	0	0

In any event, a lower average was desired. A slight lack of adhesion is preferred over a slightly melted condition, so an average leaning slightly in the negative direction would be better than one that is slightly positive. To reduce the mean, a second confirmation test was run in the same manner as the first, except that the signal factor, C, was set at its low level. The data from this run is given in Table 12. The average is now $\bar{y} = -0.031$. As was desired, the signal factor did seem to move the average without adversely affecting the variation.

Table 12. Data From Second Confirmation Experiment:
$A_1 B_1 C_1 D_2 E_3 F_3$

Outer Array Condition	1	0	0	0	0	0	0	0	0	0	0	0	0	0	0	0
	2	0	0	0	0	0	0	0	0	0	0	0	0	0	0	0
	3	0	0	0	0	0	0	0	0	0	0	0	0	0	0	0
	4	0	0	0	−2	0	0	0	0	0	0	0	0	0	0	0

8. Quality Improvement After Confirmation

Figure 4 contains histograms that compare the process performance before and after the experiment was run. The "before" data was collected with the process settings that were used before this study was conducted. The "after" data is the data from the second confirmation experiment. In each case, the sample size is 64.

The figure clearly shows that the process performance has been greatly improved by using the optimal combination that was determined through the experiment. At the optimal combination, the process produces good adhesions much more consistently than before.

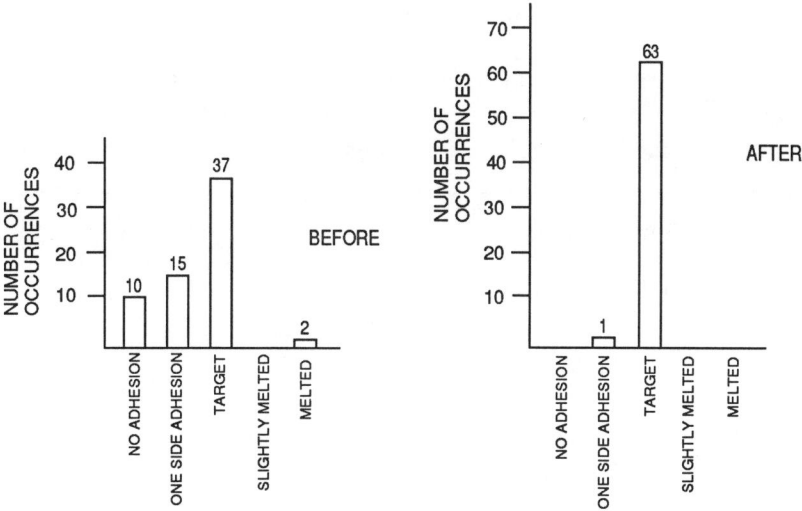

Figure 4. Comparison of Before and After Experiment

9. Cost Reduction Using the Loss Function

Operating at the optimal condition determined from the experiment, an estimated annual savings of $18,000 should be realized in the reduction of material and labor costs associated with scrap and rework. The actual savings is likely much greater than this when hidden costs and long-term effects are also considered.

In an attempt to quantify the overall savings when the hidden and long-term losses are included, the QLF was used. As can be seen in Table 13, the savings via the QLF is estimated at $80,580 per year. The loss at the "before" condition was calculated using a trimmed version of the data shown in the first histogram of Figure 4. It was thought that using the full distribution would inflate the loss unfairly, since the product is inspected by two people before being shipped and, hence, very few of the "–8" or "8" hinges produced actually reach the customer. The "after" calculation was made using the data from the second confirmation experiment (see Table 12).

Since the QLF calculation is highly dependent on the coding scheme (and the coding scheme was somewhat arbitrary), the calculation was repeated for a less severe coding scheme and the annual savings were estimated to be about $50,000.

Table 13. Loss Function

$$A = \$\,1.50 \qquad LD-50: -8, +8 \qquad k = \frac{1.50}{64} = .023$$

BEFORE	AFTER
$\overline{y} = -0.85 \quad \sigma^2 = 2.7556$	$\overline{y} = -0.03 \quad \sigma^2 = 0.0615$
$L = (.023)\left[(-0.85)^2 + 2.7556\right]$	$L = (.023)\left[(-0.03)^2 + 0.0615\right]$
$= \$\,0.080$	$= \$\,0.001$

SAVINGS/UNIT = 0.080 – 0.001 = $0.079
SAVINGS/MONTH (85,000 production) = $6715.00
SAVINGS/YEAR = $80,580.00

The total savings will likely be much greater than the savings due to just reducing scrap and rework. Total annual savings is probably $50,000 to $80,000.

10. Summary and Conclusions

Significant quality improvements and cost reduction were realized through the parameter-design experiment conducted on the heat-staking process. Good adhesions are now achieved much more consistently than before and should result in a total annual savings of about $50,000 to $80,000. The reduction of scrap/rework alone should give an annual savings of $18,000.

An accumulation analysis identified three factors that significantly affect adhesion. In addition, it was found that coding the classified attributes data, and thereby treating it as variables data in the analysis, provided additional information that aided in the selection of factor levels. The nominal-the-best strategy of minimizing variation and shifting the mean to the target appeared to work reasonably well in this case, in spite of the somewhat arbitrary coding scheme that was used.

References

Taguchi, Genichi, *System of Experimental Design*, UNIPUB/Kraus International Publications, White Plains, New York and American Supplier Institute, Dearborn, Michigan, 1987.

Acknowledgments

The authors would like to thank Dr. Thomas Snabb of the University of Michigan—Dearborn for the assistance he provided through numerous discussions of various aspects of this study.

Q & A

Q. The characteristic measured in this case study is a classified attributes type used to evaluate the effectiveness of a heat-staking process. The staking coding scheme is:

Too much melt	$y = 8$
Some melt	$y = 2$
Good	$y = 0$
One-sided adhesion	$y = -2$
No adhesion	$y = -8$

and y is treated as a nominal-the-best characteristic. Why can't they simply take:

Good staking	$y = 1$
Fair staking	$y = 2$
Bad staking	$y = 4$

and analyze y as a smaller-the-better characteristic?

A. Bad staking can result from many different failure modes. Too much melt—too much energy applied—is bad. Insufficient adhesion is bad; a result of not enough energy. It is necessary to distinguish between different failure modes to reduce the variability of energy transfer in the manufacturing process and product functions. Therefore, it is better to take y and specify its failure mode.

There may be a better substitutional characteristic to evaluate staking. The importance of selecting a good characteristic should be emphasized. The ability to select a good quality characteristic is directly related to the following:

- Understanding the principal function of the system
- Feasibility of measurement
- Cost of measurement.

The poorer the quality characteristic, the less the technological understanding of the company. When using measurement characteristics such as:

y = yield y = number of defects y = number of failures

to evaluate product/process function, the engineer has an inadequate understanding of product/process function.

Q. This case study shows three analyses: Using $S/N = -10 \log V_e$, analysis of the mean, and accumulation analysis. It seems that the S/N ratio analysis shows clearer results. Is this a correct analysis?

A. The mean data analysis and accumulation analysis in A, B, and C are strong, and the S/N analysis show B, D, E, and F as being strong. They reported better levels, according to the S/N analysis, and the confirmation run shows a tremendous reduction of variability. This shows that the way they weighted the five classes according to the energy level was appropriate. Variability can be checked using accumulation analysis; however, using S/N analysis, especially when variability is the concern, is recommended.

However, there still remains a problem since the characteristic is not a non-negative continuous variable. For example, suppose one condition results +8, +8, +8, +8, i.e., where all pieces melted using $S/N = -10 \log V_e$ becomes infinity since there is no variability, and this condition will be evaluated as an excellent condition. The results are questionable. It may be a good condition after adjusting the mean, but it may not be a good condition from an engineering standpoint. In the experiment, this condition did not occur and the result was beautifully reproduced; therefore, it was not necessary to take this situation into account. But we should recognize the importance and potential danger of this condition occuring. Selecting a better characteristic would eliminate this concern.

2. Sheet-Molded Compound Process Improvement

P. I. Hsieh and D. E. Goodwin
Chrysler Motors Engineering

The objective of this study was to identify controllable and significant material and process variables that could minimize the effect of Sheet-Molded Compound (SMC) formulation. An L_{16} orthogonal array was used to conduct the experiment. First-time-through capability of the finished product improved from 77% to 96%. Supplier scrap was reduced from 16% to 1.7%. Reduced inspection cost repair and costs due to optimization are estimated at $900,000 per year.

Editor's Note: *The following case study is an example of an experiment that resembles a Taguchi Methods experiment through its use of an L_{16} orthogonal array. Please reveiw the question-and-answer summary following the study's conclusion for a brief comparison of Taguchi Methods and traditional design of experiments techniques and an explanation of why this study is not representative of Taguchi Methods.*

1. Introduction

Grille opening panels are shipped to Chrysler Corp. assembly plants from SMC suppliers and assembled into the car prior to the paint process. Surface imperfections in the paint finish ("pops") after the paint process caused a low first-time capability (FTC) of approximately 77% for one assembly plant. The fact that the imperfections were not detectable until the components were shipped, assembled, and painted created serious productivity concerns for the assembly plant and the supplier.

From the *Fourth Symposium on Taguchi Methods*™, pp. 13–21, Copyright © 1986, American Supplier Institute, Inc., Dearborn, Michigan.

2. THE MOLDING PROCESS

The process studied in this experiment included raw material mixing to part finishing at the supplier, Eagle Picher. The finished parts were packaged and shipped to Chrysler plants. Figure 1 shows the process for producing GOP at Eagle Picher.

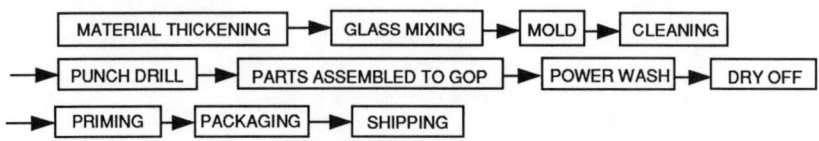

Figure 1. The Process

3. THE CAUSE-AND-EFFECT DIAGRAM FOR POROSITY

In a brainstorming session, the Chrysler Task Force and the supplier engineering team constructed a cause-and-effect diagram focused on the product and the process. An abbreviated version of the diagram appears in Figure 2.

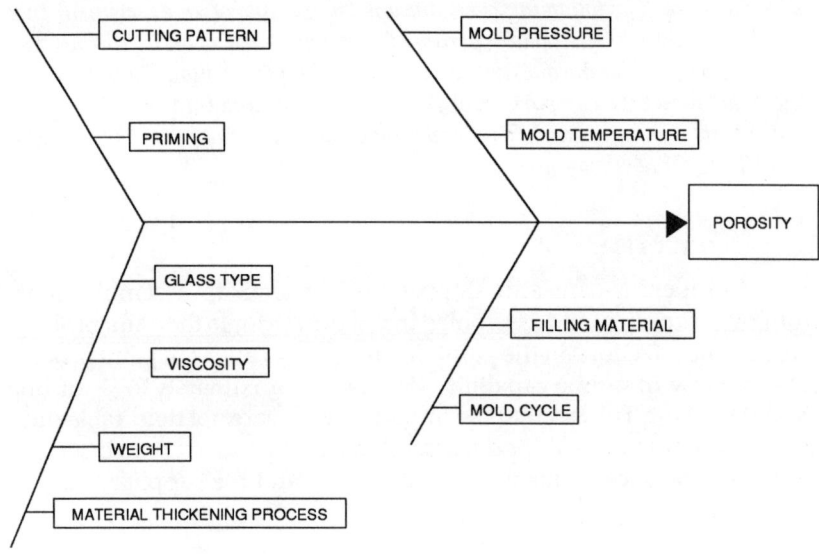

Figure 2. The Cause-and-Effect Diagram

4. Factors and Layout of the Experiment

Using the cause-and-effect diagram, an experiment was set up that included nine main variables:

Variable		No. of Levels	Level 1	Level 2
1. Mold Pressure	(A)	2	Low	High
2. Mold Temperature	(B)	2	Low	High
3. Mold Cycle	(C)	2	Low	High
4. Cutting Pattern	(D)	2	Method I	Method II
5. Priming	(E)	2	Method I	Method II
6. Viscosity	(F)	2	Low	High
7. Weight	(G)	2	Low	High
8. Material-thickening Process	(H)	2	Process I	Process II
9. Glass Type	(I)	2	Type I	Type II

In addition to these nine main factors, the following five potential interactions were investigated in this experiment:

$A \times B$
$A \times C$
$A \times D$
$B \times F$
$F \times H$

With these experimental considerations, an L_{16} orthogonal array layout was chosen to conduct the experiments. The array arrangement and responses of porosity observations can be seen in Table 1. Two responses were run per experiment. Response values are the number of "pops" found.

5. Analysis and Optimization

An analysis of variance (ANOVA) indicates that:
1. Mold pressure (A), priming (E), and mold cycle (C) were significant in contributing to the experimental variation.

Table 1. L_{16} Orthogonal Array

Exp. No.	(1) A	(2) B	(3) A x B	(4) F	(5) G	(6) B x F	(7) E	(8) C	(9) A x C	(10) H	(11) I	(12) D	(13) A x D	(14) F x H	(15) (e)	R1	R2
1	1	1	1	1	1	1	1	1	1	1	1	1	1	1	1	56	10
2	1	1	1	1	1	1	1	2	2	2	2	2	2	2	2	17	2
3	1	1	1	2	2	2	2	1	1	1	1	2	2	2	2	2	1
4	1	1	1	2	2	2	2	2	2	2	2	1	1	1	1	4	3
5	1	2	2	1	1	2	2	1	1	2	2	1	1	2	2	3	1
6	1	2	2	1	1	2	2	2	2	1	1	2	2	1	1	4	13
7	1	2	2	2	2	1	1	1	1	2	2	2	2	1	1	50	49
8	1	2	2	2	2	1	1	2	2	1	1	1	1	2	2	2	3
9	2	1	2	1	2	1	2	1	2	1	2	1	2	1	2	1	3
10	2	1	2	1	2	1	2	2	1	2	1	2	1	2	1	0	3
11	2	1	2	2	1	2	1	1	2	1	2	2	1	2	1	3	2
12	2	1	2	2	1	2	1	2	1	2	1	1	2	1	2	12	2
13	2	2	1	1	2	2	1	1	2	2	1	1	2	2	1	3	4
14	2	2	1	1	2	2	1	2	1	1	2	2	1	1	2	4	10
15	2	2	1	2	1	1	2	1	2	2	1	2	1	1	2	0	5
16	2	2	1	2	1	1	2	2	1	1	2	1	2	2	1	0	8

2. Material-thickening process (*H*) and viscosity (*F*) were both insignificant with *F* values of 0.4854 and 0.0539 respectively.
3. The interaction *FxH* was significant. A similar observation was seen in *B* x *F*.
4. As anticipated, the interaction *A* x *C* was seen as significant. The completed ANOVA table is presented in Table 2 with the level sum of the variables.

Table 2. ANOVA

Source	df	S	V	S'	ρ%
A	1	800.000	800.000	731.788	11.04
B	1	45.125	45.125	—	—
A x B	1	15.125	15.125	—	—
F	1	4.500	4.500	—	—
G	1	0.500	0.500	—	—
B x F	1	595.125	595.125	526.913	7.95
E	1	990.125	990.125	921.913	13.91
C	1	351.125	351.125	282.913	4.27
A x C	1	630.125	630.125	561.913	8.48
H	1	40.500	40.500	—	—
I	1	50.000	50.000	—	—
D	1	78.125	78.125	—	—
A x D	1	120.125	120.125	51.913	0.78
F x H	1	924.500	924.500	856.288	12.92
e	1	648.000	648.000	579.788	8.75
Error	16	1335.000	83.438		
(pool)	(23)	(1568.873)	(68.212)	2114.571	31.90
Total	31	6628.000	213.807		

Sum Variables	A	B	C	D	E	F	G	H	I
First Level (1)	220	121	193	115	229	134	138	122	120
Second Level (2)	60	159	87	165	51	146	142	158	160

To have a clear idea of the experimental results, the effects of each significant factor is graphed. These graphs represent what was observed in the ANOVA (Table 2). The factors are arranged so that the most significant is on the left.

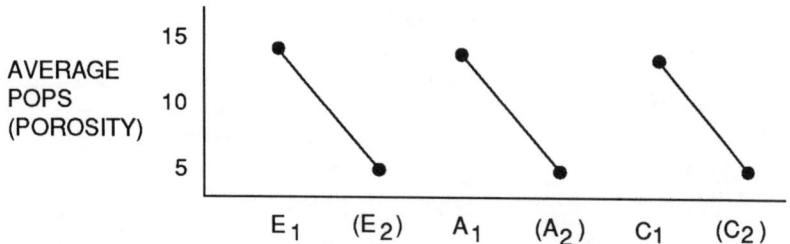

( ) denotes the desired condition; i.e., level E_2 is preferred over E_1.

Figure 3.

It is observed that B, F, and H are not significant factors to influence the "pops" being measured. However, interactions are presented between B and F ($B \times F$) as well as F and H ($F \times H$).

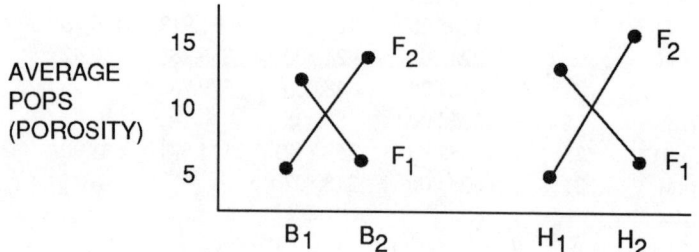

Therefore, (B_2, F_1); (H_1, F_1) are recommended.

Figure 4.

The best condition based on the levels of factors as identified in this experiment is:

Mold pressure:	High
Mold temperature:	High
Mold cycle:	High
Cutting pattern:	Method II
Priming:	Method II
Viscosity:	Low
Weight:	Low
Material thickening process:	Process II
Glass type:	Type I

6. Confirmation of Results

Confirmation experiments were carried out by the supplier in its own plant. Our assembly plant conducted a before and after study on the optimum process. Results revealed an increased first-time capability of 77% to 96%.

7. Conclusion

The experiment is considered unique and successful due to the following aspects:

1. Both supplier and Chrysler engineers were very enthusiastic about participating in the design of experiments. The supplier was particularly pleased that a joint effort was made to assist them in improving their process.
2. The supplier and Chrysler have learned the power of Taguchi Methods in DOE.
3. The supplier has expanded the use of DOE to other products.
4. The ability of the supplier to optimize internal processes for Chrysler-sourced parts resulted in price reductions for Chrysler.
5. Chrysler realized an improvement in first-time through capability from 77% to 96% in the assembly plant. The estimated savings from reduced inspection and repair is $900,000 per year.
6. There are additional savings that cannot be accurately dollarized. These areas include fewer material handling personnel and reduced GOP inventory in the assembly plant and the supplier plant.

Q & A

Q. This experiment solved a serious problem of a Sheet-Molded Compounded (SMC) process. The SMC products had porosity problems causing pops in paint finishes. This is a fire-fighting type of experiment. Nine SMC process controllable factors and five two-factor interactions were assigned to an L_{16} orthogonal array. No noise factor was used but replication of size two was taken. Analysis of the raw data was conducted using:

y = # of pops detected after the painting process

Signal-to-Noise (S/N) analysis was not conducted. What does this study indicate?

A. This case study is not a Taguchi Methods experiment but a fractional-factorial experiment. Design of experiments (DOE) make up a part of Taguchi Methods, and DOE has been used in Japanese industry for the past 40 years as a Statistical Quality Control method. Dr. Genichi Taguchi, is regarded as a pioneer in industrial applications of experimental design. The evolution of Taguchi Methods developed as a direct result of Dr. Taguchi's quest for more efficient, economical experimentation for industry, begun in the 1940s.

Dr. Taguchi and his colleagues gradually developed Taguchi Methods based on their experience and the pragmatic application of designed experiments to industrial engineering. When Taguchi Methods were first introduced to U.S. industry in the early 1980s, many people mistakenly thought they were nothing more than DOE. The characteristic that distinguishes Taguchi Methods is an efficient research method for designing, not in order to find responses but to reduce deviations from ideal functions through the use of:

1) Design of experiments for the evaluation and improvement of quality
2) The role of the orthogonal array
3) The search for additivity in characteristics distinguished by engineering objectives

The greatest difference between Taguchi Methods and Design of Experiments is the belief that it is useless and counter-productive to assign interactions, whether or not there are interactions. Orthogonal arrays should be used to help us discover experimental failures when interactions exist. An experiment utilizing an orthogonal array has value only when the estimated value of the process average and the confirmatory trial do not match. The advantage of using orthogonal arrays is not that reliability is increased by an orthogonal array, rather it is that the reliability becomes known. This is very important for product/process function.

Q. This experiment reduced scrap/rework cost by $900,000/year and triggered the implementation of Taguchi Methods company wide. Companies having success in the implementation of Taguchi Methods often experience this type of dramatic cost reduction at the early stages of implementation, don't they?

A. The use of orthogonal arrays is not enough to ensure reliability; it is the S/N Ratio that is important. We are pleased that a cost savings was realized, but it is not through the use of Taguchi Methods. Design of experiments can have dramatic results, but a robust product/process cannot be ensured. It is the stability of a product/process under a variety of usage conditions that ensures its robustness.

3. Instrument Panel Process Development

*Coloman G. Adam,
Davidson Instrument Panel — Textron*

This paper demonstrates the effectiveness of Taguchi Methods in the early detection of critical parameters in the development of an automobile instrument panel. An L_{12} orthogonal array was used in a screening trial to give direction for reducing defects. The study resulted in conformation of the three largest contributors to surface defects. The direction for the setting of other tested variables was also indicated. Additional experimentation is required to address other problems related to the reduction of surface defects.

1. Introduction: Objectives of the Experiment

To compete in terms of quality and cost, Davidson Instrument Panel—Textron is constantly searching for improved processes and constructions for automobile instrument panels (also called crash pads or dashboards). New processes for producing the outer covering (skin) and for filling the skin with urethane foam have been developed to achieve the objectives of improved quality and lowered cost.

The objectives of the new part-process-development program were:
1. To define which major factors had an effect on surface quality
2. To establish an estimate of the relative contribution of each factor
3. To identify a process that would produce defect-free instrument panels
4. To improve the interaction and communication of the various groups involved in the three main processes that make up the manufacture of an instrument panel.

To accomplish these objectives, we have adopted Taguchi Methods of designed experiments to efficiently develop processes for new instrument panels.

2. Selection of Variables for Study

A brainstorming group was organized consisting of people knowledgeable in the various processes involved in producing this new instrument panel. The first task of this group was to define the following:

1. The objective: The elimination of surface defects on the new instrument panel.
2. The quality characteristic: The size and rated severity of the surface defect as measured by visual and tactile operator inspection of each panel.
3. The Quality Loss Function type: Smaller-the-better. This was used as a statement of direction, but no actual calculations were done.

The brainstorming session generated a list of 30 possible variables that would fall under the following three main categories:

1. Tooling: Pour mold and retainer
2. Foaming process
3. Skin-making process

The three categories listed above are also the three main processes involved in the development work. These were used as categories instead of the usual five Ms for cause-and-effect diagrams, because only the main variables of each process were of interest.

From the brainstorming list the variables were narrowed down to 10 by a combination of voting and consensus. An L_{12} orthogonal array was chosen as the smallest array to fit the 10 variables (see Table 1).

The 11th column of the L_{12} was left empty and used as an estimate of error. The 10 variables were assigned to the columns of the L_{12} by the difficulty of making changes and the number of times changes are required in each column. For instance, changing the foam formulation is time-consuming and tedious; thus, it was assigned to column 1 for ease of experimentation.

Table 1. L_{12} (2^{11})

No.	1	2	3	4	5	6	7	8	9	10	11
1	1	1	1	1	1	1	1	1	1	1	1
2	1	1	1	1	1	2	2	2	2	2	2
3	1	1	2	2	2	1	1	1	2	2	2
4	1	2	1	2	2	1	2	2	1	1	2
5	1	2	2	1	2	2	1	2	1	2	1
6	1	2	2	2	1	2	2	1	2	1	1
7	2	1	2	2	1	1	2	2	1	2	1
8	2	1	2	1	2	2	2	1	1	1	2
9	2	1	1	2	2	2	1	2	2	1	1
10	2	2	2	1	1	1	1	2	2	1	2
11	2	2	1	2	1	2	1	1	1	2	2
12	2	2	1	1	2	1	2	1	2	2	1
	1					2					

The independent variables, the levels, and the column assignments are shown in Table 2.

Table 2.

Column No.		Independent Variables	Levels (1 and 2)
1	A	Foam formulation	Current and new
2	B	Venting A	No and yes
3	C	Skin weight	Low and high
4	D	Tooling aid A	Old and new type
5	E	Foam throughput	Low and high
6	F	Foam shot weight	Low and high
7	G	Diverter	No and yes
8	H	Tooling aid B	No and yes
9	I	Venting B	No and yes
10	J	Cure time	Short and long
11	e	Error column	

The dependent variable, the quality characteristic, was the size and rated severity of the surface defects found by inspection of each panel.

3. The Experiment

The trial was run on two days, and was split using the foam formulation levels in column 1. Note that the first factor (foam formulation) was confounded with the day, but fortunately this factor was not found to be significant.

All other variables were held constant and monitored during the trial.

A sample of two parts was generated for each run in the experiment. Each part was inspected visually and by feel over its entire surface. Table 3 shows the weighted values for surface defects found on each panel.

Table 3. Trial Results By Run Number For Rated Surface Defects Per Pad

Run No.	Panel A	Panel B	Sum	Difference
1	4.9	2.0	6.9	2.9
2	3.2	4.3	7.5	1.1
3	0.7	1.1	1.8	0.4
4	1.6	0.9	2.5	0.8
5	2.6	12.2	14.8	9.6
6	1.4	2.8	4.2	1.4
7	2.3	1.5	3.8	0.8
8	3.7	2.7	6.6	1.2
9	0.6	6.7	7.3	6.1
10	0.0	1.8	1.8	1.8
11	11.7	6.7	18.4	4.0
12	0.0	0.2	0.2	0.2

4. Response Analysis of Surface Defects

The sum of the rated surface defects by run ranged from 0.2 to 18.4. The range of responses caused by the chosen levels of the independent variable seems to be large enough. Two parts had no surface defects, proving it is possible to achieve this goal. Run 12 has the lowest sum and also the smallest difference between the two parts made. There seems to be a large range in the difference between the two parts made and in the difference between parts made at the same conditions. Run 5 has the largest difference and run 12 the smallest. The large difference suggests that the variability of the process needed to be studied, so Signal-to-Noise (S/N) analysis was later performed.

Rearranging the data by column number (variable) and level studied results in the following:

Table 4. Average Results, Rated Surface Defects, By Variable Level

Column No.	Level 1	Level 2	Difference
1	3.14	3.18	0.04
2	2.02	3.49	1.47
3	3.57	2.75	0.82
4	3.15	3.17	0.02
5	3.55	2.77	0.78
6	1.42	4.90	3.48
7	4.25	2.07	2.18
8	3.18	3.14	0.04
9	4.42	1.90	2.52
10	2.44	3.87	1.44
11	3.10	3.22	0.12

Columns 6, 9, 7, 2, and 10 show the largest change in defects for a change in variable level. Columns 1, 4, 8, and 11 show very little change in defects for the change in level of those variables and are not seen as important variables—or the change in the levels was too small. The difference in the averages for the change in level of column 11, the empty column being used for error, is small. Since we are interested in surface defects being reduced, the lower average level of each variable is desirable.

Plotting this data yields the following:

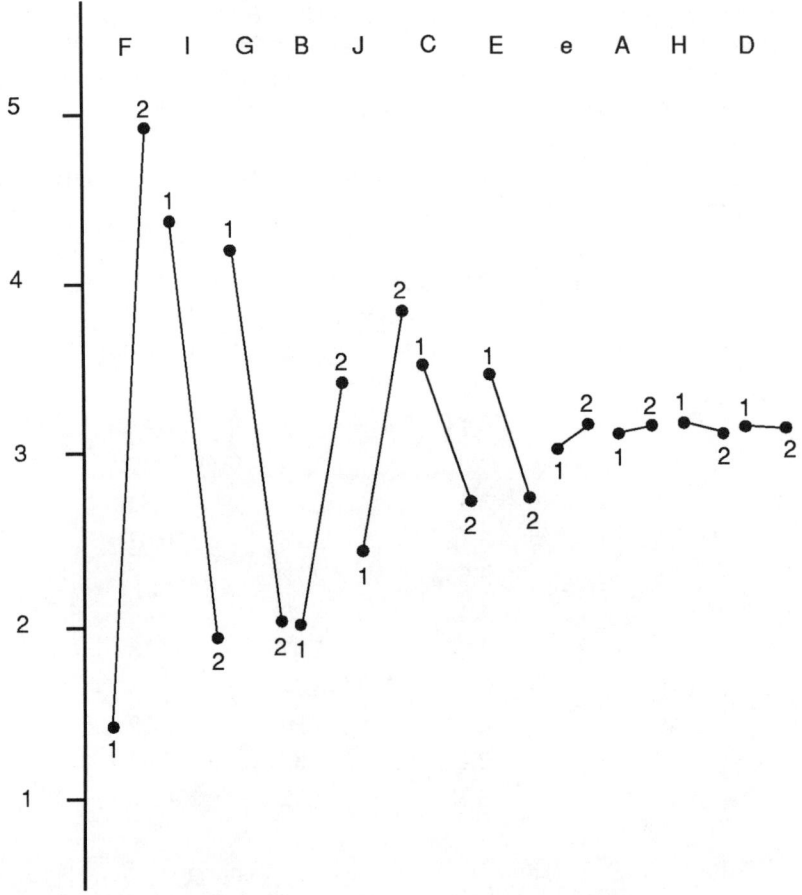

Figure 1.

The variables are shown Pareto-style to illustrate the rank order of variable contribution.

5. Analysis of Variance (ANOVA) of the Mean

The next step undertaken was analysis of variance (ANOVA), to determine the variance within the levels of the variables. First, there were 24 parts made or 24 degrees of freedom. One degree of freedom is lost due to the analysis, leaving 23. Each of the 11 variables has one degree of freedom. For each of the 12 runs there was one repetition or 12 degrees of freedom. The sum of squares is calculated for each variable and the error terms. The mean squares are calculated by dividing the sum of squares by the degrees of freedom. The percent contribution can also be calculated for each variable column.

Table 5 shows these calculations:

Table 5. ANOVA Table of Variables for Surface Defects

Source		Degrees of Freedom	Sum of Squares	Mean Square
Column	1	1	0.01	0.01
	2	1	2.67	2.67
	3	1	4.00	4.00
	4	1	0.00	0.00
	5	1	3.68	3.68
	6	1	72.80	72.80
	7	1	28.60	28.60
	8	1	0.01	0.01
	9	1	38.00	38.00
	10	1	12.33	12.33
	11	1	0.08	0.08
Sum Total		(11)	162.18	
Repetition		12	85.98	7.16
Total		23	248.16	

Columns 6, 9, 7, and 10, in decreasing order of importance, are the main contributors to the change in surface defects from changes in variable levels. These are the same columns that showed the largest difference between levels in Table 4.

Table 6 was generated from Table 5, by pooling columns 1, 2, 3, 4, 5, 8, and 11.

Table 6. Pooled ANOVA Table of Variables For Surface Defects

Source		Degrees of Freedom	Sum of Squares	Mean Square	% Contrib.	Best Level
Column	6	1	72.80	72.80	27.29	1
	7	1	28.60	28.60	9.48	2
	9	1	38.00	38.00	13.27	2
	10	1	12.33	12.33	2.92	1
Column Error		7	10.45	1.49		
Sum Total		(11)	(162.18)			
Repetition Error		12	85.98			
Total		23	248.16			
Pooled Error		(19)	96.43	5.08		

The values for percent contribution change slightly because of the smaller pooled error mean-square term.

The important columns (6, 7, 9, and 10) are retained from the ANOVA table. Their confidence level and best level are added at the table. The best level for the variable can easily be picked from Table 4 as the level giving the lowest weighted value or surface defects.

Note that the four significant variables only explain about 50% of the variability in results seen during the trial, so there is still a lot more to learn about making defect-free instrument panels and controlling variability. Further trails are needed to add new variables or try different levels of these variables.

6. S/N RATIO ANALYSIS

S/N analysis was done because of the large amount of variation seen between parts (see Table 3). This is one of the methods of analysis Dr. Genichi Taguchi developed. A large S/N Ratio is desirable. The signal is the effect caused by the variable, and the noise is the process and measurement variability.

In this case we are striving to reduce the number of surface defects, so we chose the formula for smaller-the-better. For smaller-the-better the

Instrument Panel Process Development

goal is to reduce both the mean and the variation.

The S/N Ratio can be calculated as follows (for smaller-the-better):

$$\eta = -10 \log \frac{1}{n} \sum_{i=1}^{n} y_i^2 \qquad (3.1)$$

The calculated S/N Ratio results for smaller-the-better are as follows:

Run 1: $\eta = -10 \log \frac{1}{2} \left(4.9^2 + 2.0^2 \right) = -11.46$

Run 2: $\eta = -10 \log \frac{1}{2} \left(3.2^2 + 4.3^2 \right) = -11.57$

Table 7. Trial Results by Run Number Transformed to S/N

Run No.	Transformed Results
1	− 11.46
2	− 11.57
3	+ 0.71
4	− 2.27
5	− 18.91
6	− 6.90
7	− 5.76
8	− 10.51
9	− 13.55
10	− 2.10
11	− 19.59
12	+ 16.99

Note that there is only one value per run after the transformation. The values range from +16.99 to −19.39.

Again rearranging the data by column number (variable) and level studies yields Table 8.

Table 8. S/N Average Results by Variable Level
For Smaller-the-Better

Column No.	Level 1	Level 2	Difference
1	−8.40	−5.75	2.65
2	−8.49	−5.46	3.03
3	−6.91	−7.25	−0.34
4	−6.25	−7.89	−1.64
5	−9.56	−4.59	4.97
6	−0.65	−13.50	−12.85
7	−10.82	−3.34	7.48
8	−5.13	−9.03	−3.90
9	−11.42	−2.74	8.68
10	−7.80	−6.36	1.44
11	−6.60	−7.55	−0.95

Variables (or columns) 6, 9, 7, 5, and 8 show the larger changes between levels. Columns 11, 3, and 4 show the smaller changes between levels.

Columns 6, 9, and 7 also showed larger changes between levels in Table 4.

In graphical form, the results appear in Figure 2. Again a Pareto approach is used to demonstrate rank order.

ANOVA on the S/N Ratio data is shown in Table 9:

Columns 3 and 11 were pooled into column error due to their small contribution.

Columns 6, 9, and 7 have the largest contribution for moving the mean and reducing variability.

Columns 1, 2, 5, and 8 contribute 15.39%. The remaining columns, 4 and 10 contribute 1%. The number of significant variables has increased from the mean ANOVA table as columns 1, 2, 5, and 8 are shown to be significant in addition to 6, 9, and 7.

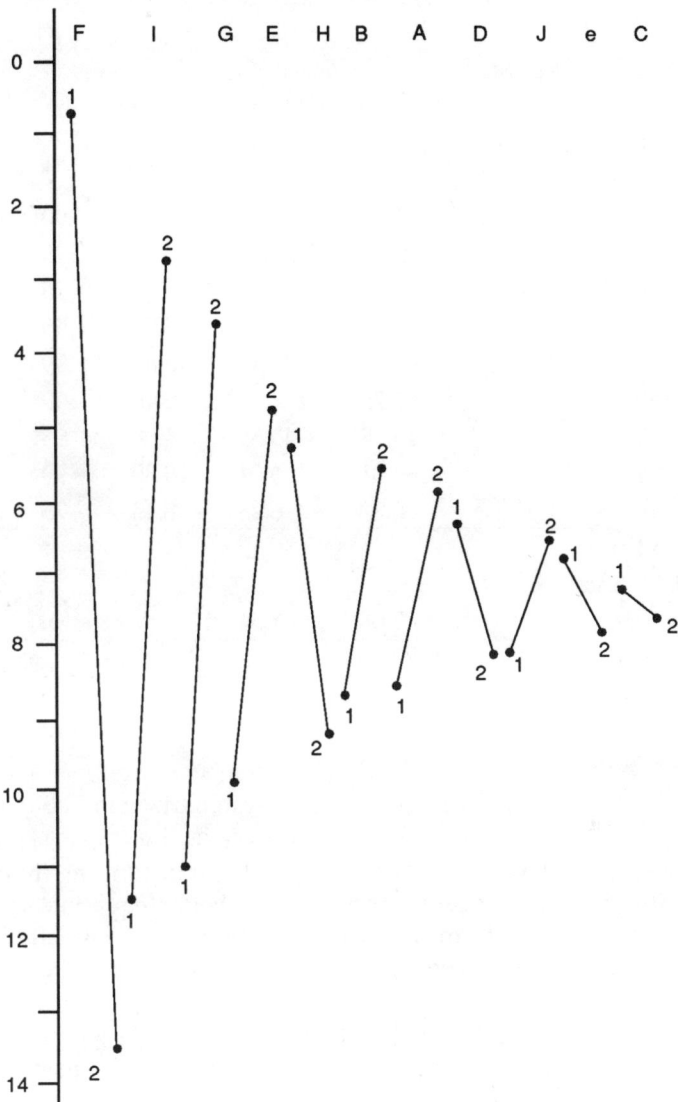

Figure 2. Graph of Reverse S/N Ratio Effects, Surface Defects, By Variable

Table 9. S/N Ratio ANOVA Table

Source	Degrees of Freedom	Sum of Squares	Mean Square	Percent Contrib.	Conf. Level	Best Level
Column 1	1	21.06	21.06	1.81	90	2
2	1	31.31	31.31	1.76	95	2
4	1	7.99	7.99	0.6	75	1
5	1	74.22	74.22	6.74	95	2
6	1	495.82	495.82	45.81	99	1
7	1	167.75	167.75	15.40	99	2
8	1	45.58	45.58	4.08	95	1
9	1	266.01	266.01	20.80	99	2
10	1	6.23	6.23	0.43	75	2
Column Error (3 and 11) and Pooled Error	(2)	3.08	1.54			
Sum total	11	1079.06				

7. Summary and Conclusions

The results of analysis of the trial are summarized in Table 10.

The defect sum is the sum of the defects in the two panels made per run. The column labeled "S/N" is the result of transforming the data to S/N Ratios using the formula for smaller-the-better (equation 3.1). With the data shown in this form, it is easier to see the level-change effect of the variation in the results. The significant effect of columns 6, 9, and 7 can be seen.

The two ANOVA tables agree that the three factors with the largest and best effect on the surface defects and their best levels are in decreasing order of importance:

1. Foam shot weight (low)
2. Venting (use additional, more)
3. Foam diverter (yes, use).

This agrees well with past experience that these variables could have a large influence on the reduction of surface defects in instrument panels.

Table 10. Independent and Dependent Variables Data Array

Run No.	Variables 1 A	2 B	3 C	4 D	5 E	6 F	7 G	8 H	9 I	10 J	11 e	Defect Sum	S/N
1	1	1	1	1	1	1	1	1	1	1	1	6.9	−11.46
2	1	1	1	1	1	2	2	2	2	2	2	7.5	−11.57
3	1	1	2	2	2	1	1	1	2	2	2	1.8	+0.57
4	1	2	1	2	2	1	2	2	1	1	2	2.5	−2.27
5	1	2	2	1	2	2	1	2	1	2	1	14.8	−18.91
6	1	2	2	2	1	2	2	1	2	1	1	4.2	−6.90
7	2	1	2	2	1	1	2	2	1	2	1	3.8	−5.76
8	2	1	2	1	2	2	2	1	1	1	2	6.6	−10.51
9	2	1	1	2	2	2	1	2	2	1	1	7.3	−13.55
10	2	2	2	1	1	1	1	2	2	1	2	1.8	−2.10
11	2	2	1	2	1	2	1	1	1	2	2	18.4	−19.59
12	2	2	1	1	2	1	2	1	2	2	1	0.2	+16.99

Summarizing the ANOVA data:

Table 11. Summarizing the ANOVA Data

Column No.		Variables	Mean ANOVA Analysis		S/N For Smaller-the-Better ANOVA Analysis	
			Percent Contrib.	Best Level	Percent Contrib.	Best Level
1	A	Foam Formul.			1.81	2
2	B	Venting A			2.76	2
3	C	Shell Weight				
4	D	Tooling aid A			0.60	1
5	E	Foam throughput			6.74	2
6	F	Foam shot wt.	27.29	1	45.81	1
7	G	Diverter	9.48	2	15.40	2
8	H	Tooling aid B			4.08	1
9	I	Venting B	13.27	2	20.80	2
10	J	Cure time	2.92	1	0.43	2
11	e	Error column				

The cure time variable (*J*) was left out of the above list because of its small contribution and the conflict in best level from the two ANOVA tables.

The trial also gave us a direction for setting the levels of the other variables (from the S/N Ratio ANOVA) to reduce variation:

1. Foam formulation at *B*
2. Venting, yes
3. Tooling aid A, use old type
4. Foam throughput, use higher
5. Tooling aid B, don't use.

Q & A

Q. This is an example of plastic product development. Is this an unusual case study?

A. Yes. In the U.S. there are very few case studies of chemical product development published.

Q. Is it good that only main effects were assigned to the L_{12} orthogonal array?

A. Yes. However, 30 factors were discussed in the brainstorming session, and one column among 11 was reserved for the estimate of error. As a rule, if any columns are empty, one of the remaining factors should be assigned. Using only one degree of freedom for the estimation of error is not recommended.

Q. Factor *A* is foam formulation and it is tedious to change, so the factor was assigned to column one. Then, the experiments were conducted following the order of columns one through 12. This violates the rule of randomization. I have discussed this problem many times with engineers, and they say their advisers always insist upon randomization. Should they continue this practice?

A. As a rule, randomization is desirable. But engineers do not always have the luxury of time and money to do it. The advice is typical of consultants who have little to do with the economic considerations or the reduction of the product-development cycle. This is a problem. The order of experiments should be determined by the engineers in such a way that it is easiest to run. Design of experiments for

Instrument Panel Process Development

Quality Engineering is quite different from agricultural experimentation, which was developed by R.F. Fisher in the 1920s.

Q. Without randomization, effects of the factors not considered in the experiment might confound with other factors. How do you avoid this?

A. This reveals an important comparison between industrial experimentation and agricultural experimentation. In Quality Engineering, we include noise factors in the experiment. Factor levels that are robust against these noise factors have a very good chance of being robust against unconsidered factor effects.

Q. Can you prove this?

A. There are many successful case studies without randomization.

Q. Weighted values for surface defects were used as a quality characteristic. Was this a good choice?

A. It is not clearly described. It would be better not only to count the number of defects, but also to take the size of defects into consideration. If the number of defects varies in such a range as this case indicates, they may be considered continuous variables for data analysis.

Q. Why are there no noise factors?

A. It is better to have noise factors, of course. It takes time to set up these experiments.

Q. Is it necessary to analyze both raw data and the S/N Ratio?

A. This is an example of a smaller-the-better case. There is also a large variation between repetitions. Therefore, only the S/N Ratio analysis is necessary.

4. Thermoplastic Extrusion Process Improvement: An Application of Dynamic Characteristics

Joseph F. Dick
Flex Technologies, Inc.

The objective of this study was to deduce extrusion settings that would make thermoplastic tubing outer diameter more sensitive to changes in the extruder screw rpm. An L_{12} orthogonal array was selected to test 11 extrusion control factors, and considerable replications of data were captured. Dynamic analysis was performed on the tubing outer diameter measurements. A comparison of previous quality to experimentally optimized quality was made using the Quality Loss Function. Sensitivity to screw rpm, with reduction of tubing outer diameter variance, can be translated into an annual savings of $64,800.

1. Objective

Flex Technologies is a major supplier of vacuum harnesses to the automotive industry. Variance encountered in the extrusion of the thermoplastic tubing that is a subassembly of the vacuum harness represents a cascading problem that affects many facets of downstream production processes. The objective endeavor of this experiment is to deduce extrusion settings that will make the tubing's outer diameter (O.D.) more sensitive to changes in the extruder screw rpm. To solve this problem Dr. Genichi Taguchi's method of multivariate experimental design was utilized to increase the linearity between the extruder rpm and the tubing's O.D. while simultaneously reducing the variability of the screw rpm and the O.D. relationship. Figure 1 shows the desired relationship.

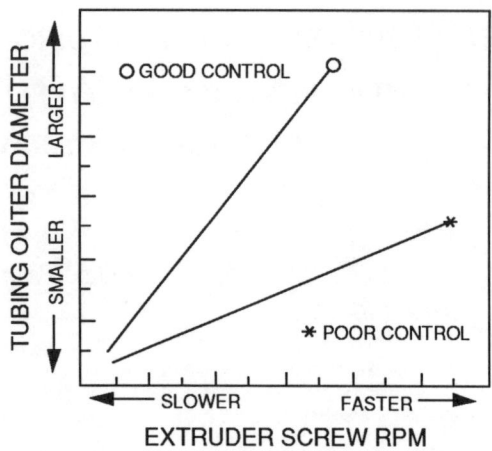

Figure 1. Graph Showing Desired Linear Relationship

2. Experimental Overview

Figure 2 depicts the actual configuration that the extrusion plant maintains for tubing production where a "LaserMike" is used to control the tubing's O.D. The LaserMike instrumentation samples the tubing's O.D. via a helium neon laser and processes measurement samplings from a two-axis alignment. The LaserMike then uses this information to decide whether the O.D. of the tubing should be increased or decreased. If the tubing O.D. is to be altered, a signal is sent back to the controlling system of the extruder, which corrects the screw rpm in accordance with the desired change.

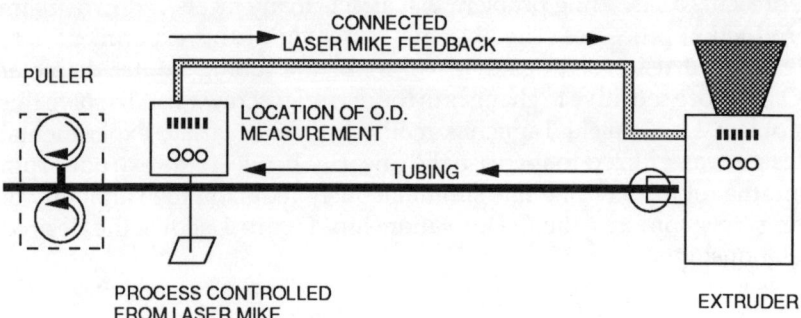

Figure 2. Extrusion Process Configuration

Since the LaserMike is used primarily for tubing O.D. control, it was decided to negate its effect relating to this study by disconnecting the LaserMike feedback conductor, which connects to the screw rpm control circuitry found in the main extrusion housing. A determined oscillatory event of sampling and correction delays caused by the LaserMike was an unnecessary contributor to the tubing outside diameter variance and was isolated from the experiment. This led to the complete control of the tubing's O.D. using the microprocessor circuitry of the extrusion unit to become the preconceived experimental intent. Figure 3 is the configuration that was used in performing this experiment.

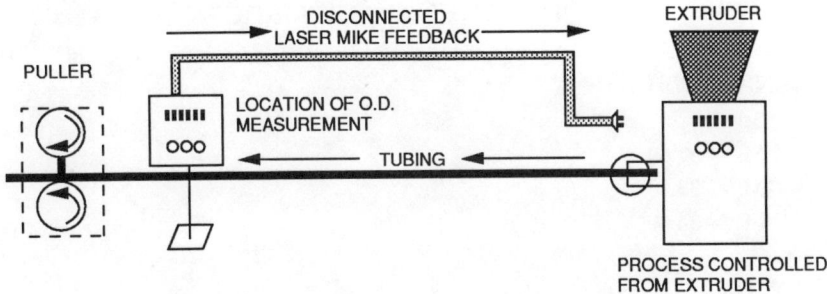

Figure 3. Configuration Used in the Experiment

A brainstorming session was held to deduce those factors believed associated with tubing O.D. variance. Extrusion plant management and others knowledgeable with this type of process were in attendance. Figure 4 shows the Ishikawa diagram that resulted from this session.

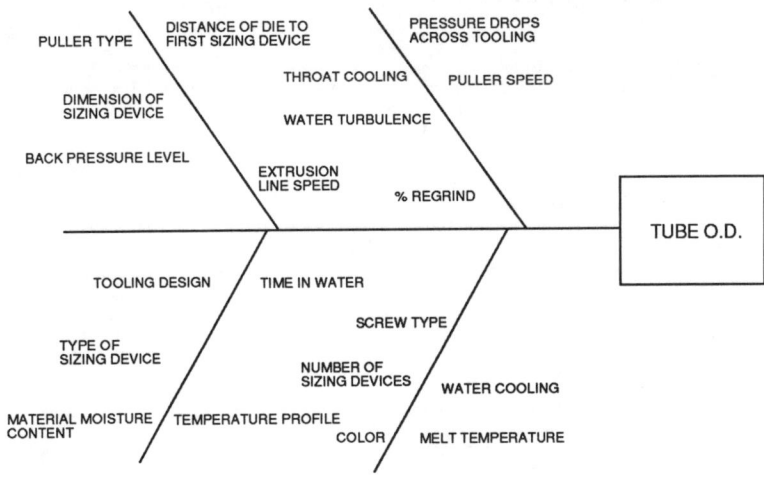

Figure 4. Cause-and-Effect Diagram

Voting on factor hierarchy took place after the cause-and-effect meeting so that assignment to an orthogonal array could be made. Concluding that the extruded tubing O.D.output process should be sensitive to screw rpm, a dynamic approach to this analysis was chosen where the signal factor would be represented by screw rpm. At the end of the meeting, the consensus of factors were reduced to 11; this would lend itself to an L_{12} orthogonal array where three levels of signal would be used for the dynamic study. The following pages show the actual factors selected and the assignment to the selected array.

QUALITY CHARACTERISTIC
Tube O.D.

SIGNAL FACTOR
    Screw rpm
    M_1 — 32.60
    M_2 — 33.60
    M_3 — 34.60

CONTROL FACTORS
    A. SCREW TYPE
        1. Standard
        2. Alternate
    B. DIMENSIONS OF SIZING DEVICE
        1. In use
        2. Larger than in use
    C. TOOLING DESIGN
        1. Minimum
        2. Maximum
    D. PULLER TYPE
        1. Hydraulic
        2. DC drive
    E. PRESSURE DROPS ACROSS TOOLING
        1. Standard in use
        2. Less than standard
    F. WATER COOLING
        1. Ambient
        2. Chilled to standard
    G. WATER TURBULENCE
        1. No turbulence
        2. Standard turbulence

H. BACK PRESSURE LEVEL
    1. Level 1
    2. Level 2
I. MOISTURE CONTENT
    1. 0.2% as received
    2. Less than 0.1%
J. TEMPERATURE PROFILE
    1. Set 1
    2. Set 2
K. MELT TEMPERATURE
    1. Temperature 1
    2. Temperature 2

$L_{12}(2^{11})$

Table 1. Experiment Layout

No./Col.	A	B	C	D	E	F	G	H	I	J	K	M_1	M_2	M_3	S/N Ratios
1	1	1	1	1	1	1	1	1	1	1	1				
2	1	1	1	1	1	2	2	2	2	2	2				
3	1	1	2	2	2	1	1	1	2	2	2				
4	1	2	1	2	2	1	2	2	1	1	2				
5	1	2	2	1	2	2	1	2	1	2	1				
6	1	2	2	2	1	2	2	1	2	1	1				
7	2	1	3	3	1	1	3	3	1	2	1				
8	2	1	2	1	2	2	2	1	1	1	2				
9	2	1	1	2	2	1	2	2	1	1					
10	2	2	2	1	1	1	1	2	2	1	2				
11	2	2	1	2	1	2	1	1	1	2	2				
12	2	2	1	1	2	1	2	1	2	2	1				

Examination of the array assignment and previously shown factor selection, shows that noise factors were not designated. This was based on the following reasoning:

Experimental time encompassed two eight-hour days that introduced, as sufficient, pertinent noise into the system.
1. Temperature differentials of 20 degrees
2. Various unexpected delays
3. Tooling setup variation.

Experimental control factor levels were performed in conjunction with the orthogonal array, where 12 data points were captured for each level of signal. The measurement of the tubing O.D. entailed the following:
1. Attain tubing sample for an associated experimental run
2. Measure the O.D. of the tubing sample approximately 1 in. from either cut end
3. Record the data points
4. Twelve tubes were measured for each level of signal providing 36 pieces of information per experimental run.

3. Raw Data and S/N Ratios

Table 2 provides the raw data attained for each experimental run, along with its associated Signal-to-Noise (S/N) Ratio.

4. S/N Ratios for Dynamic Characteristics

The following calculation method was used in computing the dynamic S/N Ratio. Experimental run 1 is used as the example.

$$S_T = 0.148^2 + 0.145^2 + \ldots + 0.152^2 + 0.155^2 - \frac{(\text{Total for run \#1})^2}{36}$$

$$= 0.8043200 - \frac{(5.38)^2}{36} = 0.0003088889 \qquad (4.1)$$

$$S_\beta = \frac{\left((m_1 - \overline{m}) \cdot M_1 + (m_2 - \overline{m}) \cdot M_2 + (m_3 - \overline{m}) \cdot M_3\right)^2}{\left(r_0 \cdot \left((m_1 - \overline{m})^2 + (m_2 - \overline{m}) + (m_3 - \overline{m})^2\right)\right)} \qquad (4.2)$$

where

$m_1 = 32.6 \quad m_2 = 33.6 \quad m_3 = 34.6 =$ Screw RPM Signal Levels

Table 2. Data

EXPERIMENT RUN	M_1				M_2				M_3				S/N Ratios
1	.148 .145 .147	.147 .145 .145	.147 .146 .148	.145 .146 .147	.148 .149 .149	.150 .148 .147	.148 .149 .150	.151 .151 .149	.153 .154 .153	.152 .154 .151	.152 .152 .154	.153 .152 .155	8.751
2	.158 .158 .157	.156 .158 .158	.157 .159 .158	.157 .156 .159	.160 .161 .160	.161 .160 .159	.161 .160 .160	.160 .160 .161	.161 .162 .164	.163 .163 .162	.160 .162 .162	.163 .163 .162	8.128
3	.169 .169 .167	.171 .168 .165	.167 .168 .166	.165 .163 .165	.171 .171 .171	.171 .169 .170	.170 .166 .168	.169 .171 .168	.173 .172 .175	.170 .172 .171	.173 .173 .174	.171 .173 .172	3.879
4	.147 .147 .146	.146 .148 .146	.147 .147 .145	.146 .146 .147	.148 .149 .148	.148 .148 .149	.148 .148 .149	.149 .148 .149	.151 .149 .152	.151 .151 .151	.149 .149 .151	.151 .151 .150	8.943
5	.161 .162 .161	.159 .160 .160	.158 .159 .159	.159 .158 .158	.165 .162 .164	.163 .162 .163	.162 .163 .163	.162 .163 .164	.169 .163 .164	.166 .165 .164	.166 .164 .166	.165 .164 .166	6.523
6	.159 .158 .158	.160 .159 .158	.157 .158 .156	.156 .158 .158	.162 .161 .162	.161 .159 .162	.159 .160 .159	.160 .161 .160	.163 .165 .163	.164 .163 .164	.163 .164 .162	.163 .165 .166	8.047
7	.202 .199 .208	.205 .203 .205	.207 .208 .207	.199 .208 .208	.210 .205 .212	.212 .202 .211	.205 .205 .210	.211 .204 .210	.210 .205 .204	.212 .213 .209	.208 .207 .213	.214 .210 .209	-3.770
8	.190 .195 .189	.199 .199 .199	.194 .189 .196	.190 .192 .194	.195 .194 .191	.193 .192 .192	.190 .191 .192	.193 .187 .199	.193 .198 .195	.207 .190 .187	.200 .195 .199	.200 .199 .200	-10.701
9	.184 .182 .183	.182 .182 .184	.183 .185 .180	.184 .182 .182	.188 .188 .186	.187 .185 .184	.183 .184 .182	.184 .183 .185	.187 .188 .189	.187 .185 .184	.189 .188 .189	.188 .189 .186	2.836
10	.213 .212 .215	.219 .209 .214	.219 .218 .206	.209 .215 .202	.223 .207 .211	.210 .208 .207	.210 .211 .212	.213 .214 .208	.215 .209 .222	.230 .225 .229	.207 .210 .213	.215 .214 .212	-11.366
11	.173 .175 .174	.174 .175 .172	.176 .178 .177	.175 .180 .170	.183 .184 .189	.182 .179 .184	.189 .190 .180	.182 .181 .184	.186 .185 .191	.192 .187 .185	.183 .182 .190	.192 .193 .184	4.702
12	.184 .185 .184	.184 .184 .185	.184 .184 .185	.180 .183 .178	.187 .185 .186	.186 .186 .185	.186 .185 .186	.185 .184 .185	.186 .187 .189	.190 .190 .188	.186 .188 .181	.183 .189 .190	-0.789

and
$M_1 = 1.756 \quad M_2 = 1.789 \quad M_3 = 1.835 =$ Signal Level Totals Per Run

and
$$\overline{m} = \frac{(m_1 + m_2 + m_3)}{3} = 33.6 \quad r_o = 12$$

calculating

$$S_\beta = \frac{[(32.6 - 33.6) \cdot 1.756 + (33.6 - 33.6) \cdot 1.789 + (34.6 - 33.6) \cdot 1.835]^2}{\left[12 \cdot \left((32.6 - 33.6)^2 + (33.6 - 33.6)^2 + (34.6 - 33.6)^2\right)\right]}$$

$= 0.0002600417$

$S_e = ST - S_\beta = 0.0000488472$ (4.3)

$$V_e = \frac{S_e}{V_{(df)}} \quad (4.4)$$

$$= \frac{.0000488472}{34} = 0.0000014367$$

$$\hat{\eta} = \frac{\left[\left(\frac{1}{r}\right) \cdot (S_\beta - V_e)\right]}{V_e} \quad (4.5)$$

where
$$r = \left[r_o \cdot \left((m_1 - \overline{m})^2 + (m_2 - \overline{m})^2 + (m_3 - \overline{m})^2\right)\right] \quad (4.6)$$

$$= \left[12 \cdot \left((32.6 - 33.6)^2 + (33.6 - 33.6)^2 + (34.6 - 33.6)^2\right)\right] = 24$$

so
$$\hat{\eta} = \frac{\left[\left(\frac{1}{24}\right) \cdot (0.0002600417 - 0.0000014367)\right]}{0.0000014367} = 7.50006 \quad (4.7)$$

$\hat{\eta}\, dB = 10 \cdot \log(7.50006) = 8.751\ dB$ (4.8)

* All calculations are subject to the rounding error encountered by transferring spreadsheet to text.

Below is the summary response table for the orthogonal array.

Table 3. Summary Response Table

Factor	Description	Level 1	Level 2	Level Difference
A	Screw type	44.270	−19.068	63.339
B	Diameter/sizing device	9.122	16.080	6.958
C	Tooling design	32.591	−7.389	39.980
D	Puller type	0.566	24.636	24.071
E	Press Drp/tooling	14.491	10.711	3.780
F	Water cooling	5.688	19.534	13.866
G	Water turbulence	15.324	9.878	5.445
H	Back press level	13.908	11.294	2.614
I	Moisture content	14.448	10.754	3.694
J	Temp profile	6.509	18.693	12.184
K	Melt temperature	21.618	3.584	18.034

The following represents the average effects of tube's O.D. Only those factors from Table 3 that maintained the largest level difference (difference ≥ 12.18) are shown. By choosing the factors with the largest level difference, we are able to essentially deduce the same information that will result from the analysis of variance (ANOVA) provided on the following page.

Figure 5 presents the average effects for the experiment.

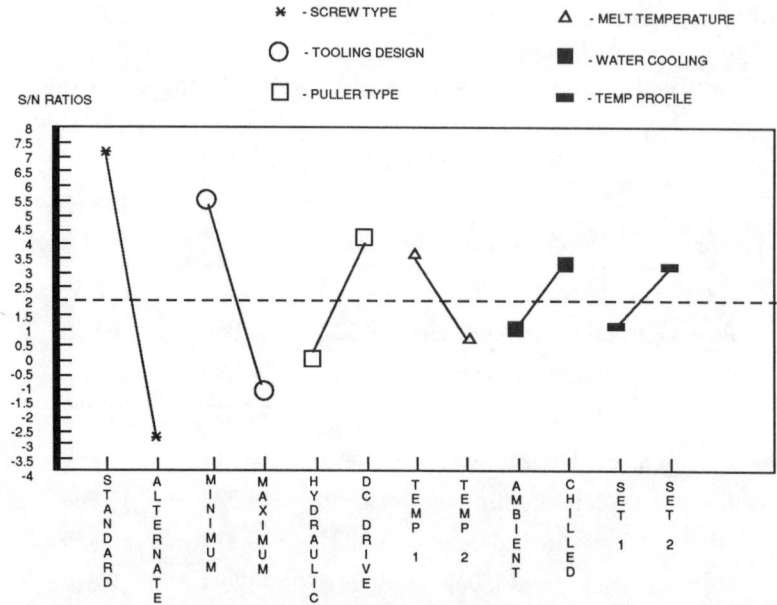

Figure 5. Factorial Effects

An ANOVA was performed on the S/N Ratios and the following was derived:

Table 4. ANOVA

Source	df	S	V	S'	ρ (%)
A	1	334.314	334.314	332.434	57.248
B	1	4.035	4.035	pool	
C	1	133.198	133.198	131.317	22.614
D	1	48.284	48.284	46.404	7.991
E	1	1.191	1.191	pool	
F	1	16.022	16.022	14.142	2.435
G	1	2.471	2.471	pool	
H	1	0.569	0.569	pool	
I	1	1.137	1.137	pool	
J	1	12.370	12.370	10.490	1.806
K	1	27.101	27.101	25.220	4.343
e'	5	9.403	1.881	20.687	3.562
T	11	580.693		580.693	100.000

5. Confirmation Run

Upon completion of the analysis, a confirmation was conducted to validate the experimental results. This involves selecting and setting factors at levels that are experimental optimum, reduce costs in production, or are easily maintainable in the process. Since all factor levels would be easy to control in a production, the method used for deriving factor levels for this analysis was attained from Table 2, where the highest-level value witnessed for each factor was chosen. Our selection for the confirmation run became the following selections:

$$A_1, B_2, C_1, D_2, E_1, F_2, G_1, H_1, I_1, J_2, K_1.$$

To realize a successful confirmation, a prediction of the S/N Ratio expected to result from the confirmation run must be calculated. The calculation of the predicted result does not use all factor levels selected for the confirmation run, but only includes those factors that maintain significance pertaining to percent contribution found in the right column of the ANOVA table (Table 3). The factors used for the prediction are as follows:

$$A_1, C_1, D_2, F_2, J_2, K_1$$

6. Calculation of the Predicted and Confirmed S/N Ratio

The S/N Ratio that is expected to result from confirmation run is calculated below:

$$\overline{A_1} - \overline{T} = 7.378 - 2.100 = 5.278$$
$$\overline{C_1} - \overline{T} = 5.432 - 2.100 = 3.332$$
$$\overline{D_2} - \overline{T} = 4.106 - 2.100 = 2.006$$
$$\overline{F_2} - \overline{T} = 3.256 - 2.100 = 1.156$$
$$\overline{J_2} - \overline{T} = 3.115 - 2.100 = 1.015$$
$$\overline{K_1} - \overline{T} = 3.603 - 2.100 = 1.503$$
$$+ \overline{T} = 2.100 = 2.100$$
$$\text{Predicted Value} = 16.390 \text{ dB}$$

To determine the 95% confidence interval:

$$C.I. = \sqrt{\left(\frac{F_{(1.5)} \times V_e}{n_e}\right)} \quad (4.9)$$

$$= \sqrt{\left(\frac{6.61 \times 1.88}{\left(\frac{12}{7}\right)}\right)} = 2.69$$

The following represents the raw data and S/N Ratio that resulted from the confirmation run:

Table 6. Confirmation Run

	M_1	M_2	M_3	S/N Ratio
Confirm	.151 .150 .151 .150 .151 .151 .152 .151 .151 .151 .151 .151	.155 .156 .156 .155 .155 .155 .155 .156 .155 .155 .155 .155	.158 .159 .158 .159 .158 .159 .159 .158 .158 .159 .158 .159	16.670

The confirming result is well within the confidence interval and is conducive to a successful experiment. Table 7 provides a summarization of factor contribution.

An evaluation of quality was an objective that was believed critical to this analysis. This was done by measuring a group of 50 test samples eight months prior to this experiment and analyzing the associated Quality Loss Function (QLF). Since the tubing's O.D. is a Nominal-the-Best characteristic, the QLF becomes:

$$k = \frac{(\$ \text{ Cost for Scrapped Ft. Tubing})}{(\text{Tolerance})^2} \quad (4.10)$$

Where the cost incurred for scrapped tubing of our sample length is $0.019125
(sample length is = 12 in.)
and
        Lower Specification = 0.147 in.
        Upper Specification = 0.153 in.
                Target = 0.150 in.

Table 7. Summary Table of Experimental Results
Quality Characteristic — Tube O.D.

Factor	Level	Description	ρ (%)	Choice
A		SCREW TYPE	57.25%	A_1
	1	Standard	7.378	
	2	Alternate	–3.178	
B		DIMENSIONS OF SIZING DEVICE	—	
	1	In use		
	2	Larger than in use		
C		TOOLING DESIGN	22.61%	C_1
	1	Minimum	5.432	
	2	Maximum	1.231	
D		PULLER TYPE	7.99%	D_2
	1	Hydraulic	0.094	
	2	DC drive	4.106	
E		PRESSURE DROPS ACROSS TOOLING	—	
	1	Standard in use		
	2	Less than standard		
F		WATER COOLING	2.44%	F_2
	1	Ambient	0.945	
	2	Chilled To Standard	3.256	
G		WATER TURBULENCE	—	
	1	No turbulence		
	2	Standard turbulence		
H		BACK PRESSURE LEVEL	—	
	1	Level 1		
	2	Level 2		
I		MOISTURE CONTENT	—	
	1	0.2% as received		
	2	Less than 0.1%		
J		TEMPERATURE PROFILE	1.81%	J_2
	1	Set 1	1.085	
	2	Set 2	3.115	
K		MELT TEMPERATURE	4.34%	K_1
	1	Temperature 1	3.603	
	2	Temperature 2	0.597	
T Bar		EXPERIMENTAL AVERAGE	2.10	
μ Prediction		$A_1\ C_1\ D_2\ F_2\ J_2\ K_1$	16.390	
Confidence Interval			2.693	

making Tolerance = 0.003 in.

and, $k = \dfrac{(\$0.019125)}{(0.003)^2} = 2125$

The data collected over the eight months yielded an average of 0.150013 in. and a standard deviation of 0.0013757.

Using the QLF:
   Loss = $k\ [\sigma^2 + (\bar{y} - \text{target})^2]$ (4.11)

This yields
   Loss = $2125\ [0.0013757^2 + (0.150013 - 0.150)^2]$ = \$0.0040/piece

After the confirmation run was complete, the screw rpm control circuitry was tuned so that the tubing O.D. output would target at 0.150 in. Fifteen minutes was allowed to pass before 50 tubing samples were extracted to be measured for a quality comparison against the tubing previously run. Sample measurements produced an average of 0.149880 in. with a standard deviation of 0.000773. The following is the quality evaluation for this sample run.

Using the QLF this yields:
   Loss = $2125\ [0.000773^2 + (0.149880 - 0.150)^2]$ = \$0.0013/piece

7. Conclusion

Extensive knowledge can be acquired by making quality comparisons between existing level conditions and experimental optimum conditions that give realization of improvement. Due to the dissimilarity between the detailed existing machine setting condition and the levels used in this experiment, only the actual quality improvement between the previous extrusion run of eight months, which represented typical O.D. variation, and the experimental optimum from this study could be considered for quality evaluation.

As shown previously by the QLFs, a total savings of \$0.0027 per piece has been extracted by this experiment. This improvement can be translated into a total yearly savings of \$64,800 when production of our sample length entails 24,000,000 units.

The study has been considered successful in deducing those factors that allow the extruded tubing O.D. output to be more sensitive to small changes in screw rpm, but the improvement to extrusion output does not end here. The next step will be to connect the LaserMike system while still using our machine settings and improve the product even more via a parameter designed experiment using the LaserMike's control setting.

Acknowledgments

Special thanks to: Flex Technologies Midvale Extrusion Plant 1, George Spahr, Gene Stefani, and Jim Walton.

Q & A

Q. Equation (6), for the S/N Ratio in the text does not belong to any of the S/N Ratio equations that I am familiar with, i.e., Nominal-the-Best, Smaller-the-Better, and Larger-the-Better. This is the first time I have seen it. Can this be explained?

A. This is an equation for dynamic characteristics, explained thoroughly in Chapter 24 of Dr. Genichi Taguchi's two-volume work *System of Experimental Design*. The equations you see are the equations for static or nondynamic characteristics. With nondynamic characteristics, we try to optimize by determining the best control factor level combination. Once the best condition is determined, we assume that there will be no periodic adjustment of parameter levels.

But with a dynamic characteristic, adjustment is necessary. We study dynamic characteristics in order to find the best combination for easy adjustment with small variability.

Q. For a Nominal-the-Best case, the S/N Ratio is the ratio of the mean squared to the variance. What does the equation for S/N Ratio mean in the case of dynamic characteristics?

A. It is the ratio of the slope (beta) squared to the variance. Beta is the magnitude of an output characteristic caused by a unit change of a signal factor. The output response resulting from the input must be linear and its slope steep.

Q. It makes sense for the response to be linear because this would make adjustment easier. But why does the slope have to be steep?

A. In this case, rpm is used to adjust the outside diameter. But the degree to which the system can adjust the outside diameter is not great. Therefore, it is necessary to amplify the sensitivity of adjustment.

Q. Is there any case in which the beta value becomes too large and the system becomes too sensitive after parameter design of a dynamic characteristic?

A. This is possible. But in such a case, we can easily adjust the slope downward most of the time. For example, in the design of a steering system of a car, when the steering angle becomes too sensitive to the turning radius, it is always possible to reduce the sensitivity by using gears.

Q. Why is it necessary to increase the slope only to reduce it later?

A. When a parameter is used to adjust the slope without affecting the S/N Ratio, such as with gears in a car, variability will be reduced when the slope is adjusted downward.

Q. So increasing the sensitivity has the same effect as reducing variability?

A. Exactly. That is the beauty of Taguchi Methods.

5. Factors Affecting Solvent-Bonded Connector Durability: Optimization of the Strength of an Emission Control Harness Assembly

Jim Quinlan
Flex Technologies, Inc

This paper investigates the improvement of automotive emission control harnesses. This product must conduct vacuum signals to various devices that alter the combustion engine's performance to minimize emissions. A low but noticeable number of solvent-bonded harnesses were found separated in finished assemblies. Taguchi experimentation resulted in a reduction in parts failure from 17% to 1.1%. As a result, an inspection cost savings of $200 per 1,000 pieces was realized on monthly production of 500,000.

1. The Thermoplastic Assembly

The product under test in this experiment was an automotive emission control harness. This thermoplastic assembly consists of thermoplastic tubing, thermoplastic connectors, thermoset connectors, tape, shielding, and valves. The purpose of this product is to conduct vacuum signals to the various devices that alter the combustion engine's performance to minimize emissions into the atmosphere.

Such products must conduct vacuum to the correct points, have a low leak rate, function in engine compartment environments, and survive "normal" handling both prior to assembly on the engine and in service.

2. The Production Operation

The operation under test in this experiment is the point at which the thermoplastic connector was assembled to the thermoplastic tubing (see Figure 1). The tubing raw material was specified by the customer as

---

From the *Second Symposium on Taguchi Methods*™, pp. 78–100, Copyright © 1984, American Supplier Institute, Inc., Dearborn, Michigan.

either Type 6 nylon or Type 6/6 nylon. The connectors were molded from Type 6 nylon only.

During this operation the tubing has a nylon solvent applied to it. It is then pushed by hand into the connector. The solvent forms a nylon-to-nylon bond that had proved to be strong and reliable over the past six years.

After this operation, the product is required to exceed 20 lbs. of force when tensile tested to destruction at 4 in./min., not to leak above a specified level, and not to produce a plugged or severely restricted tube.

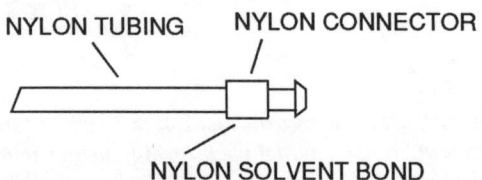

Specified Performance Requirements:

1. When pull tested to destruction at 4 in./min., the force required to destroy the bond must exceed 20 pounds.

2. The bond must not leak.

3. The bond must not plug tube.

Figure 1. The Operation

At the time of this experiment, these operations were occurring at our assembly plant at a rate of 500,000 times per month.

3. THE PROBLEM

A very low, but noticeable, number of solvent-bonded connections were being found separated in finished assemblies. Sometimes, when the products reached the 100% test station, connectors were found missing.

At our customer's plants, we would sometimes hear comments that some assemblies had connectors missing, although we had not received formal rejections. Very few were found, the samples weren't retained, and it was assumed that extreme violence had been done to the assembly as it was removed from the box and put on the engine.

Due to concern over product quality, the plant took the step of having a person "tug" on each nylon connector of finished parts after the parts were packaged. This operation found that approximately 1 in 1,000 connectors had failed. It also cost $200 per 1,000 assemblies and did nothing to solve the problem.

4. THE CAUSE-AND-EFFECT DIAGRAM

Since there was a plethora of theories on why the connectors were failing, it was decided to bring together all personnel knowledgeable about the process and product (including the production operators) to construct a cause-and-effect diagram.

An abbreviated version of the diagram appears in Figure 2.

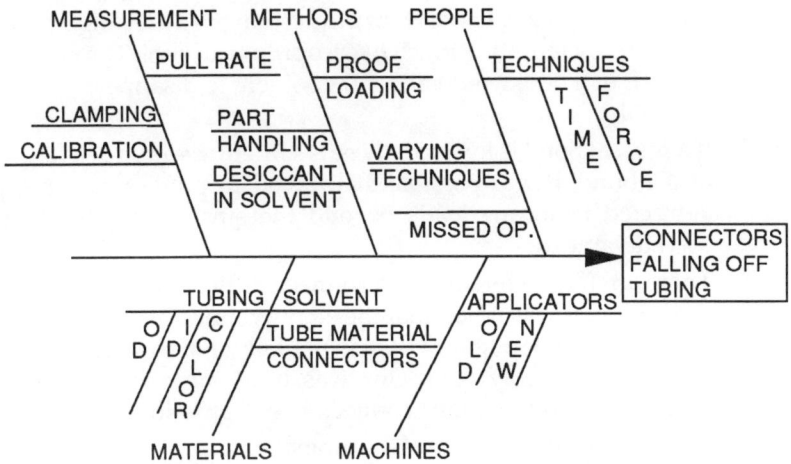

Figure 2. Cause-and-Effect Diagram

The following information was derived from the meeting and diagram:

1. The "missed operation" theory assumes that the operator forgot to dip the tube in the solvent, which was not correct. All failed parts showed evidence of having been dipped in the solvent.
2. The solvent applicator had recently been changed. The traditional dip cup had been replaced by an applicator that coated the outer diameter of the tubing with solvent. This improvement was instituted to reduce the number of plugged and restricted connections that failed at 100% test.

3. The tubing raw material had been changed from Type 6 nylon to Type 6/6 nylon due to a temporary advantage in pricing.
4. Repeated pull-testing to the 20 lb. requirement was strongly suspect. Such "proof-loading" had become a frequent test in an effort to locate the problem connections.
5. The type of base in the color concentrate was suspected to have an effect. Pigments are "carried" in pellets of various polymeric types. It was possible that an olefinic-based color concentrate had found its way into the nylon tubing rather than the more preferable polyamide-based color concentrate.
6. Another suspected factor was the time that lapsed after the operator applied the solvent and before he inserted the tubing into the connector. The solvent in question has a very high vapor pressure, evaporating much like isopropyl alcohol. The passage of too much time would allow the solvent to disappear prior to assembly.
7. If a solvent bond is torqued, there is sometimes a sudden failure of the bond. It was possible that the failed product was being subjected to torque loads beyond the survival limits of the solvent bonds.
8. There are five different nylon connectors that are assembled to the tubing. It was noted that the elbow connector seemed to be the most common failure. It was not known if this was simply because the elbow connector was used more frequently or whether it was due to the connector configuration.
9. The head history and age of the tubing were deemed significant. Some of the group thought using older tubing was better, and some did not. In the production process, some tubes might also see some short-time heating.

The cause-and-effect diagram proved to be a very useful tool in reducing the fog of theories into some testable factors.

5. Control and Noise Factors

From the above exercise, several factors were listed (see Table 1). The levels of the factors were set by the engineering, quality, and production personnel. The outside (noise) factors were primarily set by engineering, because it was essential that the noise factors were sufficiently severe to produce the type of failure under investigation while not being so severe as to fail all the parts. Some very quick testing was done to verify the levels of the noise factor.

Table 1. Factor Listing

INSIDE FACTORS		
Factor	Level	Description
A	1	Tubing Raw Material = Nylon 6
	2	Tubing Raw Material = Nylon 6/6
B	1	Color Concentrate Type = Diofinic
	2	Color Concentrate Type = Polyamide
C	1	Connector Type = Straight Connector
	2	Connector Type = Elbow Connector
D	1	Applicator Design = Old Design
	2	Applicator Design = New Design
E	1	Time from Solvent to Assembly = 1 sec.
	2	Time from Solvent to Assembly = 2 sec.
	3	Time from Solvent to Assembly = 3 sec.
	4	Time from Solvent to Assembly = 4 sec.
OUTSIDE FACTORS		
F	1	Preheating of Tubing = Ambient Temp.
	2	Preheating of Tubing = 350°F/15 min.
	3	Preheating of Tubing = 400°F/10 min.
G	1	Turns on Connector = None
	2	Turns on Connector = One
	3	Turns on Connector = Two
H	1	Number of 201 Proof Leads = None
	2	Number of 201 Proof Leads = Five
	3	Number of 201 Proof Leads = Ten

It should be noted that the inside factor, C, might be considered uncontrollable, because the customer specifies which connector is to be used. The reason this factor is inside is that we have design latitude in the area of the bond interface, allowing equalized solvent bond performance between connectors.

The temperature levels shown in factor F are only machine settings. They are not indicative of the actual temperature used on the tubing.

The noise factor, G, was very pragmatic. Rather than exert a known torque on the bond (something that is difficult to do with flexible plastic parts), the tubing was secured 25 mm from the connector and the connector twisted the requisite number of turns. This produced a non-quantifiable but repeatable amount of torque on the bond.

The proof-loading of factor H was done with a hand-pull gage. It should be noted that this proof-loading was performed prior to the torque of factor G.

6. Layout of the Experiment

One of the benefits of Taguchi Methods is the ease with which an experiment can be designed. By using the linear graphs shown in Figure 3, column assignments are made to factors.

The ease with which a layout can be made to accommodate in this case two, three, and four-level factors is, in my experience, unmatched by any other multivariate experimental technique.

A weakness in this design is the fact that one column of the L_9 array is used to estimate error. I much prefer to test factors with open columns. In this case, however, it was decided that the noise factor that would be most worthy of testing was too expensive to run, and, therefore, the column remained unassigned.

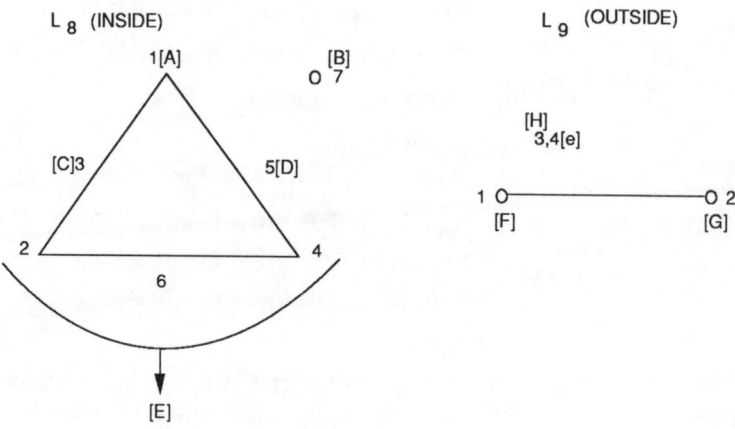

Figure 3. Linear Graphs

7. The Experimental Results

Table 2 shows the actual results obtained from the experiment in the proper position in the array. Results are in pounds of force. The samples producing a pull-off force of 1 lb. are, in fact, parts that failed in either the proof load or the torque section of the experiment. The result is shown as 1 lb. simply for the calculation of the Signal-to-Noise Ratio, which uses the reciprocal of the result and, therefore, precludes the use of zeroes.

The objective of producing a sufficient amount of failures was met. Of the 72 samples tested, 32 failed in either the proof-loading or the torque-testing sections.

Table 2. Layout and Results: Pull-Off Forces at 4 in./min.

					3	3	3	2	2	2	1	1	1	F
					3	2	1	3	2	1	3	2	1	G
					2	1	3	1	3	2	3	2	1	H
					1	3	2	2	1	3	3	2	1	e
	A	B	C	D	E	\multicolumn{9}{c	}{Data}	S/N

	A	B	C	D	E										S/N
1	1	1	1	1	1	1	61	51	1	63	64	25	35	70	6.524
2	1	2	1	2	2	1	1	68	35	1	10	42	10	30	4.739
3	1	2	2	1	3	37	70	68	1	51	58	33	25	38	9.520
4	1	1	2	2	4	1	47	68	1	1	35	1	1	46	3.520
5	2	2	2	2	1	1	1	1	1	1	1	1	1	54	6.511
6	2	1	2	1	2	1	1	40	1	26	25	47	55	63	4.764
7	2	1	1	2	3	1	1	40	1	1	1	1	56	33	1.760
8	2	2	1	1	4	1	1	42	1	1	58	57	68	64	3.520

Note: A value of 1 denotes a part that did not survive to final pull test.

Run 1: $-10 \log \frac{1}{9}\left(\frac{1}{1^2} + \frac{1}{61^2} + \frac{1}{51^2} + \frac{1}{1^2} + \frac{1}{63^2} + \frac{1}{64^2} + \frac{1}{25^2} + \frac{1}{35^2} + \frac{1}{70^2}\right)$

$= 6.524$

Run 2: $-10 \log \frac{1}{9}\left(\frac{1}{1^2} + \frac{1}{1^2} + \frac{1}{68^2} + \frac{1}{35^2} + \frac{1}{1^2} + \frac{1}{10^2} + \frac{1}{42^2} + \frac{1}{10^2} + \frac{1}{30^2}\right)$

$= 4.739$

8. Summary Results Table for Pull-Off Data

Table 3 shows the tabulated results from the experiment. The numbers are simply the sum of the results for that particular combination of variables. For example, the 356 in the upper left-hand position is the sum of the results of the 12 samples that contained level 1 of factor A and level 1 of factor F. Other values are similarly obtained. The total effect of level 1 of factor A is shown under the T column, which is the sum of the F_1, F_2 and F_3.

Summary result tables are essential to constructing the analysis of variance (ANOVA) for the experiment. Such tables also allow the calculation of the average effect of a factor level. For example, the average for all samples containing level 1 of factor A is simply the total for A_1 (1151) divided by the number of samples containing level A_1 (36) or 32.0 lbs. The experimental average is 1900/72 = 26.4 lbs.

9. ANOVA: Regular Analysis

Table 4 is the condensed ANOVA for the regular analysis of the pull-off force. Factors and interactions not appearing on this ANOVA were insignificant when compared to the error estimate and were pooled into the error estimate, e'.

The most significant factor was the noise factor, G, the torque applied to the assembly. This was designed to be very severe and is, thereby, significant.

The next most significant factor was D, the applicator design type. This was something of a surprise. Perhaps the improved design had detrimental effects on product durability.

As the ANOVA demonstrates, the next most significant items are the interaction of the tubing raw material and the preheating of the tubing, $A \times F$, the preheating of the tubing itself, F, and the effect of the tubing raw material type, A.

Table 4. Condensed ANOVA—Regular Analysis: Pull-Off Force 0 at 4 in./min.

Factor	df	S	V	S'	%
A	1	2244	2244	1954	4.1
D	1	6962	6962	6671	13.9
F	2	3673	1837	3091	6.5
G	2	11439	5720	10858	22.7
A x F	2	5239	2620	4657	9.7
e'	63	18318	291	20644	43.1
T	71	47875	—	47875	100.0

Factors Affecting Solvent-Bonded Connector Durability

Table 3. Summary Results Table—Pull-Off at 4 in./min.

	F_1	F_2	F_3	T	G_1	G_2	G_3	T	H_1	H_2	H_3	T	S/N	Sm
A_1	356	321	474	1151	606	366	179	1151	401	278	472	1151	23.334	156.834
A_2	500	118	131	749	422	213	114	749	222	269	258	749	10.555	137.888
T	856	439	605	1900	1028	579	293	1900	623	547	730	1900	33.889	294.722
B_1	433	220	313	966	536	348	82	966	326	276	364	966	15.599	150.154
B_2	423	219	292	934	492	231	211	934	297	271	366	934	18.290	144.567
T	856	439	605	1900	1028	579	293	1900	623	547	730	1900	33.889	294.721
C_1	491	237	269	997	531	299	167	997	299	306	392	997	16.542	151.095
C_2	365	202	336	903	497	280	126	903	324	241	338	903	17.347	143.627
T	856	439	605	1900	1028	579	293	1900	623	547	730	1900	33.889	294.722
D_1	580	350	374	1304	641	457	206	1304	372	428	504	1304	24.329	162.440
D_2	276	89	231	596	387	122	87	596	251	119	226	596	9.560	132.282
T	856	439	605	1900	1028	579	293	1900	623	547	730	1900	33.889	294.722
E_1	186	131	116	433	241	162	30	433	188	103	142	433	7.035	68.150
E_2	247	98	112	457	236	94	127	457	131	102	224	457	9.503	75.114
E_3	186	113	217	516	238	204	74	516	144	178	194	516	11.280	75.140
E_4	237	97	160	494	313	119	62	494	160	164	170	494	6.071	76.316
T	856	439	605	1900	1028	579	293	1900	623	547	730	1900	33.889	294.720
e_1	587													
e_2	671													
e_3	642													
T	1900													

A_1 S/N Total = 6.524 + 4.739 + 9.520 + 3.520 = 23.334
A_2 S/N Total = 6.511 + 4.764 + 1.760 + 3.520 = 10.333

10. Response Graphs of the Regular Analysis

The graphic representations of the significant effects is an essential step in demonstrating the results of any experiment. All the graphs of Figure 4 are of the same scale.

The effect of material is shown in the upper left-hand graph. It demonstrates that the average of all samples containing level 1 of factor A (Type 6 nylon raw material) was 11.2 lbs. higher than the average of the samples using Type 6/6 nylon raw material. The arrow on the A_1 point is the 90% confidence range for the estimate of the average.

The graph showing the interaction between tubing preheating, F, and tubing raw material type, A, is of particular interest. The tubing made from Type 6/6 nylon performs better when not subjected to heat than does the Type 6 nylon, but its performance suffers significantly when subjected to heat prior to pull-testing. This result proved of interest because when this material was designated as an alternate, only the specified quality characteristics were checked. On the basis of these tests, Type 6/6 nylon was deemed superior for pull-off.

The graph of this interaction demonstrates one of the strengths of Dr. Genichi Taguchi's use of orthogonal arrays—that is, to test product performance against outside noise and thereby obtain a more realistic perception of a change or improvement in product quality.

11. S/N and Sensitivity Analysis

Tables 5 and 6 show condensed ANOVAs for S/N and sensitivity analysis. To be perfectly honest, an L_8 array is not the best choice for such analysis, because there are barely enough degrees of freedom to calculate a pooled estimate of error.

Table 5. Condensed ANOVA—S/N Analysis Pull-Off Force at 4 in./min.

Factor	df	S	V	S'	%
A	1	20.41	20.41	18.54	32.5
D	1	27.26	27.26	25.39	44.5
e'	5	9.38	1.9	13.12	23.0
T	7	57.05	—	57.05	100.0

Factors Affecting Solvent-Bonded Connector Durability 83

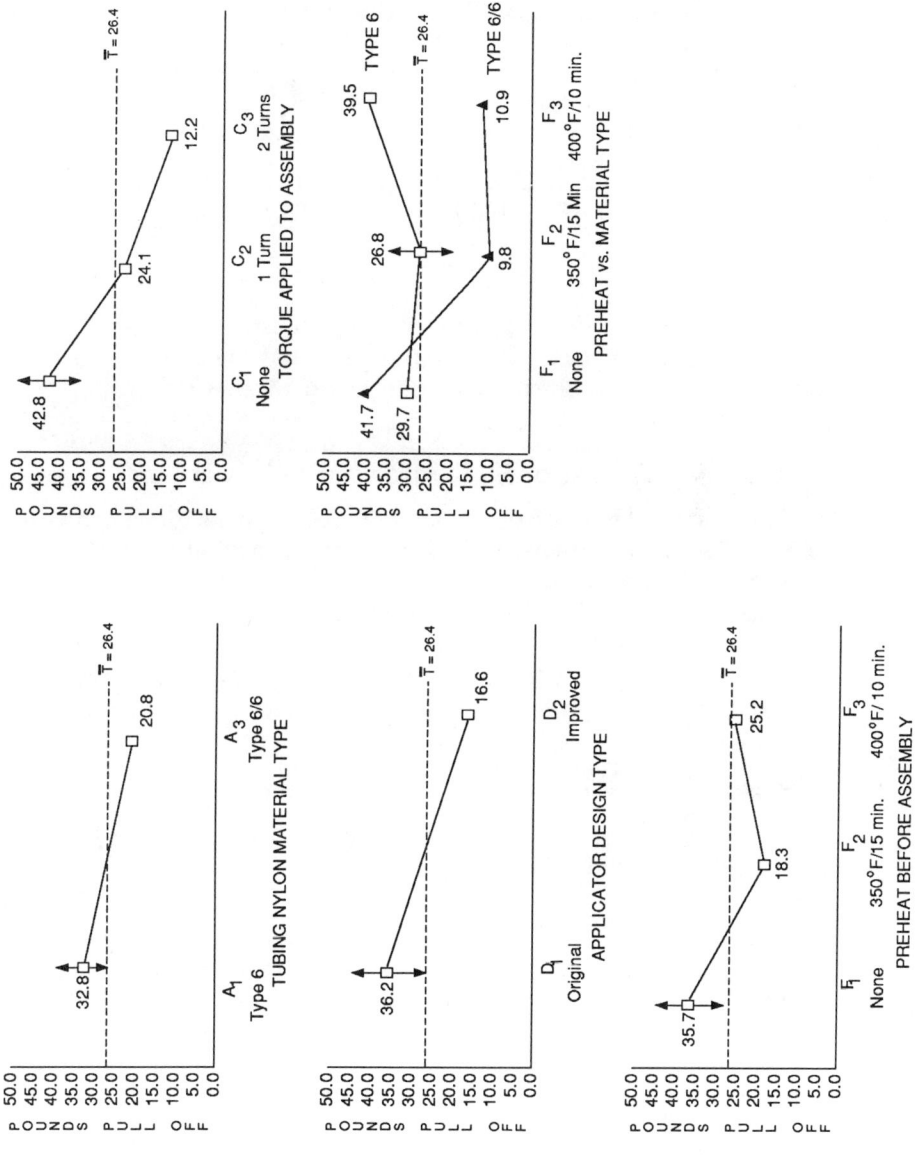

Figure 4. Graphs of Regular Analysis Pull-Off Data

Table 6. Condensed ANOVA—Sensitivity Analysis Pull-Off Force at 4 in./min.

Factor	df	S	V	S'	%
A	1	44.9	44.9	38.6	20.3
D	1	113.7	113.7	107.4	56.5
e'	5	31.5	6.3	44.1	23.2
T	7	190.1	—	190.1	100.0

These ANOVAs do result in supportive information regarding the significant effect of factor A (raw material) and factor D (applicator design type) over the outside noise the product was subjected to.

12. Response Graphs of S/N and Sensitivity Analysis

The graphs of Figure 5 demonstrate the effects of factors A and D on S/N and sensitivity analysis. Both S/N and sensitivity lines for the subject factors have similar slopes. If a level of one of these factors produced a low S/N Ratio while producing a higher sensitivity, I would have concluded that the better sensitivity was obtained with a marked increased in the variability of the results. It might, therefore, not have been a good choice to simply select the factor that performed the best.

13. The Summary

The summary of all the significant effects of the factors and interactions of the experiment are shown in Table 7. Such tables present a coherent view of the results.

This table demonstrates that inside factors A and D were significant in all the analyses, while noise factors F and G were significant in the pull-off. (By definition, F and G could not be significant in S/N and sensitivity analysis.)

Two interactions between inside and outside factors were significant as well.

While looking at this table, it should be noted that graphs can and sometimes should be made of insignificant interactions. For example, in the survivability column neither $A \times F$, $A \times G$, or $A \times H$ are significant. This means, essentially, that the superior performance of A_1 over A_2 is consistent over the varying levels of F, G, and H. In presenting the results of this

Factors Affecting Solvent-Bonded Connector Durability

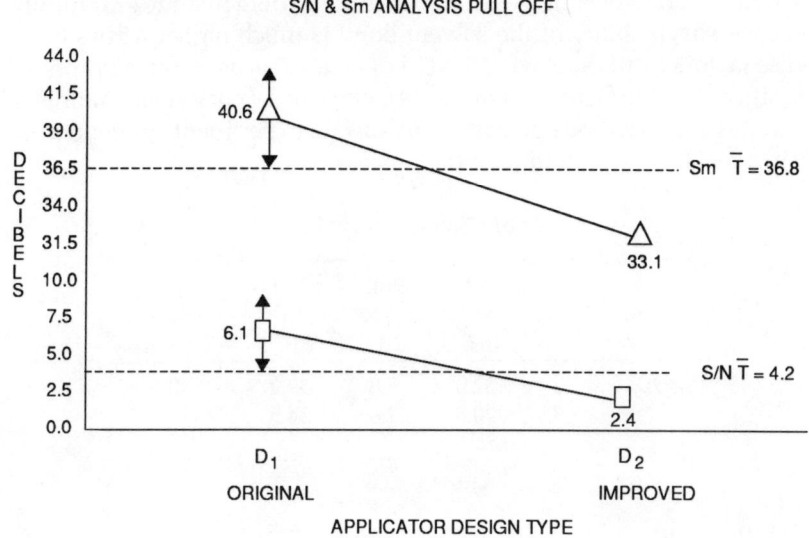

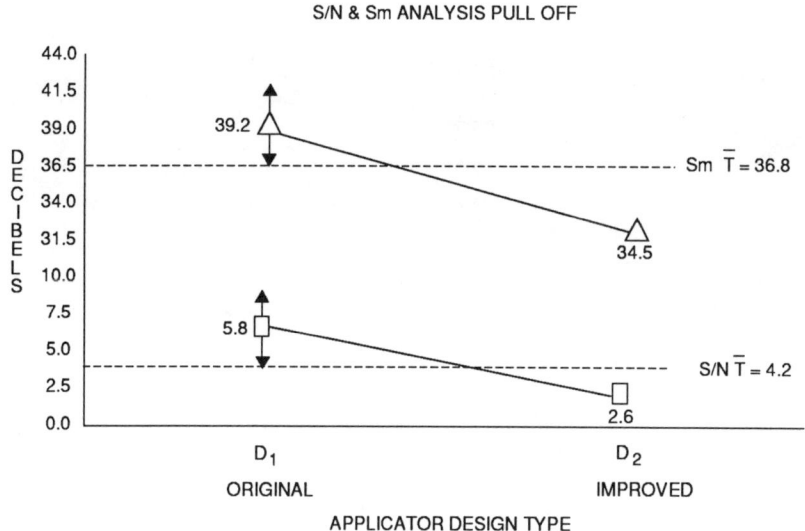

Figure 5. Effects of Factors *A* and *D* on Signal-to-Noise and Sensitivity

experiment, however, it would be beneficial to demonstrate graphically that the survivability of the solvent bond is much higher across these noise factors in all cases when level 1 of factor A is used. Such graphs of significant inside factors versus noise factors allow personnel unfamiliar with Taguchi Methods or with multivariate experiments in general to gain a feel for the operation of the process.

Table 7. Summary Table

Factor	Level	Pull Avg. lbs.	Pull S/N dB	Pull Sm dB	Choice
A	1	32.0	5.8	39.2	0
	2	20.8	2.6	34.5	—
B	1	—	—	—	—
	2	—	—	—	—
C	1	—	—	—	—
	2	—	—	—	—
D	1	36.2	6.1	40.6	0
	2	16.6	2.4	33.1	—
E	1	—	—	—	—
	2	—	—	—	—
F	1	33.7	—	—	—
	2	10.3	—	—	—
	3	25.2	—	—	—
G	1	42.0	—	—	—
	2	24.1	—	—	—
	3	12.2	—	—	—
A x F	11	29.7	—	—	—
	12	26.8	—	—	—
	13	39.5	—	—	—
	21	41.7	—	—	—
	22	9.8	—	—	—
	23	10.9	—	—	—
D x H	11	—	—	—	—
	12	—	—	—	—
	13	—	—	—	—
	21	—	—	—	—
	22	—	—	—	—
	23	—	—	—	—
Avg.	—	26.4	4.2	36.8	—

14. THE EXPERIMENTAL CONFIRMATION

Dr. Taguchi's methods allow for the confirmation of the experimental results by selecting levels for each factor, preparing an additional sample(s), and performing a 90% confidence test on the mean of these additional samples.

This process is shown in Table 8. This is an extremely useful part of the technique. Most of the more than 200 experiments that I've been involved in during the past three years have confirmed using this technique. More importantly, the predictions made from these experiments have been realized in production at a much higher rate than with the old "one-factor-at-a-time" experimental approach.

When an experiment does not confirm, there has invariably been an assignable cause for the lack of confirmation. The problem is usually in experimental techniques but also, infrequently, in interactions.

Table 8. Confirmation of Experiment at $A_2D_2F_1G_1$*

Calculation of estimated mean:

$$\hat{\mu} = 36.2 + 42.8 + 41.7 - 52.8$$
$$= 67.9 \pm 9.8 \text{ lbs}$$

Estimate for average of additional five samples at $A_2D_2F_1G_1$:

$$\bar{x} = \hat{\mu} \pm \sqrt{F\,1,63 \times V_e' \times \left(\frac{1}{ne} + \frac{1}{5}\right)} \quad (5.1)$$

$$= 67.9 \pm 18.2 \text{ lbs.}$$
$$= 49.7,\ 86.1$$

Actual results from five samples:

1. 56
2. 63
3. 46
4. 61
5. 53

$\bar{x} = 55.8$ Experiment Confirmed

---

*Estimate using strong effects: $\hat{\mu} = \overline{D} + \overline{G} + \overline{A \times F} - 2\overline{T}$ (5.2)

15. The Estimate of Survival Percentage

At this point, it was decided to predict the survival percentage at given levels of factors (see Table 9). Of course, A_1 and D_1 are preferable to A_2 and D_2. In selecting the noise factors, the preheat, F, was selected at level 1. This is because very few tubes actually are heated to the temperature, prior to assembly, that F_2 and F_3 represent. Similarly, it was decided that the type of torque used in the experiment was rarely seen by a part, so level 1 was selected for G. Proof-loading, H, however, is something that assemblies routinely see. Therefore, level 2 of H was selected.

The new method should reduce the percentage of failures by a significant amount. Remember, only a very low percentage of parts actually see the proof-loading phenomenon. The practical result of changing the levels of factor A and factor D was to essentially eliminate the problem. No report of missing connectors have been received from our customers or from our plant since changes have been made.

Table 9. Estimate of Survival Percentage at $A_1D_1F_1G_1H_2$ (Suggested Method) and $A_2D_2F_1G_1H_2$ (Existing Method)*

Suggested Method
$\hat{\mu} = 0.69 + 0.79 + 0.88 + 0.75 - 1.68$
$\phantom{\hat{\mu}} = 3.48 + 5.75 + 8.65 + 4.77 - 3.15(\text{dB})$
$\phantom{\hat{\mu}} = 19.50(\text{dB})$
$\phantom{\hat{\mu}} = 0.989 \pm 0.041$
1.1% Failure

Existing Method
$\hat{\mu} = 0.42 + 0.79 + 0.88 + 0.33 - 1.68$
$\phantom{\hat{\mu}} = -1.40 + 5.75 + 8.65 + 3.00 - 3.15(\text{dB})$
$\phantom{\hat{\mu}} = 6.77(\text{dB})$
$\phantom{\hat{\mu}} = 0.826 \pm 0.148$
17.4% Failure

*Estimate using strong effects: $\hat{\mu} = \overline{A} + \overline{F} + \overline{G} + \overline{D \times H} - 3\overline{T}$ (5.3)

16. Conclusion

This experiment was selected as a case study because of the following considerations:

1. The usefulness of Dr. Taguchi's orthogonal arrays in problem-solving is demonstrated.
2. The importance of being able to test process factors against a range of noise or environmental factors is demonstrated.
3. A traditionally "tough" type of problem to solve—i.e., a very low percentage problem—was successfully dealt with.
4. An optional raw material, which looked satisfactory under traditional verification methods, had some weaknesses when analyzed from a durability standpoint.
5. A process improvement in applicator design turned out to have significant side effects on product durability.

In terms of quantifiable results, we realized the removal of $200 per 1,000 assembly inspection costs. Less substantively, we all gained an appreciation of the process factors. The original design applicator was improved in regard to plugging performance so that some of the gain obtained by the improved applicator was realized. We can still use the optional material, but we realized that an additive to the solvent was required to improve performance.

For the small cost of the experiment, the process has not only been improved, but also has become more intelligible.

Q & A

Q. This study used an L_8 inner orthogonal array with four 2-level main effects and one 4-level main effect. The outer array was an L_9 with three noise factors. Can you comment on this experimental design?

A. An L_8 orthogonal array allows the inclusion of seven main effects; therefore, four levels of factor E—from solvent bond to assembly—were examined. Three columns were used to create the four-level factor using the multi-level technique. I would recommend either an L_{12} with more control factors or an L_{18} where the four-level factor E could be created by columns 1 and 2, leaving six columns available to test the additional three-level main effects.

Q. But wouldn't that require more experiments to be conducted?

A. No, instead of the L_9 outer array a compounding of noise factors, i.e.,

N_1 — condition giving good results

N_2 — condition giving poor results

the actual number of test pieces produced using an L_{18} would be 18 x 2 = 36. In this study 8 x 9 = 72 pieces were produced.

Q. In the original study of 0,1 data,

y = 0 if survived

y = 1 if did not survive

was analyzed in addition to the S/N Ratios to determine the percent survival of test pieces. What were the results of this analysis?

A. The results of the 0,1 analysis showed the same optimization. However, 0,1 data analysis is less sensitive because it is essentially classified attributes data with two classes, i.e., yes/no or good/bad. Therefore, 0,1 data, such as number of defects, percent survival, or percent failure, tend to be poor quality characteristics.

Q. By conducting 0,1 data analysis, noise main effects and interactions were obtained between control and noise (see ANOVA below). Was this a regular analysis?

Condensed ANOVA

Factor	df	S	S'	ρ%
A	1	1.39	1.27	7.2
D	1	2.00	1.89	10.6
F	2	2.03	1.80	10.1
G	2	4.19	3.97	22.3
D x H	2	1.08	0.86	4.8
e'	63	7.08	7.98	44.9
T	71	17.77	17.78	99.9

A. Yes, conducting "regular analysis" enables the experimenter to obtain additional technical information in addition to optimization. But instead of 0,1 data, raw data y = pull-off should have been used. It was good that the author tried and compared two analysis techniques. This is very common. Additional analysis serves two purposes: First, it provides a contrast for S/N analysis and second, alternative analysis increases technological understanding of the product/process being investigated, leading to the possibility of a technological breakthrough.

6. Optimization of the Strength of Diesel Injection

Steve Crisp
Lucas Girling Ltd.

This case study describes parameter design experimentation performed to reduce the rework rate of a diesel injector on the assembly and test operation. The quality characteristic was nozzle opening reduction. The analysis used 16 parameters in the first-stage experiment based upon the finding of the first stage, a second experiment was conducted to further investigate the six most significant factors. Quality improvement was realized by a 17% reduction in rework after the first stage, and another 4% reduction after the second. This equates to an annual cost savings of 14,880 pounds sterling.

1. The Hot-Plastic Forming Process

Lucas Girling is a major operations company within the international manufacturing group Lucas Industries. It enjoys a truly comprehensive involvement with the world of transport. Lucas Industries' products can be found on virtually all forms of vehicles, and it is against this background that Lucas Girling has specialized to become a world leader in braking technology.

With the increased use of lightweight plastics in modern automotive braking equipment, development work is in progress to utilize their full potential. One area of research is hot-forming a metal insert into a premolded plastic component to improve production fabrication techniques. To investigate the load-supporting capabilities of a hot-forming plastic retaining ring, it was decided to conduct tests on an existing component that uses a simple hot-forming process.

The process involved the hot forming of an annular ring of plastic

---

From the *Fourth Symposium on Taguchi Methods*™, pp. 786–805, Copyright © 1986, American Supplier Institute, Inc., Dearborn, Michigan.

material onto a circular steel disc positioned in the top of a servovalve body (see Figure 1). A preheated die was forced down upon the ring at the top of the valve body, by the action of air pressure in a 16 sq. in. standard air chamber. The secured steel inserts were then pulled out of the body and the force required to break the formed ring noted.

The forming process, although fairly simple, involves a number of different production factors, some of which may be interrelated. Attempts to optimize these proved unsuccessful using the traditional technique of varying a single factor at a time, as this did not allow for the interaction between different factors. Also, there were only a limited number of valve bodies available for testing, and the number of time-consuming tests needed to be minimized.

It was decided that production parameters could best be optimized by the application of Taguchi Methods, which define a comprehensive test procedure and also make best use of the development engineer's time.

Experience gained during ring development allowed parameters to be defined. A set of reference tests was conducted to give an indication of the expected experimental error.

2. Control and Noise Factors

After analysis of the hot-forming process, the following variables were identified as important to the final product quality:
1. Staking temperature (die temperature during hot forming)
2. Hold time (die-to-work piece contact time)
3. Batch number (valve body production molds 1 and 2)
4. Dimensional variation
5. Depth of stake (thickness of formed lip)
6. Material variation
7. Maximum force during hot forming (regulated by pressure in air chamber)
8. Rate of hot forming
9. Strain rate during testing
10. Force application rate (restrictor in air pressure line to air chamber).

These 10 major factors were categorized as follows:

Controllable Production Factors
1. Staking temperature
2. Hold time

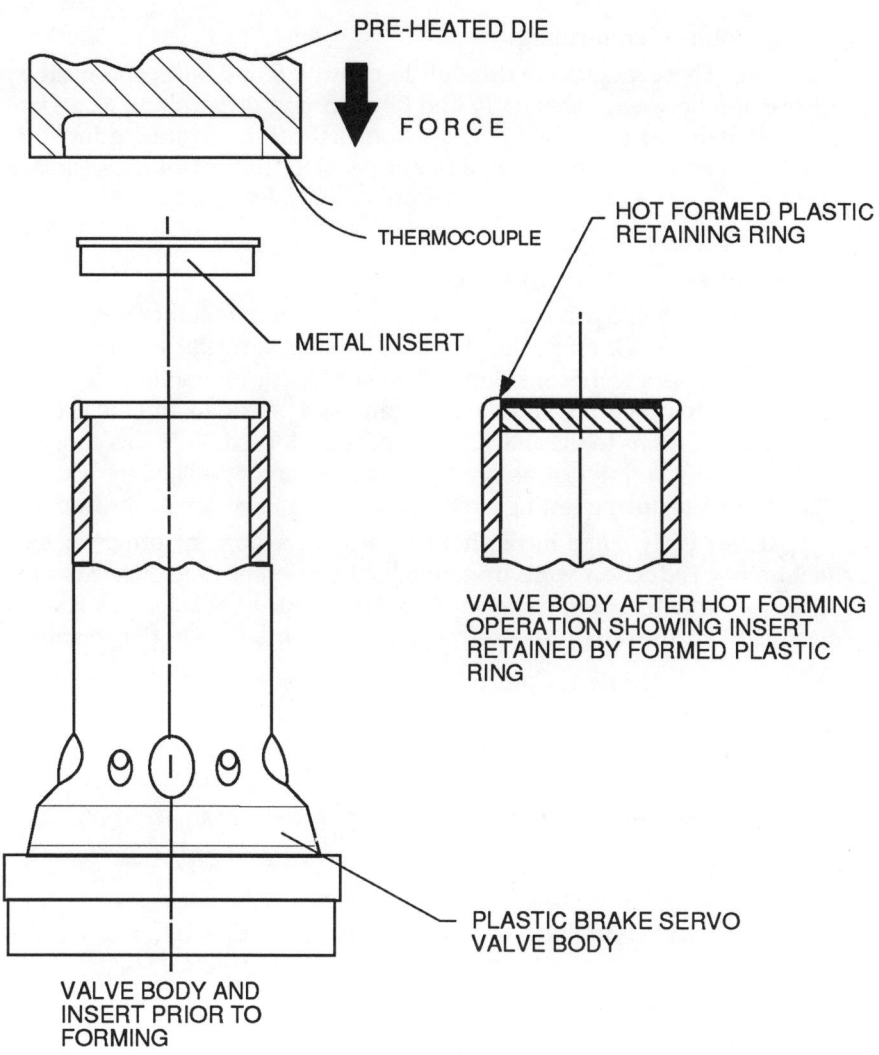

Figure 1. Hot Forming Process

3. Batch number
7. Force of operation (maximum)
10. Force application rate

Random Production Factors (Noise)

4. Dimensional variation
5. Depth of stake
6. Material variation

8. Rate of hot forming

Note: These factors are difficult to control: 5 and 8 depend on the interaction between valve body and hot-forming press; 4 and 6 can be controlled during valve-body production. In the test, current production valve bodies were used, so it was not possible to control these noise factors.

Test Factors (Noise)

9. Strain rate during testing

Table 1 lists the production controllable factors together with their assigned values. One four-level factor, staking temperature, and four two-level factors were considered. The facility for interaction between the staking temperature and the hold time was provided and the necessary modifications to the analysis procedure adopted. This was considered of particular interest, as preliminary tests suggested an interaction. The strain rate during testing was introduced as a two-level noise factor.

At this early stage in the hot-forming development program the factors of production were undefined. The reference factor levels are listed in Table 10. Having specified the basic controllable factors, it was necessary to formulate the orthogonal-array matrix for the forming operation.

Table 1. Controllable Production Factors

Code	Factor	Level	df	Specific values
A	Temperature (°C)	4	3	$A_1 = 180, A_2 = 200,$ $A_3 = 220, A_4 = 240$
B	Hold time (sec)	2	1	$B_1 = 5, B_2 = 15$
C	Batch Number	2	1	$C_1 = 1, C_2 = 2$
D	Force (kN)	2	1	$D_1 = 6, D_2 = 7$
E	Force rate (kN/s)	2	1	$E_1 = 5, E_2 = 1$

3. Layout of the Experiment

Using Taguchi Methods, detailed with the Quality Engineering manual, the test parameters were analyzed and an L_{16} orthogonal array produced to determine the test procedure. Table 2 shows the 11-column L_{16} array that specifies the total test procedure. The first three columns, 2, 6, and 4, are arranged to produce the four-level temperature factor, A, and columns 3, 5, and 7 form the interaction between the temperature and the staking time.

Table 2. Orthogonal Array for Test Procedure

	A			B	A*B			C	D	E
Test	2	6	4	1	3	5	7	8	9	10
1	1	1	1	1	1	1	1	1	1	1
2	1	1	1	1	1	1	2	2	2	2
3	1	2	2	2	1	1	2	2	1	1	1
4	1	2	2	2	1	1	2	2	2	2	2
5	2	2	1	3	1	2	1	2	1	1	2
6	2	2	1	3	1	2	1	2	2	2	1
7	2	1	2	4	1	2	2	1	1	1	2
8	2	1	2	4	1	2	2	1	2	2	1
9	1	1	1	1	2	2	2	2	1	2	1
10	1	1	1	1	2	2	2	2	2	1	2
11	1	2	2	2	2	2	1	1	1	2	1
12	1	2	2	2	2	2	1	1	2	1	2
13	2	2	1	3	2	1	2	1	1	2	2
14	2	2	1	3	2	1	2	1	2	1	1
15	2	1	2	4	2	1	1	2	1	2	2
16	2	1	2	4	2	1	1	2	2	1	1
				STAKING TIME	HOLD TIME			BATCH NO	FORCE	FORCE APPLY

Staking Temperature °C $A_1 = 180$ $A_2 = 200$ $A_3 = 220$ $A_4 = 240$
Hold Time (Seconds) $B_1 = 5$ $B_2 = 15$
Batch Number $C_1 = 1$ $C_2 = 2$
Process Force (KN) $D_1 = 6$ $D_2 = 7$
Force Apply Rate (kN/S) $E_1 = 5$ $E_2 = 1$

4. **TEST PROCEDURE AND RESULTS:**

   A. Ten valve bodies were formed in accordance with the reference test factors (see Table 10). The failure load at a strain rate of 100 was found (the results are shown in Table 3).

   B. Valve bodies from both production batches were formed under the action of the hot-staking press according to the layout of the orthogonal array. For each of the 16 combinations, two tests were conducted at different strain rates and the pull-out loads noted. Table 5 shows the results of the 16 pairs of tests. A standard Hounsfield tensometer fitted with a 0–5 kN beam was applied for testing. Strain was applied automatically using the motor-drive system at rates of 50 and 150 units. Failure load was recorded on an *X-Y* plotter.

   C. Ten valve bodies were formed using the determined optimum factor levels and the pull-out noted for a strain rate of 100 (see Table 4).

Table 3. Reference Conditions — Pull-Out Loads (kN)

No.	E_1	E_2	E_3	E_4	E_5	E_6	E_7	E_8	E_9	E_{10}
Load	2.52	2.49	1.91	2.00	2.61	2.74	2.26	2.49	2.25	2.75

Mean = 2.35 kN
Standard Deviation = 0.28 kN
S/N Ratio = 7.424 dB

Table 4. Recommended Conditions — Pull-Out Loads (kN)

No.	T_1	T_2	T_3	T_4	T_5	T_6	T_7	T_8	T_9	T_{10}
Load	4.62	4.51	4.25	4.54	3.78	4.37	4.56	4.05	4.21	4.44

(T_5 result due to machine error)

Mean = 4.40 kN
Standard Deviation = 0.28 kN
S/N Ratio = 12.836 dB

Table 5. Results from the 16 Individual Tests

Test No.	A Temp	B Time	C Batch	D Load	E Load Rate	Load 1 kN	Load 2 kN	Avg. kN	S/N dB
1	1	1	1	1	1	2.18	2.10	2.14	6.60
2	1	1	2	2	2	2.68	2.65	2.67	8.51
3	2	1	1	1	1	2.46	2.57	2.52	8.00
4	2	1	2	2	2	2.92	2.59	2.76	8.76
5	3	1	1	1	2	2.83	2.74	2.79	8.89
6	3	1	2	2	1	3.61	3.22	3.42	10.63
7	4	1	1	1	2	3.31	3.40	3.36	10.51
8	4	1	2	2	1	4.02	3.98	4.00	12.04
9	1	2	1	2	1	3.08	3.14	3.11	9.85
10	1	2	2	1	2	3.07	2.97	3.02	9.60
11	2	2	1	2	1	3.35	3.15	3.25	10.23
12	2	2	2	1	2	3.46	3.21	3.34	10.44
13	3	2	1	2	2	3.42	3.81	3.62	11.12
14	3	2	2	1	1	3.56	3.70	3.63	11.20
15	4	2	1	2	2	4.33	4.90	4.62	13.23
16	4	2	2	1	1	4.77	4.70	4.74	13.51
							TOTAL	52.94	163.12
							AVERAGES	3.31	10.2

5. ANALYSIS OF RESULTS

In accordance with Taguchi Methods, the Signal-to-Noise (S/N) Ratio was calculated for the larger-the-better characteristic. The formula is shown below.

$$(\eta_{dB}) \; S/N \text{ ratio} = -10 \log \frac{1}{n} \sum_{i=1}^{n} \frac{1}{y_i^2} \tag{6.1}$$

S/N Ratio Larger-the-Better

Example:

$$\text{Run 1: } -10 \log \frac{1}{2} \left(\frac{1}{2.18^2} + \frac{1}{2.10^2} \right) = 6.60 \text{ dB}$$

$$\text{Run 3: } -10 \log \frac{1}{2} \left(\frac{1}{2.46^2} + \frac{1}{2.57^2} \right) = 8.00 \text{ dB}$$

The S/N Ratio is very sensitive to variation within a set of results, and because it is additive it gives a clearer indication of abnormalities with a set of results. The calculated S/N Ratios for each of the tests are shown in Table 5. To demonstrate the improvement achieved by optimizing production methods using Taguchi experimental design, predicted S/N Ratios and means were calculated and the values checked by experimentation.

The first step in the analysis of the multivariate hot-forming experiment was to sum all the results containing the level of a particular factor. The average was then calculated, and these results are shown in Table 6.

Table 6. S/N Ratio Response Table

	A	B	C	D	E
Level 1	8.64	9.24	9.81	9.84	10.26
Level 2	9.36	11.14	10.59	10.55	10.13
Level 3	10.46				
Level 4	12.32				
Difference	3.68	1.90	0.78	0.71	−0.13

Any improvement in the pull-out performance is noticed by an increase in the average S/N Ratio between levels of a certain factor. Therefore, improvements are obtained if the average S/N Ratio increases for a certain factor between different levels of the factor, and it would be advisable to change production techniques in accordance with these increases. Graphs of the S/N Ratios for each of the factors are shown in Figure 2.

The results can be analyzed in the following ways:
A. S/N Ratio analysis
B. Regular data anlaysis (raw data)

A) S/N Ratio Analysis

The suspected interaction between factors A and B was investigated by plotting their S/N levels on a simple graph (see Figure 3). Table 7 shows the interaction data (totals).

Figure 3 shows that the interaction between A and B using S/N ratio analysis is not significant; the lines are virtually parallel, hence there is little interaction.

Optimization of the Strength of Diesel Injection

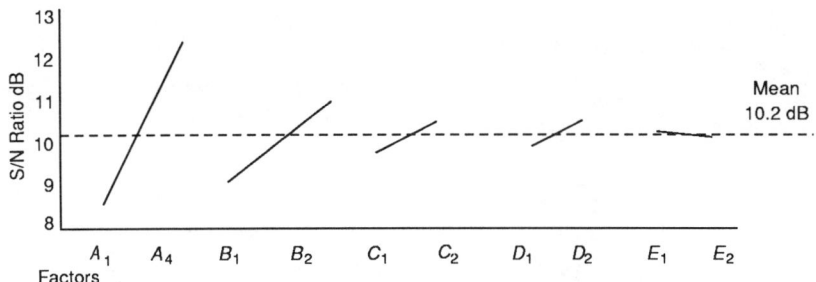

Figure 2. Significant Effects Shows Variation in S/N Ratios

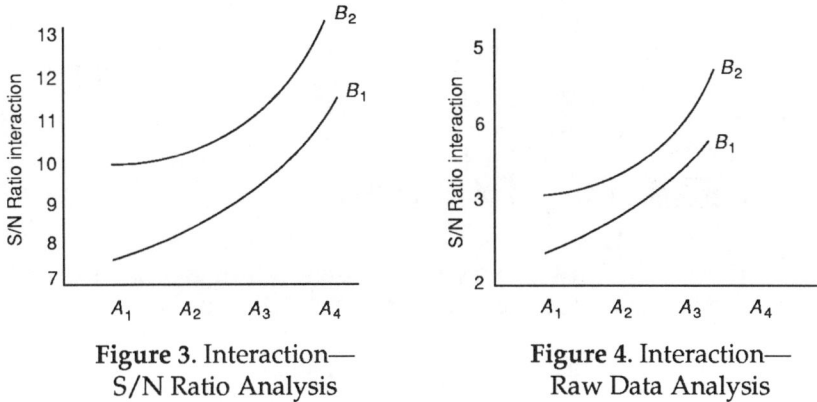

Figure 3. Interaction— S/N Ratio Analysis

Figure 4. Interaction— Raw Data Analysis

Table 7. S/N Ratio A*B Interaction Response Table

	B_1	B_2
A_1	7.56	9.73
A_2	8.38	10.34
A_3	9.76	11.16
A_4	11.27	13.37

Having decided that little interaction occurs between factors A and B (Figure 3), and that factor E is not significant (see Figure 2), a comparison can be made between the reference S/N Ratio and the optimum S/N Ratio.

$\overline{T}$ is the average S/N Ratio over the 16 different test conditions:

$\overline{T} = 10.2$

1. Reference - $A_2 B_1 C_1 D_1 E_1$
   (E_1 is not significant and therefore need not be included in the analysis)

$$\text{S/N Ratio} = A_2 + B_1 + C_1 + D_1 - 3\overline{T} \qquad (6.2)$$
$$= 9.36 + 9.24 + 9.81 + 9.84 - 30.585$$
$$= 7.665 \text{ dB}$$

2. Recommended = $A_4 B_2 C_2 D_2 E_1$ (But E_1 not included – see above)

$$\text{S/N ratio} = A_4 + B_2 + C_2 + D_2 - 3\overline{T} \qquad (6.3)$$
$$= 12.32 + 11.14 + 10.59 + 10.55 - 30.585$$
$$= 14.015 \text{ dB}$$

B) Regular Data Analysis (Raw Data)

Table 8 is the raw-data response table and information is taken from Table 5. The figures are averaged across the test procedure.

Table 8. Regular Analysis Response Table

	A	B	C	D	E
Level 1	2.74	2.95	3.18	3.19	3.35
Level 2	2.97	3.66	3.45	3.43	3.27
Level 3	3.36				
Level 4	4.18				

The interaction between factors A and B was again investigated Table 9 shows the interaction data.

Figure 4 shows that the interaction between A and B using the regular raw-data analysis is not significant; hence, interaction data will not be included in the analysis.

$\overline{T}$ is the average put-out load over the 16 different test conditions:
$$\overline{T} = 3.31$$

Table 9. Regular Analysis $A*B$ Interaction Data

	B_1	B_2
A_1	2.41	3.10
A_2	2.64	3.30
A_3	3.11	3.63
A_4	3.68	4.68

1. Reference = $A_2 B_1 C_1 D_1 E_1$ (E_1 not significant)

$$= A_2 + B_1 + C_1 + D_1 - 3\overline{T} \qquad (6.4)$$
$$= 2.97 + 2.95 + 3.18 + 3.19 - 9.93$$
$$= 2.36 \text{ kN}$$

2. Recommended = $A_4 B_2 C_2 D_2 E_1$ (E_1 not significant)

$$= A_4 + B_2 + C_2 + D_2 - 3\overline{T} \qquad (6.5)$$
$$= 4.18 + 3.66 + 3.45 + 3.43 - 9.93$$
$$= 4.79 \text{ kN}$$

6. Recommendations and Verification of Predictions

At this stage in the investigation of hot-plastic forming, recommendations for the process can be made, the accuracy of the predictions determined, and further investigation procedures formulated to improve or further support the recommendations suggested.

From the analysis the following process factors have proved most suitable, with predicted increases in pull-out load and a drop in variance, when compared to the reference test:

Hot-forming die temperature .... 240°C
Die contact time .... 15 seconds
Batch number .... Noise Factor
Force applies .... 7 kN
Rate of application of force .... Not significant

As detailed in Section 4, 10 valve bodies were tested under the reference conditions (test procedure A) and 10 valve bodies were tested under the recommended conditions (test procedure C). The results from these two tests are shown in Figures 4 and 5. From these figures the mean, standard deviation, and S/N Ratios for the pull-out loads from the 10 samples can be calculated.

These figures calculated from specimen tests can be compared with the mean and the S/N Ratio predicted from the analysis of results obtained from the orthogonal array (test procedure B), as shown in Table 10.

Table 10. Confirmation Test Results

		Predicted (Taguchi analysis)	Actual (confirmation run)
Reference Test Factors $A_2 B_1 C_1 D_1 E_1$	Mean (kN)	2.36	2.35
	Std. Deviation	—	0.28
	S/N Ratio (dB)	7.665	7.424
Recommended Test Factors $A_4 B_2 C_2 D_2 E_1$	Mean (kN)	4.79	4.40
	Std. Deviation	—	0.18
	S/N Ratio (dB)	14.015	12.836

7. Discussion of Results

Performance for valve bodies formed under the optimum conditions was satisfactory, with a high mean pull-out load and low variability. The improvement in performance over the reference conditions is shown in Table 10. There is a good correlation between the predicted and actual results for both the S/N Ratio and the means. On calculation, no significant difference was evident in the S/N Ratio for the two strain rates (noise factors). This means that strain rate as a noise factor need not be considered in further tests.

As this particular hot-forming process does not apply to a present production item, the Quality Loss Function, with regard to cost savings, is not applicable at this stage.

8. Conclusions

The application of Taguchi Methods in Lucas Girling's development program has proved profitable. The main advantage of this methodical test procedure has been the efficient use of the development engineer's time. The analysis technique has highlighted those factors of greater importance and served to eliminate those of lesser importance, hence simplifying the test routine. The interaction between the two important factors has been tested and proved to be insignificant. However, very high temperatures may encourage an interaction due to a breakdown in the microstructure of the polymer and consequent damage.

9. FURTHER INVESTIGATION

The next step in the analysis of the hot-forming process is to develop another test routine. This will investigate the expected peak in the performance trends shown by the factors. This second test procedure discounts factors of little or no significance (the suggested layout is detailed briefly in the appendix). The analysis of process data will be achieved by considering three 3-level factors arranged in an L_9 orthogonal array, together with one 2-level noise factor. Two tests for each factor combination at each noise level will be carried out. The Taguchi experimental design technique reduces the test procedure for evaluation from 108 tests (full factorial to 36 tests).

APPENDIX TO THE STUDY
Further Experimental Investigation

The following factors are to be investigated (See Table A):

Table A. Factors and Levels for Further Investigation

Factor	Level 1	Level 2	Level 3
1. Temperature of die (°C)	235	245	255
2. Die contact time (sec.)	10	15	20
3. Staking force (kN)	5	7	9
Noise Batch Number	1	2	

The higher forces are obtained by replacing the type 16 air chamber with a larger type 24. No interactions are suspected and the layout of the test procedure is shown in Table B on the following page.

Table B. L_9 Orthogonal Array

Test Number	Temperature	Time	Force	Results B_1 B_2
1	1	1	1	
2	1	2	2	
3	1	3	3	
4	2	1	3	
5	2	2	2	
6	2	3	1	
7	3	1	3	
8	3	2	1	
9	3	3	2	

Q & A

Q. This is a case with one 4-level factor and its interaction with a 2-level factor.

A. An L_{16} orthogonal array was used to assign a 4-level factor and four 2-level factors. Since all factors are continuous variables, it is better to use a 3-level orthogonal array and assign more control factors. If it is necessary to assign more than three levels for temperature, an L_{18} orthogonal array may be used. From the horizontal combinations of columns 1 and 2, a 6-level column can be prepared. Therefore, temperature can be assigned up to six levels.

Q. How is a 4-level factor assigned to a six-level column?

A. Two of the six levels are repeated. This is called "dummy treatment."

Q. If this is done, is there a way to assign the interaction?

A. From the nature of factor A, temperature, and factor B, time, it is better to use "sliding levels." The experimenter sets different time conditions (or ranges) at each level of temperature to effectively cancel out the effect of the interaction.

Q. Isn't factor C, batch number, a noise factor?

A. Yes it is. It should be assigned to the outer array.

Q. If batches are assigned to the outer array, then the number of experiments will be doubled.

A. Instead of assigning batches as a noise factor, we might look for a noise factor associated with deterioration.

Q. Why are the S/N Ratio and raw data both analyzed?

A. For larger-the-better characteristics, raw data analysis is not necessary. The effect of the mean is included in the S/N Ratio.

Q. Is this the case study of Taguchi Methods from the UK?

A. Yes, it is. The application in the UK has increased during the last two years.

7. Cruise Control Vacuum Valve Improvement Study

John J. McCarte
Malco Montgomeryville

This case study demonstrates the application of Taguchi Methods in the optimization of a cruise control vacuum valve. Failures were attributed to the lack of an optimized design at the process stage. An L_{16} orthogonal array, using eight parameters, was used to investigate plunger push-out force and to reduce plunger processing variability. Simultaneous improvement in push-out force of the plunger and reduction of process variability of the plunger was achieved. Through process optimization, push-out force was increased 17%. Variability of push-out force was decreased by 50%, and the reduction in average percent defective was reduced by 19%. The reduction in the percent defective resulted in a savings of $17,000 per year.

1. The Product and Objective of the Study

The cruise control vacuum valve had been failing in the assembly operation at significantly high levels because the spring-loaded plunger was breaking away from the body of the valve. The failures were attributed to the lack of an optimum design in the assembly process. This investigation was conducted to seek out the optimum processing condition.

We had two quality characteristics to consider. The first deals directly with the objective — the plunger breaking away from the body, the characteristic being push-out force. The second is the travel distance of the plunger.

From the *Second Symposium on Taguchi Methods*™, pp. 101–124, Copyright © 1984, American Supplier Institute, Inc., Dearborn, Michigan.

2. Quality Characteristics

Quality Characteristics	Specification	Description
P = Push-out force	30 lb. minimum	Force to push plunger through the top of the valve.
t = Travel distance	0.280 in. to 0.320 in.	The mininum and maximum distance to make and break vacuum.

The push-out force was considered to be more important at this time, because this is where the high failure rate was occurring. The travel distance average was not achieving the nominal of 0.300 in. so it would be appropriate to find a condition to increase t. Therefore, the objective is to find a process condition to:

1. Maximize P and t, with the emphasis on P.
2. Minimize the variability of P and t.

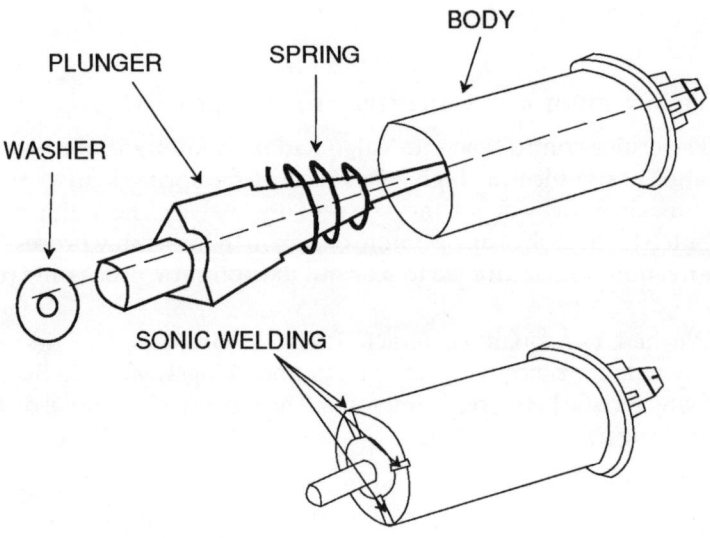

Figure 1. Illustration of Vacuum Valve

3. Factors and Factor Levels

Factor Parameters

A. Material — The plastic material that the body of the valve is made of was chosen since there are two acceptable variations. One type has a lower melt point index and is slightly less expensive.

B. Table Dwell Time — This refers to the speed in which the dial table indexes. The faster it goes, the less residence time each assembly spends under the equipment. It also means an increase in productivity.

C. Heat Gun Temperature — Each of the assemblies passes under a preheating station to soften the material.

D. Bracker Pressure — This is an assembly fixture sometimes known as an orbital riveter. It is used in this process to actually roll the top of the plastic body over the washer and lock the plunger in place. The pressure is the amount of pressure applied to the top of the valve.

E. Sonic Weld — The sonic weld station was designed to put four stakes on the assembly to keep the washer stable.

F. Sonic Weld Pressure — This refers to the pressure applied by the horn on the welder to the top of the valve.

G. Sonic Weld Time — The amount of time the horn stayed on the assembly.

H. Bracker Travel Time — This is the relation of distance and time the bracker head traveled to the top of the valve.

Table 1. Layout Factors and Levels

Factors (Parameters)	Levels	Unit
A. Material	$A_1^* = X \quad A_2 = Y$	
B. Table Dwell Time	$B_1^* = 2.7 \quad B_2 = 2.2$	sec.
C. Heat Gun Temperature	$C_1^* = 410 \quad C_2^* = $ ambient	°F
D. Bracker Pressure	$D_1 = 40 \quad D_2^* = 60 \quad D_3 = 80$	lb.
E. Sonic Weld	$E_1 = $ No $\quad E_2^* = $ Yes	
For E_2, F = Sonic Weld Press G = Sonic Weld Time	$F_1^* = 20 \quad F_2 = 40$ $G_1^* = 0.4 \quad G_2 = 0.8$	lb. sec.
H. Bracker Travel Time	$H_1 = $ Low $\quad H_2^* = $ Normal $H_3 = $ High	

NOTE: 1. Levels with * are the existing process condition. Hence, the existing conditions were $A_1, B_1, C_1, D_2, E_2, F_1, G_1,$ and H_2.
2. Table dwell time is essentially the processing time directly relating to productivity.
3. Factors F and G are nested with E, F and G. They take values only when E on the sonic weld is applied. (See Table 2 and Appendix 1 to this Study).

4. Layout of Control Factors

The full factorial experiment will take $2 \times 2 \times 2 \times 3 \times 3 \times (1 + 2 \times 2) = 360$ combinations. However, a 16-combination experiment was designed using an L_{16} orthogonal array. Because 3-level factors have to be allocated to a 2-level system, such as an L_{16}, and because of the existence of nested factors, special techniques called the "Idle Column Method" and "Orthogonal Nesting" were applied. (See Appendix 1 to this Study.)

Table 2. L_{16} and Allocation of Factors

No.	B 1	2	3	G 4	H 5	F 6	7	C 8	E 9	A 10	IDLE 11	D 12	13	14	15	DATA
1	1	1	1	1	1	1	-	1	1	1	1	1	-	-	-	
2	1	1	1	1(G_1)	1(2')	1(F_1)	-	2	2	2	2	2(3)	-	-	-	
3	1	1	1	2	2	2	-	1	1	1	1	2	-	-	-	
4	1	1	1	2(G_2)	2(3)	2(F_2)	-	2	2	2	2	1(2')	-	-	-	
5	1	2	2	1	1(2')	2	-	1	1	2	2	1(2')	-	-	-	
6	1	2	2	1(G_2)	1	2(F_2)	-	2	2	1	1	2	-	-	-	
7	1	2	2	2	2(3)	1	-	1	1	2	2	2(3)	-	-	-	
8	1	2	2	2(G_2)	2	1(F_1)	-	2	2	1	1	1	-	-	-	
9	2	1	2	1(G_1)	2(3)	1(F_1)	-	1	2	1	2	1(2')	-	-	-	
10	2	1	2	1	2	1	-	2	1	2	1	2	-	-	-	
11	2	1	2	2(G_2)	1(2')	2(F_2)	-	1	2	1	2	2(3)	-	-	-	
12	2	1	2	2	1	2	-	2	1	2	1	1	-	-	-	
13	2	2	1	1(G_1)	2	2(F_2)	-	1	2	2	1	1	-	-	-	
14	2	2	1	1	2(3)	2	-	2	1	1	2	2(3)	-	-	-	
15	2	2	1	1(G_1)	1	1(F_1)	-	1	2	2	1	2	-	-	-	
16	2	2	1	2	1(2')	1	-	2	1	1	2	1(2')	-	-	-	

5. Results

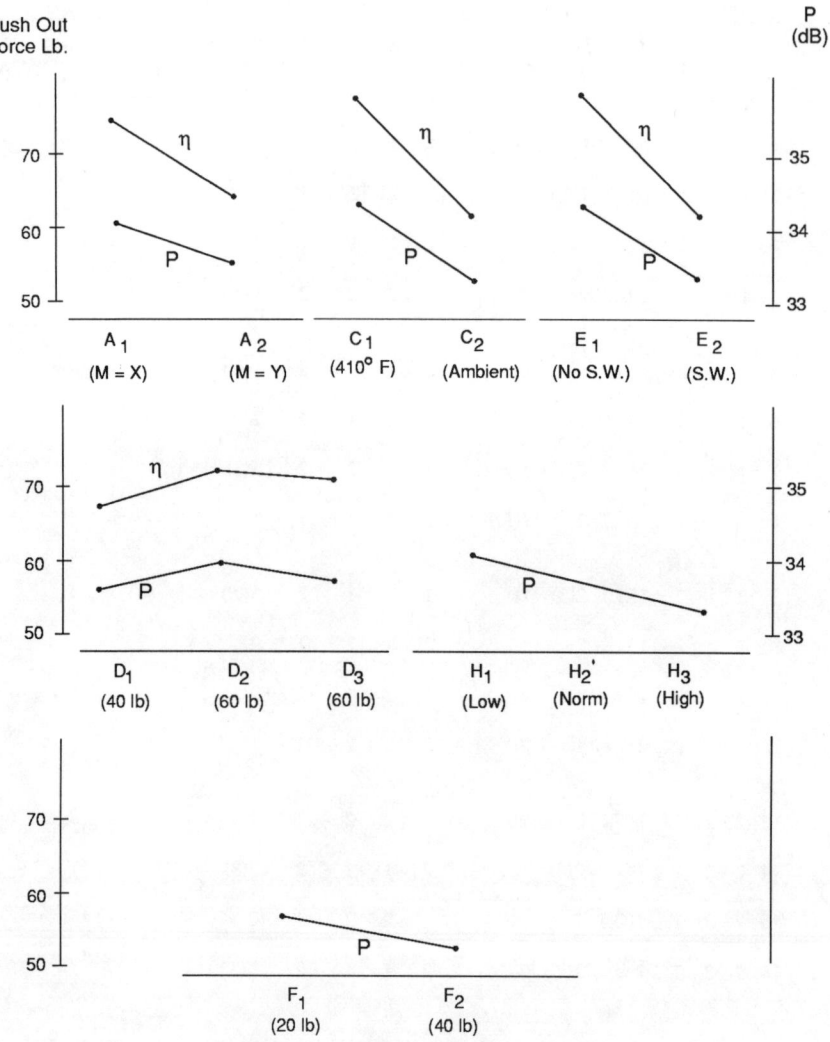

Figure 2. Significant Factor Response
Push-Out Force

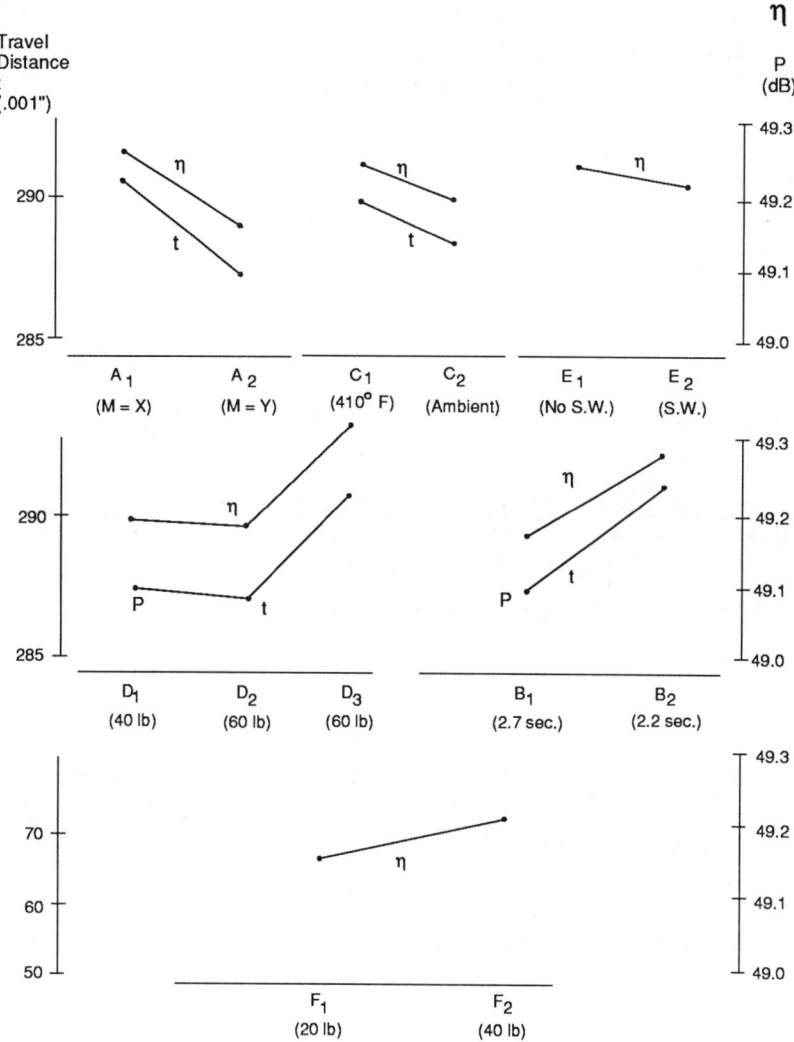

Figure 3. Significant Factor Response
Travel Distance

Table 3 shows the expected characteristic response for each factor. The factor effect is either significant or insignificant. For each significant factor, its preferred level is indicated by *, and the number of asterisks shows the significance level. The insignificant factor level is indicated by a dash.

The table also shows that S/N Ratio analysis and ordinary analysis result in the same preferred level and significance in most of the cases. The following gives a discussion for each factor.

6. Optimization of the Characteristic

***: 0.01, **: 0.05, *: 0.10, °: Statistically insignificant, —: The non-optimal level of significant factors

Recall:
- ηp = S/N Ratio of push-out force
- p = Push-out force in pounds.
- ηt = S/N Ratio of travel distance
- t = Travel distance in 0.001 in.

NOTE: Level with * symbols indicates the preferred level of the significant factor.

A: **Material** — $A_1 : M = X$. The existing material is preferred for all of our characteristic responses.

B: **Table Dwell Time** — The table dwell time is not contributing to push-out force, i.e., either level can be used without affecting the push-out force. On the other hand, this factor is significant to travel distance, and surprisingly, B_2: 2.2 sec. leads to better travel distance. Hence, B_2 should be included in the optimum process condition, while B_1 is the existing condition.

C: **Heat Gun Temperature** — C_1: 410°F is preferred for all four cases. C_2: Ambient would result in 10 lb. less push-out force.

D: **Bracker Pressure** — Here is a decision problem. D_2: 60 lb. is preferred for push-out force while D_3 leads to better travel distance. Since push-out force is more important, let D_2 be the optimum. Of course, if travel distance has to be increased later, then D_3 can be chosen.

E: **Sonic Weld** — Surprisingly, E_1: No Sonic Weld is preferred for both characteristics, especially this factor resulted in a very strong significant effect on push-out force. E_2, the existing level, has been used for the last six years in production.

F: **Sonic Weld Pressure and** G: **Sonic Weld Time** — Since E_1 is chosen for the optimum condition, let the discussion on these two nested factors be omitted.

G: **Bracker Travel Time** — Factor H is insignificant to almost all characteristic responses. It showed 5% significance in the ordinary analysis of push-out force, H_1: Low being preferred. However, it is insignificant to the S/N Ratio. The reason is that even though H_1 maximizes push-out force, H_1 leads to higher variation of push-out force. H_1 should be chosen as optimum if maximization has more importance than having a bit more variation.

Table 3. Overall Analysis

	Factor (Parameter)		Level	Push Out Force ηP (dB)	Push Out Force P (lb)	Travel Distance ηt (dB)	Travel Distance T(.001")
	A:	Material	A_1:M = X	35.3653***	60.62***	49.2616***	290.63***
			A_2:M = Y	34.4660—	56.44—	49.1506—	287.06—
	B:	Table Dwell Time	B_1:2.7 sec.	34.7626 °	56.98 °	49.1499—	286.94—
			B_2:2.2 sec.	35.0688 °	58.30 °	49.2622***	290.69***
	C:	Heat Gun Temperature	C_1:410°F	35.6960**	62.67***	49.2338***	289.75*
			C_2:Ambient	34.1353–	52.61—	49.1784—	287.88—
	D:	Bracker Pressure	D_1:40 lb.	34.7840–	55.26—	49.1952—	288.49 °
			D_2:60 lb.	35.1623*	59.18**	49.1880—	288.21 °
			D_3:80 lb.	35.0474–	56.96—	49.2532***	290.34 °
	E:	Sonic Weld	E_1: No	35.6483***	61.96***	49.2203**	289.31 °
			E_2: Yes	34.1830—	53.31—	49.1918—	288.13 °
E_2	F:	Sonic Weld Pressure	F_1:20 lb.	34.4813 °	55.28**	49.1675—	287.50 °
			F_2:40 lb	33.8748 °	51.35—	49.2161***	289.13 °
	G:	Sonic Weld Time	G_1:0.4 sec	34.2680 °	54.20 °	49.1828 °	288.00 °
			G_2:0.8 sec	34.0981 °	52.43 °	49.2008 °	288.63 °
	H:	Bracker Travel Time	H_1: Low	35.2345 °	59.87**	49.2130 °	289.06 °
			H_2: Normal	34.7015 °	55.84—	49.2042 °	288.78 °
			H_3: High	35.0252 °	52.67—	49.2028 °	288.67 °

7. Process Estimation Using the Experimental Data

The following are calculations for estimates of the characteristic response for the existing and optimum conditions. These estimates were made using the result of data analysis in this experiment. Here the additivity of factorial effects is assumed. Moreover, only significant factors were used in making this estimation.

1. The existing condition: $A_1B_1C_1D_2E_2F_1G_1H_2$

$$\eta P = \overline{A_1C_1} + \overline{D_2} + \overline{E_2} - 2\overline{T} = 35.8412 + 35.1623 +$$
$$34.1830 - 2 \times 34.91565 \quad (7.1)$$
$$= 35.3552 \pm 1.4429 \text{ (dB)}$$

$$P = \overline{A_1C_1} + \overline{D_2} + \overline{E_2} + (\overline{F_1} - \overline{E_2}) + \overline{H_2} - 3\overline{T} = 61.12 \pm 3.27 \text{ (lb.)} \quad (7.2)$$

$$\eta t = \overline{A_1C_1} + \overline{B_1} + \overline{D_2} + \overline{E_2} + (\overline{F_1} - \overline{E_2}) - 3\overline{T} = 49.1399 \pm 0.0484 \text{ (dB)} \quad (7.3)$$

$$t = \overline{A_1C_1} + \overline{B_2} + \overline{D_2} - 2\overline{T} = 291.6500 \pm 2.85 \text{ (.001 in)} \quad (7.4)$$

2. The optimum condition: $A_1B_2C_1D_2E_1H_2$

$$\eta P = \overline{A_1C_1} + \overline{D_2} + \overline{E_1} - 2\overline{T} = 35.8412 + 35.1623 + 35.1623 - 2 \times 34.91565$$
$$= 36.8205 \pm 1.4429 \text{ (dB)} \quad (7.5)$$

$$P = \overline{A_1C_1} + \overline{D_2} + \overline{E_1} + \overline{H_2} - 3\overline{T} = 67.7975 \pm 3.06 \text{ (lb.)} \quad (7.6)$$

$$\eta t = \overline{A_1C_1} + \overline{B_2} + \overline{D_2} + \overline{E_1} - 3\overline{T} = 49.3702 \pm 0.0475 \text{ (dB)} \quad (7.7)$$

$$t = \overline{A_1C_1} + \overline{B_2} + \overline{D_2} - 2\overline{T} = 291.6500 \pm 2.85 \text{ (.001 in)} \quad (7.8)$$

NOTE: The above confidence intervals were calculated using the following formula:

Confidence Interval
for ηP
$$= \pm \sqrt{F_{1', 9, 0.05} \times V_e \times \left(\frac{\text{df used in the est.}}{\text{total df}} + 1\right)} \quad (7.9)$$

$$= \pm \sqrt{5.12 \times 0.3098 \times [(5/15) + 1]}$$

$$= \pm 1.4429$$

Where V_e is MS error from ANOVA

NOTE: The confidence intervals for the S/N Ratio can be constructed using a more accurate formula. Here, the above formula is used for simplification.

8. CONFIRMATION EXPERIMENT AND COMPARISON OF RESULTS

To check the reproducibility of this experiment, data was collected under the optimum condition for the purpose of confirmation. Its sample size is 25, and the result is compared with the result from the existing condition. Note that the estimations made in the previous section agree with the figures based on these data.

1. Push-out Force Specification: 30 lb. minimum

	Avg.	3σ	S/N Ratio	C_p
Existing Condition ($n = 150$)	57.27	25.25	27.0109	1.08
Optimum Condition ($n = 25$)	69.80	12.43	36.8294	3.20

2. Travel Distance Specification .280 in./.320 in.

	Avg.	3σ	S/N Ratio	C_p
Existing Condition ($n = 150$)	289.80	15.90	49.2378	1.26
Optimum Condition ($n = 25$)	289.20	12.00	49.2216	1.67

NOTE: The figures for the above existing condition are based on the data collected from control charts over a period of two weeks. Data outside of the control limits were discarded for the calculation.

The figures for the optimum condition are based on the data from the confirmative production run of 25 pieces. Hence, they do not include day-to-day and week-to-week variations, as do the existing condition figures.

The real comparison can be made only after the process is changed and data collected for a month or so.

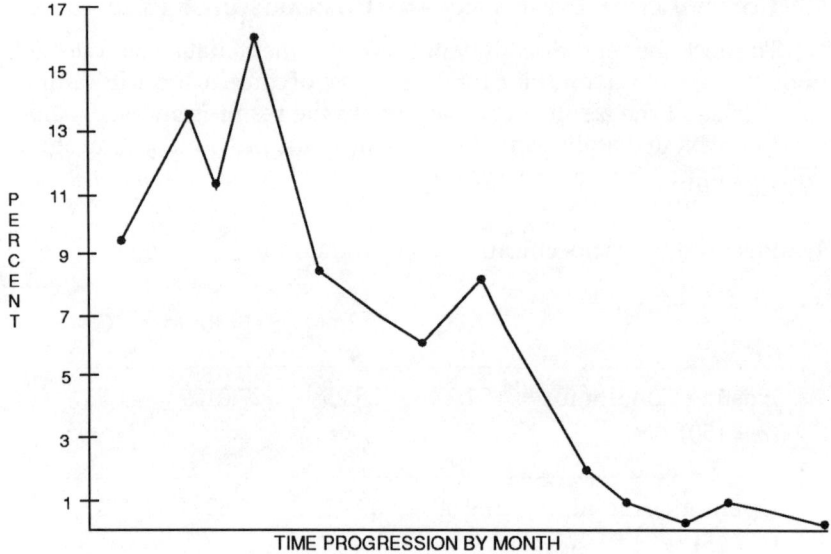

Figure 4. Cruise Control Vacuum Valve Percent Defective Time Progression by Month

9. Improvement After the Study

Through Taguchi Methods design of experiments, we were able to accomplish the following:

1. Increase push-out force by 17%.
2. Reduce variability of average and standard deviation of push-out force by 50%.
3. Reduce variability of travel distance by 18%.
4. Reduce average % defective by 19%.
5. Remove sonic welding station.
   A. The reduction of the % defective resulted in a saving of $17,000 per year.

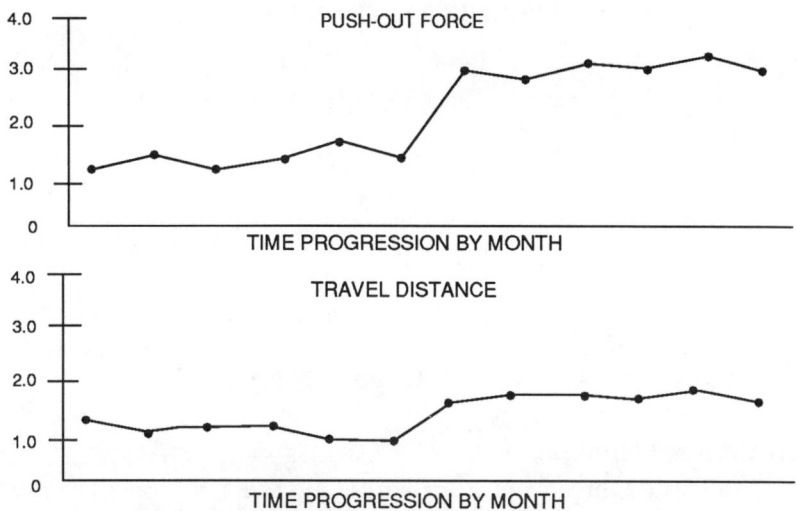

Figure 5. Cruise Control Vacuum Valve CP Index
Push-Out Force

B. The removal of the sonic weld station is a savings of approximately $800 per year.
C. The reduction of table dwell time is an increase in productivity of approximately 21%.

REFERENCES

Taguchi, Genichi, and Yuin Wu. *Introduction to Off-Line Quality Control*, Central Japanese Quality Control Association, 1979.

Taguchi, Genichi. *System of Experimental Design: engineering methods to optimize quality and minimize cost*, Volume 1, for UNIPUB/Kross International Publications and American Supplier Institute, Inc., 1987.

ACKNOWLEDGMENTS

Thank you to Professor Yuin Wu and Shin Taguchi for instruction in these techniques.

APPENDIX TO THE STUDY

APPENDIX 1 — NOTES ON "IDLE COLUMN METHOD" AND "ORTHOGONAL NESTING"

1. Refer to Chapter 6 of *Off-Line Quality Control* by Dr. Genichi Taguchi and Yuin Wu for allocation of factors to an orthogonal table using a linear graph.
2. Refer to *System of Experimental Design: Engineering Methods to Optimize Reality and Minimize Cost*, Volume 1, by Genichi Taguchi for "Idle Column Method" and "Orthogonal Nesting."

IDLE COLUMN METHOD:

To allocate a three-level factor, e.g., D and H in this report, to a two-level system, such as L_8, L_{16}, L_{32}, etc., a column of the orthogonal table is used as an idle column. Let us use factor D to illustrate the procedure of allocation. In this report, Column 11 is chosen as the idle column (see Figure A1). The linear graph of L_{16} gives a line segment corresponding to Column 7 connecting the idle column and the point corresponding to Column 12. Then Column 7 and Column 12 can be used to allocate 3-level factor D. The line segment column, Column 7, is deleted in L_{16} and then the combination of Column 12, and the idle column gives the level of D, as shown below. The table below also shows the decomposition of degree of freedom.

Idle (Col. 11)	Col. 12	Col. 7	Level of D
1	1	—	D_1
1	2	—	D_2
2	1	—	D_2
2	2	—	D_3

Source	df		Source	df
Idle Column (Col. 11)	1 - A	→	Idle	1
Col. 12	1 - A		D_1D_2	1
Col. 7 (Interaction Col .11 x Col. 12)	1 - A		D_2D_3	1

Figure A1.

Similarly, factor H is allocated using the same idle column and Column 14 and Column 5. In other words, D and H are sharing the same idle column. Therefore, the sum of squares calculated from the idle column includes some portion of factor effects and some experimental error.

ORTHOGONAL NESTING:

In this report, factors F and G are taking levels only when E_2 occurs. Here, E is allocated to Column 9 of an L_{16} orthogonal array. (See Figure A2.) Then as in the idle column method, a point and its line segment to Column 9, in the linear graph, are used for allocation of the nested factor. Figure A2 shows Column 6 and Column 15 are used for F, Column 15 and Column 13 for factor G. Then the line segment columns, i.e., Column 15 and Column 13, are deleted from the L_{16}. Finally, factor F takes its level according to Column 6, but only when Column 9 takes level two. The sum of squares from Column 6 when Column 9 takes level 1 is used to evaluate experimental error e_1. Similarly, the factor effect of G and experimental error e_2 are calculated from Column 4. The table below illustrates the discussion.

	Col. 9 (E)	Col. 6 (F, e_1)		
E_1	1	1		
	1	2		Experimental error e_1
	2	1	F_1	Factor effect of F
E_2	2	1	F_2	

Source	df		Source	df
Col. 9 (E)	1-A		Col. 9 (E)	1
Col. 6	1-A		F	1
Col. 15 (Interaction			Experimental	
Col. 9 x Col. 6)	1-A		error e_1	1

Figure A2.

Appendix 2 — Analysis of Variance Calculations

Example: Push-out Force

Table A-1. Layout of Data

Exp. No.	Raw Data	$\Sigma \eta p_1$	$\Sigma \eta p_1^2$	ηp
1	72, 68, 64, 49, 64, 72, 62, 74, 61, 75	661	44251	36.2049
2	— — — — — — — — — —	473	22741	33.2869
3	— — — — — — — — — —	627	40013	35.6914
4	— — — — — — — — — —	470	22880	33.0540
5	— — — — — — — — — —	674	45602	36.5224
6	— — — — — — — — — —	510	26750	33.7500
7	— — — — — — — — — —	691	48081	36.6832
8	— — — — — — — — — —	452	20738	32.9071
9	— — — — — — — — — —	686	48140	36.4042
10	— — — — — — — — — —	499	25629	33.5831
11	— — — — — — — — — —	575	33389	35.0644
12	— — — — — — — — — —	467	22275	33.1118
13	— — — — — — — — — —	499	25199	33.6307
14	— — — — — — — — — —	670	45089	36.4635
15	— — — — — — — — — —	600	36550	35.3669
16	— — — — — — — — — —	668	44814	36.4366

Table A-2. Calculation of ANOVA for ηp

Factor	Level 1	Level 2	Sum of Squares	df
Idle	274.7362	283.9152	5.2670	1
A	282.9221	275.7283	3.2344	1
B	278.0999	280.5505	0.3753°	1
C	285.5681	273.0823	9.7434	1
D (D_1,D_2)	135.8545 (D_1)	138.8807 (D_2)	1.1447	1
(D_2,D_3)	142.4172 (D_2)	141.4980 (D_3)	0.1057°	1
E	285.1862	273.4642	8.5878	1
F	137.9651	135.4491	0.7601°	1
e_1	143.3971	141.7891	0.3232°	1
G	137.0718	136.3924	0.0577°	1
e_2	143.2632	141.9230	0.2245°	1
H (H_1,H_2)	138.4336	136.3016	0.5682°	1
(H_2,H_3)	141.3103	142.6049	0.2095°	1
e_3	276.8900	281.7604	1.4825	1
e_4	280.1349	278.5155	0.1639°	1
TOTAL			32.2479	15

Sum of squares with ° are pooled with SSE

ANALYSES

For each of 16 combinations, i.e. each row of orthogonal array L_{16}, 10 readings were taken for both characteristics (replication = 10). For each set of data, the S/N Ratio, denoted by η, was calculated using the following formula:

$$\eta = -10 \log \left(\frac{1}{10} \left(\frac{1}{y_1^2} + \frac{1}{y_2^2} + \ldots + \frac{1}{y_{10}^2} \right) \right) (dB) \qquad (7.10)$$

Where y_i is i_{th} data. $i = 1, \ldots 10$.

A higher value represents either a higher average or less variation or combination of both. Hence, the higher the value the better the process. According to the layout of the L_{16}, the combination No. 1 has the process condition $A_1, B_1, C_1, D_1, E_1, H_1$. No. 2 has A_1, B_2, C_2, E_1, H_2. The raw data sets and S/N Ratios were recorded as follows:

Table A-3. Raw Data and S/N Ratios

Comb. No.1	1	2	3	4	5	6	7	8	9	10	S/N Ratio
Push-Out Force	72	68	64	49	64	72	62	74	61	75	36.2049
Travel Distance	290	297	295	296	285	290	300	280	295	285	49.28109

•
•
•

Comb. No.1	1	2	3	4	5	6	7	8	9	10	S/N Ratio
Push-Out Force	42	48	39	57	55	45	49	40	44	54	33.2869
Travel Distance	285	275	285	275	285	280	280	280	275	290	48.97019

•
•

Comb. No.1	1	2	3	4	5	6	7	8	9	10	S/N Ratio
Push-Out Force	62	58	69	70	64	66	66	68	73	72	36.4366
Travel Distance	285	285	290	300	290	300	290	300	285	285	49.27195

The analysis of variance was conducted on the following four characteristic responses:

1. ηp = S/N Ratio of push-out force (dB)
2. ηt = S/N Ratio of travel distance (dB)
3. p = raw data of push-out force (lb.)
4. t = raw data of travel distance (.001 in.)

The comparisons between ηp analysis and p analysis, and ηt analysis and t analysis, should show the power of S/N Ratio analyses.

Q & A

Q. What is a "pseudo factor"(or nested factor)?

A. The pseudo factor method is a technique used to assign an experiment where some factors are nested into specific levels of another factor. In this study, factor E is welding methods: regular resistance welding and ultrasonic welding. In ultrasonic welding there are two factors, welding pressure and welding time, which are nested. But, these two factors do not exist in resistance welding. Therefore, comparison of resistance welding and ultrasonic welding must be done after the optimum condition of ultrasonic welding is determined. This makes the assignment and data analysis complicated.

Q. Can a separate experiment for ultrasonic welding be conducted?

A. Of course. By conducting a separate experiment on ultrasonic welding, its optimum condition is found. Then that condition is set and compared with resistance welding. But when there are some common factors for the two welding methods, it would be more efficient to design a nested factor experiment.

Q. What is an idle column?

A. The idle column method is the technique used to assign a 3-level factor in a 2-level series orthogonal array. A more complete explanation is in the appendix of this study. An L_{16} orthogonal array is used in the experiment, with 3-level factors D and H.

Q. Can it be assigned in a 3-level orthogonal array?

A. Yes, it can. When 2-level factors are assigned in a 3-level orthogonal array, the third level of the column, where a 2-level factor is assigned, will be dummy-treated.

Q. Which way is better, using a 3-level or a 2-level orthogonal array?

A. It is practical to select the orthogonal array by the number of levels the majority of the factors possesses.

Q. The characteristic "push-out force" is a larger-the-better characteristic but "travel distance to break vacuum" is a nominal-the-best characteristic. Why is the larger-the-better characteristic used?

A. When it is very hard to move the mean up to the target or when sensitivity is not strong enough, a larger-the-better characteristic may be used for travel distance.

Q. There are no noise factors assigned in this experiment. Is this all right?

A. It would be better if there were noise factors included to help ensure a more robust design and reproducibility. However, reproducibility was confirmed in the trial production.

8. Optimization of a Hot-Stamping Process

Steve Sykes and William Ross
Kenkor Division, North American Reiss

Traditionally, during the design phase of a new product engineers specify what is needed to meet form, fit, and functional requirements. Unfortunately, this is typically done at the expense of product manufacturability. This case study demonstrates the use of Taguchi parameter design to assist design engineers in developing a product that both meets their needs and is manufacturable. In less than one month, a hot-stamping process was both established and optimized. The results not only yielded 100% conformance, but enable the design engineers to develop realistic product requirements in less than half the normal time.

1. Introduction to the Experiment

Problem: To improve adhesive, color contrast, and uniformity of coverage characteristics of a hot-stamping operation performed on injection-foam-molded parts.

Procedure:
1. Assembly of a cross-functional, problem-solving team including: engineering, quality, process control, line personnel, and setup personnel.
2. Problem and goal qualification based on quality and cost concerns.
3. Training: George Eckes, manager of the Supplier Quality Assistance Group at StorageTek, provided 16 hours of training on advanced problem solving including Taguchi Methods.

From the *Sixth Symposium on Taguchi Methods*™, pp. 407–414, Copyright © 1988, American Supplier Institute, Inc., Dearborn, Michigan.

4. Process flowcharting: A detailed manufacturing flowchart was developed including the identification of controllable and uncontrollable process variables.
5. Brainstorming: After constructing a cause-and-effect diagram, 71 potential causes were identified. Factors were then ranked (eliminating noise factors from consideration), and the five most probable factors, were selected for experimentation.
6. Factor level selection: Four of the five factors had a linear relationship, with output over a realistic range. For the last factor, an attribute, four levels were chosen.
7. Design selection: An L_8 (2^7) orthogonal array was selected to identify sources of variation.
8. Results were categorized into one of four categories. Accumulation analysis was used with analysis of variance (ANOVA) to quantify the contributions to variation. Five parts were hot-stamped at each experiment condition (approximately 40 opportunities) and the entire design was replicated once.
9. Following completion of the experiment, a confirmation run verified the results. A follow-up experiment was performed to pinpoint more specifically an optimum level for significant factors.

2. Factors, Experimental Layout and Results

Experimental setup and analysis: Table 1 shows the factors and levels. Table 2 shows the L_8 (2^7) Orthogonal Array. Table 3 shows the results of the experiment. Table 4 is the completed ANOVA. Figure 1 shows the optimization of the significant factors.

Table 1. Factors and Levels

	FACTORS	LEVELS	
		1	2
A	Temperature	350°F	450°F
B	Tape	4 Types	
C	Pressure	60 lb.	80 lb.
D	Time	0.4 sec	0.7 sec
E	Delay	1/4 turn	1/2 turn

Optimization of a Hot-Stamping Process

Table 2. L_8 (2^7) Orthogonal Array

$L_8(2^7)$

	A	B	C	D	E
1	1	1	1	1	1
2	1	2	1	2	2
3	1	3	2	1	2
4	1	4	2	2	1
5	2	1	2	2	2
6	2	2	2	1	1
7	2	3	1	2	1
8	2	4	1	1	2

Five samples at each condition; replicate once

Table 3. Results — Hot-Stamp Design (Accumulation Analysis)

	Good	G/M	B/M	Bad	Cumulative			
					I	II	III	IV
1	4	0	1	5	4	4	5	10
2	0	0	1	9	0	0	1	10
3	0	0	0	10	0	0	0	10
4	0	0	0	10	0	0	0	10
5	8	2	0	0	8	10	10	10
6	4	6	0	0	4	10	10	10
7	0	6	4	0	0	6	10	10
8	0	0	10	0	0	0	10	10

Table 4. ANOVA — Hot-Stamp Design

	f	S	V	s'	ρ%
A	3	91.51	30.5	90.52	37.7
B	9	56.80	6.31	53.83	22.4
C	3	12.31	4.10	11.32	4.7
D	3	1.05	.35	.06	0.1
E	3	6.26	2.09	5.27	2.2
e	216	72.07	.33	79.00	32.9
TOTAL	237	240.0		240.0	100.0

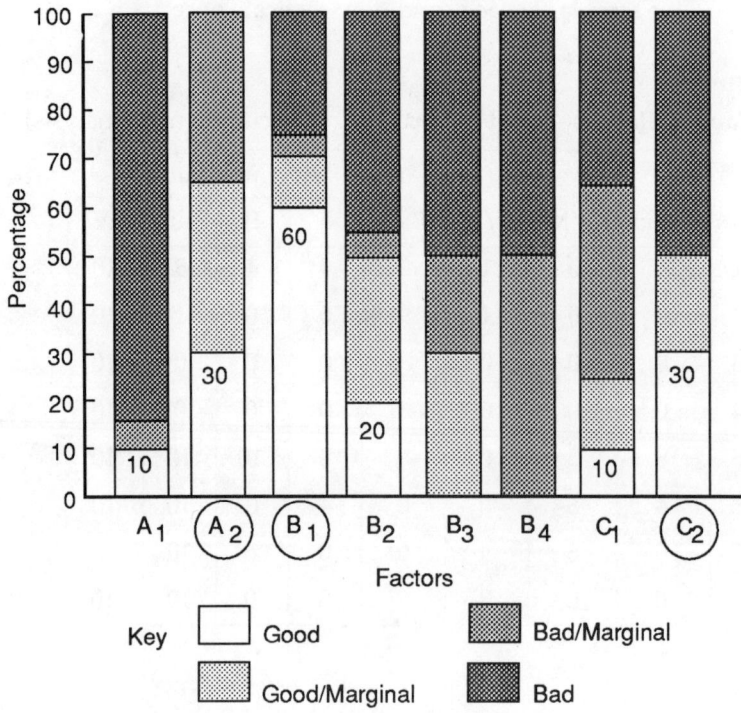

Figure 1. Optimization—Hot-Stamp Design

3. THE OPTIMAL CONDITION AND CONFIRMATION

Upon completion of the experimental analysis, factors *A*, *B*, and *C* were optimized:

A at level 2

B at level 1

C at level 2

A confirmation run verified the expected results. The estimate of optimum conditions (using Omega transformation) is as follows:

$\hat{\mu} = 91.9\% \pm 38\%$

With a final multi-level optimization experiment, 100% yield was consistently achieved.

4. IMPROVEMENT

The following is an itemized list of the results of the experiment:
- Parts acceptance at StorageTek went from 0% to 100%.
- North American Reiss saved more than $20,000 in processing costs.
- Critical factors were identified for further improvement in the future.
- 100% coverage of the target area was consistently achieved.
- Adhesive properties were significantly increased.
- Color achieved was functional.
- Parts are potential candidates for parts certification at StorageTek.
- Proper process control was put in place to ensure consistency of critical variables.

ACKNOWLEDGMENTS

North American Reiss–Kenkor Division would like to acknowledge Storage Technology Corporation of Louisville, Colorado, for its assistance in training and application of its Taguchi Methods. George Eckes, manager of the Supplier Quality Assistance Group, was instrumental in establishing the framework upon which Statistical Process Control could be implemented and successfully utilized. In addition, the assistance of Allen Collier and Pete Neumann of StorageTek and Bob Geist, James Schue, and Hwang Ngo of Kenkor was instrumental in completing this project.

Q & A

Q. Is this a simple experiment with five factors in an L_8 orthogonal array?

A. Yes, but we still recommend the assignment of more factors in a larger array, such as an L_{12} or L_{18} orthogonal array. Also, the inclusion of three-level factors is more desirable.

Q. Accumulation analysis is tedious when software programs are not available.

A. There is a way to make the analysis simpler. In this experiment, there are four categories: good, good/marginal, bad/marginal, and bad. A weight is considered and assigned for each category. The S/N Ratio for smaller-the-better characteristics is then used. For example, S/N Ratios of experiments No. 1 and No. 2 are calculated as follows:

Table 5. Weighted Data

Class	Good	Good/Marginal	Bad/Marginal	Bad
Weight	0	1	2	3
Frequency				
No.1	4	0	1	5
No.2	0	0	1	9

$$\eta(\text{No. 1}) = -10 \log \frac{1}{10}\left(0^2 \times 4 + 1^2 \times 0 + 2^2 \times 1 + 3^2 \times 5\right)$$
$$= -6.90 \, (\text{dB})$$
$$\eta(\text{No. 2}) = -10 \log \frac{1}{10}\left(0^2 \times 0 + 1^2 \times 0 + 2^2 \times 1 + 3^2 \times 9\right)$$
$$= -9.29 \, (\text{dB})$$

Table 6. S/N Ratios — Smaller-the-Better

No.	1	2	3	4	5	6	7	8
η (dB)	-6.90	-9.29	-9.54	-9.54	7.00	2.22	-3.42	-6.63

Table 7. Response Table (Average)

Factor Level	A	B	C	D	E
1	−8.82	0.05	−6.56	−5.21	−4.41
2	−0.21	−3.54	−2.47	−3.81	−4.82
3		−6.48			
4		−8.09			
Difference	8.61	8.59	4.09	1.4	0.21
Order	1	2	3	4	5

Q. How is the weight selected? Is it arbitrary?

A. The determined weight is proportional to the loss.

Q. Suppose only the products in the class "bad" are rejected. In that case, should a weight of "0" be assigned to the rest of the classes?

A. No, there are losses for those in the classes of "good/marginal" and "bad/marginal." Think about the Quality Loss Function. When quality deviates from the target, which is "good," there is a specific monetary loss.

9. Automatic Wave Soldering of Electronic Printed Circuit Assemblies

Robert A. Miller,
Body and Assembly, Ford Motor Company

Charles A. Phaneuf and Joseph F. Rypl
Electrical Division, Wickes Manufacturing Company

This case study demonstrates the application of Taguchi Methods in automatic wave soldering. Automatic wave soldering is a mature process, but increasing demands to improve product reliability to the range of 200 ppm defective is critical to remain competitive. First-run yield needed to be increased to 99% for improved field reliability. This study was conducted to quantify and optimize wave-soldering factors that impact solder quality and reliability. As a result of this study, first-run solder process capability was improved from 97% to 99.5%. This translates into an 83% reduction in solder touch-up and repair and an annual savings of $60,000.

1. The Wave Soldering Process

Automatic wave soldering is a critical process in high-quality manufacturing of electronics and to their subsequent field reliability. In an electronics assembly plant producing a variety of products, the wave-solder machine must accommodate varying artwork configurations, solder joint densities, component lead configurations, and solderability conditions in a random sequence. The many wave solder machine adjustments offer many opportunities to "control" the process with many combinations of machine settings to accommodate the differences in products and soldering conditions. Optimum soldering results across all products are thus difficult to achieve and consistently maintain.

Automatic wave soldering is a mature process in many respects in that it has operated in the electronics industry for many years with process yields typically in the 90s. Dramatic decreases in quality defects

---

From the *Third Symposium on Taguchi Methods*™, pp. 212–233, Copyright © 1985, American Supplier Institute, Inc., Dearborn, Michigan.

and manufactured cost may thus be elusive. New and increasing demands from our customers to deliver product reliability in the range of 200 ppm, however, necessitated re-evaluating this established process to increase first-run yields to greater than 99% for improved field reliability, customer/consumer satisfaction, and future business potential.

This study was conceived to quantify and optimize wave soldering controllable and uncontrollable factors that impact solder quality and reliability. The objective is to define an optimum combination of machine settings that will produce excellent solder quality on a variety of products and gain those difficult few percentage points to exceed 99% first-run yield.

2. Design of the Experiment

The experimental control factors, levels, and noise factors (Table 1) were crystallized in a brainstorming session with product, quality, and industrial engineers plus production personnel and supervisors (Table 2).

The L_{18} orthogonal array describes the layout of the experiment, showing which factor levels are active in each of the 18 experiments.

The explanations of the control factors are mostly self-evident. Flux Flow describes the rate of flux-foaming as controlled by the air pressure on the foamer stone. Flux Air Knife refers to the flux-pot air knife that blows excess flux off the circuit board.

Factor levels one and three were created as artificial operating conditions (except factor A) to generate extreme process results to define the linear or quadratic performance curves of each factor. The noise factors represent the difficult to predict and control variants in EEC timer and fan controller configurations and their solderability conditions (oxide).

The defects to be analyzed are solder bridges and solder fillet holes (i.e., incomplete fillets). For purposes of this study, no differentiation would be made between fillet holes considered acceptable to industry standards and fillet holes requiring repair, as the goal is to eliminate them completely.

The fan controller and EEC timer (Figure 1) were selected as representative of relatively high density and low density soldering conditions and represent extremes of lead masses and topside masses.

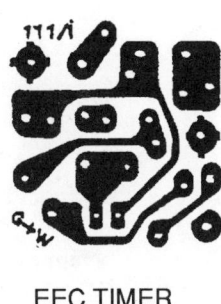

EEC TIMER

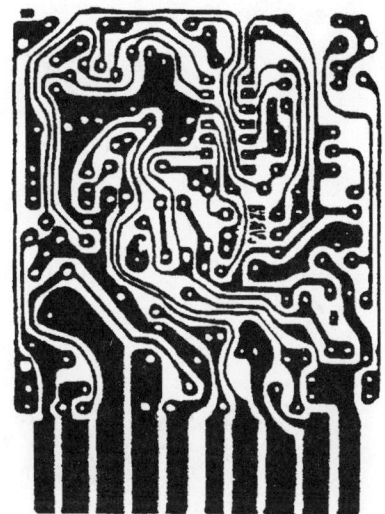

FAN CONTROLLER

Figure 1. EEC Timer and Fan Controller

3. Analysis of Experimental Results

The responses by noise level and by experiment are detailed in Table 2 next to the L_{18} orthogonal array. The response table (Table 3) sums the gross number of defects (by category) generated whenever each of the control factors was active. To put the tallies in the response table in perspective, the number of solder joints in the experiment totaled 57,000 on the fan control and 59,600 on the EEC timer. For example, the number "55" under "fan holes" on the factor A_1 line in Table 3 represents the gross number of holes produced on fan controllers when level one of factor A was active in experiments one through nine.

The response table is the principal analysis tool of the designed experiment.

The EEC Signal-to-Noise (S/N) Ratio column in the response table represents the S/N evaluation of EEC holes response data.

Significant factors can be relied on to repeatedly deliver the same results in production that were demonstrated in the experiment.

Table 1. Experimental Parameters

	Control Factor	Level One	Level Two	Level Three
A	FLUX TYPE	Organic Acid	Synthetic	—
B	FLUX DENSITY (spec gravity)	High 0.900	Nominal 0.875	Low 0.850
C	SOLDER TEMP	460°F	490°F	520°F
D	FLUX FLOW +	Normal +	High +	Normal +
E	SOLDER WAVE HEIGHT	Shallow	Shallow	Deep
F	PREHEAT SETTING	1	3	6
G	CONVEYOR SPEED	5 ft/min	8 ft/min	10 ft/min
H	FLUX AIR KNIFE ANGLE	45 degrees	90 degrees	reverse
I	FLUX AIR KNIFE PRESSURE	low	current	high
	Noise Factors			
	OXIDE	Unoxidized (normal)	Oxidized PCBs	Oxidized PCBs + components
	DENSITY	EEC TIMER normal	FAN CONTROL high	

Table 2. Experimental Layout and Results

L_{18} ARRAY CONTROL FACTORS								RESPONSES BY NOISE LEVEL									
E X P E R I M E N T	FLUX SPECIFIC GRAVITY	DENSITY	SOLDER WAVE WIDTH	FLUX HEIGHT + HEAT	PREHEAT	CONVEYOR ANGLE	KNIFE FEED RATE	KNIFE FEED ANGLES	FAN CONTROL HOLES			FAN CONTROL BRIDGES			EEC HOLES			EEC SIGNAL TO NOISE
									NORMAL	OX PCB	OX ALL	NORMAL	OX PCB	OX ALL	NORMAL	OX PCB	OX ALL	
	A	B	C	D+E	F	G	H	I	1	2	3	1	2	3	1	2	3	
1	1	1	1	1	1	1	1	1	0	1	2	0	0	0	28	31	22	−17.28
2	1	1	2	2	2	2	2	2	0	9	1	0	0	0	22	26	25	−17.62
3	1	1	3	3	3	3	3	3	0	1	0	1	0	0	27	29	24	−17.08
4	1	2	1	1	2	2	3	3	1	3	3	0	8	5	13	21	26	−14.52
5	1	2	2	2	3	3	1	1	1	3	0	1	5	5	27	34	34	−19.68
6	1	2	3	3	1	1	2	2	1	3	2	0	0	0	41	23	42	−20.23
7	1	3	1	2	1	3	2	3	3	6	9	39	29	27	10	23	31	−15.94
8	1	3	2	3	2	1	3	1	1	1	2	0	0	0	26	28	41	−19.37
9	1	3	3	1	3	2	1	2	0	0	2	1	0	0	17	15	39	−16.92
10	2	1	1	3	3	2	2	1	3	4	9	0	0	0	36	32	45	−20.16
11	2	1	2	1	1	3	3	2	1	8	8	1	2	1	20	14	38	−17.39
12	2	1	3	2	2	1	1	3	0	3	3	0	0	0	46	40	48	−21.27
13	2	2	1	2	3	1	3	2	2	20	5	0	0	0	49	38	51	−21.59
14	2	2	2	3	1	2	1	3	2	0	13	0	0	1	41	34	34	−19.34
15	2	2	3	1	2	3	2	1	3	2	5	1	2	1	48	31	36	−20.10
16	2	3	1	3	2	3	1	2	4	16	4	0	1	0	44	33	54	−21.44
17	2	3	2	1	3	1	2	3	8	7	2	0	0	0	56	37	58	−22.63
18	2	3	3	2	1	2	3	1	1	2	3	0	0	0	57	24	59	−21.96
	CONTROL FACTOR LEVELS								RESPONSES BY NOISE LEVEL									

Table 3. Response Table

CONTROL FACTOR		FAN HOLES		FAN BRIDGES		EEC HOLES		S/N EEC HOLES TOTAL		OPT LVL
FLUX TYPE	A_1	55	s*	122	s	935	s*	-158.64	s*	A_1
	A_2	138	s	10	s*	1093	s	-185.88	s	
FLUX DENSITY	B_1	53		5	s	553	s*	-110.80	s*	B_1
	B_2	69		39	s	633	s	-115.46	s	
	B_3	71		88	s	642	s	-118.26	s	
SOLDER TEMP	C_1	95	s	110	s	587	s*	-110.93	s*	
	C_2	67	s	16	s	605	s	-116.03	s	
	C_3	31	s*	6	s*	636	s	-117.56	s	C_3
FLUX FLOW + SOLDER WAVE HT	DE_1	56		32	s	550	s*	-108.84	s*	DE_1
	DE_2	71		97	s	644	s	-118.06	s	
	DE_3	66		3	s*	634	s	-117.62	s	
PREHEAT SETTING	F_1	65		91	s	562	s*	-112.14		
	F_2	61		28	s	608	s	-114.32		F_2
	F_3	67		13	s*	658	s	-118.06		
CONVEYOR SPEED	G_1	63		0	s*	705	s	-122.37	s	
	G_2	56		25	s	556	s	-110.52	s*	G_2
	G_3	74		107	s	567	s	-111.63	s	
FLUX AIR KNIFE ANGLE	H_1	54		14	s*	631		-115.93		
	H_2	77		90	s	622		-116.68		
	H_3	62		28	s	575		-111.91		H_3
FLUX AIR KNIFE PRESSURE	I_1	43	s*	15	s	639		-118.55	s	I_1
	I_2	86	s	6	s*	591		-115.19	s	
	I_3	64	s	111	s	598		-110.78	s*	
NOISE FACTORS	UNOX	31	s*	45		618	s			
	OX PCB	90	s	47		513	s*			
	OX ALL	73	s	40		699	s			

s Significant Factor
* Optimum Level

In reviewing the response table, the optimum level for all factors can be concluded from their response tallies in the priority of significant factors first followed by insignificant factors. The significant factors, graphically displayed in Figures 2, 3, 4, and 5, are from the second regular S/N Ratio analysis.

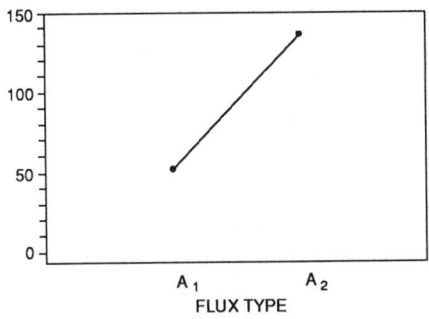

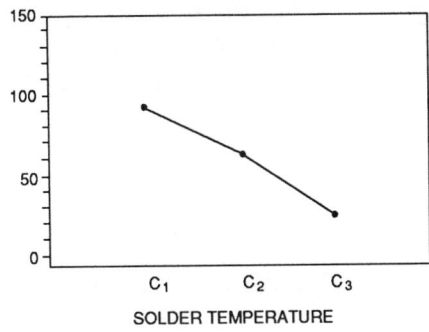

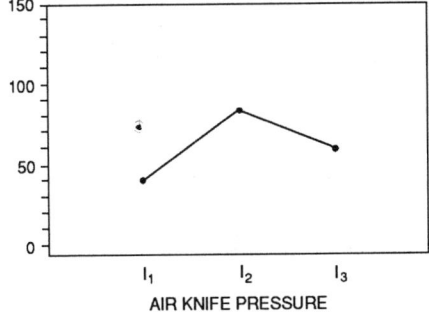

Figure 2. Fan Control Holes Significant Factor Performance

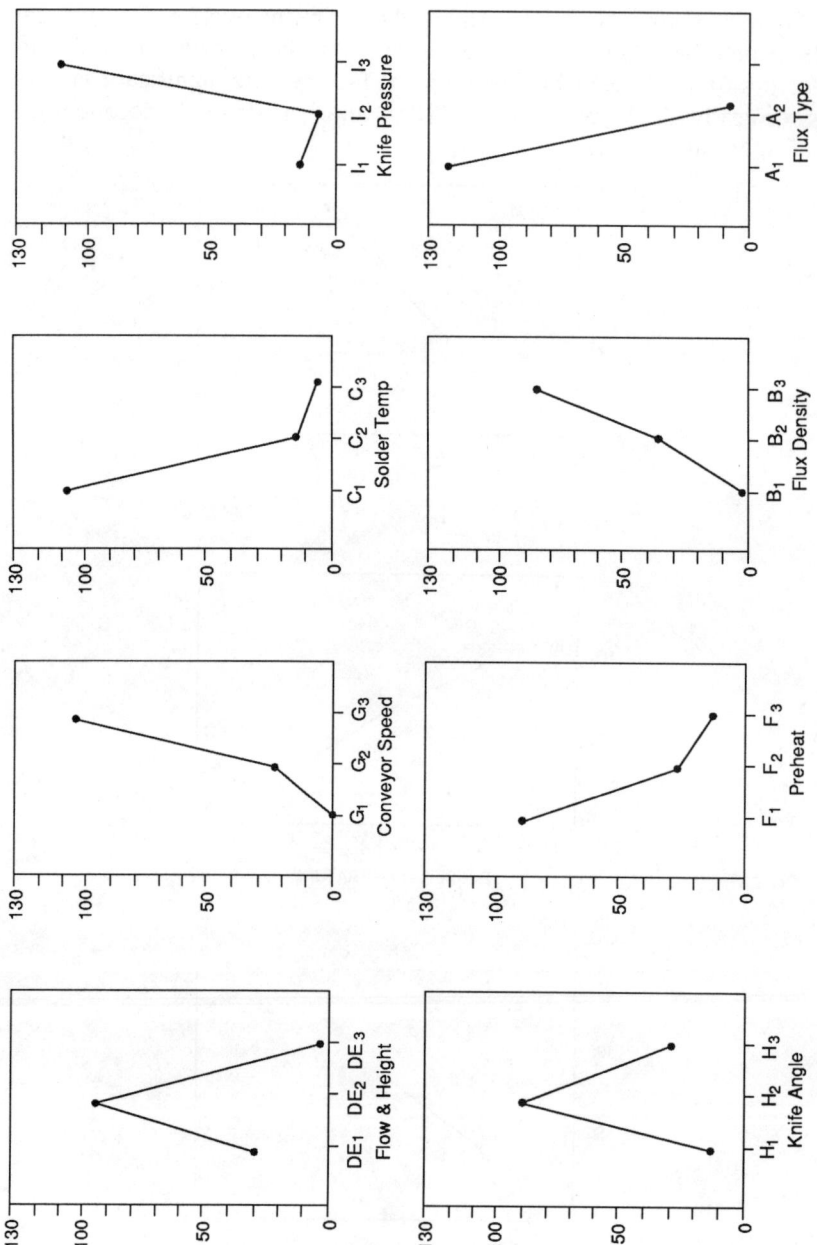

Figure 3. Fan Control Bridges
Significant Factor Performance

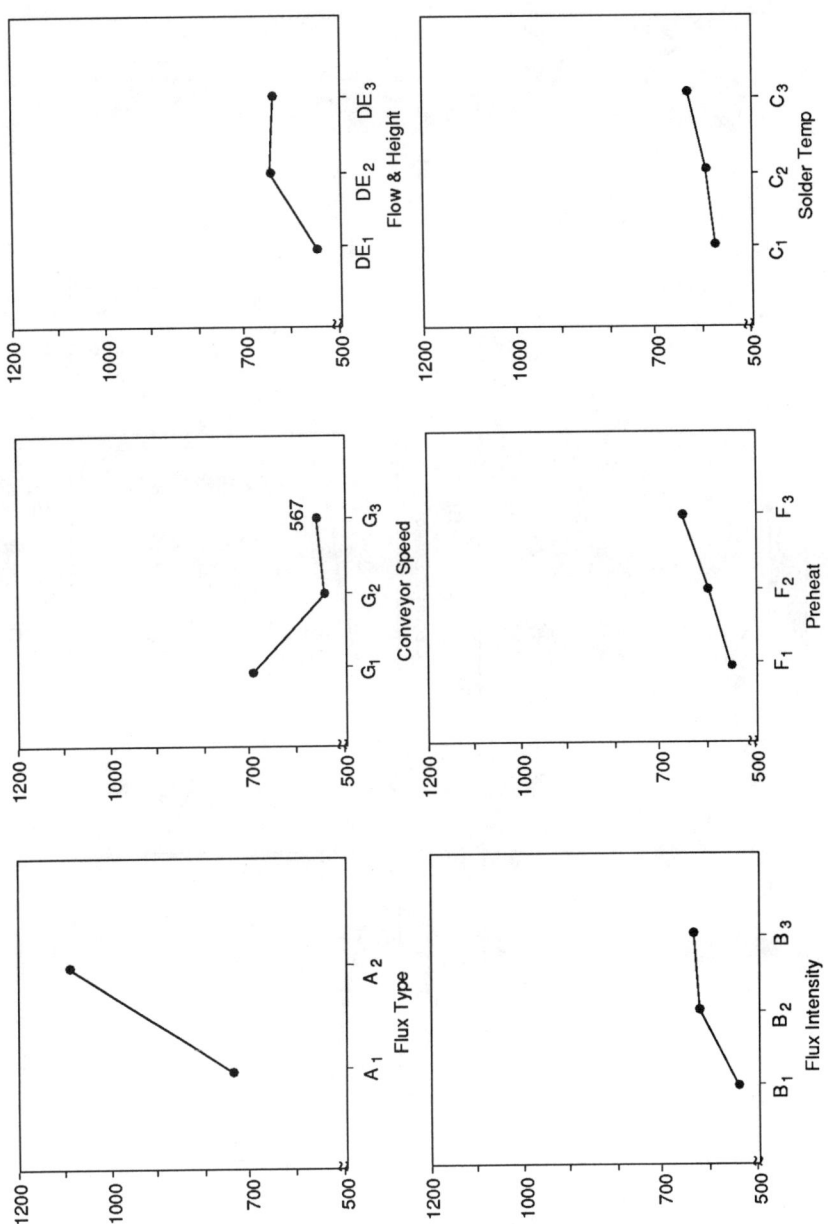

Figure 4. EEC Holes
Significant Factor Performance

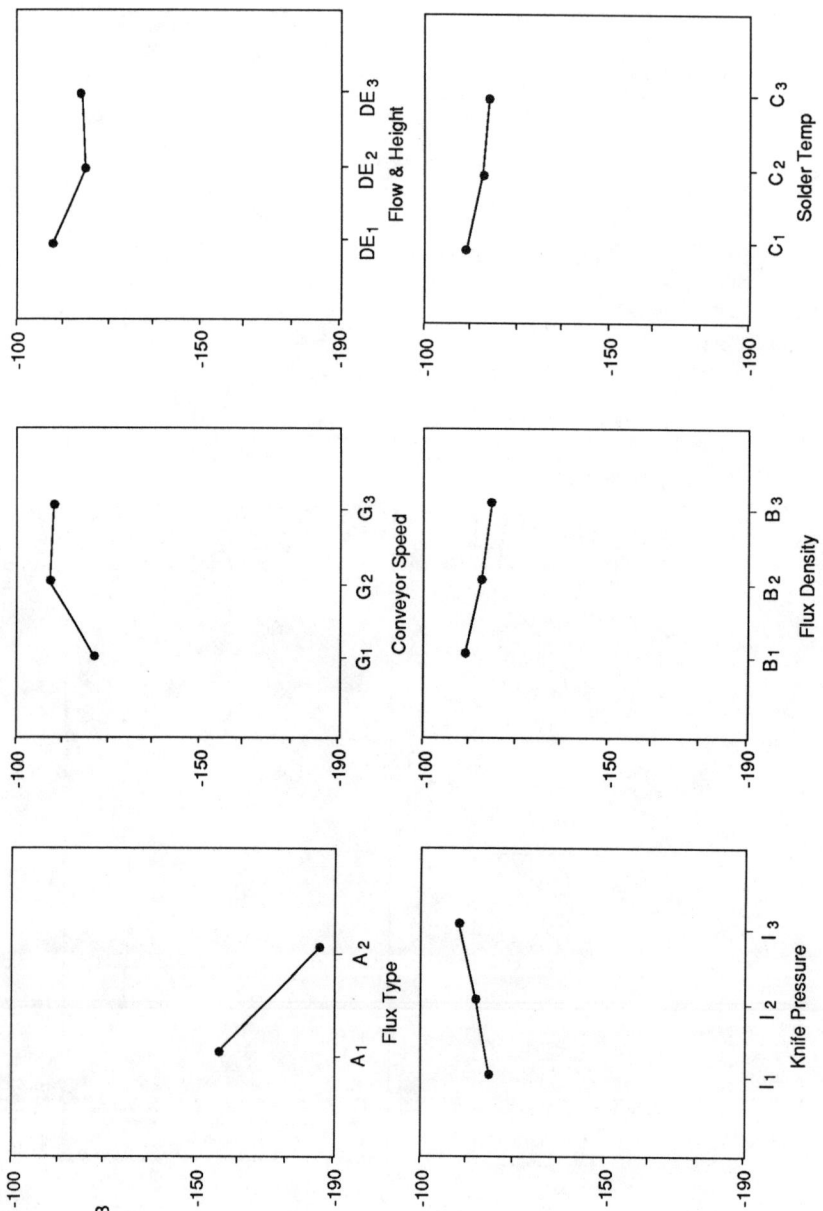

Figure 5. EEC Holes S/N Significant Factor Performance

4. Conclusions and Confirmation

The basic laws of soldering are supported by this data with its emphasis on flux, oxide, solder temperature, and conveyor speed. The interesting discovery of this experiment, however, is that these factors contributed less than 50% to process variability.

Fan controller solder bridges are heavily influenced by controllable machine settings, where holes are heavily influenced by the oxide noise factor.

EEC timer solder bridges did not create enough overall data to be analyzed, which suggests we enjoy a very robust design that resists bridging within the scope of this experiment and reasonable operating conditions. EEC holes were not reduced to the same extent as fan holes, however, suggesting that untested control factors impact solder holes. This is cause for further study.

The oxide noise-factor level two showed an interesting and significant improvement in EEC holes. For this experiment, the PCB was artificially oxidized in an oven at an elevated temperature over an arbitrary time cycle. This baking process may have coincidentally driven off PCB board house processing residues, which have been suspected of adversely affecting solder quality. This phenomenon will be further studied.

These conclusions are based on the experimental results of the designed experiment and are thus limited to the scope of the experiment. As was mentioned above, levels one and three were perceived as extreme conditions where the process would likely produce poor results. Yet it was at these extremes that EEC solder temperature and flux density optimized. These results encourage the careful exploration of control-factor levels beyond these perceived boundaries of acceptable process performance. This process will be studied further.

A confirming experiment has been accomplished with actual production data supporting the conclusions of the experiments. First-run solder process capability has increased from 97% to 99.5% in the confirming study. This translates into an 83% reduction in solder touch-up and repairs, which will generate approximately $60,000 in annual cost improvement. Less obvious is the product reliability improvement forecasted to be 50 ppm with its coincident customer and consumer satisfaction improvement and return sales potential gain. Also less obvious is a 38% increase in solder-machine capacity (resulting from increased conveyor speed), which will reduce long-run capital overhead and contribute to higher profits, lower prices, increased sales, or any combination of the above.

5. Summary

The Taguchi designed experiment has demonstrated an exciting methodology in analyzing process control factors' weighted impact on solder quality when uncontrollable forces (noise) interact with the wave soldering process. This analysis tool will be used on follow-up wave soldering analyses to further reduce process variability and define optimum soldering conditions for other products. This methodology has already been used to optimize sonic and resistance welder setup parameters and will continue to be applied in new processing applications and troubleshooting of existing processes.

Currently the Taguchi-designed experiment technique is also being applied to a circuit-design analysis to quantify the factors that introduce product performance variability at the design level. While the manufacturing organization constantly strives to optimize its processes, product performance variability inherent in design is extremely difficult to overcome. The design-level Taguchi analysis will be evaluated as a potential tool for qualifying design functions prior to production release and to identify the major control factors for manufacturing to focus control efforts on from production start forward.

Q & A

Q. There are two types of quality characteristics in this study: holes and bridges. Solder holes, which are incomplete fillets, and solder bridges, both of which resulted in short circuits and in defects. For simplicity of analysis, can we add the numbers of these defects together?

A. Definitely not, and the reasons are very important. Holes are the result of insufficient energy input into the system, while bridges are the result of too much energy. Suppose there are two control factors, A and B. The lower level is the condition of less energy, and the higher level is more energy. Combination A_1B_1 results in less energy and causes holes. A_2B_1 and A_1B_2 are moderate energy conditions, meaning less holes would result. Since A_2 is better than A_1 and B_2 is better than B_1, the best condition judged from the results might be A_2B_2. But that condition might be the worst because under the condition A_2B_2, too much energy would be put into the system, and many bridges would be formed. This is the result of an interaction.

Q. I learned that an interaction is caused by selecting a poor quality characteristic. Is this true?

A. A bad characteristic has poor additivity. Additivity means that when you combine a good effect with another good effect, the result should be better than each independent effect. In the above example, A_2 is better than A_1 and B_2 is better than B_1. Therefore, the combined effect, A_2B_2, should be much better than each individual effect. But the result of A_2B_2 is too many bridges. The best condition we predicted became the worst condition, this is due to interaction of effects. By selecting a good quality characteristic, we could minimize interactions. Interactions should be dealt with by techniques of the specific technology and appropriate analysis techniques, such as 1) changing to characteristic values possessing additivity, 2) consideration of the interrelationships between the levels chosen for different factors, and 3) the case of categorized values, the use of a correct method of analysis.

Q. Is it all right to analyze holes and bridges separately?

A. Yes. But the number of holes is still not a good characteristic. It is attributes data. We should always try to convert the quality characteristic into a continuous variable.

Q. How would this be done?

A. We can prepare boards of different density and use them for the experiments. In this experiment, we would then observe at what density holes start to occur, and at what density bridges start to occur. Treat the density when the holes start to occur as a smaller-the-better characteristic and the density when the bridges start to occur as a larger-the-better characteristic.

Q. In a wave-soldering process, we have to solder the boards of different density. When the density is quite different, the operating condition might not be the same. How is this compensated for?

A. You can pick up a factor that will be used to adjust the energy, which is known as a signal factor, and then use the dynamic characteristic approach to maximize the Signal-to-Noise (S/N) Ratio.

Q. There are a few control factors that can adjust energy. Which one should be used?

A. If you do not know, you can put those control factors in the inner orthogonal array and study which factor is the best to use. When you discover a factor that can adjust the energy, the factor becomes the signal factor. In the next experiment, the signal factor is then put outside the array for the calculation of S/N Ratios using the concept of dynamic characteristics.

PART 2:
MECHANICAL —PRODUCT

10. Experiment to Optimize the Design Parameters of an Elastomeric Connector and Tubing Assembly

Engineering Staff
Baylock Manufacturing Corp.

This study demonstrates the use of Taguchi Methods in the optimization of thermoplastic elastomers. The objective of the study was twofold: to reduce the force required to assemble the connector to the tubing and to increase the force necessary to separate the assembly once completed. An L_9 inner orthogonal array and L_8 outer array were used to obtain measurements of pull-off response and assembly effort. The selection of optimum levels for two opposing characteristics was determined and a confirmation run conducted. The results of the confirmation run were within the predicted values.

1. Description of the Experiment

This experiment was designed using an L_9 orthogonal array for the controllable factors and an L_8 orthogonal array for the environmental or noise factors. An estimate of the effects of three levels of four controllable factors and of two levels of three noise factors on assembly effort and pull-off was to be obtained. Signal-to-Noise (S/N) Ratios and 2-level interactions between controllable and uncontrollable factors were to be obtained for the pull-off response.

Controllable factors are shown in Figure 1:

A = Interference
B = Connector wall thickness
C = Insertion depth
D = Percent adhesive in connector pre-dip.

From the *First Symposium on Taguchi Methods*™, pp. 123–136, Copyright © 1983, American Supplier Institute, Inc., Dearborn, Michigan.

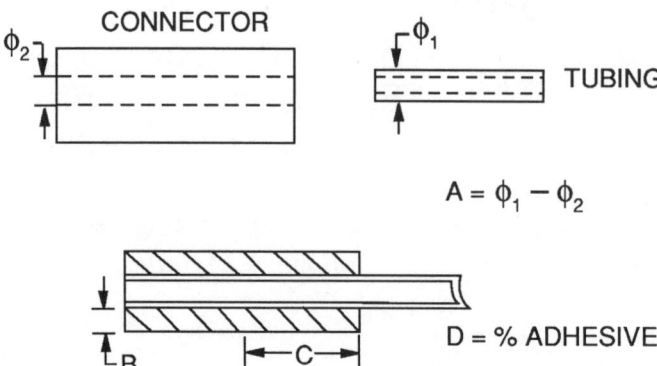

Figure 1. Controllable Factors

Noise factors involved the post-assembly conditioning of the samples prior to testing. Noise factors were:

E = Conditioning time
F = Conditioning temperature
G = Conditioning relative humidity.

The noise factors were put into an L_8 orthogonal array in order to detect any interactions between the conditioning levels. Had this not been desired, an L_4 orthogonal array could have been used at a savings of the cost to prepare and test 36 samples.

2. Assembly Effort Results

The layout in Table 1 is the assembly-effort section of this experiment. The left-hand side lists the levels of the controllable factors. Samples prepared in accordance with condition number three, for example, would consist of low interference between the tubing and connector (A_1), thick-walled connectors (B_3), deep insertion depth (C_3), and a high percentage of adhesive in the connector pre-dip (D_3).

The results are peak assembly force in pounds. These were obtained by the use of a load cell under the assembly fixture. An arbor press was used to maintain a constant rate of assembly.

The right-hand column lists the S/N Ratios in decibels. These values are calculated for the situation where a smaller-the-better response is more desirable. Lower assembly efforts are beneficial in terms of productivity, worker satisfaction with the job, and more consistent insertion depths. Consistent insertion depths reduce the variability of the pull-off response, which will be seen later in this experiment.

Design Parameters of an Elastomeric Connector

Table 1. Layout by Orthogonal Array L_9

	L_9				Inter-ference (A)	Wall Thick-ness (B)	Inser-tion Depth (C)	Percent Ad-hesive (D)	Sample 1	Sample 2	Sample 3	Sample 4	Sample 5	Sample 6	Sample 7	Sample 8	S/N Ratio (dB)
i	A	B	C	D													
1	1	1	1	1	Low	Thin	Shallow	Low	7.5	7.2	7.6	7.4	7.2	7.3	6.5	7.7	−17.28
2	1	2	2	2	Low	Med.	Med.	Med.	8.0	8.1	8.4	7.5	7.8	8.7	8.2	8.2	−18.20
3	1	3	3	3	Low	Thick	Deep	High	8.5	9.0	8.9	8.8	8.9	8.6	8.7	8.7	−18.85
4	2	1	2	3	Med.	Thin	Med.	High	8.1	8.1	8.2	8.6	7.5	8.5	8.5	8.3	−18.31
5	2	2	3	1	Med.	Med.	Deep	Low	8.7	8.7	8.9	9.0	9.2	8.8	9.1	9.4	−19.06
6	2	3	1	2	Med.	Thick	Shallow	Med.	7.9	7.5	7.8	7.6	7.6	7.6	8.0	7.6	−17.75
7	3	1	3	2	High	Thin	Deep	Med.	9.3	9.3	9.5	9.3	9.6	9.6	9.6	9.5	−19.52
8	3	2	1	3	High	Med.	Shallow	High	7.5	8.4	7.9	7.9	8.3	8.2	8.1	8.2	−18.65
9	3	3	2	1	High	Thick	Med.	Low	8.5	8.4	8.2	8.6	8.5	9.0	8.7	8.3	−18.62

$$\text{S/N Ratio} = -10 \log \frac{1}{n} \sum_{i=1}^{n} y_i^2 \qquad (10.1)$$

$$\text{Run 1: } -10 \log \left(\frac{7.5^2 + 7.2^2 + 7.6^2 + 7.4^2 + 7.2^2 + 7.3^2 + 6.5^2 + 7.7^2}{8} \right) = -17.28$$

$$\text{Run 2: } -10 \log \left(\frac{8.0^2 + 8.1^2 + 8.4^2 + 7.6^2 + 7.8^2 + 8.7^2 + 8.2^2 + 8.2^2}{8} \right) = -18.20$$

The next analysis on the assembly-effort data is performed using the S/N Ratio (see Table 2).

Table 2. ANOVA (condensed): Signal-to-Noise Ratio—Assembly Effort Data

Source	df	S	V	S'	%
A (lin.)	1	1.005	1.005	1.003	26.9
A (quad.)	1	0.045	0.045	0.045	1.2
B (quad.)	1	0.129	0.129	0.127	3.4
C (lin.)	1	2.383	2.383	2.381	63.9
C (quad.)	1	0.039	0.039	0.037	1.0
D (lin.)	1	0.122	0.122	0.120	3.2
e'	2	0.004	0.002	0.016	0.4
T	8	3.727	—	3.727	100.0

All four factors were significant on S/N Ratios. Their effects are shown below.

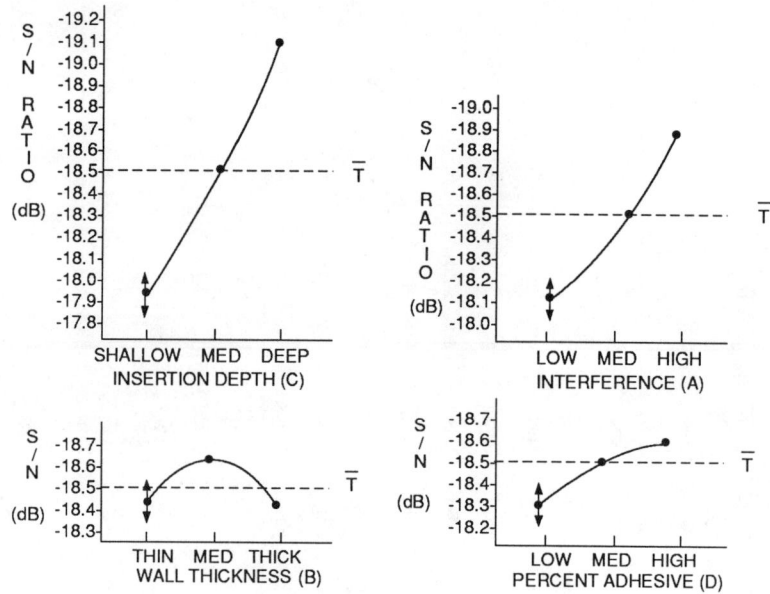

Figure 2. Effects of Factors: Signal-to-Noise Ratio—Assembly Effort

The judgment of the optimum levels based on the data in Figure 2 must await the analysis of the pull-off results of this experiment.

3. Pull-Off Force Results

The layout in Table 3 is for the pull-off force section of this experiment. It is identical to the layout for assembly forces with the exception of the L_8 orthogonal array added to the top of the layout. This section of the layout indicates the various levels of post-assembly conditioning that the sample parts underwent prior to pull testing. The pull testing was done on a tensile tester at a pull rate of 4 ipm and the results are in pounds.

In the right-hand column there is a S/N Ratio calculated in decibels. In this situation, the S/N Ratio is calculated using the formula for larger-the-better.

An analysis is performed using the S/N Ratio on the pull-off force data. This data was based on the formula for larger-the-better. As with other data, the first step is the ANOVA table. This ANOVA was decomposed into linear and quadratic effects, but there was no resulting increase in sensitivity so that only the main effects are shown (Table 4).

Table 4. ANOVA (Condensed): S/N Ratio—Pull-Off Force Data

Source	df	S	V	S'	%
A	2	1.775	0.888	1.456	27.5
C	2	2.876	1.438	2.557	48.3
e'	4	0.639	0.160	1.278	24.2
T	8	5.290	—	5.291	100.0

The two significant effects (interference and insertion depth) are then graphed.

Table 3. Layout by Orthogonal Arrays L_9 and L_8

Column assignments for L_8 (noise) array:

Col	1	2	3	4	5	6	7
Factor	0 (e_1)	E	F	E×F	G	E×G	F×G
Cond. Time (E)		120 h				24 h	
Cond. Temp. (F)			150°F				72°F
Cond. R.H. (G)					75%		

Experiment layout and results:

i	A	B	C	D	Interference (A)	Wall Thickness (B)	Insertion Depth (C)	Percent Adhesive (D)	120h / 150°F / 75%	120h / 150°F / 25%	120h / 72°F / 75%	120h / 72°F / 25%	24h / 150°F / 75%	24h / 150°F / 25%	24h / 72°F / 75%	24h / 72°F / 25%	S/N Ratio (dB)
1	1	1	1	1	Low	Thin	Shallow	Low	19.1	20.0	19.6	19.6	19.9	16.9	9.5	15.6	24.025
2	1	2	2	2	Low	Med.	Med.	Med.	21.9	24.2	19.8	19.7	19.6	19.4	16.2	15.0	25.522
3	1	3	3	3	Low	Thick	Deep	High	20.4	23.3	18.2	22.6	15.6	19.1	16.7	16.3	25.335
4	2	1	2	3	Med.	Thin	Med.	High	24.7	23.2	18.9	21.0	18.6	18.9	17.4	18.3	25.904
5	2	2	3	1	Med.	Med.	Deep	Low	25.3	27.5	21.4	25.6	25.1	19.4	18.6	19.7	26.908
6	2	3	1	2	Med.	Thick	Shallow	Med.	24.7	22.5	19.6	14.7	19.8	20.0	16.3	16.2	25.326
7	3	1	3	2	High	Thin	Deep	Med.	21.6	24.3	18.6	16.8	23.6	18.4	19.1	16.4	25.711
8	3	2	1	3	High	Med.	Shallow	High	24.4	23.2	19.6	17.8	16.8	15.1	15.6	14.2	24.832
9	3	3	2	1	High	Thick	Med.	Low	28.6	22.6	22.7	23.1	17.1	19.3	19.9	16.1	26.152

Design Parameters of an Elastomeric Connector

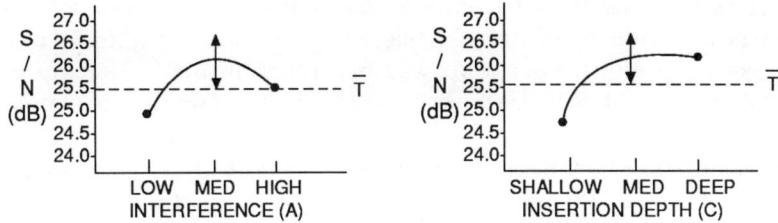

Figure 3. Effects of Factors: S/N Ratio—
Pull-Off Data

4. Review of Factors for Optimization

The next step in the experiment was to determine the optimum level for each factor based on the experimental results. The easiest way by which to accomplish this is to organize the results in the manner shown below:

Table 5. Summary Table of Results

Factors	Levels	Assembly Effort	Pull-Off Force	Cost Rating	Performance Rating Assy	Pull	Overall Rating
Inter-	1 Low	8.1	18.7	Least	Best	Worst	
ference	2 Medium	8.3	20.7	—	—	Best	X
(A)	3 High	8.7	19.5	Most	Worst	—	
Wall	1 Thin	—	—	Least	—	—	X
Thickness	2 Medium	—	—	—	—	—	
(B)	3 Thick	—	—	Most	—	—	
Insertion	1 Shallow	7.7	18.4	Least	Best	Worst	
Depth	2 Medium	8.3	20.3	—	—	—	X
(C)	3 Deep	9.1	20.6	Most	Worst	Best	
Percent	1 Low	8.3	20.5	Least	Best	Best	X
Adhesive	2 Medium	8.4	19.5	—	Worst	—	
(D)	3 High	8.4	19.2	Most	Worst	Worst	

To a great extent, the selection of factor levels involves the experience and judgment of the experimental team in conjunction with management, manufacturing, and quality assurance. The selection of the optimum levels should be geared to producing a product that is fit for use and is robust in its operating environment. The following discussion is of a general nature, since there are no hard and fast rules for selection.

The selection for factor A (interference) was at A_2. This level resulted in the best pull-off performance while being mid-range in terms of cost and assembly effort. Level two was mid-range in the S/N Ratio of assembly effort, while it was the best in S/N Ratio and sensitivity of pull-off force.

The selection for factor B (wall thickness) was at B_1. Since, within the ranges selected in this experiment, wall thickness had no significant effect, this selection was made at the lowest cost level of this variable.

The selection for factor C (insertion depth) was at C_2. This involved selecting the mid-range level of C in terms of cost, assembly effort, and pull-off force. This selection was due to the requirements for pull-off in the finished product. Had C_1 produced acceptable pull-off forces, that level would have been selected.

The selection for factor D (percent adhesive in connector pre-dip) was D_1. This level was the most attractive in terms of cost, assembly effort, and pull-off force. This level also produced the best S/N Ratio in terms of assembly effort as well.

The table indicates that the product will see all levels of the environmental or noise factors. The adhesive is known to cure and improve with time and use. Long-term testing has been conducted that demonstrates that fact. Unfortunately, this characteristic has not been exploited by reducing the pull-off requirement shortly after assembly since the product is used very close to the time of assembly. Another avenue that this could open (but did not in this case) is to minimize the cost of the product and then post-cure the bonds. This is not applicable due to the fact that the cost of the curing is greater than the savings in producing a product with a lower initial pull-off.

The point to be noticed is that with meaningful data, the options available to a manufacturer of this product can be analyzed in terms of dollars and cents. Creative approaches can be made toward problems due to the quantification of the process factor effects and of the effects of the environment.

5. Confirmation of Experimental Results

Dr. Genichi Taguchi's method of experimental design using orthogonal arrays allows the experimenter to confirm the results of the experiment in a very quick and efficient manner. A 90% confidence band is calculated for the average of a number of samples prepared to levels selected in the above paragraphs. If the average of the additional samples falls within this range, it is considered to confirm the experiment. If the average does not fall within the calculated range, the experiment must be reviewed to find the fault. Such problems could arise from a number of causes, some of which could be "hidden" factors not included in the design, confounding interactions, and poor experimental technique.

Such confirmation is very important to conduct and should accompany every experiment. In this case, five additional samples were constructed and tested at the levels of A_2, B_1, C_2, and D_1, and conditioning levels of E_1, F_1, and G_1.

Table 6. Confirmation Results

Assembly Efforts:	
Calculated 90% confidence band	= 8.3 ± 0.3 pounds
Results of five samples	= 8.0
	8.2
	8.3
	8.0
	8.1
Total	40.6
Average	8.1 (within range)
Pull-off Force:	
Calculated 90% confidence band	= 18.1 ± 2.2 pounds
Results of five samples	= 19.8
	16.9
	21.0
	18.3
	19.5
Total	95.5
Average	19.1 (within range)

6. Advantages of Such Experimentation

- Lower costs for research, development, and optimization
- Better understanding of the system of factors involved in products and processes
- More creative solutions to problems once the effects of factors are discovered
- Improved competitive position due to optimization of products and processes in terms of cost and fitness for use
- Continuous improvement in engineers' abilities

- More harmonious relationships with production due to the increased efficiencies and lack of foul-ups upon the introduction of new processes and products
- Ease of designing and analyzing experiments.

In short, multivariate experimental designs in general, and Dr. Taguchi's orthogonal arrays in particular, are one of the most important tools in ensuring a good competitive position of American business in all markets by designing quality into our products and processes.

Q & A

Q. Is this study a good example of parameter design?

A. Yes, however an L_9 is a rather small orthogonal array. It would be better to have more control factors and assign them to a larger array, such as an L_{18}.

Q. In the analysis of variance, effects are decomposed in linear and quadratic components. Is this necessary?

A. It is not really necessary since indices can be observed by plotted curves.

Q. Is decomposition done in order to create more degrees of freedom for the error after pooling the smaller components, so that the F test can be conducted more effectively?

A. The F-test is only for reference. In the case of Signal-to-Noise Ratios, the F-test is not necessary. It is more important to know how much decibel gain is achieved rather than the test significance.

Q. In the confirmatory experiment, why was only one noise factor condition, E_1, F_1, and G_1 used?

A. It is better to vary noise factors at both the optimum condition and the current condition in order to compare robustness.

11. AN EXPERIMENT TO REDUCE POST-EXTRUSION SHRINKAGE OF A SPEEDOMETER CABLE CASING

Jim Quinlan and Engineering Staff
Flex Products, Inc.

This paper demonstrates the use of Quality Engineering in the reduction of post-extrusion shrinkage of a speedometer cable casing. An L_{16} orthogonal array, incorporating 15 two-level factors, was used. A long-standing problem of 15 years was resolved, resulting in cost reduction from $2.12 per unit to $0.13 per unit. The standard deviation was reduced from 0.05 to 0.025.

1. THE PRODUCT UNDER TEST

The product under test in this experiment was extruded thermoplastic speedometer casing, shown in Figure 1. This product is used to cover the mechanical speedometer cable on automobiles. The product consists of an extruded polypropylene inner liner, a layer of braided wire, and a co-extruded casing.

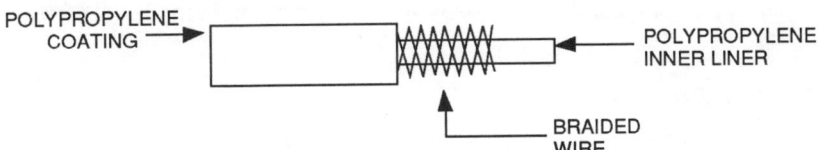

Figure 1. Extruded Thermoplastic Speedometer Cable Casing

This product has been produced for more than 15 years. Prior to manufacture by Flex Products, the casing under test had been produced by a division of General Motors Corp. That division had conducted much one-factor-at-a-time experimentation with high costs and disappointing results.

From the *Third Symposium on Taguchi Methods*™, pp. 367–384, Copyright © 1985, American Supplier Institute, Inc., Dearborn, Michigan.

2. The Quality Characteristic

The quality characteristic of concern is the post-extrusion shrinkage of the casing. Excessive shrinkage can cause noise in the assembly, which has been one of the larger problems with mechanical speedometer cable assemblies. The post-extrusion shrinkage is approximated with a two-hour heat-soak test, as shown in Figure 2.

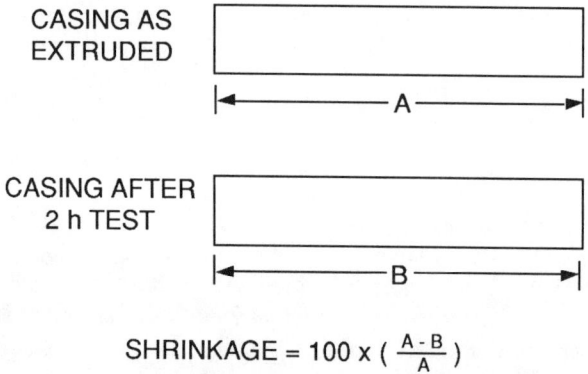

Figure 2. Percent Shrinkage after a two-hour heat-soak test.

The percent shrinkage is obtained by measuring a length of casing that has been properly conditioned, placing that casing in a two hour heat soak in an air-circulating oven, reconditioning the sample, and measuring the length. The post-test length is then subtracted from the original length, divided by the original length, and then multiplied by 100 to obtain a percent result. The approximate length of the samples is 600 mm.

3. The Process

The production process for this product is to 1) extrude the polypropylene liner, cool it, and coil it, 2) uncoil the liner and braid wire around the liner and recoil it, and 3) uncoil the wire coated liner and extrude the coating onto it and then cut the product to the finished length.

There are three separate operations. Most of the efforts at reducing post-extrusion shrinkage had been directed at the final operation, since many of the characteristics were specified by the engineering drawing. In addition, in discussions regarding post-extrusion shrinkage, the final operation seemed the most logical operation where factors that significantly effect shrinkage would exist.

4. The Cause-and-Effect Diagram for the Experiment

In the preliminary design of the experiment, cause-and-effect diagrams are the most useful for generating a listing of the factors for the test. Cause-and-effect diagrams lend more structure to ideas than the traditional brainstorming methods. Figure 3 is a greatly abbreviated version of the actual cause-and-effect diagram.

In this experiment, we obtained the opinions of our customers, the production personnel, the quality personnel, and the engineers involved in the product and the process to develop a list of factors that could contribute to post-extrusion shrinkage. By obtaining input from all informed personnel, the probability of conducting a successful experiment is increased dramatically.

This large diagram of potential factors was then reduced to the 15 most likely candidates by a consensus process.

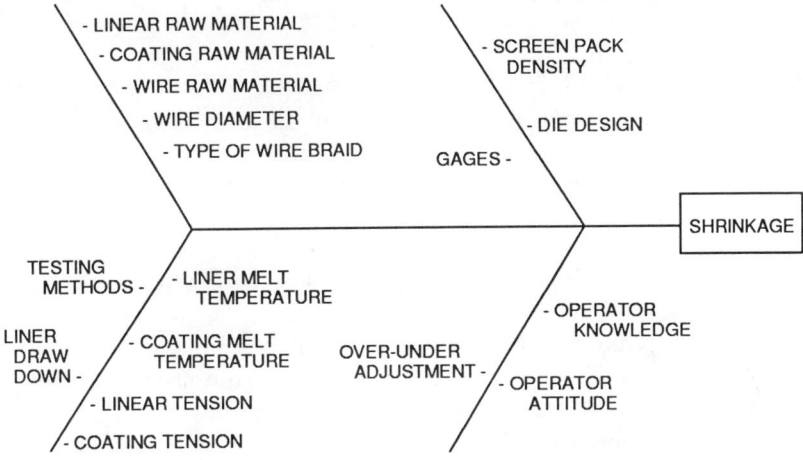

Figure 3. The Cause-and-Effect Diagram for the Experiment

5. The Factor Listing

The final result was a listing of the 15 2-level factors shown in Table 1. Note that the first four factors concern the first step of the production process, the next three concern wire braiding, and the final eight concern the coating process.

The levels of the factors were selected by personnel familiar with the process. This group was essentially the same as that which participated in the cause-and-effect diagram, with the exception that our customer's personnel were not included.

Table 1. Factor Listing

Liner Process	A. Liner O.D. B. Liner Die C. Liner Material D. Liner Line Speed	A_1 = Existing B_1 = Existing C_1 = Existing D_1 = Existing	A_2 = Changed B_2 = Changed C_2 = Changed D_2 = 80% of Existing
Wire Braiding	E. Wire Briad Type F. Braiding Tension G. Wire Diameter	E_1 = Existing F_1 = Existing G_1 = Smaller	E_2 = Changed F_2 = Changed G_2 = Existing
Coating Process	H. Liner Tension I. Liner Temp. J. Coating Material K. Coating Die Type L. Melt Temperature M. Screen Pack N. Cooling Method O. Line Speed	H_1 = Existing I_1 = Ambient J_1 = Existing K_1 = Existing L_1 = Existing M_1 = Existing N_1 = Existing O_1 = Existing	H_2 = More I_2 = Preheated J_2 = Changed K_2 = Changed L_2 = Cooler M_2 = Denser N_2 = Changed O_2 = 70% of Existing

6. THE LAYOUT AND RESULTS OF USING L_{16} ORTHOGONAL ARRAY

Table 2 shows an L_{16} orthogonal array, the four separate shrinkage results, and the Signal-to-Noise (S/N) Ratio. The L_{16} allows the testing of up to 15 two-level factors. Of course, this type of design runs the risk of confounding the interactive effects with the factorial effects. To eliminate this risk entirely is only possible if all of the 32,768 combinations on the factors were tested. To minimize the risk, the experiment must be tested for reproducibility.

Since a minimum of 3,000 ft. of finished product was the smallest quantity that could be manufactured at a given combination of factors, 48,000 ft. of product was committed to this experiment.

The experiment itself was quite complicated to run through our extrusion plant. In an effort to minimize the confusion, summary sheets for each operation were provided to the foremen and operators. These sheets listed the combination of the factors and the order of production, which were randomized as much as possible.

Even with the use of the summary sheets, the conduct of this experiment was not easy. The management and production operators at our extrusion facility deserve much of the credit for the success of this experiment.

After random samples were selected for each 3,000 ft. sample, four separate short-term heat-soak tests were performed. One test was performed each day. Shrinkage was calculated from the above formula and recorded.

Table 2. Layout Using Orthogonal Array L_{16}

A	B	C	D	E	F	G	H	I	J	K	L	M	N	O	Test 1	Test 2	Test 3	Test 4	S/N Ratio
1	1	1	1	1	1	1	1	1	1	1	1	1	1	1	0.49	0.54	0.46	0.45	6.26
1	1	1	1	1	1	1	2	2	2	2	2	2	2	2	0.55	0.60	0.57	0.58	4.80
1	1	1	2	2	2	2	1	1	1	1	2	2	2	2	0.07	0.09	0.11	0.08	21.04
1	1	1	2	2	2	2	2	2	2	2	1	1	1	1	0.16	0.16	0.19	0.19	15.11
1	2	2	1	1	2	2	1	1	2	2	1	1	2	2	0.13	0.22	0.20	0.23	14.03
1	2	2	1	1	2	2	2	2	1	1	2	2	1	1	0.16	0.17	0.13	0.12	16.69
1	2	2	2	2	1	1	1	1	2	2	2	2	1	1	0.24	0.22	0.19	0.25	12.91
1	2	2	2	2	1	1	2	2	1	1	1	1	2	2	0.13	0.19	0.19	0.19	15.05
2	1	2	1	2	1	2	1	2	1	2	1	2	1	2	0.08	0.10	0.14	0.18	17.67
2	1	2	1	2	1	2	2	1	2	1	2	1	2	1	0.07	0.04	0.19	0.18	17.27
2	1	2	2	1	2	1	1	2	1	2	2	1	2	1	0.48	0.49	0.44	0.41	6.82
2	1	2	2	1	2	1	2	1	2	1	1	2	1	2	0.54	0.53	0.53	0.54	5.43
2	2	1	1	2	2	1	1	2	2	1	1	2	2	1	0.13	0.17	0.21	0.17	15.27
2	2	1	1	2	2	1	2	1	1	2	2	1	1	2	0.28	0.26	0.26	0.30	11.20
2	2	1	2	1	1	2	1	2	2	1	2	1	1	2	0.34	0.32	0.30	0.41	9.24
2	2	1	2	1	1	2	2	1	1	2	1	2	2	1	0.58	0.62	0.59	0.54	4.68
																		Total	193.47

7. THE SIGNAL-TO-NOISE RATIO

Dr. Genichi Taguchi has extended the audio concept of S/N Ratio to multivariate experimentation. The formulae for S/N are designed so that the experimenter can always select the highest value to optimize the experiment. Therefore, the method of calculating the S/N Ratio differs depending on whether a larger response, a smaller response, or an on-target response is desirable.

Table 3 S/N Ratio When Smaller Response is Better

Formula:
$$S/N = -10 \times \log\left(\frac{1}{n} \sum_{i=1}^{n} y_i^2\right) \quad (11.1)$$

Examples:

Case	Avg.	y_1	y_2	y_3	y_4	S/N
1	.50	.56	.44	.54	.46	5.94
2	.15	.21	.09	.19	.11	16.00
3	.15	.15	.16	.14	.15	16.47

Case 3 is best — same average as case 2 but less variability

In cases such as this where the smaller amount of shrinkage is better, the formula is shown in Table 3. In this case, either a reduction in the mean shrinkage and/or a reduction in the variability will improve the situation. The figure shows the improvement in S/N Ratio when either of those characteristics improve.

8. THE TOTAL FOR EACH FACTOR LEVEL

The first step in the analysis of all multivariate experiments is to sum all the results containing one level of a factor and comparing it to the other level of the factor. If level one of factor A, for example, either decreased the average shrinkage or substantially reduced the variability, then the total S/N Ratio for A_1 would be larger than that for A_2.

Since the experiment was conducted using an orthogonal array, each total for a factor level contains eight S/N Ratios. By definition the totals for both levels of a given factor equal the total of the experiment results. i.e., 193.47. By reviewing the numbers in Table 4, a feeling for the effect of each factor can be obtained by noting the difference in S/N totals for a given factor level. The greater the difference between Level 1 and Level 2 to a factor, the greater that factor's effect.

Table 4. S/N Ratio Totals for Each Factor Level

$A_1 = 105.88$	$E_1 = 67.96$	$I_1 = 92.82$	$M_1 = 94.97$
$A_2 = 87.59$	$E_2 = 125.51$	$I_2 = 100.64$	$M_2 = 98.50$
$B_1 = 94.40$	$F_1 = 87.89$	$J_1 = 99.40$	$N_1 = 94.51$
$B_2 = 99.07$	$F_2 = 105.58$	$J_2 = 94.07$	$N_2 = 98.96$
$C_1 = 87.61$	$G_1 = 77.74$	$K_1 = 106.25$	$O_1 = 95.01$
$C_2 = 105.86$	$G_2 = 115.73$	$K_2 = 87.22$	$O_2 = 98.46$
$D_1 = 103.19$	$H_1 = 103.24$	$L_1 = 93.50$	
$D_2 = 90.28$	$H_2 = 90.22$	$L_2 = 99.97$	

The greater the difference in level totals for a factor, the greater the significance of that factor.

9. THE ANALYSIS OF VARIANCE TABLE

Table 5 is the ANOVA table for the experiment. The analysis is performed by noting the sources of variation in the left-hand column, which are, of course the 15 factors under test in the experiment. The column labeled df indicates the degrees of freedom for the factor. The next column, labeled S, is the sum of squares for the factor. The column labeled V is the mean sum of squares, i.e., the sum of squares for the factor divided by the degrees of freedom in that factor. The column labeled F is the results of the traditional Fisher test for significance, and an asterisk denotes whether the factor was significant at 95 or 99% confidence.

Notice that seven degrees of freedom, seven factorial effects in this case, have been pooled into an estimate of error. This estimate of variance, or mean sum of squares for error, is used as the denominator of the F test.

The column labeled S' is the pure effect of each factor. Since all multivariate experimental designs assume that error is allocated equally over all the degrees of freedom within the experiment, each significant effect contains an amount of error which must be subtracted out. The error is added to our estimate of error in the S' column. Notice that the totals for S_T and S_T' are equal—the total variation within the experiment is constant. The final column is the S' value for each significant factor divided by the total variation, S_T'. This column indicates the percent of contribution to variance by each factor.

Table 5. Analysis of Variance Table

Source	df	S	V	S'	ρ (%)
A	1	20.9128	20.9128	19.1513	4.6
B	[1]	[1.3612]	1.3612	—	—
C	1	20.8282	20.8282	19.0667	4.6
D	1	10.4171	10.4171	8.6556	2.1
E	1	207.0275	207.0275	205.2660	49.5
F	1	19.5625	19.5625	17.8010	4.3
G	1	90.1788	90.1788	88.4173	21.3
H	1	10.5963	10.5963	8.8348	2.1
I	[1]	[3.8226]	3.8226	—	—
J	[1]	[1.7765]	1.7765	—	—
K	1	22.6350	22.6350	20.8736	5.0
L	[1]	[2.6146]	2.6146	—	—
M	[1]	[0.7782]	0.7782	—	—
N	[1]	[1.2355]	1.2355	—	—
O	[1]	[0.7418]	0.7418	—	—
e	7	12.3304	1.7615	26.4222	6.4
T	15	414.4886	—	414.4886	100.0

From this table, it is easy to see that factors E and G are the most important in terms of shrinkage. These two factors account for more than 70% of the experimental variance.

10. Response Graphs of Significant Effects

To obtain a clear idea of the experimental results, the effect of each significant factor is graphed. The factors are arranged so that the most significant is on the left. These graphs indicate what was observed in the table of summary results—that the greater the difference between levels, the greater the effect. The points are calculated by taking the total of the factor level shown in Figure 4 and dividing by the number of data points in that total to obtain an average effect. In the case of E_1 for example, the average effect is 67.96 divided by 8, or 8.5 dB. The experimental average of 12.1 dB is obtained by dividing the total for the experiment (193.47) by the number of data points (16).

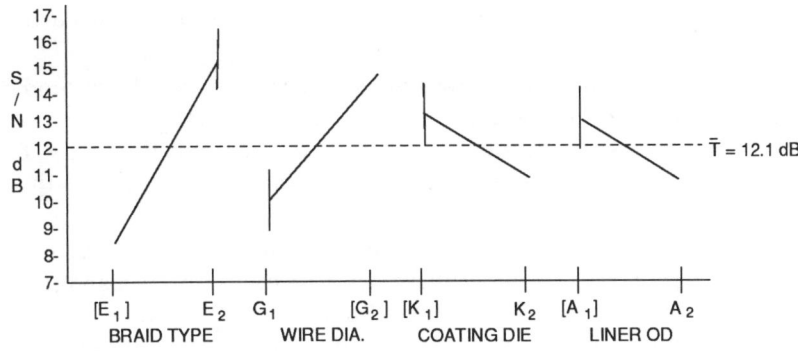

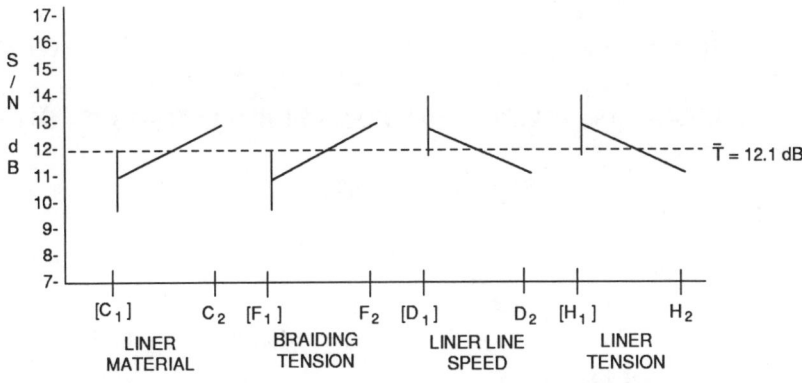

[ ] = EXISTING CONDITION

Figure 4. Graphs of Significant Effects

The vertical bar is the 90% confidence range for the estimate of the factor level's mean. This is based on our estimate of error and the degrees of freedom therein.

Since the higher S/N Ratio is more desirable, it can be seen that the best level of the factors under test were being used in five of the eight significant cases. The most significant factor, however, was specified by the engineering drawing at an undesirable level.

11. Comparison of Existing and Optimum Conditions

If each factor was selected for the best S/N Ratio, what would be the effect on post-extrusion shrinkage as measured by the two-hour test? And, since the actual production condition was not tested in this experiment, what does the experiment predict shrinkage to be in current production?

These questions can be answered using a simple formula for prediction from the experimental results. Since the assumption has been made that each factor is independent, i.e., no significant interactions exist, the factorial effects are assumed to be independent. Figure 5 shows these calculations and their results.

Note that the term "optimum" reflects only the optimum levels of the factors as defined by this experiment. The true optimum combination of these factors could be wildly different than the combination shown in Figure 5. This optimization is based only on the knowledge obtained from the experiment.

I. Existing = $A_1 C_1 D_1 E_1 F_1 G_1 H_1 K_1$ (11.2)
$\hat{\mu} = A_1 + C_1 + D_1 + E_1 + F_1 + G_2 + H_1 + K_1 - 7 \times \overline{T}$
$\hat{\mu} = 13.24 + 10.95 + 12.90 + 8.50 + 10.99 + 14.47 + 12.91 + 13.28 - 86.64$
$\hat{\mu} = 12.60 \pm 4.18$
$$\frac{1}{n} \sum_{i=1}^{n} y_i^2 = 0.0595$$

II. Optimum = $A_1 C_2 D_1 E_2 F_2 G_2 H_1 K_1$ (11.3)
$\hat{\mu} = A_1 + C_2 + D_1 + E_2 + F_2 + G_2 + H_1 + K_1 - 7 \times \overline{T}$
$\hat{\mu} = 13.24 + 13.23 + 12.90 + 15.69 + 13.20 + 14.47 + 12.91 + 13.28 - 84.64$
$\hat{\mu} = 24.28 \pm 4.18$
$$\frac{1}{n} \sum_{i=1}^{n} y_i^2 = 0.0037$$

Figure 5. Calculation of Existing Versus Optimum Mean S/N Ratio

A 90% confidence band is shown on both estimates. This band again reflects the estimate of error within the experiment and the degrees of freedom that the estimate of mean is based. The term of the sum of squares divided by the number of sample is calculated from the estimated mean as well. Since this is basically an estimate of the average squared plus the square of the standard deviation, it will be used later in our discussion of the Quality Loss Function (QLF).

12. THE ACTUAL RESULTS VERSUS THE PREDICTION

To test the results of our experiment, a comparison was made between the prediction and the actual results. Had these not compared within the 90% confidence range, the experimental results would be suspect. Either a significant hidden factor could exist, the conduct of the experiment might be flawed, or a strong interactive effect could exist.

Table 6. Actual Results in the Process

	$\bar{x}$	S	S/N	Predicted Range
Before	0.26	0.05	11.64	8.42/16.78
After	0.05	0.025	25.05	20.10/28.46

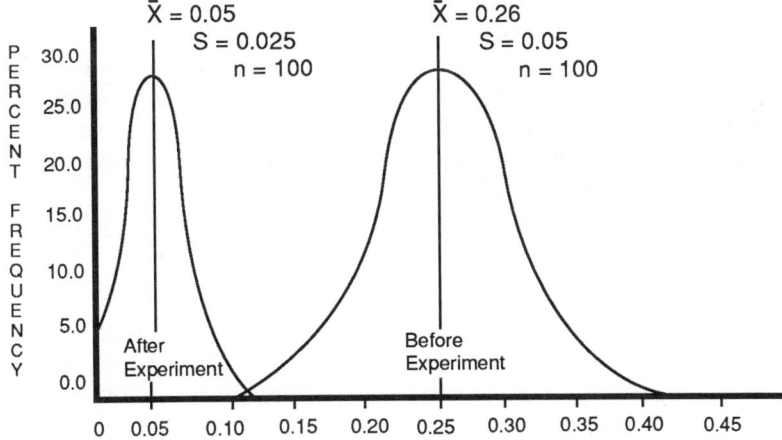

Figure 6. Short Term Shrinkage in Percent

As can be seen in Table 6, the experiment successfully predicted the actual S/N Ratio of the process both at the existing and the optimized condition.

The effect this had on the distribution of post-extrusion shrinkage can be seen in Figure 6. This dramatic improvement, it should be noted, was only achieved by changing one of the design criteria of the product. The control-charting efforts that had been assiduously applied to this process and product could not have been successful in reducing the average post-extrusion shrinkage by the amount shown.

If Shrinkage = 1.50%, then Customer Complains.
Warranty Cost to Replace Cable Assembly = $80.
Therefore:
$$k = [80/(1.5)^2] = \$35.56$$
and:
$$L = k \text{ (MSD) (for smaller-the-better MSD} = \bar{y}^2 + \sigma^2) \quad (11.4)$$
Therefore:
Existing Condition L_e = 35.56 x 0.0595 = $2.12 per unit.
Optimum Condition L_o = 35.56 x 0.0037 = $0.13 per unit.

Figure 7. Loss Function for Speedometer Casing

13. THE QUALITY LOSS FUNCTION

One of Dr. Taguchi's concepts that has been gathering slow acceptance is that of the QLF. Since quality is defined by Dr. Taguchi as the loss a product causes to society, both producer and consumer costs must be considered. In most cases, lower producer costs lead to higher consumer costs and the sum of those two costs to society can be approximated by L = k (MSD), mean square deviation.

Using this formula allows reduction in variability to be a quantified gain (Figure 7). This formula is used to calculate the gain to society caused by a process improvement.

While much of this formula is approximation, I feel more and more comfortable with its use. The savings shown in Figure 8 go somewhere, either to the producer or to the consumer. By minimizing the cost of our products to society, American manufacturers can continuously improve their competitive position in world markets.

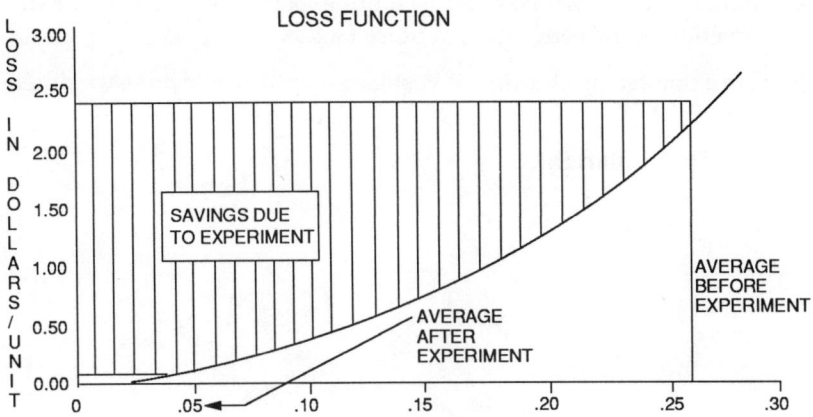

Figure 8. Post Extrusion Shrinkage as a Percentage of Original Casing Length

Q & A

Q. This case study won the Taguchi Application Award at the 1985 Symposium on Taguchi Methods. Fifteen control factors were assigned to an L_{16} orthogonal array with all interactions confounded to the main effects. The experimental results are beautifully reproduced. Any comments?

A. As long as good characteristics are selected, effective noise factors are taken, an appropriate S/N Ratio is used for data analysis, and an orthogonal array such as an L_{12}, L_{18}, L_{36}, or L_{54} is used without assigning interactions, all experiments will become reproducible.

Q. There are no noise factors taken in this experiment. Is this a correct procedure?

A. Shrinkage occurs when the product is exposed to a high temperature and high humidity. In this experiment the product, after extrusion, was placed in a two-hour heat soak in an air-circulating oven. This is similar to compounded or worst noise factor conditions.

Q. When noise factors are to be compounded, what is the process when there are noise factors but the best noise-factor level is unknown?

A. In that case, we would conduct a pre-experiment to investigate the direction of the compounded noise factor.

Q. Can a one-factor-at-a-time investigation be used for pre-experimentation?

A. Yes. That is all right.

12. Robust Design of a Disk-Brake System: An Analytical Simulation Study Using Taguchi Methods

Edward Lumsdaine and John G. Cherng
University of Michigan—Dearborn
School of Engineering

This case study demonstrates the potential of coupling simulation with Taguchi Methods in the design process. A two-dimensional transient heat-transfer model is used to simulate the axial and radial temperature field of a disk-brake rotor. The simulation results are then used as input into Taguchi methods to identify the most dominant design parameters in order to optimize the design. The optimum design is compared with the existing design to determine the effectiveness of the recommended design changes. The results show the influence of such design parameters as rotor type (solid or vented) and rotor taper, as well as material characteristics (particularly conductivity). A further step investigates the influence of the rotor thickness and the rotor/brake-pad area ratio, together with an approach that makes the design robust against different types of braking action. Without interfacing the thermal simulation model with Taguchi Methods, it is very difficult to determine the dominant parameters or parameter interaction in order to obtain an optimum disk-brake rotor design.

1. Introduction to the Experiment

The disk-brake system of a motor vehicle endures severe thermal and mechanical stresses. In particular, the load applied to the rotor disk is irregular, nonperiodic, and intermittent, causing significant temperature gradients and stress concentration that can lead to rotor deformation. Although disk brakes are less prone to fade (loss of braking capacity due to overall high temperature in the rotor disk) than drum brakes, large temperature increases can result in brake surface rupture. The conventional experimental or analytical methods consider the design parameters of the disk-brake system on a one-parameter-at-a-time basis. These methods not only waste much time and effort, but also are unable to take the interaction effects between the design parameters into account. In addition, the experimental results are often not repeatable, such as between bench and prototype testing or between laboratory and field testing.

Thus, the objective of this study was to interface Taguchi Methods with an analytic model of the disk-brake system to identify the most dominant design parameters that cause rotor failure, in order to obtain significant reduced and repeatable results. Taguchi Methods has recently been introduced to U.S. industry for quality control of manufactured products. The Quality Loss Function concept and the Signal-to-Noise (S/N) Ratio[1] are receiving increasing attention in engineering fields. An optimum design for the disk-brake system will be determined by evaluating the level of the S/N Ratio for each dominating design factor. The Taguchi method of parameter design is an iterative process that consists of seven key steps:

1. selection of the control factors,
2. selection of the noise factors,
3. choice of an appropriate orthogonal array to determine the analytic runs,
4. analytical simulation (or experimental tests),
5. calculation of the S/N Ratio for each control factor,
6. calculation of the analysis of variance (ANOVA) table and determination of the percentage contribution for the control factors, and
7. summary of results.

The steps are repeated if results are not satisfactory or new areas need to be investigated.

The thermal stresses, σ, in a rotor resulting from the difference between the temperature at the outer surface and the temperature at the center ($z = 0$) are given by:[2]

$$\sigma = -\frac{E}{1-w}\alpha\left(T_s - T_i\right) \tag{12.1}$$

where

E = elastic modulus
w = Poisson's ratio
σ = thermal expansion coefficient
T_s = temperature at outer surface
T_i = temperature at the center of the rotor disk

In addition, surface stress varies almost as a linear function of the initial temperature gradient existing at the surface of the rotor disk.[3] Thus, the present study considers two conditions: (a) maximum temperature differences and (b) maximum temperature gradients existing in the axial and radial directions of the rotor. This paper will first discuss the physical model of the disk-brake system, followed by an analytical analysis. The application of Taguchi Methods is then presented, including the selection of control and noise factors, the setup of the orthogonal array, and the interface of the analytic program with Taguchi Methods, followed by a discussion of system-design optimization and conclusions. The objective of using Taguchi Methods is to optimize the design parameters to achieve the smallest temperature difference and temperature gradient in both the radial and axial directions.

2. Physical Model of Disk-Brake System

The key components of the disk-brake system are the brake pads and the rotor disk. The physical parameters impacting the design and performance are the density, heat capacity, conductivity, ratio of the disk-pad area to the rotor-disk area, thickness of the rotor disk, taper of the rotor disk, vent gap and type of vent material properties of the pad, and friction coefficient. Figure 1 shows a schematic diagram of the disk/pad configuration, together with the dimensional parameters.

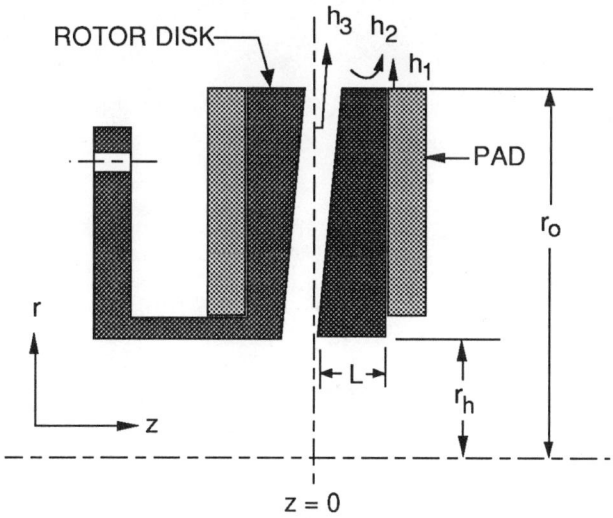

Figure 1. Definition of Disk/Pad Parameters

3. ANALYTICAL ANALYSIS

Governing Equations: The analytical method of the disk-brake system is based on a radially tapered, ventilated rotor with two calipers. The transient, two-dimensional governing equation in dimensionless units is:

$$\frac{\partial^2 \phi}{\partial y^2} + \frac{1}{y}\frac{\partial \phi}{\partial y} + \frac{\partial^2 \phi}{\partial Z^2} + \frac{\ddot{q}(t) r_o^2}{kT_o} = \frac{1}{F_o}\frac{\partial \phi}{\partial \beta} \qquad (12.2)$$

with boundary and initial conditions:
Convective heat transfer at the outer rim of the rotor disk:

$$\frac{\partial \phi}{\partial y}(1, Z, \beta) = Nu\, r_o \phi(1, Z, \beta) \qquad (12.3)$$

Conduction from the hub (inner radius):

$$\frac{\partial \phi}{\partial y}(y_n, Z, \beta) = \left\{\frac{-\rho C_p V_h}{k(2\pi y_h L) t_o}\right\}\frac{\partial \phi}{\partial \beta}(y_h, Z) \qquad (12.4)$$

Convection from the inner surface of the vented rotor disk:

$$\frac{\partial \phi}{\partial Z}(y, 0, \beta) = Nu_3 \phi(y, 0, \beta) \qquad (12.5)$$

Heat input on the rotor-disk surface and convection:

$$\phi(y, Z, 0) = \frac{[f(y, Z) - T_o]}{T_o} = F(y, Z) \qquad (12.6)$$

Temperature of the rotor at the initial state:

$$\frac{\partial \phi}{\partial z}(y, 1, \beta) = \left[\frac{\ddot{q}_o(L)}{kT_o}\right]\left[\frac{A}{A_t}\right] - Nu_L \phi(y, 1, \beta) \qquad (12.7)$$

where

$$\phi = \frac{(T - T_o)}{T_o}, \quad y = \frac{r}{r_o}, \quad y_h = \frac{r_h}{r_o}$$

$$Z = \frac{Z}{L}, \quad \beta = \frac{t}{t_o}, \quad F_o = \alpha \frac{t_o}{r_o^2}, \quad \alpha = \frac{k}{(\rho C_p)},$$

$$Nu_{ro} = \frac{h_2 r_o}{k}, \quad Nu_3 = \frac{h_3 L}{k}, \quad Nu_L = \frac{h_1 L}{k}$$

and

A/A	= area ratio of the pad to the rotor disk
Cp	= heat capacity of the rotor disk
h_1, h_2, h_3	= film coefficients as defined in Figure 1
K	= conductivity of the rotor disk
L	= rotor-disk thickness
Nu	= Nusselt number
$\ddot{q}(t)$	= internal heat generated
$\ddot{q}_o(L)$	= heat of friction
r_h	= radius at the hub of the rotor disk
t_o	= total elapsed time
r_o	= radius at the tip of the rotor disk
ϕ	= dimensionless temperature
T_o	= temperature at time zero
ρ	= density of the rotor disk
t	= time
V_h	= volume of the hub.

The governing equation allows the introduction of internal heat generation. The assumptions for using this equation include: pad pressure is uniform over the rotor surface; no circumferential temperature or pressure changes occur; moments of inertia are negligible; average temperature is used to determine the friction coefficient in the calculation of heat generation; and the kinetic energy of the rotor is used to determine the heat generation (which appears as heat input on the rotor surface).

The heat flux at the rotor surface is calculated using the following equations[4]:

$$\ddot{q}_0(L) = \left(\frac{\mu p v}{778}\right) \times 3600 \frac{\text{Btu}}{\text{h} - \text{ft.2}} \qquad (12.8)$$

where

μ = pad/rotor friction coefficient

p = mechanical pressure computed by dividing the normal force between the pad and rotor by the friction area of the rotor in lb./ft.^{2}

v = relative sliding velocity between pad and rotor in.- ft./s.

The sliding velocity between the pad and the rotor is described by:

$$v = (1-s) V \left(\frac{r_m}{R}\right) \qquad (12.9)$$

where

V = vehicle velocity

s = tire slip

R = tire radius

r_m = effective rotor radius

Thus the heat flux at the rotor surface can be expressed as:

$$\ddot{q}_0(L) = \frac{\mu p (1-s) V \times r_m \times 3600}{778 R} \qquad (12.10)$$

Finite-difference Solution and ANSYS Program: The heat-transfer equation together with the boundary and initial conditions (equations 12.3–12.7) are solved using finite difference. A computer program called NDHT (School of Engineering, University of Michigan-Dearborn) was used to calculate the axial and radial temperatures of the rotor disk for the vented and unvented rotors. A separate paper[5] describes the thermal stresses on the disk rotor using the ANSYS program and a nonlinear, stress-strain relationship. These results are used to tentatively determine rotor design. Although the boundary conditions are for a uniform rotor, taper is introduced numerically in NDHT as stepwise changes in the radial direction.

4. Taguchi Methods Analysis

Control Factor Selection: Control factors are those design parameters that can be specified by the designer, such as dimensions, materials, or manufacturing processes. For the disk-brake system, the following control factors were selected:

- A = thickness taper of the rotor disk from the tip to the hub
- B = type of rotor structure
- C = rotor material
- D = type of braking action.

Each control factor is assigned three different values (levels) or ranges for investigation, as shown in Table 1. The chosen control factor levels (and thus their combinations) cover a wide range of values for the design parameters.

Table 1. Control Factors

Control Factor	Level 1	Level 2	Level 3
A = Thickness Taper	0.068/0.0050	0.058/0.058	0.050/0.068
B = Rotor Structure	$h_1 = h_2 = 6$	$h_1 = h_2 = 6$	$h_1 = h_2 = 6$
	$h_3 = 0.01$	$h_3 = 6$	$h_3 = 24$
C = Rotor Material	Gray Iron	Cast Iron	Steel
	k = 30	k = 32	k = 27
	Cp = 0.12	Cp = 0.13	Cp = 0.12
	p = 460	p = 430	p = 480
D = Braking Type	Single	Pumping	Intermittent

Thickness taper is the difference in thickness between the tip and the hub of the rotor disk. The three levels of tapering investigated include positive taper ($L_1/L_h > 1$), no taper ($L_1/L_h = 1$), and negative taper ($L_1/L_h < 1$). Three different rotor types were considered: solid structure, vented with straight vanes, and vented with curved vanes. The difference in the structure is represented by the value of the third heat-transfer-film coefficient, h_3 in Btu/hr.-ft.^{2}-°F. Three different materials were selected for the rotor: gray iron, cast iron, and steel. These are distinguished by their physical properties of conductivity (Btu/hr.-ft.-°F), heat capacity (Btu/lb.-°F), and density (lb./ft.^{3}).

Three types of braking action were selected: single braking, brake pumping, and intermittent braking. The time-dependent heat flux functions of these three braking types are shown in Figure 2. Single braking simulates a quick, short stop of a vehicle and leads to a sudden temperature increase (thermal shock). For simulating quick brake pumping, the heat-flux function is repeated three times. Intermittent braking simulates the action of a driver who steps on the brake and releases it for a short period before repeating the process twice more. Such heating and cooling cycles cause thermal fatigue in the rotor-disk material. Thermal shock and thermal fatigue are the two major reasons that lead to surface rupture of the rotor[3].

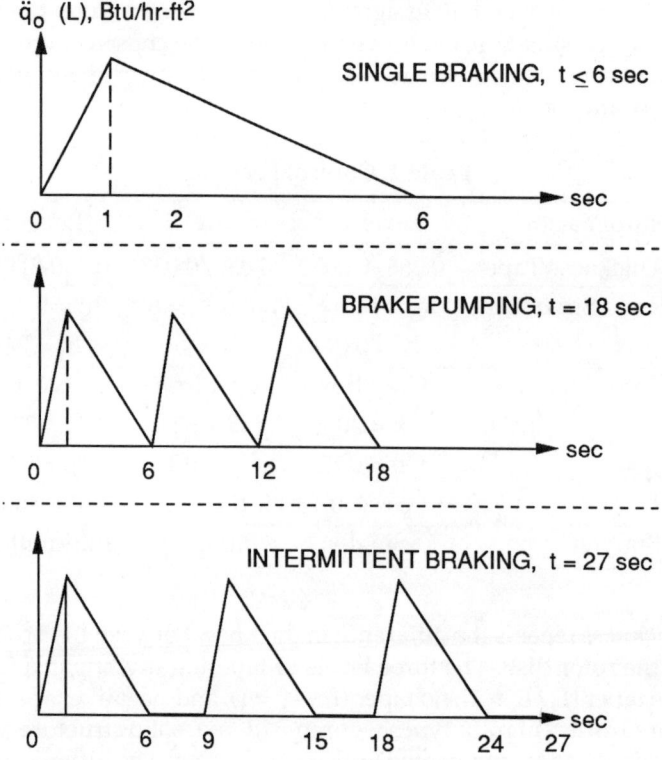

Figure 2. Type of Braking Action Investigated

Noise Factor Selection: Noise factors are the parameters that cause the performance of the product to deviate from its design specifications. These are usually outside the control of the designer, such as environmental factors, impurities of the material, and non-uniformity of the manufactured parts. In this study, five noise factors were identified:

- A'' = conductivity of the rotor material, Btu/hr.-ft.-°F
- B'' = heat capacity of the rotor material, Btu/lb.-° F
- C'' = density of the rotor material, lb./ft.^{3}
- D' = heat-transfer-film coefficients, Btu/hr.-ft.^{2}-°F
- E' = ambient temperature, °F.

For simplicity, the assigned levels of the noise factors relating to material properties take into account a ± 10% deviation from nominal values, and the ambient temperature levels represent summer and winter conditions. They are listed in Table 2.

Table 2. Noise Factors

Noise Factors	Level 1	Level 2
A' = Conductivity	0.1	−0.1
B' = Heat Capacity	0.1	−0.1
C' = Density	0.1	−0.1
D' = Firm Coefficient	0.1	−0.1
E' = Ambient Temp.	25	100

Orthogonal Array: Standard orthogonal arrays have been developed for the purpose of assigning experiments. Since this parameter-design study involves control factors and noise factors, two orthogonal arrays are required. The inner (main) array is used for the control factors; the outer array for the noise factors is offset at a 90° angle above the control-factor array, as show in Table 3. An $L_{18}(2^1 \times 3^7)$ orthogonal array was selected for the inner array, where the subscript denotes the number of lines (or experimental runs required), the numeral in parentheses is the number of levels assigned to the control factors, and the exponent the number of columns to which the factors are assigned. Columns may be assigned not only to individual control factors, but also to errors and interactions between factors.

The chosen outer array was an $L_8(2^5)$ because the objective of this parameter-design study is to obtain the smallest temperature difference or gradient possible. Since the nominal value levels for the noise factors do not provide any significant information about the problem, they were not included. The L_{18} size for the inner array was selected because it provides for an even distribution of the interactions between factors

Table 3. Inner/Outer Orthogonal Array for Parameter Design

L_{18}	A B C D		L_8	1	2	8				
		⋯ ⋯ B' A'		Noise Factors						
1	⎫			$y_{1\text{-}1}$	$y_{1\text{-}2}$ ...	$y_{1\text{-}8}$	u_1	u_1'	u_1''	u_1'''
2	Controllable			...	...	...	...	...	...	...
3	Factors ⎭			...		...				
..				...		...				
..				...		...		(S/N Ratio)		
...				...		...				
18				$y_{18\text{-}1}$		$y_{18\text{-}8}$	u_{18}	u_{18}'	u_{18}''	u_{18}'''

among all columns. The effort involved in using a larger array was not justified for this initial investigation.

Analytical Simulaton: The analytical simulation of the disk-brake system was integrated into the DISBK program (School of Engineering, University of Michigan-Dearborn). All key parameters, time, and space-integration intervals were defined according to the orthogonal array and then passed to the numerical simulation subroutine. The complete simulation was accomplished in a loop fashion to carry out 144 (or 18 × 8) runs for a given temperature reference condition. For each temperature reference (temperature difference or temperature gradient), both axial and radial directions were evaluated. The simulation was repeated with different values for the control factors or even for different control factors when additional information was desired.

Calculation of S/N Ratio: The analytical simulation results for the axial and radial temperature difference (or gradient) of each test run are used to calculate the S/N Ratio. For this study, which is a case of "smaller-the-better," the S/N Ratio is determined by the following formula[1]:

$$S/N = -10 \log \frac{1}{n} \sum_{i=1}^{n} y_i^2 \tag{12.11}$$

where

    S/N = S/N Ratio in decibels (dB)
    y_i = performance/simulation results (calculated ΔT or gradient)
    n = number of simulation runs

Calculation of the Analysis to Variance (ANOVA) Table: The analysis of variance (ANOVA) calculations consist of the sum of squares of the S/N Ratio, the degree of freedom, the variance, the variation ratio (F-ratio), pure variation, and the percent contribution for each control factor.

The sum of squares of each control factor is calculated by the following equation:

$$S_A = \frac{\left(\sum_{i=1}^{M} A_i^2\right)}{d} - \frac{\left(\sum_{i=1}^{M} A_i\right)^2}{n} \tag{12.12}$$

where

    S_A = sum of squares for control factor A
    A_i = sums of the S/N Ratios at each level
    M = number of levels
    d = number of data points of each level
    n = total number of test runs

Table 4 lists the mean of the S/N Ratio of the control factors for the case of maximum temperature difference and for the maximum temperature gradient. In addition, the following calculations were performed for the ANOVA tables shown in Table 5 for the axial temperature difference and Table 6 for the radial temperature difference (similar tables were obtained for the axial and radial temperature gradients):

(a) Error sum of squares (S_e):

$$S_e = S_T - \left(\sum_{i=1}^{N} S_i\right), \quad N = \text{number of control factors} \tag{12.13}$$

$$S_T = y_1^2 + y_2^2 + \ldots + y_n^2 - \frac{(y_1 + y_2 + \ldots + y_n)^2}{n} \tag{12.14}$$

Table 4. Calculated Mean of the S/N Ratio of Each Level

Control Factor	Axial			Radial		
	Level 1	Level 2	Level 3	Level 1	Level 2	Level 3
	Maximum Temperature Difference					
A	49.0	54.5	49.3	154.2	254.4	154.5
B	51.2	51.3	50.2	183.6	176.4	202.9
C	51.6	54.4	46.8	177.8	208.8	176.5
D	57.3	46.9	53.6	233.5	219.9	109.6
	Maximum Temperature Gradient					
A	−97.6	−93.9	−97.3	3.1	103.2	3.3
B	−95.7	−96.2	−96.8	32.5	25.3	51.8
C	−96.0	−92.8	−99.9	26.6	57.6	25.3
D	−96.0	−98.9	−93.8	82.3	68.8	41.6

Table 5. ANOVA Table of Control Factors for the Axial Temperature Difference

Control Factor	df	S	V	S'	ρ (%)
A	2	3.223	1.612	3.180	25.070
B	2	0.119	0.060	0.075	0.595
C	2	4.845	2.423	4.802	37.857
D	2	4.299	2.150	4.255	33.550
Error	9	0.197	0.022	0.371	2.928
Total	17	$S_t = 12.684$	—	12.684	100.000

Table 6. ANOVA Table of Control Factors for the Radial Temperature Difference

Control Factor	df	S	V	S'	ρ (%)
A	2	1111.074	555.537	1018.28	31.301
B	2	62.937	31.469	0	0
C	2	111.535	55.768	0	0
D	2	1538.949	769.475	1446.16	44.453
Error	9	428.684	47.693	788.74	24.246
Total	17	S_t = 3253.179	—	3253.18	100.000
Pooled Error	13	603.156	46.397	—	—

y_i = S/N ratios of each run

(b) Variance and degree of freedom: The variance is the sum of squares divided by its degree of freedom. The degree of freedom of each control factor is equal to the number of its levels minus one. The total degree of freedom is equal to the total number of the test or simulation runs minus one. The degree of freedom of the error is the total degree of freedom minus the sum of the degree of freedom of all control factors, or 17 − (2 + 2 + 2 + 2) = 9 in this study. The error variances, V_e, is the error sum of squares, S_e, divided by the degree of freedom of the error.

(c) Pure variation (S'_A):

$$(S'_A) = S_A - (\text{degree of freedom of } A) \times (\text{error variance}) \quad (12.15)$$
$$= S_A - 2V_e$$

(d) Variation ratio: The variation ratio is the variance of the control factor divided by the error variance. If this value is smaller than 2, its contribution will be negligible. The sum of squares of the control factor will then be "pooled" into the error factor, thus generating a new error variance. For example, in Table 6, both control factors B and C had variation ratios smaller than 2.

Hence,

$$V_e' = \frac{(S_B + S_C + S_e)}{(2 + 2 + 19)} \quad (12.16)$$

(e) Pure variation of error (S'_e):

$S'_e = S_e +$ (sum of degree of freedom of
control factors not pooled) x (error variance)

Therefore,

$S'_e = S_e + 8V_e$ (for Table 5) \hfill (12.17)
$S'_e = S_e + 4V_e$ (for Table 6)

(f) Degree of contribution (in percent) for each control factor:

$$\rho_A = \frac{S_A'}{S_T'} \times 100, \quad S_T' = S_T \hfill (12.18)$$

5. Discussion of Results

Analyzing simulation results (more than 500 test runs in this case) could present a difficult task. Taguchi methods is an improvement over the traditional statistical F-ratio method; it is not only a parameter-design tool, but also constitutes a means of sorting out the important information and presenting it in a simple and clear fashion that enables the designer to plan and optimize the testing program and then interpret the test results.

Figure 3 shows the S/N Ratio (S/N) plots for the case of maximum temperature difference, and Figure 4 shows similar plots for the maximum temperature gradient. In both figures, the solid line indicates temperatures in the axial direction and the dashed line the radial direction. The results in Table 4 are used to make these plots. Since higher S/N Ratios mean better performance, those levels of the control factors that result in the highest S/N Ratios will yield the smallest temperature difference on the disk rotor. Therefore, the performance characteristics of each control factor at each level can easily be identified from the S/N plots. The results for each control factor are discussed in more detail below.

Thickness Taper (Control Factor A): From Figures 3 (a) and 4 (a), it can be seen that for both the axial and radial temperature fields, the rotor with uniform blade thickness performs best. In particular, taper increases the radial temperature difference (and thus stress) in the rotor blade considerably and is undesirable. When comparing the slopes of the graphs in Figures 3 and 4, the factors with the steepest slopes are the most sensitive and important to performance. Thus, rotor-blade taper is seen to be a sensitive control factor for the thermal performance of the rotor.

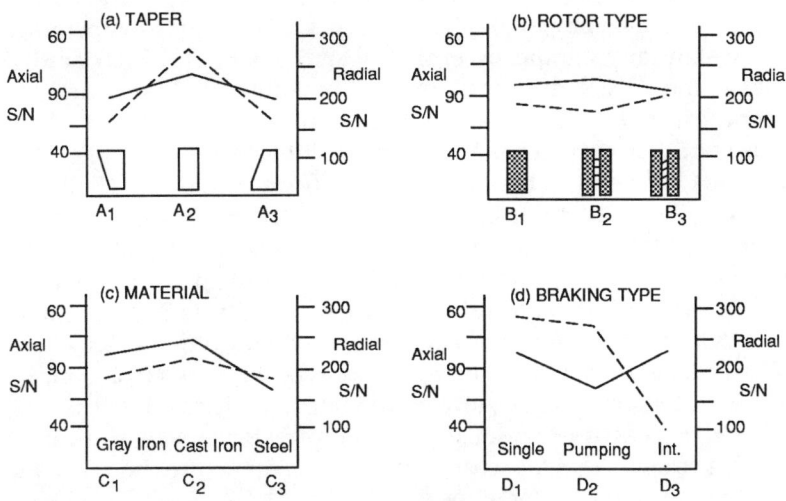

Figure 3. S/N Ratio Plots (in dB) for Each Control Factor (Maximum ΔT_z, ΔT_r)

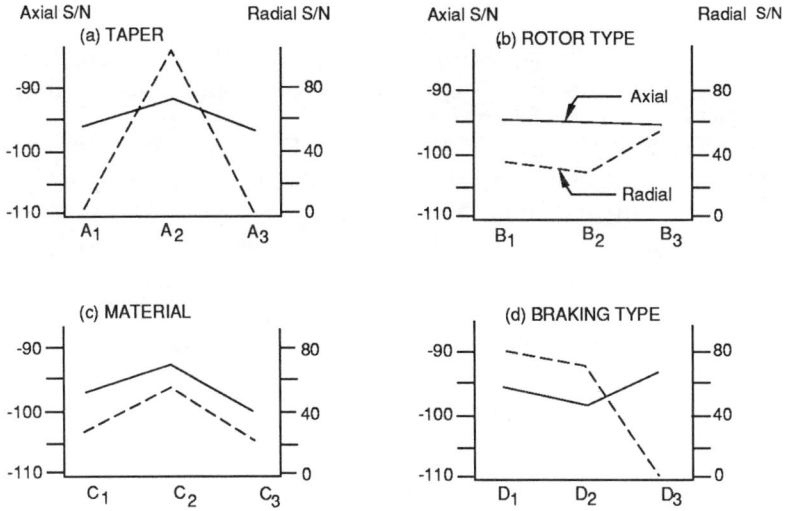

Figure 4. S/N Ratio Plots (in dB) for Each Control Factor (Maximum $\Delta T/\Delta z$, $\Delta T/\Delta r$)

Rotor Structure (Control Factor B): As shown in Figures 3 (b) and 4 (b). Neither the axial temperature difference nor the axial temperature gradient show any significant sensitivity to rotor structure. In the radial direction, the S/N Ratios for both the temperature difference and the temperature gradient decrease slightly with the straight vane model but increase with the curved vanes (over the solid rotor). This implies that unless the film coefficient can be dramatically improved, the small vent in the middle of the rotor could cause more harm than good to the temperature variation in the radial direction. The inner heat-transfer-film coefficient, h_3, ranges from 3.48 to 10.6 Btu/hr.-ft.^{2} per °F for a vented rotor having an outer diameter of 1.25 ft., rotating from 350 rpm (at 20 mph) to 800 rpm (at 60 mph) (4) Higher values for the film coefficient can only be obtained when the rotor speed exceeds 2000 rpm (= 130 mph), which is not a situation encountered by most vehicles. However, the calculated percent contribution for this control factor (as shown in Tables 5 and 6) is so small that low cost and ease of manufacture should be the overriding design considerations.

Rotor Material (Control Factor C): The three materials under investigation were gray iron, cast iron, and steel. They are identified by their important physical parameters: conductivity, heat capacity, and density. Both the radial and the axial temperature difference strongly indicate that cast iron would have the best performance and steel the worst performance.

In a subsequent study on rotor material [6], the influence of conductivity, heat capacity, and density was investigated by treating these parameters as separate control factors for brass, cast iron, and steel, while leaving the noise factors unchanged. The results show that density and specific heat were not significant parameters, but that conductivity is the most dominant control factor for the axial temperature difference. From that study, it could also be deduced that braking type affects temperature more in the radial direction than in the axial direction and that the radial-temperature-difference analysis exhibits a large error contribution, which may imply that the results have large variations.

Types of Braking (Control Factor D): Three braking actions—single, pumping, and intermittent—were investigated. Single braking has a thermal impact on the rotor. Pumping and intermittent braking cause thermal fatigue in the rotor. From Figures 3 and 4, it can be seen that the sensitivity of this control factor is different for the temperature difference and the temperature gradient among the three braking types. In the axial temperature filed, single braking and intermittent braking have higher S/N Ratios than brake pumping, whereas radial single braking shows the highest S/N Ratio. Since the axial temperature difference is the dominant parameter in the brake system (as will be shown later in Table

11), driving habits and conditions that lead to the use of single or intermittent braking are most propitious for longer brake life. Long stretches of continuous braking (a condition that has been simulated with "brake pumping") should be avoided if at all possible.

When braking type was used as a noise factor and not as a control factor as a follow-up to the study on rotor materials, it was found that conductivity also emerged as the most dominant parameter for the radial temperature difference, while the error contribution was reduced to a negligible amount when compared to the results reported in Lumsdaine and Cherng[6].

6. Further Investigation

The original study found that a rotor with uniform thickness (no taper) is the best design. However, this was determined under the assumption that the braking pressure is uniformly distributed on the surface of the disk rotor and that the ratio of braking pad area to rotor area is 1.0 (full coverage). A further investigation was made to identify the optimum design parameters when the braking pressure is not uniformly distributed on the rotor surface and to determine the influence of changes in area ratio.

Therefore, area ratio was added as a new control factor (see Table 7), and the heat flux generation due to braking as given in boundary condition 4 was changed to a step function equation:

(a) for $\frac{r_h}{r_o} \leq y \leq \frac{r_p}{r_o}$:

$$\frac{\partial \phi}{\partial z}(y, 1, \beta) = -Nu_L \phi(y, 1, \beta) \tag{12.19}$$

(b) for $\frac{r_p}{r_o} \leq y \leq 1$:

$$\frac{\partial \phi}{\partial z}(y, 1, \beta) = \left[\frac{q_o(L)}{kT_o}\right]\left[\frac{A}{A_t}\right] - Nu_L \phi(y, 1, \beta) \tag{12.20}$$

This means that heat-flux is only generated when the radial distance is greater or equal to the radius of the brake pad. A linear heat-flux distribution (i.e., heat flux equal to a minimum value at the inner radius

Table 7. Revised Set of Control Factors

Control Factor	Level 1	Level 2	Level 3
A = Rotor Taper	0.068/0.050	0.058/0.058	0.050/0.068
B = Rotor Type	Solid $h_3 = 0.01$	Straight Vanes $h_3 = 6$	Curved Vanes $h_3 = 24$
C = Material	Grey Iron	Cast Iron	Steel
D = Area Ratio	0.25	0.50	1.00

of the brake pad and equal to a maximum value at the outer radius) is used in the heat-flux calculation. Such a linear distribution approximates actual braking conditions more closely than a uniform heat-flux distribution. The tip of the rotor is generally at a higher temperature because of its higher velocity and because the brake calipers touch the tip before they are in full contact with the rotor surface.

To make the final design robust against braking type, this parameter was treated as a noise factor. The other noise factors remained the same.

Table 8 presents the new ANOVA calculations for the axial temperature difference simulation and Table 9 for the radial temperature difference. The temperature gradient simulations show similar sensitivity patterns and contributions.

Table 8. ANOVA Table of Axial Temperature Difference (Further Study)

Control Factor	S	V	S'	ρ (%)
A	16.956	8.478	16.956	73.087
B	0.004	0.002	0.004	0.018
C	6.239	3.120	6.239	26.892
D	0.000	0.000	0.001	0.003
Error	0.000	0.000	0.000	0.000

Table 9. ANOVA Table of Radial Temperature Difference (Further Study)

Control Factor	S	V	S'	ρ (%)
A	30.602	15.301	30.602	24.189
B	0.256	0.128	0.256	0.202
C	8.610	4.305	8.610	6.806
D	85.673	42.837	85.673	67.719
Error	1.371	0.000	1.371	1.084

The analysis shows that:
1. The rotor thickness taper and the rotor material are the two most dominant factors for the axial temperature difference.
2. The rotor thickness taper and the area ratio are the two most dominant factors for the radial temperature difference.
3. Rotor type and material exhibit similar trends as in the original analysis and do not appear to be affected by the change in braking type from control factor to noise factor.
4. Area ratio has little effect on axial temperature difference or axial temperature gradient.

Figures 5 and 6 present the S/N Ratio plots for the temperature difference and temperature gradient for each of the control factors. These plots are consistent with the analytical observations 1 and 2 listed above. The solid line again represents axial temperatures, and the dashed line represents radial temperatures. For rotor thickness taper, the positive taper (which has the thicker tip) demonstrates better performance in both the axial and radial directions. Rotor structure and rotor material show similar results as in the original study. The area ratio in the radial direction indicates that this may be an exponential relationship, with the highest ratio being best.

7. Comparison of Current and Optimum Design

This step involves a calculation of performance gain between the optimum design, as indicated by the S/N Ratio results of the Taguchi Methods given in Figures 5 and 6, and the existing design. Since area ratio has a significant effect in the radial direction only, and since the braking pad can never be made to fully cover the rotor for economic and design

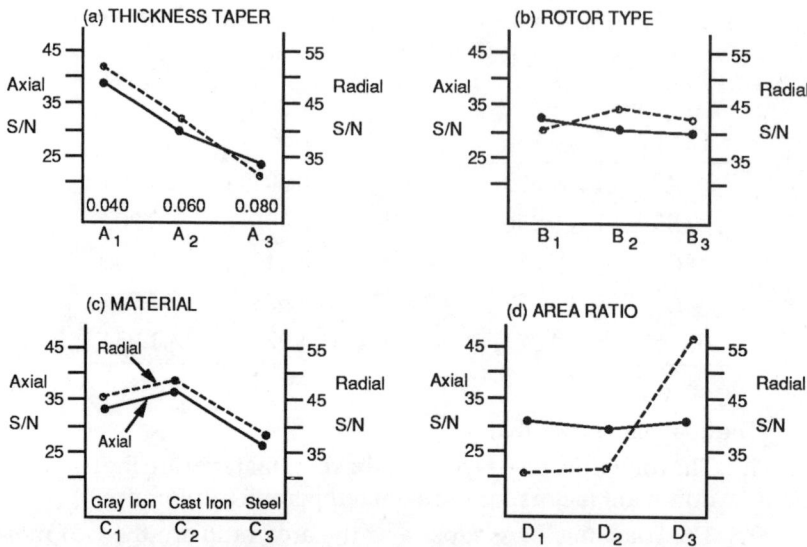

Figure 5. S/N Ratio Plots (in dB) for Revised Control Factors
(Maximum $\Delta T_z/\Delta T_r$)

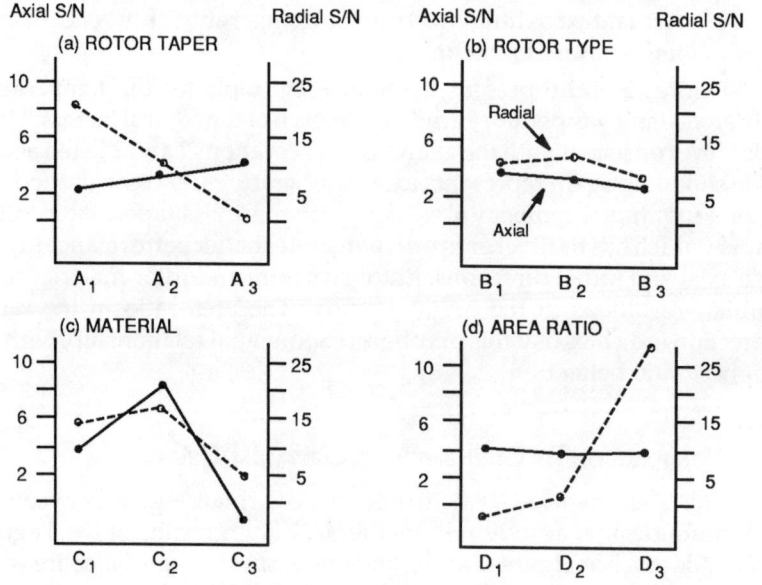

Figure 6. S/N Ratio Plots (in dB) for Each Control Factor
(Maximum $\Delta T/\Delta z$, $\Delta T/\Delta r$)

reasons, it is not included in this step. Both gray iron and cast iron are presently used to manufacture brake rotors. For the calculation, gray iron is specified for the existing brake rotor, together with uniform thickness. Its performance will be compared with an optimized design made of cast iron and a rotor with positive taper. The calculation is performed under intermittent braking conditions for the maximum temperature difference simulation, since this condition is the most realistic operating mode for a brake system. Table 10 lists the calculated S/N values for the two factors. The current design is A_2, C_1. The optimum design is A_1, C_2 since these have the highest S/N Ratios.

Table 10. S/N Ratios for Taper (A) and Rotor Material (C)

Axial Temp.	Difference	Radial Temp.	Difference
$A_1 = 39.5$	$C_1 = 33.2$	$A_1 = 52.4$	$C_1 = 45.2$
$A_2 = 32.8$	$C_2 = 36.4$	$A_2 = 43.7$	$C_2 = 47.7$
$A_3 = 25.3$	$C_3 = 27.9$	$A_3 = 34.9$	$C_3 = 38.0$

The performance gain can be calculated for both the axial and radial direction in the following manner:

Axial Direction:

Current Design =

$$\mu_c = \frac{(A_2 + C_1)}{6} - \frac{T}{18} \qquad T = A_1 + A_2 + A_3 \qquad (12..21)$$

$$= \frac{(32.8 + 33.2)}{6} - \frac{(39.5 + 32.8 + 25.3)}{18}$$

$$= 11.00 - 5.42 = 5.58$$

Optimum Design =

$$\mu_o = \frac{(A_1 + C_2)}{6} - \frac{T}{18} \qquad (12..22)$$

$$= \frac{(39.5 + 36.4)}{6} - 5.42$$

$$= 12.65 - 5.42 = 7.23$$

Therefore, the gain is equal to $7.23 - 5.58 = 1.65$ dB

Radial Direction:

Current Design =

$$\mu_c = \frac{(43.7 + 45.2)}{6} - \frac{(52.4 + 43.7 + 34.9)}{18}$$
$$= 14.82 - 7.28 = 7.54$$

Optimum Design =

$$\mu_o = \frac{(52.4 + 47.7)}{6} - 7.28$$
$$= 16.68 - 7.28 = 9.40$$

Therefore, the gain is equal to 9.40 – 7.54 = 1.86 dB

It can be seen that both the axial and radial directions have positive performance gain, but not in a significant amount. These relatively minor performance gains indicate that the current design is quite close to the optimum design. Therefore, the cost related to each design becomes an important factor. For example, if the cost of manufacturing a rotor with positive taper is much higher than the cost of manufacturing a rotor with uniform thickness, the latter would be the better choice. Table 11 presents the mathematical confirmation for the current and optimum design. The optimum design has a higher S/N Ratio and a lower maximum temperature difference. The improvement in the temperature difference ranges from 17.5% in the axial direction to 25% in the radial direction.

Table 11. Comparison of Optimum and Current Design

Design	S/N Ratio		Max. Temp. Diff.	
	Axial	Radial	Axial	Radial
Current	5.4	10.83	611	349
Optimum	7.09	13.52	504	292

8. Conclusions

1. Through the systematic application of Taguchi's parameter design method, the optimum design for a disk-brake system was identified as a solid rotor having a disk with positive taper and made of cast iron. Thermal conductivity was found to be the

most significant property of the rotor material in terms of minimizing the temperature difference between the center and the outer surface of the rotor.
2. Both the axial and radial temperature differences are very sensitive to rotor taper, with positive taper being the optimum design.
3. The structure of the rotor (solid or vented) does not have a significant effect on the thermal performance of the brake system. However, inefficient venting may cause larger temperature gradients than would occur in a solid rotor.
4. Area ratio (pad area to rotor area) may have an exponential effect on the radial temperature difference and the radial temperature gradient; this effect does not appear in the more important axial direction.
5. The mathematical model has shown a reliable sensitivity with regard to the input design parameters. This also proves that Taguchi Methods can be used as an optimization tool for engineering design application.

9. Recommendation

This study has demonstrated a unique application of interfacing Taguchi Methods with an analytical model as applied to the design of a disk-brake system. Due to limited time and resources, a more in-depth investigation could not be undertaken. However, a recommendation was made for continuation of this study with the objectives of using better simulation models, such as a three-dimensional heat transfer model integrated with a three-dimensional stress analysis model, together with cost analysis and experimental confirmations. Further studies should include the following steps:
1. Two prototype disk rotors, one with the current design specifications and one for the optimum design, need to be tested for experimental confirmation.
2. A detailed cost analysis needs to be interfaced with the Dr. Taguchi's Quality Loss Function to provide important information during product development.
3. A three-dimensional mathematical model, which includes both a heat transfer and a stress analysis, should be developed to simulate the actual field operation of the disk brake system.

References

1. Wu, Yuin and W.H. Moore. *Quality Engineering—Product and Process Design Optimization*, American Supplier Institute, Inc. Dearborn, Michigan, June 1986.

2. Boley and Weiner. *Theory of Thermal Stress*, John Wiley & Sons, New York, 1967.

3. Limpert, Rudolf. "An Investigation of Thermal Conditions Leading to Surface Rupture of Cast Iron Rotors," SAE Paper No. 720447.

4. Limpert, Rudolf. "Cooling Analysis of Disk Brake Rotors," SAE Paper No. 751014.

5. Lumsdaine, Edward and Shen-Rong Wu. "Non-Linear Thermal Stress of Disk Brake Rotors Using ANSYS," School of Engineering, University of Michigan-Dearborn (in preparation).

6. Lumsdaine, Edward and John G. Gherng. "Parameter Design for a Disk Brake System," *Proceedings*, Fifth Symposium on Taguchi Methods, American Supplier Institute, Inc., Dearborn, Michigan. pp. 803–819, October 1987.

Acknowledgements

The authors gratefully acknowledge the assistance provided on Taguchi Methods analysis by Mr. Yuin Wu, Vice-Chairman, American Supplier Institute, Inc., Dearborn, Michigan. They also appreciate the work done by Mrs. Monika Lumsdaine, who did the editing, word processing, and final drawings.

Q & A

Q. This is a case of simulation using $L_{18} \times L_8$. Why were these chosen?

A. I was told that because a small computer was used, it took a longer time to compute. That is why an L_{18} orthogonal array was used. An L_{36} could be used if a main frame is available.

Q. In the first simulation, the type of braking action was assigned in the inner array. This sounds like a noise; why was it assigned to the inner array?

A. That's right, it is a noise. So it should have been assigned to the outer array. They probably wanted to know the effect of different types of braking action. The results showed pumping is the worst. By the attitude of tolerance design, the results might be used to inform customers not to pump the brake.

In the second simulation, this factor was not assigned in the inner array.

Q. Can noise factors be compounded into one?

A. Yes, we can prestudy the effect of each noise factor on temperature and then compound them.

It might be a good idea to assign an indicative factor, e.g., car speed, in the simulation.

Q. What is an "indicative factor"?

A. An indicative factor has technical meaning like a control factor, but nothing to do with the selection of the optimum level. Car speed is an example. In parameter design, we want to find a control-factor level combination that is least affected by noise factors, including application conditions. Therefore, indicative factors might be treated as noise factors. It depends on the objective of the study.

Since the effects of noise factors at slow speed and high speed are different, it is better to determine and compare Signal-to-Noise Ratios at different speeds.

Q. Is temperature the output characteristic of this case?

A. Yes. In the study of brake systems, it is necessary to study a car's travel distance from the point the brake is pushed. I don't know if models exist, but it is necessary to study the distance to stop at different speeds and try to make it closer to the ideal target or ideal curve the engineer considers.

Part 3:
Electrical —Process

13. COMPUTER RESPONSE-TIME OPTIMIZATION USING ORTHOGONAL ARRAY EXPERIMENTS

T.W. Pao, M.S. Phadke, and C.S. Sherrerd
AT&T Bell Laboratories

This study describes a method of experimentation for systematically and efficiently obtaining a system's performance under a specified range of load and environmental conditions. This is achieved by simultaneously studying a large number of system parameters, as opposed to experimenting with only one parameter at a time. The study included an experiment to optimize the response time of a VAX™ 11-780 machine under UNIX™ system Release 5.0 operation. The effects of eight system parameters — three hardware and five software parameters—were evaluated using only 18 orthogonally designed test configurations. The resulting optimum system configuration gave a 60% reduction in mean response time.

1. INTRODUCTION: THE RESPONSE TIME EXPERIMENT

Think of yourself at 3 p.m. trying to use a time-share computer to prepare a few viewgraphs for a presentation the next morning. But the computer response time is unbearably slow. Wouldn't you wish that you could get a quick enough response from the computer?

If virtually every user is experiencing unbearable response time, the "common-sense" solution would be to buy more hardware (e.g., a more powerful computer). But if we want to incur the extra expense, we might need to quantitatively justify it. Problems of this nature constantly arise in industry. Before we make such an investment, we ought to see if we can improve the response time through better administration of the machine.

Computer system administrators are very skillful in setting approximately satisfactory administration parameter values. Nevertheless,

---

From the June 23–26, 1985 *IEEE International Conference on Communications*, pp. 890–895. New York: IEEE Communications Society.

computer performance reflects a very complex hierarchy of internal queuing (of tasks, process, data transfer, etc.), which defies modeling with sufficient accuracy to more precisely optimize response times. Experimentation is often necessary, therefore, to obtain the information needed to do that optimization.

We describe a method of experimentation that is a very efficient way to determine the system configuration that gives optimum performance under a specified range of load and environmental conditions, by simultaneously studying a large number of system parameters.

We describe the method by an actual example: an experiment we ran in 1984 to simultaneously study eight system parameters (factors) of a VAX 11-780 machine under UNIX operating system, Release 5.0, to optimize performance under actual load conditions. The eight parameters of that study were:

- A. disk-drive configuration;
- B. distribution of key system and user files among disks;
- C. memory size;
- D. system buffer size;
- E. number and selection of "sticky bits" sets;
- F. number of KMCs used (devices for computer-to-terminal communications);
- G. size of "INODE" table; and
- H. sizes of certain other system tables.

Parameters A and F were studied at two levels each, and the other parameters at three levels each. An 18-row orthogonal array design matrix was used. Each row represented a distinct system configuration of these eight parameters. Performance data on each of these test configurations was collected over 2-1/2 days of normal operation. The data was analyzed to determine how each of the eight parameters influences the system performance. That information was then used to determine an optimum system configuration, that is the setting of all eight parameters to give the least overall response times. Confirmatory experiments under those optimum conditions showed about 60% reduction in mean response time for the particular computer installation.

The paper is divided into nine sections. The description of the optimization problem is given in Section 2. The micro and macro modeling approaches to optimization are compared in Section 3. In Section 4, we describe the eight parameters and their levels chosen for this study. The design of the orthogonal array experiment is given in Section 5, followed in Section 6 by a description of the experimental procedure. The analysis of the experimental data is presented in Section 7. The optimum system configuration and the results of a confirmatory experiment are given in Section 8. Concluding remarks are given in Section 9.

2. FORMULATION OF THE RESPONSE TIME PROBLEM

This study was conducted on the UNIX operating system, Release 5.0 on a VAX 11-780 computer. It had 48 user terminal ports, 2 remote job entry links, 4 megabytes of memory, and 5 disk drives. The average number of users logged on at one time was between 20 and 30.

For an objective measurement of the response time, we used two specific, representative commands called "standard" and "trivial." The standard command consisted of creating, editing, and removing a file; whereas the trivial command was simply the UNIX system "date" command (not involving I/O). The response times were measured by submitting these commands automatically and clocking the time taken for the computer to respond.

Figures 1a and 1b show the variation of the response times as functions of time of day. Notice that prior to the beginning of the experiment, the average response time increased as the afternoon progressed. The increase in response time correlated well with the increase in the work load during the afternoon. Our objective in the experiment was to make the response time uniformly small throughout the day, even when the load increased as usual.

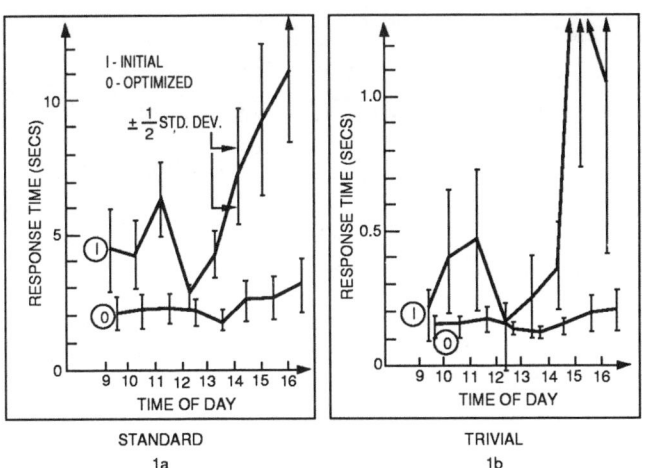

Figure 1. Comparison of Response Times

3. Approaches to Optimization

There are two broad approaches to optimization: micro modeling and macro modeling.

Micro Modeling

The approach called micro modeling is based on an in-depth understanding of the system. It begins with developing a mathematical model of the system, which in this case would be the complex internal queuing of the UNIX operating system. When systems are complex, as is the present case, it takes a lot of simplifying assumptions, as well as a considerable effort, to develop the model. Furthermore, the more simplifying assumptions that are used, the less realistic the model, and hence the less adequate the model for precise optimization. But once an adequate model is constructed, a number of well-known optimization methods can be used to find the best system configuration.

Macro Modeling

In the approach called macro modeling, the step of building a detailed mathematical model of the system is bypassed. Instead, the UNIX system is viewed as a "black box," as illustrated in Figure 2. The parameters that influence the response time are identified and divided into two classes: noise factors and control factors.

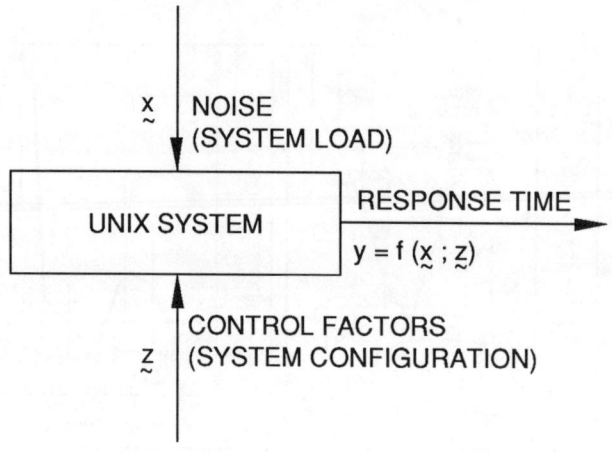

Figure 2. System Model

Noise factors are those factors that we cannot, or we choose not to, control during the normal operation of the system. Load variations during the usage of the machine (from day-to-day and as a function of time of day) constitute the main noise in this problem. The number of users, cpu demand, I/O demand, and memory demand are some of the more important load measures. Temperature and humidity variations in the computer room and fluctuations in the power supply voltage are also noise factors, but normally are of minor consequence.

Control factors are those parameters that the system administrator can set at desired levels. Examples of control factors are the memory size, the partitioning of the memory into system buffers and user memory blocks, etc. The job of the system administrator is to set the levels of all control factors such as to give the shortest response time under all load conditions encountered by the machine.

The next step in macro modeling is to judiciously select a small number of system configurations, as defined by the different levels of the control factors, and experimentally evaluate the system performance for each of those configurations. While evaluating the system performance, the noise is allowed to vary over its normal range. The performance data are then analyzed to determine the best system configuration. The best system configuration in all probability will not be one of those tried earlier.

When one is primarily concerned only with obtaining the optimum system configuration, and not with obtaining detailed understanding of the system itself, the macro modeling gives the specific information needed for optimization with a minimum of expenditure of experimental resources.

This paper addresses how we used the macro modeling approach to optimize one particular installation of the UNIX operating system.

4. Selection of Factors and Levels

Discussion with computer scientists and system administrators led to the selection of the eight factors listed in Table 1 for improving the response time:

Let's discuss a few of these factors. When a sticky bit for a command such as "rm," "ed," "etc," is set, the system during initialization continuously copies the executable module of that command into the swap area of the disk, so that every time that command is needed again but not found in memory, it is brought back expeditiously, i.e., in a single operation, rather than block-by-block as otherwise happens. Factor F specifies how many and which commands should have their sticky bit set.

KMCs are special devices used to assist the main central processor unit (cpu) in handling the terminal and remote job entry traffic. They attempt to reduce the number of interrupts faced by the main cpu. In this experiment only, the KMCs used for terminal traffic were changed.

The number of entries in the INODE table determines the number of user files that can be simultaneously handled by the system.

Of these eight control factors, A, C, and F are hardware factors. Changing them usually involves much effort and capital investment. (Actually, for factor F we kept the physical KMC devices and only changed the software specifications for handling terminal ports.) The other five factors are software-related, and they can be easily changed by the system administrator.

The potential operating levels for the control factors are listed in Table 1. The pre-experiment levels are marked with an asterisk (*). The file system distribution a, b, and c refer to three specific distributions of the user and system files among the disk drives. Obviously, the actual distribution depends on the number of disk drives used in a particular system configuration. Procedures were followed in moving file systems to preserve their internal entropy (order/disorder).

Note that for disk drives, levels two and three are identical. Originally, we had planned to consider level three with an RP07 disk and a faster memory controller; but for scheduling reasons that was impractical. So we took level three to be the same as level two, in order to complete the experiment in a reasonable time frame. But still regarding these as three levels rather than two helped in the layout of the orthogonal array design matrix discussed in the following section.

In Table 8, the system buffer size levels are expressed as fractions of the total memory used for system buffers, rather than absolute buffer sizes. Level two of factor E stands for three specific, most frequently used, commands. And level three of factor E stands for the eight specific, most frequently used, commands, including the three of level two.

5. THE ORTHOGONAL ARRAY EXPERIMENTAL DESIGN

The full-factorial experiment to explore all possible factor-level combinations would require $2^2 \times 3^6 = 2916$ experiments. This is obviously prohibitively large. Also, it is unnecessary to perform the full-factorial experiment; a system's behavior can usually be adequately characterized by relatively few parameters.

Table 1. Control Factors and Levels

Label	Factor Name	Levels 1	2	3
A	Disk Drives (RM05 & RP06)	4&1*	4&2	4&2
B	File Distribution	a*	b	c
C	Memory Size (MB)	4*	3.5	3
D	System Buffers	1/5	1/4	1/3*
E	Sticky Bits	0*	3	8
F	KMC's Used	2*	0	
G	INODE Table Entries	400	500	600*
H	Other System Tables	a	b	c*

* Denotes Pre-experiment Levels

For our optimization study, we set the following statistical and pragmatic requirements and constraints:

1. Obtain an average picture over the entire region spanned by the eight factors.
2. Only a small number of system configurations can be tried.
3. Disk configuration changes were to be kept to an absolute minimum (we changed it only once). File distribution was the next hardest factor to change, since that involved unloading all files and reloading them according to the new configuration. So, changes in file-system distribution were also minimized.
4. Contrasts in any factor should be orthogonal to contrasts in every other factor. That means we seek the best additive or superposition model for predicting system behavior throughout the eight-dimensional region spanned by the chosen factor levels.

Requirements 1 and 4 imply that we should use an orthogonal array design for the experiment. A number of orthogonal arrays have been tabulated by Dr. Genichi Taguchi, and Yuin Wu, along with associated linear graphs that can be used to conveniently construct orthogonal designs for any experimental situation. The appropriate design for this UNIX system response time optimization study was the L_{18} orthogonal array, shown in Table 2. The assignment of factors to the columns of the array is also shown in the table. It has 18 rows; each row represents a different system configuration. For instance, row one is composed of level one for each of the eight control factors.

The matrix in Table 2 is characterized by the fact that in every pair of columns, all combinations of levels occur, and they occur an equal number of times. This is the combinatoric property that ensures the orthogonality of the contrasts specified in requirement 4, listed above.

Table 2. Experimental Design — L_{18}

Row No.	F 1	A 2	B 3	C 4	D 5	E 6	G 7	H 8
1	1	1	1	1	1	1	1	1
2	1	2	1	3	2	2	2	2
3	1	3 = 2'	1	2	3	3	3	3
4	1	2	2	1	1	2	3	3
5	1	3 = 2'	2	3	2	3	1	1
6	1	1	2	2	3	1	2	2
7	1	3 = 2'	3	1	2	1	2	3
8	1	1	3	3	3	2	3	1
9	1	2	3	2	1	3	1	2
10	2	2	1	1	3	3	2	1
11	2	3 = 2'	1	3	1	1	3	2
12	2	1	1	2	2	2	1	3
13	2	1	2	1	2	3	3	2
14	2	2	2	3	3	1	1	3
15	2	3 = 2'	2	2	1	2	2	1
16	2	3 = 2'	3	1	3	2	1	2
17	2	1	3	3	1	3	2	3
18	2	2	3	2	2	1	3	1

6. Experimental Procedure

We next describe the experimental procedure followed in each of the 18 experiments. Prior to understanding the study, we looked at the day-to-day fluctuation in response time and load. It revealed that the load was roughly similar for all the five week days. So we decided to run these experiments for 2-1/2 days each, thus completing two experiments per week. Experimental data consisted of response-time measurements taken once every ten minutes from 9:00 a.m. to 5:00 p.m. (The exact moments were chosen so as to avoid other automatically invoked system operations). For both standard and trivial response times, we took approximately 120 sets of measurements per experiment, to span the "noise domain" defined by various load levels and types.

The 18 experiments were conducted in the order of convenience. That is, experiments with disk drives at level one were conducted first, followed by those at levels two and three. Even within a given level of disk drives, the experiments were conducted so that the file-system distribution was changed the least number of times.

The experiments were conducted over a period of about three months. To avoid biases, care had to be taken to eliminate outliers. Thus, days that were obviously unusual were eliminated from the data; for example, a day of a severe snowstorm when the system load was very low, and days during the Easter week when many normal users were on vacation.

7. Data Analysis for Response Time

We next show the analysis of the standard response time. Analysis of the trivial response time was done similarly.

As a measure of the user's perception of response time, we used the quadratic loss function. That is, the objective of our optimization was to maximize, where

$$\eta = -10 \log_{10} \text{(mean squared response time)} \qquad (13.1)$$

Maximization of η is clearly equivalent to minimization of the mean squared response time, since the log function is monotonic. The log transform has been used to improve the additivity of the factorial effects. η is also referred to as the Signal-to-Noise (S/N) Ratio.

The objective function, η, and the mean response time were calculated for each of the 18 experiments. These values are tabulated in Table 3. From the 18 values of η, we have to compute how η changes as a function of each of the eight control factors. Because of the orthogonality of the design matrix, this can be done easily. For example, the average for the first level of factor F (KMCs used for terminal communication) is the average of the nine experiments (experiments one through nine), which were conducted with level one of factor F. Likewise, the average for the second level of factor F is the mean of experiments 10 through 18, which

Table 3. Standard Response Times

Row #	Mean (sec)	$-10\log_{10}$ (mean square) η (dB)
1	4.65	−14.66
2	5.28	−16.37
3	3.06	−10.49
4	4.53	−14.85
5	3.26	−10.94
6	4.55	−14.96
7	3.37	−11.77
8	5.62	−16.72
9	4.87	−14.67
10	4.13	−13.52
11	4.08	−13.79
12	4.45	−14.19
13	3.81	−12.89
14	5.87	−16.75
15	3.42	−11.65
16	3.66	−12.23
17	3.92	−12.81
18	4.42	−13.71

were conducted at level two of factor F. Let us denote the averages for levels one and two of F by m_{f1} and m_{f2} respectively. Here $m_{f1} = -13.94$ dB and $m_{f2} = -13.50$ dB. Table 4 lists the average η values for the levels of all eight control factors. These averages are graphically displayed in Figure 3. To determine the relative importance of the eight factorial effects, standard analysis of variance (ANOVA) was performed. Table 4, Figure 3, and the ANOVA results showed that the factors that have the biggest effects compared to the error are sticky bits (E), memory size (C), and disk drives (A). For the levels considered, the file system distribution (B), KMCs used for terminal communication (F), and INODE table entries (G), have the least influence on η. The other two factors, namely system buffers (D), and other system tables (H), have moderate effects.

Table 4. Factorial Effects for Standard Response Time

Factor		Average η (dB)		
		Level 1	Level 2	Level 3
A	Disk drives	−14.37	−13.40	
B	File system distribution	−13.84	−13.67	−13.65
C	Memory size	−13.32	−13.28	−14.56
D	System buffers	−13.74	−13.31	−14.11
E	Sticky bits	−14.27	−14.34	−12.55
F	KMCs used for terminals	−13.94	−13.50	
G	INODE table entries	−13.91	−13.51	−13.74
H	Other system tables	−13.53	−14.15	−13.48

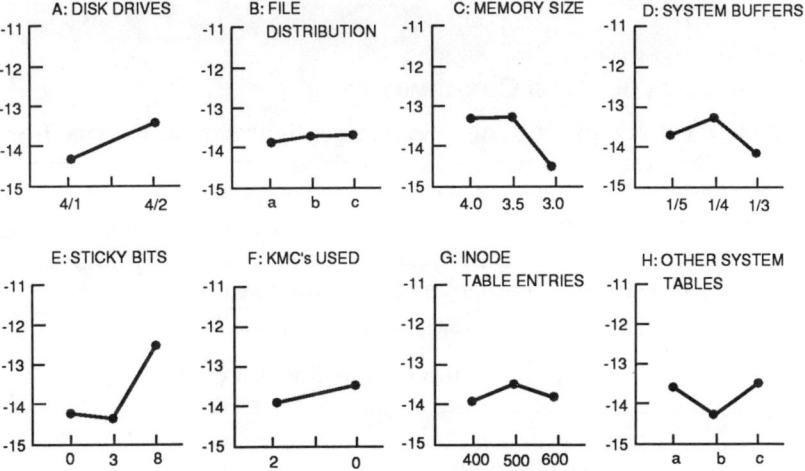

Figure 3. Analysis of Factorial Effects
[−10 log (Mean Square Standard Response Time)]

The following conclusions can be made from the plots of the factorial effects. Note that these conclusions are valid only for the particular load characteristics of our machine.

1. Going to 3 Mbytes of memory leads to a significant increase in response time. On the other hand, buying more than 4 Mbytes of memory would probably not improve the response time, as implied by the flatness of the plot between 3.5 Mbytes and 4 Mbytes.

2. Going from setting 0 sticky bits to those of the three most-used commands does not improve the response time. This is probably because, regardless of setting sticky bits, these three commands tend to stay in the memory as a result of their very frequent use. However, when sticky bits are set on the five next-most-used commands, the response time improves greatly. Perhaps one should, in any next round of experiments, study setting even more than sticky bits.
3. Adding one more disk drive leads to better response time. Perhaps even more disks should be considered for improving the response time. Of course, this would mean more cost, so proper trade-offs would have to be made.
4. KMCs do not help in improving response time for this type of computer environment. Therefore, they may be eliminated as far as terminal handling is concerned, thus reducing the cost of the hardware.

8. Optimization and Confirmation

The recommended optimum system configuration, as inferred from the data analysis, is shown in Table 5 along with the starting system configuration. Changes were recommended in the levels of disk drives, system buffers, and sticky bit setting because they lead to faster response times. KMCs were eliminated because they did not help in improving response, and eliminating them meant saving hardware.

Table 5. Optimum Control Factor Levels

Label	Factor Name	Start	Optimum	Changed
A	Disk Drives (RM05 & RP06)	4&1	4&2	*
B	File Distribution	a	a	
C	Memory Size (MB)	4	4	
D	System Buffers	1/3	1/4	*
E	Sticky Bits	0	8	*
F	KMCs Used	2	0	*
G	INODE Table Entries	600	600	
H	Other System Tables	c	c	

* Denotes a level change was recommended.

Subsequently, the optimum configuration was implemented. The average response times for the standard and trivial commands for more than two weeks of operation under the optimum conditions are plotted in figures 1a and 1b. Comparing the response time under the starting configuration with that under the optimum configuration, we see that under the optimum conditions the response time is small, even in the afternoon when the load is high. In fact, the response time is uniformly low throughout the day.

The data from the confirmation experiment are summarized in Table 6. For the standard response time, we see that the mean response time was reduced from 6.15 sec. to 2.37 sec., which amounts to a 61% improvement. Similar improvement was seen in the rms response time. On the $-10 \log$ (mean square) scale, the improvement was 8.39 dB. Likewise, for the trivial response time, the improvement was seen to be between 70% and 80% of the mean value, or 12.45 dB, as indicated in Table 6.

Table 6. Comparison of Response Times

Measure	Standard Response Time			Trivial Response Time		
	Starting Levels	Optimum Levels	Improvement	Starting Levels	Optimum Levels	Improvement
Mean (sec)	6.15	2.37	61%	0.521	0.148	71%
RMS (sec)	7.59	2.98	61%	0.962	0.200	79%
$-10\log$ (MS)	-17.60	-9.21	8.39dB	+0.34	+13.98	13.64dB

9. Concluding Remarks

By systematically conducting a small number of experiments we have accomplished over 60% reduction in response time of a UNIX operating system Release 5.0. This is a demonstration of how carefully planned experiments using orthogonal arrays can be used to efficiently generate information about a large number of parameters so that their optimum levels can be determined.

In practice, running real-life experiments to optimize every computer installation is obviously not practicable. Instead, more benefits can be achieved by performing off-line orthogonal array experiments to optimize over several different load conditions. The information gained from these off-line experiments can be used to map the operating system parameter space. This catalog of experimental results can then be used to improve the performance of different machines.

Reprinted from IEEE Communications Society, "IEEE International Conference on Communications," June 23–26, 1985, Chicago, Illinois.

Q & A

Q. In this simulation example, an L_{18} orthogonal array is used. There are eight control factors. If there are more than 8 factors, say 10 or 12 factors, which orthogonal array should be used?

A. If time is not critical, it is better to use an L_{36} orthogonal array.

Q. Since there are only 12 factors, why isn't an L_{27} used which has 13 columns?

A. By using an L_{36} orthogonal array, interactions are uniformly distributed to the other columns.

Q. Should interactions still not be assigned even if it is obvious from the model that interactions do exist?

A. That's correct. It is not good to assign interactions even if there are interactions. Interactions between control factors are of little value. This means that the main effects of the interaction are inconsistent. We would rather try to discover main effects that are consistent, or reproducible downstream.

Q. Then how do we handle interactions?

A. You can either conduct experiments downstream or brainstorm to improve the quality characteristics.

Q. Wouldn't it be costly to conduct an experiment downstream?

A. Yes, that's why we do not recommend it. We must select good quality characteristics.

Q. How is this done?

A. There is no generic answer. Each quality characteristic is examined case by case. The engineers' knowledge of the product/process is invaluable in selecting quality characteristics. S/N Ratios are generally good quality characteristics, because they are directly related to the output of product/process performance. By taking the logarithmic scale, we can expect better additivity.

Q. What does additivity mean?

A. When there is additivity, there are no interactions.

Q. If there are no interactions, can we then use one-factor-at-a-time type experiments for simulation?

A. Yes. But we would still not know if interactions were strong. That is why we must use orthogonal arrays to prove the interactions insignificant.

14. Process Optimization and Gold Usage Reduction Utilizing Taguchi Methods

Michael G. White
Military/Aerospace Division, ITT Cannon

This paper describes how two designed experiments were successfully conducted on gold plating of pin contacts. The quality characteristic measured was gold-plating thickness. The objective of the experiment was to identify the optimum operating levels for both the control factors that minimize variability and for the signal factors that adjust the mean closer to the target value. This application of Taguchi Methods required a total of 25 tests. First, an L_{16} orthogonal array was conducted on nine variables to identify the significant factors. Next, an L_9 was conducted to optimize the levels of the resulting significant factors. As a result of the process optimization, the variation in gold-plating thickness was reduced by more than 60%. This tightening of the distribution curve lowered the average plating thickness while maintaining the minimum specified thickness of 50 µin.

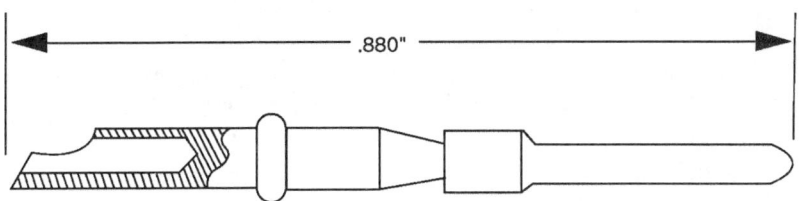

Figure 1. Size #20 Beryllium Copper Pin Contact

1. Factors and Layout for the First Test

The first experiment was conducted in a smaller, manual plating tank in order to reduce the costs associated with the 16 necessary tests. The purpose of the first test was to identify which of nine possible

From the *Third Symposium on Taguchi Methods*, pp. 269–283, Copyright © 1988, American Supplier Institute, Inc., Dearborn, Michigan.

controllable process variables were statistically significant in controlling either the mean or the variability in gold-plating thickness. Five factor interactions were also tested for significance (see Table 1).

Table 1. Factors and Levels in First Experiment

Factor	Factor Description	Test Level 1	Test level 2
A	Gold Concentration	.70 –.75 oz./gal.	1.10 – 1.15 oz./gal.
B	Temperature	100°F	110°F
C	pH	4.25	4.40
D	Current Density	1.0 amps/ft^2	2.0 amps/ft^2
E	Barrel Speed	18 rev/min	9 rev/min
F	Load Size	1/3 Full	1/2 Full
G	Anode Size	1/4" x 3"	1" x 3"
H	Anode Placement	Max. distance	1/2 way to barrel
I	Nickel Concentration	620 ppm	700 ppm

Interactions: $A \times B, A \times C, A \times I, B \times C, E \times F$

An L_{16} orthogonal array was selected and is shown in Table 2. A linear graph was drawn to depict the selected interactions, and array columns were assigned according to a table in Appendix 11 of *System of Experimental Design* by Dr. Genichi Taguchi.

2. Data Analysis for the First Test

After the 16 experiments in Table 2 were run in random order, samples of 10 contacts were measured by a calibrated X-ray machine for gold-plating thickness for each experiment.

The nominal-the-best case was used for the Signal-to-Noise (S/N) Ratio, (n), calculations. The ANOVA identified the factors that are statistically significant in their contribution to piece-to-piece variation. It also showed the contribution of each individual factor to total variation. Table 3 is the completed analysis of variance (ANOVA).

Another ANOVA was performed on the actual raw data (the plating thickness reading). This ANOVA identified the statistically significant factors affecting the mean value of plating thickness (see Table 4).

Table 2. L_{16} Orthogonal Array for First Experiment

Exp. No.	Columns Factors	1 A	2 I	3 A x I	4 E x F	5 D	6 B	7 A x B	8 G	9 H	10 B x C	11 E	12 C	13 A x C	14 e	15 F
1		1	1	1	1	1	1	1	1	1	1	1	1	1	1	1
2		1	1	1	1	1	1	1	2	2	2	2	2	2	2	2
3		1	1	1	2	2	2	2	1	1	1	1	2	2	2	2
4		1	1	1	2	2	2	2	2	2	2	2	1	1	1	1
5		1	2	2	1	1	2	2	1	1	2	2	1	1	2	2
6		1	2	2	1	1	2	2	2	2	1	1	2	2	1	1
7		1	2	2	2	2	1	1	1	1	2	2	2	2	1	1
8		1	2	2	2	2	1	1	2	2	1	1	1	1	2	2
9		2	1	2	1	2	1	2	1	2	1	2	1	2	1	2
10		2	1	2	1	2	1	2	2	1	2	1	2	1	2	1
11		2	1	2	2	1	2	1	1	2	1	2	2	1	2	1
12		2	1	2	2	1	2	1	2	1	2	1	1	2	1	2
13		2	2	1	1	2	2	1	1	2	2	1	1	2	2	1
14		2	2	1	1	2	2	1	2	1	1	2	2	1	1	2
15		2	2	1	2	1	1	2	1	2	2	1	2	1	1	2
16		2	2	1	2	1	1	2	2	1	1	2	1	2	2	1

Table 3. ANOVA on Variation for First Experiment

Source (factor)	df	S	V	S'	ρ (%)
A	1	12.68°	12.68°	—	—
I	1	3.26°	3.26°	—	—
A x I	1	0.07°	0.07°	—	—
F x E	1	74.4	74.4		
D	1	859.0	859.0	844.84	36.1%
B	1	25.6	25.6	—	—
A x B	1	259.7	259.7	254.54	10.9%
G	1	121.9	121.9	107.74	4.6%
H	1	77.3	77.3	—	—
B x C	1	19.2°	19.2°	—	—
E	1	70.2	70.2	—	—
C	1	141.6	141.6	127.44	5.4%
A x C	1	25.8	25.8	—	—
F	1	615.8	615.8	601.64	25.7%
e	1	35.6	35.6		
(e)	(5)	(70.81)	(14.16)		17.3%
Total	15	2342.2		2342.2	100.0%

° pooled into error (e)

Table 4. ANOVA on Average for First Experiment

Source (factor)	df	S	V	S'	ρ (%)
A	1	6.9	6.9	—	—
I	1	1.6	1.6	—	—
A x I	1	45.8	45.8	—	—
F x E	1	114.0	114.0	—	—
D	1	1121.3	1121.3	1100.72	6.2%
B	1	2826.3	2826.3	2805.72	15.7%
A x B	1	31.9	31.9	—	—
G	1	717.0	717.0	696.42	3.9%
H	1	261.0	261.0	240.42	1.4%
B x C	1	147.2	147.2	126.62	0.7%
E	1	492.5	492.5	471.92	2.6%
C	1	11749.1	11749.1	11728.52	65.8%
A x C	1	123.8	123.8	—	—
F	1	181.5	181.5	160.92	0.9%
e	1	16.7	16.7		
(e)	(5)	(102.9)	(20.58)		2.8%
Total	15	17836.5		17836.5	100.0%

3. Conclusions From First Test

From the ANOVAs in the initial experiment, four factors were identified for further testing. Current density and load size were selected as significant control factors and pH was selected as a strong signal factor. Anode size was also selected, because it is significant both as a control and a signal factor. The first test was designed to screen a larger number of variables to identify a small number of significant factors. Changing the level of the insignificant factors did not significantly contribute to the plating thickness variation.

4. FACTORS AND LAYOUT FOR THE SECOND TEST

The second experiment was conducted on an automatic precious metals plating line in a production mode. The purpose of the second experiment was to test the above four significant factors at three levels in order to optimize the production process. The three levels were chosen as a result of the conclusions from the first test. With three levels, a more accurate relationship curve can be drawn between the factor levels and their dependent S/N Ratios (see Table 5).

Table 5. Factors and Levels Tested in Second Experiment

Factor	Factor Description	Test Level 1	Test Level 2	Test Level 3
A	Current Density amps/ft.^{2}	1.5	2.0	2.5
B	Load Size parts/barrel	8,000	10,000	12,000
C	Anode size inches (width)	2	4	6
D	pH	4.20	4.30	4.40

Test settings were altered slightly to be compatible with the larger plating tank used in the second experiment. Setting for the other five factors (tested as not significant in the first experiment) were held constant during all tests.

To test four factors at three levels, an L_9 was selected from the available orthogonal arrays in Dr. Taguchi's reference manuals (see Table 6).

Table 6. L_9 Orthogonal Array for Second Experiment

Experiment No.	Columns Factors	1 A	2 B	3 C	4 D
1		1	1	1	1
2		1	2	2	2
3		1	3	3	3
4		2	1	2	3
5		2	2	3	1
6		2	3	1	2
7		3	1	3	2
8		3	2	1	3
9		3	3	2	1

5. DATA ANALYSIS FOR THE SECOND TEST

The same calibrated X-ray machine was operated by the same inspector to measure gold-plating thickness readings on a sample of contacts for each of the nine experiments.

A. ANOVA on Variation

An ANOVA was performed on the S/N Ratios calculated for each of the nine experiments. The completed ANOVA in Table 7 shows the contribution of each factor to total piece-to-piece variation in plating thickness.

Table 7. ANOVA on Variation for Second Experiment

Source	df	S	V	S'	ρ (%)
A	2	23.72	11.86	20.01	27.7%
B	2	27.48	13.74	23.77	33.0%
C	2	17.24	8.62	13.53	18.8%
D	2	3.71°	1.86°	—	—
	(2)	(3.71)	(1.86)		20.5%
e		0	0		
Total	8	72.13			100.0 %

° pooled into error (e)

Table 7 shows that changing the settings (between levels 1, 2, and 3) of current density, load size, and anode size contributes to nearly 80% of the total thickness variation.

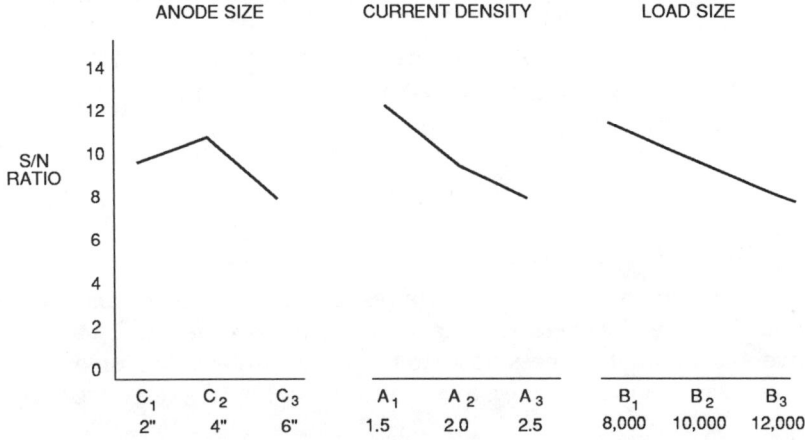

Figure 2. Response Curves on Variation for Second Experiment

B. Response Curves on Variation

Figure 2 shows a graphical representation of the relationship between the level of each factor and its corresponding impact on variation. To minimize variation from the mean value, the level with the highest S/N Ratio is selected. For anode size, level C_2 (4 in. anode width) will reduce piece-to-piece variability over the other two settings.

C. ANOVA on the Average

An ANOVA was performed on the actual raw data (the plating-thickness readings). The ANOVA in Table 8 identifies the significant factors that affect the mean value of plating thickness and their individual contribution to total variation. This ANOVA is the final result after pooling insignificant factors A and B into e (error) and then decomposing the remaining significant factors into their linear and quadratic components. Since the experimental error, e_1, was not so much smaller than repetition error e_2 both of these were pooled together into error e on the ANOVA. The high contribution of error was due to the large sample size for each experiment, which resulted in the high repetition error. This partially obscures the contribution of the significant factors. The repetition error was ignored in the first test to avoid the problem of obscuring the factors' contribution to total variance. This assumption did not alter the identification of the four most significant control and signal factors.

Table 8. ANOVA on Average for Second Experiment

Source	df	S	V	S'	ρ (%)
Cl	1	303.75	303.75	243.72	3.6%
Dl	1	1242.15	1242.15	1182.14	19.7%
Dq	1	380.02	380.02	320.01	4.7%
(e)	(86)	(5160.38)	(60.01)	—	72.0%
Total	89	6833.16			100%

D. Response Curves on the Average

Figure 3 shows the response curves between factor levels and the raw data (plating thickness readings). Levels are selected that move the average plating thickness closer to the 50 μin. target value, unless these levels were shown to increase variability in the Figure 2 response curves.

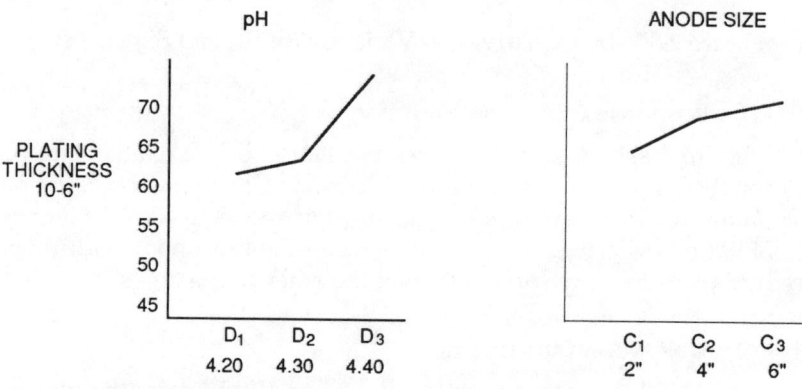

Figure 3. Response Curves on Average for Second Experiment

6. Conclusions from Second Test

The two-step procedure of parameter design was next applied. First, control factors and their optimum levels were selected to minimize piece-to-piece variability. From the ANOVA in Table 7 and the response curves in Figure 2, factor levels C_2 (anode size = 4 in.), A_2 (current density = 1.5 amps/ft.^{2}), and B_1 (load size = 8 parts/barrel) were selected.

Next, from Table 8 and Figure 3, potential signal factors were analyzed. Factor level D_2 proved to be an excellent signal factor. It was shown in the ANOVA on variation (Table 7) that it is not an important control factor. Also, it was shown in Table 8 and Figure 3 to be very significant in adjusting the process average.

In summary, the two-step parameter design leads to an optimized process setting for each of four different plating variables. This combination of optimized control factor levels should lead to a significant reduction in piece-to-piece variability. It is then possible, with the signal factor, to further adjust the average plating thickness closer to the minimum allowed plating thickness of 50 µin.

7. Confirmation and Follow-up Results

A. Confirmation Tests

There were separate confirmation tests for both the first and the second experiment. A confidence interval was calculated in which the average (mean) of the readings of the confirmation sample must fall. The interval for each optimization experiment was calculated at a 95% confidence level. The actual second confirmation test yielded a mean of 55.5 µin., which was near the center of the interval for a strong confirmation. The optimized settings resulted in a 40% reduction in the total amount of variation from the mean. The confidence interval calculations for the confirmation test on the second experiment are shown in Figure 4.

B. Follow-up Tests

Analysis of the Response Curves and the ANOVA on variation indicated that there was an excellent chance of even more variation reduction. According to Figure 2, it would not further reduce variance to experiment beyond the tested limits for anode size. However, there appeared to be a strong chance that a lower current density setting or a smaller load size would provide reduced variability.

Since an even smaller load size would increase the labor costs per plated part, a small test (one experiment) was designed with the same optimized settings as used in the confirmation test except for current density. In the follow-up test, the latter factor was set at 1.25 amps/ft². In this test, the total remaining variation was reduced by 50%.

1. Estimated sample average based on use of the two significant signal factors C_2 and D_1.
2. Formula:

$$\overline{X}_{C_2 D_1} = \hat{\mu}_{C_2 D_1} \pm \sqrt{F^1_{f_e;\,0.05} \times V_e \left(\frac{1}{n_e} + \frac{1}{r}\right)} \qquad (14.1)$$

3. Solution (where $\overline{T}$ = average of all readings and $\overline{C}_2$ = average of all C_2 readings)

   a. $\hat{\mu}_{C_2 D_1} = \overline{T} + (\overline{C}_2 - \overline{T}) + (\overline{D}_1 - \overline{T})$

   $\qquad = \overline{C}_2 + \overline{D}_1 - \overline{T}$ \qquad (14.2)

   $\qquad = 62.43 + 58.47 - 62.18$

   $\qquad = 58.72$

   b. Confidence interval:

   $F^1_{86;\,0.05} = 3.96$ (from F Table)

   $V_e = 60.01$ (from ANOVA)

   $r = 30$ (confirmation sample size)

   $$n_e = \frac{\text{total no. of experiments}}{\text{total df in est.} + 1 \text{ for } \overline{T}} = \frac{9}{5} \qquad (14.3)$$

   $\sqrt{3.96 \times 60.01 \left(\frac{5}{9} + \frac{1}{30}\right)} = 11.83$ (at 95%)

   c. $\overline{X}_{C_2 D_1} = 58.72 \pm 11.83$ (46.89, 70.55)

Figure 4. Calculations for Estimation and Confidence Interval

C. Gain from Variation Reduction

Using the S/N Ratios calculated for all the experiments, it is possible to calculate the gain in variation reduction. Figure 5 shows that the new variation due to process optimization (including the lower current density level) represents a total reduction of nearly 70% over the average historical variation.

This represents a 70% reduction in variation.

Gain:
$$10 \log \eta_{new} - 10 \log \eta_{orig.} = +5.22 \text{ dB} \qquad (14.4)$$

$$10 \log \frac{\eta_{orig.}}{\eta_{new}} = 5.22$$

$$\log \frac{\eta_{orig.}}{\eta_{new}} = .522$$

$$\frac{\eta_{orig.}}{\eta_{new}} = 3.33$$

Figure 5. Gain in Variation Reduction

8. Quality Improvement: Reduction in Gold Usage

With more than a 66% reduction in variation on the tested part through optimization of the control factors, it is possible to reduce the mean level of plating thickness closer to 50 μin by adjusting the signal factor. At ITT Cannon, the pH (signal factor) of the plating bath was reduced slightly. However, since a pH lower than the tested levels for the process bath could result in other bath irregularities (e.g., chelating agents), we reduced the time in the plating bath to achieve the desired mean thickness level. As we are now expanding this optimization to other contact designs (including socket contacts), a significant financial savings is resulting from a reduced level of gold overplating.

Appendix to the Study

Table A.
.125 Anlaysis— Average

No.	Gold Plating Thickness Reading (μin.)																				Total	$\bar{x}$
1	63	52	57	60	51	64	57	56	61	57	58	51	54	60	54	64	50	54	55	49	1,127	56.35
2	59	60	63	61	58	66	53	63	57	61	61	60	73	81	59	62	68	53	60	72	1,250	62.50
3	60	66	78	83	64	76	89	106	68	78	52	86	91	69	71	57	73	96	83	60	1,506	75.30
4	67	77	66	51	53	55	59	58	62	62	81	76	60	58	53	59	55	54	70	60	1,236	61.80
5	71	74	78	63	62	67	47	69	49	58	54	80	71	67	62	47	51	66	57	49	1,242	62.10
6	70	58	69	65	65	74	71	75	75	65	70	64	65	66	55	70	71	74	65	75	1,362	68.10
7	61	66	65	74	66	73	73	65	83	81	60	75	77	62	60	69	65	60	89	76	1,400	70.00
8	68	62	54	51	43	59	57	64	53	52	48	58	46	47	42	68	51	48	50	44	1,043	52.15
9	66	47	67	56	55	56	49	53	39	54	42	46	66	89	42	65	61	46	92	58	1,152	57.60
10	48	63	69	60	89	81	63	53	68	76	53	67	66	68	69	70	89	67	74	70	1,358	67.90
11	75	76	75	70	71	70	84	68	75	73	80	76	69	71	70	75	67	68	76	66	1,466	73.30
12	58	55	47	49	59	45	53	56	41	61	52	55	54	50	53	55	52	56	55	52	1,059	52.95
13	64	65	57	76	54	54	65	60	64	67	62	67	58	55	61	64	56	55	52	57	1,233	61.65
14	45	79	77	72	71	99	50	74	77	74	72	96	75	89	98	77	41	77	96	75	1,514	75.70
15	84	53	56	64	61	74	57	56	74	69	65	72	48	64	64	67	55	68	56	55	1,256	62.80
16	61	60	55	50	54	51	50	56	57	55	53	52	57	52	53	54	55	55	49	56	1,081	54.05

TOTAL 1014.25

Table B. Experiment Array (L_9)

Exper. No.	A 1	B 2	C 3	D 4	Thickness Readings for 030-3019-000										Total	η	Thickness Readings for 030-9036-000										Total
1	1	1	1	1	56	52	56	57	60	58	57	65	55	54	570	14.53	57	50	59	54	55	60	52	57	44	48	536
2	1	2	2	2	59	53	56	63	50	60	61	64	59	59	584	13.04	74	46	53	63	60	54	54	60	64	52	580
3	1	3	3	3	68	54	62	62	77	52	60	55	48	57	696	7.01	54	59	77	62	79	76	62	53	53	49	624
4	2	1	2	3	70	57	68	67	71	78	71	69	73	81	705	11.17	68	71	85	61	72	71	68	62	78	72	708
5	2	2	3	1	55	79	72	62	68	55	58	51	52	48	600	5.83	56	54	62	62	77	52	60	55	48	57	583
6	2	3	1	2	52	54	59	52	51	60	68	64	75	63	598	7.99	51	52	49	55	69	70	54	76	50	65	591
7	3	1	3	2	73	50	60	64	56	67	64	72	69	58	633	9.11	85	58	72	59	81	67	72	69	81	86	730
8	3	2	1	3	69	61	71	61	65	48	51	72	55	73	626	7.25	73	79	59	56	83	57	63	73	66	79	688
9	3	3	2	1	58	66	64	61	64	51	48	61	68	43	584	7.28	51	61	50	53	53	47	52	56	55	46	524

Q & A

Q. This case study is a classical example showing that reducing variability reduces cost. The characteristic chosen is "gold-plating thickness." Do you approve of the selection of the quality characteristics?

A. Yes. For plating, painting, and coating, there exist various types of defects. However, the idea is to reduce the variability of the thickness, increasing the likelihood that the other types of defects will decrease. Engineers should always think in terms of the principal function of the process/product being investigated.

Q. This study did not use any noise factors. It seems that the S/N Ratio is calculated using sample-to-sample variability and position-to-position (within-sample) variability. Is this correct?

A. Yes, samples at 10 positions in each run were measured to calculate a S/N Ratio. It is permissible not to use noise factor(s) when there is large variation between repetitions.

Q. In the second experiment, an L_9 array was used. Is this array too small?

A. In this case, it is all right, since it followed the first L_{16} array. But try to avoid using small arrays (i.e., L_8, L_9) for the first experiment. It is recommended to use arrays larger than L_{12} for the initial experiment.

Q. Is there another way to assign the experiment?

A. Yes, by designing a 3-level experiment, using an L_{18} orthogonal array, without assigning interactions.

Q. But an L_{18} array has only eight columns, while in this case there are nine factors. Are the number of columns adequate to assign all nine factors?

A. Yes, we can set six factors with three levels and three factors with two levels. One of the 2-level factors is assigned to the first column that is a 2-level column. The remaining two 2-level factors are assigned to one of the 3-level columns using the combination design.

Q. How is this accomplished?

A. Suppose there are two 2-level factors, A and B; there are four combinations between A and B. Instead of assigning all four combinations, which we normally do, take three of the four combinations and consider three combinations as a factor with three levels.

Q. Then how are the effects of A and B?

A. Suppose we use the combinations A_1B_1, A_2B_1, and A_1B_2. The effect of A is determined from the difference between the average of A_1B_1 and A_2B_1, since B_1 is common to both. The effect of B is obtained from A_1B_1 and A_1B_2.

Q. The experiment was conducted in random order. Is it necessary?

A. It is not necessary, since there are some factors whose levels are more difficult to change, such as gold concentration, pH, and nickel concentration. Also, the experiment was conducted in a 250 gallon tank; imagine how difficult it was to prepare. About randomization, refer to the case study of Davidson Instrument Panel.

Q. What about the data analysis in this experiment?

A. This is a typical example of a nominal-the-best characteristic analysis. First, we find the factors that are significant for the S/N Ratio to reduce variability, second we find a factor or factors that are insignificant to the S/N Ratio, but significant to the mean to adjust to the target value. In this experiment, the factors current density is significant to the S/N Ratio but insignificant to the mean, while pH is significant to the mean but insignificant to the S/N Ratio.

Q. Is this a fortuitous case?

A. By studying as many as nine factors, the chance of finding such factors is increased. This is one of the reasons taking as many control factors as possible is recommended.

Q. Raw data analysis is used instead of 10 log Sm to analyze the means. Why is this so?

A. For the data where the mean does not vary widely, it is all right to use raw data analysis. But 10 log Sm is used when the means are widely dispersed. The latter case is often the case in the earlier stages of product/process development (R&D).

Q. Engineers know how to adjust the mean in many cases, such as adjusting the mean of a dimension. Is thickness a dimension?

A. Yes. In this experiment, pH was used to adjust the mean only to a certain extent. Because a low pH value adversely affects the other quality characteristics, further adjustment was made using plating time. Plating time was not listed as a control factor in either experiment, but the engineers knew it could be used to adjust the thickness.

This could be a problem if variability changes when plating time changes. However, it was said that no such problem occurred. It was also reported that the standard deviation of thickness was reduced to one-half, and the mean was adjusted to a lower level. As a result, gold consumption was reduced and the annual savings was $400,000.

Q. Is it all right to reduce the average thickness to a level that meets the specification?

A. When it is too thick, the loss to the supplier becomes greater. When it is too thin, the loss to the customer becomes greater. We need to determine the level where the two losses balance. That must be determined by the product design engineer.

15. Photo-Receptor Optimization via Taguchi Methods

*Dr. H. Heil, Dr. B. Hofmann,
N. Schmidt, and J. Segain
ITT Passive Components*

This Taguchi Methods application addressed a serious welding process problem involving electrical connections on power capacitors. Due to a low capability of C_{pk} 0.25, extensive destructive testing was required to control a 30% defect rate. In this L_{16} experiment, at a cost of 800 DM (less than $400), nine factors of the process were examined. By adjusting the level setting of seven of these factors, average weld strength was increased by 29% and variation reduced by 40%, yielding a C_{pk} of 2.7. Destructive testing has been reduced significantly to that required for Statistical Process Control and the previous high-field failure complaints have dropped to zero. With no investment in technology or equipment, an annual savings of 50,000 DM ($25,000) was achieved by this Taguchi Methods application.

1. Introduction: The Product

Nurnberg Passive Components is a division of ITT's West German manufacturing group employing approximately 1,500 people on a three-shift operation. Basic product lines of this division include capacitors, hybrids, photo-receptors, and other electrical components using state-of-the-art manufacturing technologies.

2. Objective of the Experiment

Three objectives were established for the experiment at the outset. The first objective was to minimize blemishes on the surface of photo-receptors to eliminate the need for 35% rework and exposure of custom-

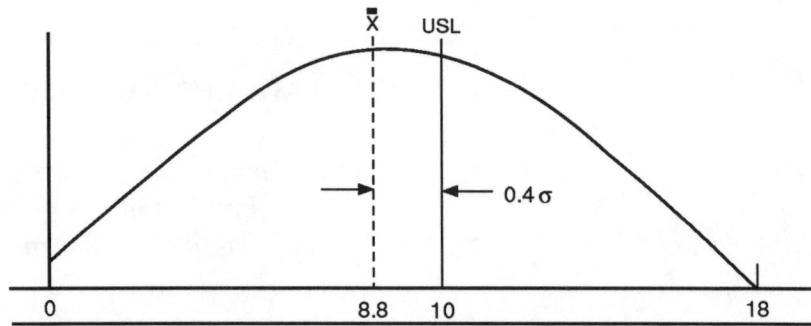

Figure 1. Blemishes/Drum

ers to poor-quality copies. The second objective was to identify process parameters and measurements that would provide an effective method for controlling the process and predicting the functional quality of the photo-receptors being produced. The final objective was to gather critical information usable in a planned product-development program, which would extend the product application into a broader, more demanding area of application. Such a breakthrough would ensure the customer an advanced performance capability at a very low cost.

To maximize total cost, the Taguchi concept of counter measures was applied.

3. QUALITY CHARACTERISTICS, FACTORS AND EXPERIMENTAL LAYOUT

The brainstorming group consisted of representatives of the Photo-Receptor Manufacturing Group, Technology & Design Engineering Group, and Quality Control Engineering personnel. Since in this case the cost of each experiment and the cost of detailed inspection is very high, some preliminary experiments were planned (see Figure 2).

The first preliminary experiment was designed to find basic causes of variation in visual defects by utilizing past data with three factors. Since all data were available, analyzing data for three-way layout was not difficult.

Factors were:

A = Different batches (3 levels)
B = Position (4 levels)
C = Location (30 levels)

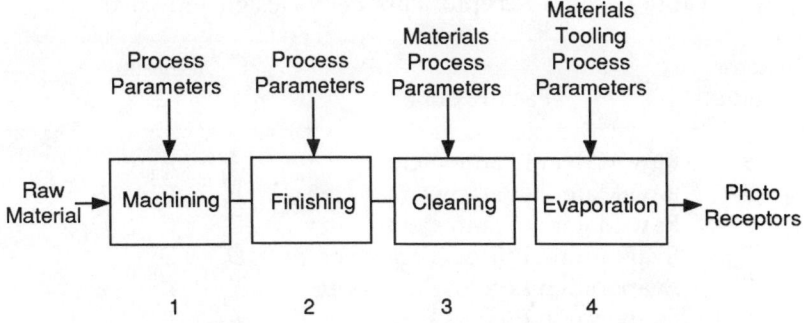

Figure 2. Photo-Receptor Manufacturing Flow Diagram

Since visual quality is classified best, good, fair, and bad, accumulation analysis was appropriate. Results of analysis showed that dominant variance occurred between batches while factor B had some influence on variance. Lab analysis on small-size defects showed some chemical residuals and defects due to fusing of raw material on substrate. The next approach was to expose each process that could contribute to the causes mentioned above. Since finishing quality characteristics were very stable, attention was focused on the cleaning process. A simple experiment was conducted on the cleaning process, including process parameters, materials, material conditions, and different sizes of substrates. Results of analysis showed that materials were the most dominant factor. Treatment of the substrate also showed some significancy. Different sizes of substrates proved insignificant. After optimizing the cleaning process (which was dominant on defects due to chemical residuals), the next step became the designing of an experiment to optimize evaporation process parameters (to minimize fusion defects, which were the defects most frequent among other visual defects). After a series of discussions, 10 factors were agreed upon to have important effects on quality characteristics of the product (including dynamic characteristics). Table 1 shows the factors and levels.

Experimental factors consisted of three product design parameters, five process parameters, and one tooling design parameter (indication of quality variation on different product locations led the group to experiment with tooling design). Quality characteristics and objectives to be optimized were selected as follows:

Table 1. Photo-Receptor Parameter Design and Levels

Factor Code	Factor Name	Levels 1	2	3
A	Raw Material Parameters	A_1	A_2	
B	Raw Material Parameters	B_1	B_2	B_3
C	Raw Material Parameters	C_1	C_2	C_3
D	Evaporation Process Parameter	D_1	D_2	
E	Evaporation Process Parameter	E_1	E_2	E_3
F	Evaporation Process Parameter	F_1	F_2	
G	Evaporation Process Parameter	G_1	G_2	
H	Evaporation Process Parameter	H_1	H_2	
I	Evaporation Process Parameter	I_1	I_2	
J	Tooling Design Parameter	J_1	J_2	J_3

v: Visual defects — Size class 1, 2, 3 (3 worse)
w: ⎫
x: ⎬ Photo and Electrical — Target M (minimum variation)
y: ⎬ Performance Characteristics — Dynamic target condition
z: ⎭ — Target M (minimum variation)
   — Minimum better

Four process observation characteristics were also included to support secondary objectives:

r: ⎫
s: ⎬ Process characteristics measured.
t: ⎬
u: ⎭

From Table 1, an L_{18} ($2^1 \times 3^7$) orthogonal array was found to be sufficient with factors DF and HI combined and assigned to columns 7 and 8, respectively. The layout of the experiment is shown in Table 2.

The great expense of conducting a full production-scale experiment in this technology led to development of an equivalent, less-expensive, laboratory experiment. While this required some ingenuity in certain areas, it was possible to create adequate equivalency in this case.

Table 3 shows a sample of the experiment layout sheets used to prevent errors in conducting the experiment and recording of data.

Table 2. Layout of Experiment Photo-Receptor
Multiple Quality Characteristics

FACTORS	G	C	A	B	E	J	(D F)	(H I)		Defects						Q.C.
# EXP	1	2	3	4	5	6	7	7	8	8	CL	CL	CL	L	M	R	Process Quality Characteristics
1	1	1	1	1	1	1	1	1	1	0	0	0	0	0	0	0
2	1	1	2	2	2	2	2	1	2	1	0	0	0	0	0	0	0
3	1	1	3	3	3	3	1	2	1	2	0	0	0	0	0	0	0
4	1	2	1	1	2	2	1	1	1	2	0	0	0	0	0	0	0
5	1	2	2	2	3	3	1	2	1	1	0	0	0	0	0	0	0
6	1	2	3	3	1	1	2	1	2	1	0	0	0	0	0	0	0
7	1	3	1	2	1	3	2	1	1	2	0	0	0	0	0	0	0
8	1	3	2	3	2	1	1	2	1	1	0	0	0	0	0	0	0
9	1	3	3	1	3	2	1	1	2	1	0	0	0	0	0	0	0
10	2	1	1	3	3	2	2	1	1	1	0	0	0	0	0	0	0
11	2	1	2	1	1	3	1	2	2	1	0	0	0	0	0	0	0
12	2	1	3	2	2	1	1	1	1	2	0	0	0	0	0	0	0
13	2	2	1	2	3	1	1	2	2	1	0	0	0	0	0	0	0
14	2	2	2	3	1	2	1	1	1	2	0	0	0	0	0	0	0
15	2	2	3	1	2	3	2	1	1	1	0	0	0	0	0	0	0
16	2	3	1	3	2	3	1	1	2	1	0	0	0	0	0	0	0
17	2	3	2	1	3	1	2	1	1	2	0	0	0	0	0	0	0
18	2	3	3	2	1	2	1	2	1	1	0	0	0	0	0	0	0

4. Optimization and Estimation

For each quality characteristic, 14 different analyses were conducted. In this section only one type of analysis will be discussed, because the primary objective was to minimize surface defects. Since one product is produced in the lab per experiment, multivariables analysis is performed instead of accumulation analysis to obtain more fundamental results.

From Table 4, Parameters A, B, and C, product design parameters, J, tool design parameter and process parameters G, E, and H become significant. To be able to determine optimum levels of significant factors, supplementary tables (Table 5) and bar graphs (Figure 3) for significant factors, were prepared.

From Figure 3, optimum levels of significant factors can be determined as:

$$A_2, B_3, C_2, E_1, G_1, J_3, \text{ and } H_2.$$

Table 3. Experiment and Data Layout Sheet

Exp. #	OA#	G	C	A	B	E	J	D	F	H	I	Constant
14	13	G_2	C_2	A_1	B_2	E_3	J_1	D_1	F_2	H_2	I_1	Parameter Values

Quality Characteristics		L	M	R
w)	Performance	0	0	0
x)	Quality	0	0	0
y)	Characteristics	0	0	0
z)		0	0	0
r)	Process	0	0	0
s)	Observation		0	
t)	Characteristics		0	
u)			0	

Visual Quality

# of Defects			Accumulated Results		
Class 1	Class 2	Class 3	I	II	III
2	2	16	2	4	20

I = # of Class 1 Defects
II = I + # of Class 2 Defects
III = II + # of Class 3 Defects

It is interesting to note from Figure 3 that significant factors were intensively causing variations of class 3 defects and have nothing at all to do with class 1 defects.

For multivariable analysis, the feasible process average estimation equation is the logarithmic additivity of significant factors. Then the process average equation can be written as:

$$\hat{\mu}_I = \frac{\left(\overline{A}_2 \times \overline{B}_3 \times \overline{C}_2 \times \overline{E}_1 \times \overline{G}_1 \times \overline{J}_3 \times \overline{H}_2\right)_i}{\overline{T}_i^6} \qquad i = i^{th} \text{ class} \qquad (15.1)$$

Then:

$\hat{\mu}_I = 0 \pm CI_I$

$\hat{\mu}_{II} = .21 \pm CI_{II}$

$\hat{\mu}_{III} = .51 \pm CI_{III}$

$CI_I = 0 \quad CI_{II} = {}^{+1.06}_{-.21} \quad CI_{III} = {}^{+1.67}_{-.51}$

5. Optimization for Multiple Quality Characteristics

Since other quality characteristics are also involved in this experiment, it is useful to make a summary table for multi-quality characteristics to be able to make sound trade-offs (see Table 6).

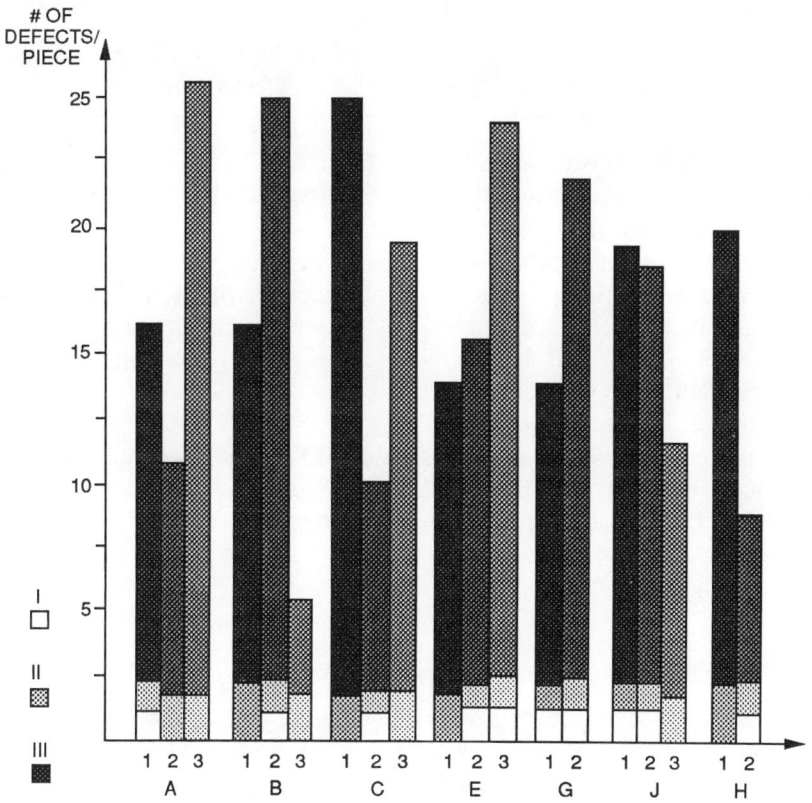

Figure 3. Bar Graphs for Significant Factors

Table 4. ANOVA Multi-Variables
Photo-Receptor # of Defects (Pooled)

Source	df	S	V	S'	ρ(%)
G	3	25.73	8.57	20.72	8.19
C	6	41.41	6.90	31.39	12.40
A	6	35.71	5.95	25.69	10.15
B	6	37.61	6.27	27.59	10.90
E	6	30.50	5.08	20.48	8.09
J	6	21.13	3.52	11.11	4.39
H	3	35.87	11.955	30.86	12.19
G x C	6	15.602	2.60		
(e)	(9)	(9.452)	(1.05)		
(e)	(15)	(25.054)	(1.67)	(85.174)	(33.69)
T	51	253.01		253.01	100.00

From the Table 6, it can be seen that 6 out of the 10 factors are changed to optimize functional quality characteristics. Results of these changes are shown below in the table.

The analyses also showed that two evaporation process readout measurements would provide excellent indication of raw-material conditions critical to photo-receptor quality. By maintaining control charts on factors G, E, J, and H, the tendency of critical functional quality characteristics can be predicted with a high degree of accuracy during processing.

As currently set up, all drums produced are screened against a 10-blemish maximum specification limit. As Figure 4 shows, the outgoing product distribution approximates a uniform distribution. The optimized distribution was developed from experiment data using very conservative factors.

6. Quality Improvement After Optimization

As can be seen from Figure 4, the potential for blemishes above the maximum allowed is virtually zero (C_{pk} 4.5) compared to 0.13 previously. Application of the Taguchi QLF analysis on outgoing quality is shown in Table 7.

Table 5. Significant Factor Level Averages

Opt. Levels	Factor Level	Class Cum.			Class Avg. Cum.			Non-Cumulative		
		I	II	III	I	II	III	Class 1	Class 2	Class 3
	A_1	2	12	96	0.33	2.0	16.00	0.33	1.67	14.00
**	A_2	1	9	17	0.16	1.5	11.83	0.16	1.34	10.30
	A_3	0	7	152	0.0	1.16	25.33	0.0	1.16	24.17
	B_1	0	13	95	0.0	2.16	15.83	0.0	2.16	13.67
	B_2	3	9	150	0.5	1.5	25.00	0.5	1.0	23.5
**	B_3	0	6	74	0.0	1.0	6.61	0.0	1.0	5.16
	C_1	1	8	150	0.16	1.33	25.00	0.16	1.17	23.67
*	C_2	2	10	59	0.33	1.66	9.83	0.33	1.33	8.17
	C_3	0	10	110	0.0	1.66	18.83	0.0	1.66	17.17
	E_1	0	4	86	0.0	.67	14.33	0.0	0.67	13.66
*	E_2	1	6	93	0.16	1.0	15.50	0.16	0.84	14.50
	E_3	2	18	140	0.33	3.0	23.33	0.33	2.67	20.33
	G_1	1	12	115	0.11	1.33	12.77	0.11	1.22	11.44
*	G_2	2	16	204	0.22	1.77	22.67	0.22	1.55	20.90
	J_1	2	12	127	0.33	2.00	21.17	0.33	1.67	19.17
	J_2	1	9	121	0.16	1.5	20.16	0.16	1.34	18.66
*	J_3	0	7	71	0.0	1.16	11.83	0.0	1.66	10.67
	H_1	0	21	258	0.0	1.75	21.5	0.0	1.75	19.75
*	H_2	3	7	61	0.5	1.16	10.16	0.5	0.66	9.00

Table 6. Summary of Results

Quality Characteristics and Level of Significance

	Performance Quality Characteristics						
Factor	Surface Defects	v	w	x	y	Optimum Level	Present Level
G	8%	Insig.	Insig.	Insig.	Insig.	G_1	G_2
C	12%	7%	Insig.	18%	Insig.	C_2	C_2
A	10%	81%	50%	7%	15%	A_2	A_2
B	10%	Insig.	30%	14%	55%	B_3	B_2
E	8%	Insig.	Insig.	8%	Insig.	E_1	E_2
J	4%	7%	Insig.	12%	6%	J_3	J_2
D	Insig.	Insig.	Insig.	5%	Insig.	D_2	D_2
F	Insig.	Insig.	Insig.	13%	Insig.	F_1	F_2
H	12%	Insig.	Insig.	5%	Insig.	H_2	H_2
I	Insig.	Insig.	Insig.	Insig.	6%	I_1	I_2

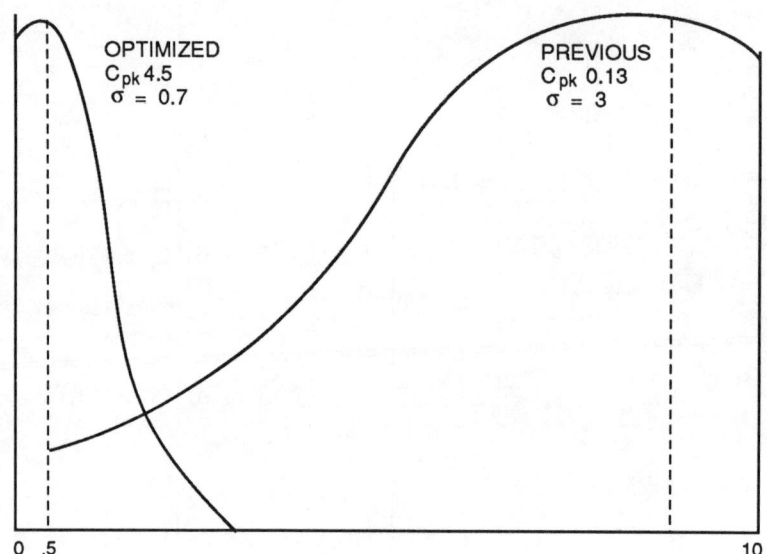

Figure 4. Blemishes/Drum

Table 7.

Condition	Distribution	Approximate Variance	Average Loss	x Gain	Annualized (100,000)
For Smaller Than Specified Value		$L = \dfrac{A_o}{\Delta_o^2}\left(\sigma^2 + \overline{y}^2\right)$ (15.2)		$A = 450$ DM $\quad$ (15.3) $\Delta_o = \text{USL} - \overline{y}$	
Present	Approximate Uniform	$3^2 + \dfrac{7^2}{12}$	58.88 DM		
Optimized	Skewed Normal	$.5^2 + .7^2$	3.33 DM	55.55 DM	5,555,000 DM

Table 8. Expected # Defects/Product

Defect Type	Present	Optimum
Class 1	.20	0.00
Class 2	.30	.22
Class 3	8.30	.30

Q & A

Q. This is a good case study. Is this the 1986 Taguchi Application award winner?

A. Yes. An L_{18} orthogonal array was used, allowing the inclusion of many control factors. Quality was improved and a great monetary savings resulted.

Q. How are ten control factors assigned in an L_{18} orthogonal array when it only has eight columns?

A. There are four 3-level factors and six 2-level factors. To assign 2-level factors in a 3-level column, the array must be modified using the combination design. The modification is made using columns seven and eight. Two 2-level factors provide four possible combinations, D_1F_1, D_1F_2, D_2F_1, D_2F_2 (combination D_2F_2 was dropped from the experiment). A new 3-level factor was created using the three remaining levels.

$$D_1F_1$$
$$D_2F_1$$
$$D_1F_2$$

Column seven is shown twice to reflect the three combinations of *DF* used. Factors *H* and *I* were assigned to column eight using the same technique.

Q. Multivariables analysis is used. What is that?

A. There is some inconsistency of technical terms used in Taguchi Methods. Different books use their own translation. I think people should follow the terms translated by someone earlier unless the terms are incorrect. This is not the place to show originality by creating new terms. That makes for confusion. For this type of characteristic, Dr. Genichi Taguchi calls it multiattribute, not multivariable.

Q. What are multiattributes?

A. They are classified integers or countable classified numbers, but the total numbers are different from case to case. In this case, the number of defects in each class is different from run to run.

16. HIGH VOLTAGE, HIGH TEMPERATURE WIRE STRIP-FORCE OPTIMIZATION

D. Bernstein and M. Koulopoulos
ITT Suprenant

This paper examines strip-force problems associated with one type of high-voltage, high-temperature wire used in the electronic OEM marketplace. Variability of strip-force is the primary cause of rejection. The objective was to minimize strip-force variation around a target value of 20 ± 10 lb. An L_{27} orthogonal array was selected to determine the optimum parameter values that cause variation between insulation materials and the metal conductors. The experiment was conducted, optimum settings selected, and a confirmation run executed. The result of optimization was an improvement from a condition in which 5.5% of the product was in specification to a C_{pk} of 1.5. As a result of bringing the process under control, an annual savings in material and production costs of $100,000 was achieved.

1. INTRODUCTION: THE STRIP-FORCE PROBLEM

ITT Suprenant is an electrical wire and cable manufacturer in a 375,000 ft. plant located in Clinton, Massachussetts. A large variety of wire and cable products is offered to the industrial market, including railroad locomotives, rapid transit, oil exploration, and engineered products, and the electronic market, including electronic OEM, Navy shipboard, defense electronic distribution.

Because of relatively short-run production and the large variety of complex products, losses tend to be high when compared to high-volume, less-complex wire and cable manufacturers.

From the *Second Symposium on Taguchi Methods*™, pp. 48–59, Copyright © 1984, American Supplier Institute, Inc., Dearborn, Michigan.

One of the most consistent and tenacious problems in manufacturing is a strip-force problem associated with one type of high voltage, high temperature wire used in the electronic OEM marketplace. This is a primary cause for rejection, both internally and externally, on many other types of wire experienced not only by Suprenant, but by the wire and cable industry as a whole. In addition to the wire and its problems is the continual improvement in wire-stripping machine design. These machines work best at higher speed when the strip-force variation is minimum.

2. Factors and Experimental Layout

Insulated wire is shipped on spools consisting of 5 to 10,000 ft. The wire is then fed into an automatic machine that cuts the wire to length and also removes a certain amount of insulation from each end of the wire. The amount of force to remove the insulation is a function of the adhesive force between the insulation and the wire. The spread in strip-force values must be controlled so the stripping machine will work.

The numerous factors that can cause variation in adhesive forces between insulation material and the metal conductor were analyzed.

A brainstorming session was held that included engineers, production, and quality and machine operators. Eleven factors were felt to have influence on the strip-force value and when incorporated in the process at various levels, an experiment could be designed that would yield some useful information. The factors and levels are shown in Table 1.

Table 1. Factors and Levels

Factors	I	II	III
C	700	1000	1300
A	A_1	A_2	A_3
B	.75	1.05	1.35
L	5	10	15
D	35	40	45
E	0	1/8	1/4
F	1	2	3
G	75	125	190
H	380	415	450
J	185	275	365
k	1	1.5	1.8

An L_{27} (3^{13}) orthogonal array was selected as the most desirable for the problem with factors as determined. In addition to the variables associated with each factor, it was also advantageous to determine the effect of time between two vital operations in the overall wire-making process. The two different time periods are shown as T_1 and T_2. In each time period, three tests were made on the finished experiment sample. The orthogonal array is shown in Table 2.

Table 2. L_{27} (3^{13}) Orthogonal Array

Factors	C	A	B	L	H	D	E	F	G	J	K	A	xH	T_1			T_2		
Exp. #	1	2	3	4	5	6	7	9	10	12	13	8	11	1	2	3	1	2	3
1	1	1	1	1	1	1	1	1	1	1	1	1	1	24	23	25	21	25	23
2	1	1	1	1	2	2	2	2	2	2	2	2	2	28	29	29	31	31	28
3	1	1	1	1	3	3	3	3	3	3	3	3	3	31	32	32	26	31	30
4	1	2	2	2	1	1	1	2	2	3	3	2	3	29	29	26	26	27	26
5	1	2	2	2	2	2	2	3	3	1	1	3	1	27	28	30	22	20	29
6	1	2	2	2	3	3	3	1	1	2	2	1	2	29	27	28	23	25	22
7	1	3	3	3	1	1	1	3	3	2	2	3	2	26	20	28	15	24	20
8	1	3	3	3	2	2	2	1	1	3	3	1	3	27	25	26	23	9	12
9	1	3	3	3	3	3	3	2	2	1	1	2	1	25	28	26	25	13	25
10	2	1	2	3	1	2	3	2	3	2	3	1	1	32	30	25	23	24	29
11	2	1	2	3	2	3	1	3	1	3	1	2	2	27	21	25	25	25	26
12	2	1	2	3	3	1	2	1	2	1	2	3	3	32	33	31	28	30	30
13	2	2	3	1	1	2	3	3	1	1	2	2	3	13	15	25	14	10	9
14	2	2	3	1	2	3	1	1	2	2	3	3	1	26	22	6	22	16	13
15	2	2	3	1	3	1	2	2	3	3	1	1	2	24	24	18	21	20	17
16	2	3	1	2	1	2	3	1	2	3	1	3	2	29	27	29	18	27	26
17	2	3	1	2	2	3	1	2	3	1	2	1	3	30	34	34	27	33	33
18	2	3	1	2	3	1	2	3	1	2	3	2	1	31	32	32	33	21	23
19	3	1	3	2	1	3	2	3	2	3	2	1	1	23	28	26	6	9	4
20	3	1	3	2	2	1	3	1	3	1	3	2	2	31	30	30	5	17	16
21	3	1	3	2	3	2	1	2	1	2	1	3	3	23	18	26	9	3	5
22	3	2	1	3	1	3	2	1	3	2	1	2	3	23	22	24	24	18	16
23	3	2	1	3	2	1	3	2	1	3	2	3	1	17	15	17	22	19	21
24	3	2	1	3	3	2	1	3	2	1	3	1	2	27	26	27	28	22	26
25	3	3	2	1	1	3	2	2	1	1	3	3	2	32	30	33	30	14	16
26	3	3	2	1	2	1	3	3	2	2	1	1	3	30	24	28	25	12	19
27	3	3	2	1	3	2	1	1	3	3	2	2	1	37	37	40	33	34	33

3. RESPONSE ANALYSIS AND ANALYSIS OF VARIANCE

Data gathered from the 27 experiments during a four-day period (four 10-hour shifts) was analyzed. Table 3 and Table 4 show the contribution of significant factors toward strip-force variability. Table 4 sites those factors affecting strip force as functions of T_1 and T_2 (the time between the last two finishing operations in the process.)

Table 3. Pooled ANOVA for Strip Force S/N[†]

Source	df	S	V	S'	ρ %
C_l	1	194.05	—	185.76	14.83
E_l	1	49.95	—	41.66	3.32
$A \times H_q$	2	45.56	—	28.98	2.04
B_l	1	566.96	—	558.67	44.61
B_q	1	107.48	—	99.19	7.92
L_q	1	49.59	—	41.30	3.30
H_l	1	36.41	—	28.12	2.25
J_q	1	29.65	—	21.56	1.70
G	2	48.21	—	31.63	3.19
(e)	(15)	(124.494)	(8.29)	(215.684)	(17.22)
T	26	1252.55		1252.55	100.00

[†]ANOVA table derived from:

$$\text{S/N Ratio Nominal-the-Best} = 10 \log \frac{1}{n} \left[\frac{(S_m - V_e)}{V_e} \right] \quad (16.1)$$

From Table 3, factors B and C were significant contributors to strip force variation. These are the factors to be improved from a variance point of view.

Secondly, the ANOVA table for time sensitivity (Table 4) shows those factors that are significant in terms of time. The major contributor in this case is factor B, but several others are also significant. Time between the final two processing operations is important, as is the maximum time for manufacturing operations. The maximum time for manufacturing purpose will be subsequently determined by further analysis.

Table 4. Pooled ANOVA for Finishing Operation (Sensitivity Analysis)

Source	df	S	V	S'	ρ %
C	2	244.33	—	217.75	2.60
A	2	527.82	—	501.24	5.98
B	2	2236.93	—	2210.35	26.37
H	2	360.11	—	333.53	3.98
G	2	560.48	—	533.90	6.37
K	2	205.48	—	178.90	2.13
T	1	1115.49	—	—	13.15
TxC	2	277.31	—	—	2.99
TxA	2	182.30	—	—	1.86
TxB	2	441.56	—	—	4.95
TxL	2	236.71	—	—	2.51
(e_3)	(140)	(1964.33)	(14.03)	(2258.96)	(26.95)
T	161	8382.27	—	8382.27	100.00

In addition to making the ANOVAs, response graphs were plotted. Each one of these was carefully reviewed, and the conclusions drawn from them contributed significantly to finding the optimum conditions.

Each significant factor was plotted and the effect of the three levels of each factor studied. The S/N Ratios were also plotted, and the effect of each factor level and the corresponding effect on variance was noted.

Finally, each factor was plotted with respect to its effect on strip-force as a function of time.

The graphs in Figures 1, 2, and 3 were of primary value in arriving at the optimum process conditions. A significant aspect of the response graphs is that all the effects of the factors were determined within the same experiment. This is a major departure from many corrective-action programs where one variable is introduced and all others kept constant.

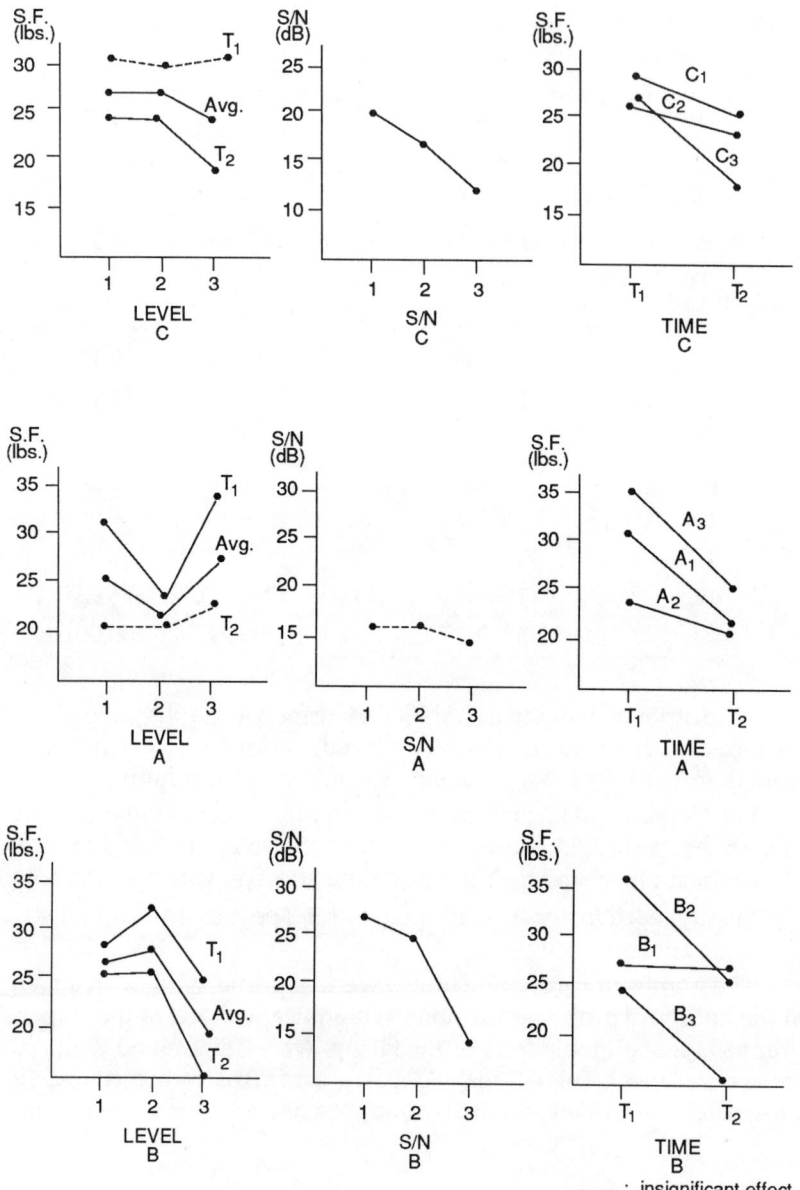

Figure 1. Response Graphs for Significant Factors
(Factors C, A, and B)

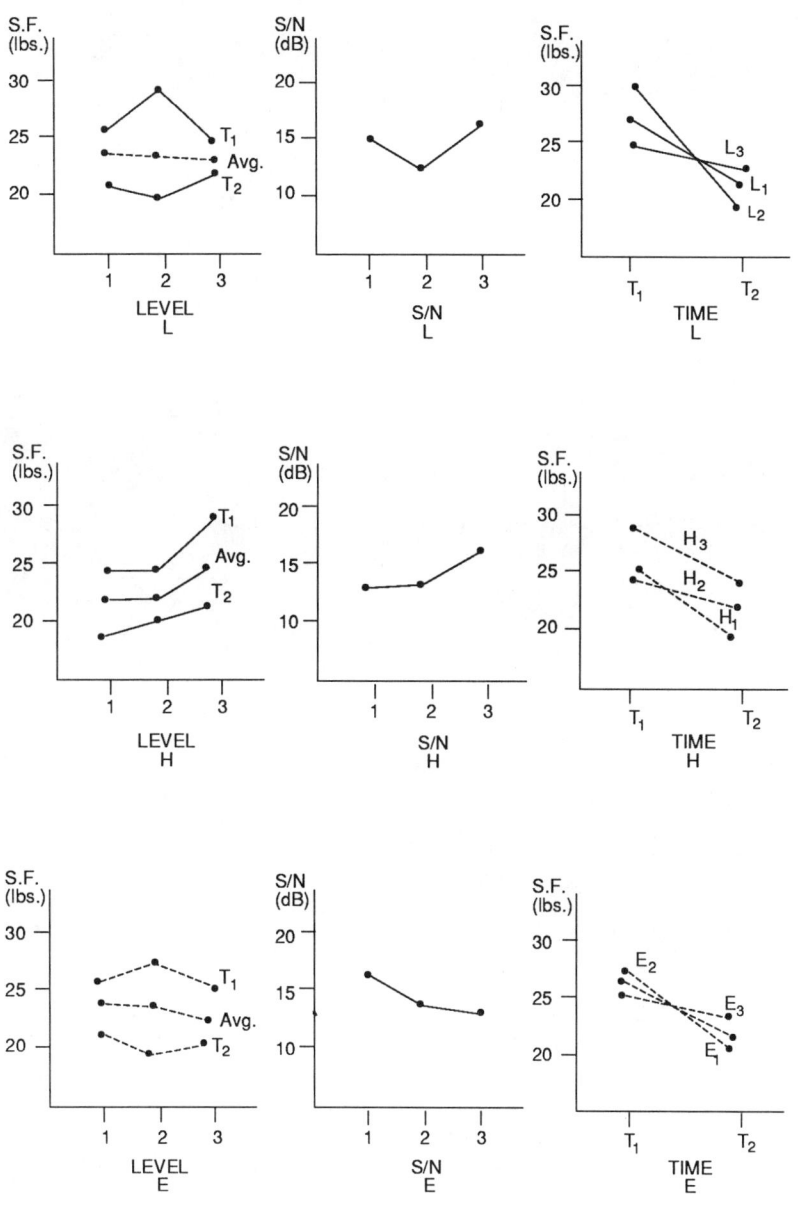

Figure 2. Response Graphs for Significant Factors (Factors *L*, *H*, and *E*)

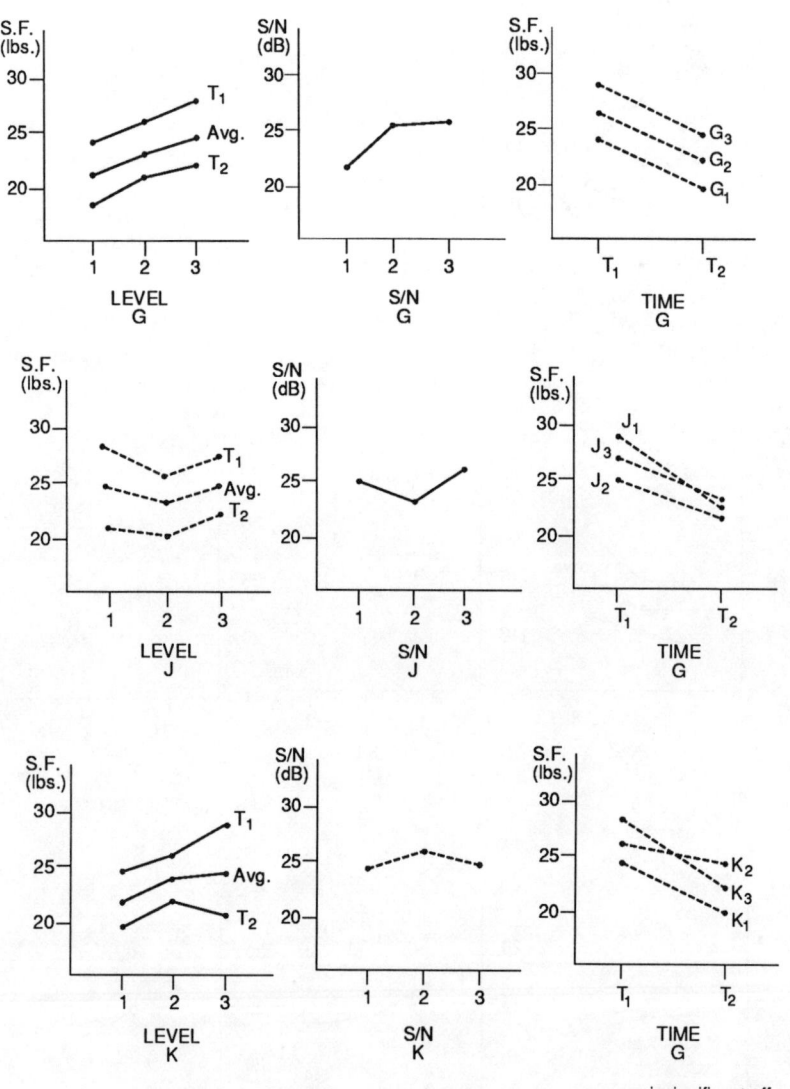

Figure 3. Response Graphs for Significant Factors
(Factors G, J, and K)

4. Optimization and Confirmation

The optimum condition after analysis is shown in Table 5.

Table 5. Optimum Condition after Analysis

Parameters	A	B	C	D	E	F	G	H	J	K	L
Present Condition	A_1	B_2	C_2	D_2	E_1	F_1	G_2	H_2	J_1	K_2	L_2
Optimum Condition	A_2	B_1	C_1	D_3	E_1	F_1	G_1	H_3	J_3	K_1	L_3

Under the optimum parameter levels, confirmation and a short-term capability study showed the following results which were within the confidence limits of the estimated value (Figure 4).

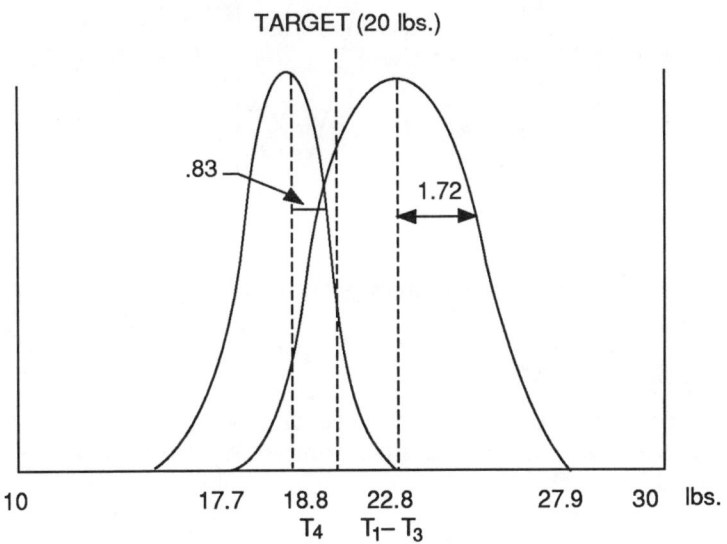

$$C_{pk} = \frac{30 - 22.8}{3 \times 1.72} = 1.4 \tag{16.2}$$

where, $\sigma = 1.72$ lbs., Avg. = 22.8 lbs.

Figure 4. Strip Force Distribution—Confirmation Experiment Results

5. Quality Improvement in Strip-Force

Figure 5 shows the overall improvement in strip-force made as a result of this experiment. It also shows that the variability has been improved and the average is centered close to the target value.

In addition to having more information relative to the causes of strip-force variation was the time window between the final two processes. This was very significant in that the window was enlarged, offering much more flexibility for manufacturing to schedule the machines to do the last operation.

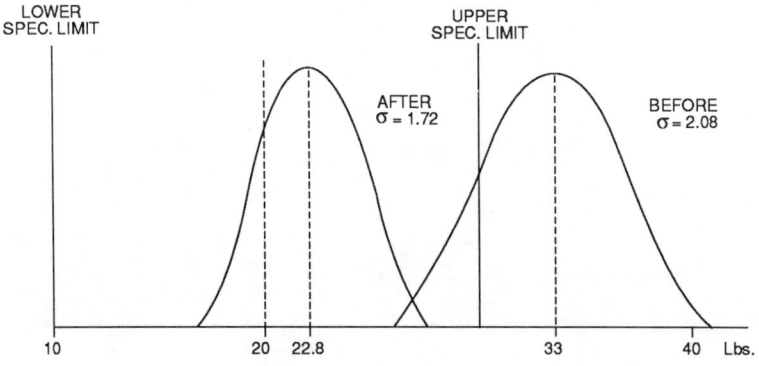

Figure 5. Overall Improvement in Strip-Force

6. Conclusion

The strip-force problem has been a major customer complaint, as well as a cause of high manufacturing losses. During the last several years this has been a very annoying, unresolved problem. As higher-speed machines are developed, the window of strip-force values seems to continually decrease. This places increasing demands on consistent manufacturing processing.

Numerous theories were expounded as to what the culprit was that caused the problem. Many changes were made (one at a time) along the way as we try to stabilize the strip-force value around some mutually acceptable level. Stability did not seem to be within our grasp.

Quality engineering looks at the total situation at one time. The influence of certain factors along with their relative impact is a tremendous guiding piece of information, which is the standard output of this technique.

Results confirm that under optimum conditions this process improved from a condition where 5.5% of the product was in specification limits to a C_{pk} of 1.5. This has also had a significant effect on material and production costs, resulting in approximate savings of $100,000 per year.

We now know the factors that require close control. We know where to invest funds should we want to refine the process further. Most of all we know the technique is a powerful tool for learning what factors vary and to what degree they vary within a given process.

Confidence in our capability to produce a product within specified strip-force limits has been readily restored.

Q & A

Q. In this case, is the objective to move the current average of 33 lb. to 20 lb.?

A. Yes. The major objective is to find the factors that are significant in affecting the mean. Therefore, analysis of the mean has a higher priority.

Q. Is it necessary to convert raw data into decibel units?

A. If there is approximately one figure difference between data, it is permissible to use raw data.

Q. Why is this?

A. When the numbers vary considerably, you will find poor additivity. In such cases, it is better to convert the data into a logarithmic function for better additivity.

Q. In the graphs, S/N Ratios and two kinds of raw data are exhibited. Why?

A. The two kinds of raw data show the same thing. In graphs, we need to show the factors that are significant to the S/N Ratio and the factors that are significant to the mean but insignificant to the S/N Ratio.

Q. Are control factor levels quite different before and after the experiment?

A. Among the 11 control factors, only two factors were correct before the experiment. I still remember the presenter of this study saying, "We thought we were experts, but Dr. Taguchi told us we were not."

Q. It was a huge success to improve the yield from 5.5% to 100%. Any comments?

A. This company was competing with two other companies. After this study, quality was dramatically improved, so the buyer designated this company as the single source. This means that an annual sale of $20 million was secured.

17. Optimization of Bond Strength and Contact Using Taguchi Methods

Dr. Pirrung
Automotive Division, ITT SWF

A Taguchi Methods application to a R&D project was developed with the objective to optimize bond strength and contact assistance involving the mounting of an integrated circuit on a metallized glass substrate material. Multiple quality characteristics were analyzed (physcial and electrical). This experiment served as a proving ground for the usefulness of Taguchi Methods in R&D applications. There was a surprising result: The copper conductor is far superior to nickel in resistance and does not affect bond strength at all. The development engineer who designed this experiment is confident that the results represent an optimization of crucial quality characteristics.

1. Introduction

The experiment described in this presentation is an R & D project concerned with developing an I.C.-controlled LCD dashboard display.

2. Objectives and Quality Characteristics

In this product's design, the I.C. chip that controls the display functions is to be mounted on a glass substrate. The mounting technique is to simply attach the I.C. posts with adhesive to the conducting paths deposited on a glass substrate. There are two quality characteristics that must be optimized: 1) the bonding strength and 2) the electrical resistance of the bond.

From the *Fourth Symposium on Taguchi Methods*™, pp. 305–316, Copyright © 1986, American Supplier Institute, Inc., Dearborn, Michigan.

3. Factors and Experimental Layout

R & D engineering personnel and representatives from manufacturing conducted brainstorming for four hours to design an experiment that would reveal which factors contribute toward the optimization of the quality characteristics.

The experimental design is summarized in the tables below.

Table 1. Factors and Factor Levels

	Level 1	Level 2	Level 3	Level 4
A. Adhesive Type	D_1	H-20-E	88-1	H-20E-175
B. Cure Time	90 min. @ 90° C	60 min. @ 120° C		
C. Conductor Mat'l	Cu	Ni		
D. Polyurethane Coating on Assembly	Yes	No		
E. I.C. Post Coating	Tin	Silver		

Since a four-level factor is present, yet only seven degrees of freedom are required, a multi-level arrangement was used to modify a standard L_8 orthogonal array into the required form. The resulting experimental array is shown in Table 2.

Table 2. Layout and Data Format

L_8	A B C D E 1 2 3 4 5	Bond Strength (pounds)	η	Bond Resistance (ohms)	η
1	1 1 1 1 1	$y_{1,1} \cdots y_{1,20}$	η_1	$y_{1,1} \cdots y_{1,10}$	η_1
2	1 2 2 2 2		η_2		η_2
3	2 1 1 2 2		η_3		η_3
4	2 2 2 1 1		η_4		η_4
5	3 1 2 1 2		η_5		η_5
6	3 2 1 2 1		η_6		η_6
7	4 1 2 2 1		η_7		η_7
8	4 2 1 1 2	$y_{8,1} \cdots y_{8,20}$	η_8	$y_{8,1} \cdots y_{8,10}$	η_8

The bond strength is to be tested by pulling the bonded I.C. post off by a standard tensile strength meter and measuring the force it took to break each post free. The bond resistance is measured with a standard resistance meter.

One I.C. chip is bonded per experiment. Every second I.C. chip post is tested for bond strength, every fourth for bond resistance (bond resistance is a more stable and repeatable quality characteristic). This will result in 20 repetitions for bond strength and 10 repetitions for resistance data.

4. ANALYSIS OF RESULTS

The following tables show the experimental results. Table 3 shows the data and S/N Ratios for resistance. Table 4 is a response table showing the factor level averages. Table 5 gives the data and S/N Ratios for bond strength. Table 6 is a response table that gives the factor level averages for mean bond strength and S/N Ratio analysis.

1. Resistance Data
   See Table 3 (on following page).

Table 4. Level Mean Tables

	Regular (Ω)				S/N (dB)			
	Level				Level			
Factor	1	2	3	4	1	2	3	4
A	242.0	317.3	2,372.5	421.9	−38.43	−35.68	−46.76	−37.38
B	1,398.2	278.7			−42.74	−36.39		
C	8.9	1,668.0			−18.55	−60.57		
D	1,346.9	330.9			−42.26	−36.86		
E	372.8	1,304.1			−39.69	−39.43		

Optimum Levels:
  Regular: A_1, B_2, C_1, D_2, E_1
  S/N: A_2, B_2, C_1, D_2

2. Bond-Strength Data
   See Table 5.

Table 3. Data and S/N Ratios for Resistance

	A	B	C	D	E	Resistance (ohms)										η
	1	2	3	4	5											
1	1	1	1	1	1	20	10	20	10	10	10	10	10	20	20	−23.42
2	1	2	2	2	2	470	470	470	470	470	470	470	470	470	470	−53.44
3	2	1	1	2	2	7	5	5	6	5	6	5	5	6	6	−15.02
4	2	2	2	1	1	800	560	530	560	450	1,110	600	660	460		−56.34
5	3	1	2	1	2	4,740	4,730	4,730	4,740	4,730	4,740	4,730	4,730	4,730	4,730	−73.51
6	3	2	1	2	1	10	10	10	10	10	10	10	10	10	10	−20.00
7	4	1	2	2	1	1,180	530	820	380	870	1,190	370	970	1,180	950	−58.99
8	4	2	1	1	2	9	8	8	6	5	5	5	4	4		−15.76

$$\eta = -10\log \frac{1}{n}\left(y_1^{\,2} + y_2^{\,2} + \dots y_n^{\,2} \right) \qquad (17.1)$$

Run 1: $-10\log \dfrac{1}{10}\left(20^2 + 10^2 + 20^2 + 10^2 + 10^2 + 10^2 + 10^2 + 10^2 + 20^2 + 20^2 \right) = -23.42$

Table 5. Bond Strength Data

A	B	C	D	E	Bond Strength (pounds)											η
1	2	3	4	5												
1	1	1	1	1	640	580	460	880	1,000	620	700	880	560	600	930	56.35
1	1	2	2	2	400	530	620	580	570	550	550	610	610	600	480	54.67
2	1	1	2	2	540	750	630	620	680	640	550	580	580	560	480	55.40
2	2	2	1	1	800	940	940	1,000	1,000	1,000	1,000	1,000	1,000	800	680	59.09
3	1	2	1	2	840	1,000	1,000	1,000	1,000	570	1,000	1,000	1,000	840	1,000	58.98
3	2	1	2	1	800	750	750	880	820	850	830	820	920	800	630	57.99
4	1	2	2	1	490	600	600	660	550	490	600	540	490	510	480	54.67
4	2	1	1	2	600	980	1,000	1,000	1,000	1,000	1,000	1,000	1,000	1,000	950	59.30

$$\eta = -10 \log \left[\frac{1}{n} \left(\frac{1}{y_1^2} + \frac{1}{y_2^2} + \cdots \frac{1}{y_n^2} \right) \right] \quad (17.2)$$

Run 4: $-10 \log \left[\frac{1}{11} \left(\frac{1}{800^2} + \frac{1}{940^2} + \frac{1}{940^2} + \frac{1}{1000^2} + \frac{1}{1000^2} + \frac{1}{1000^2} + \frac{1}{1000^2} + \frac{1}{1000^2} + \frac{1}{1000^2} + \frac{1}{800^2} + \frac{1}{680^2} \right) \right] = 59.09$

Table 6. Factor Level Averages (Bond Strength)

Factor	Regular (Pounds)				S/N (dB)			
	Level				Level			
	1	2	3	4	1	2	3	4
A	641.0	739.5	835.3	741.5	55.51	57.25	58.49	56.96
B	722.4	756.2			56.34	57.76		
C	Insig.	Insig.			57.26	56.84		
D	884.1	594.5			58.43	55.67		
E	Insig.	Insig.			57.01	57.09		

Optimum Levels:
    Regular: A_3, B_2, D_1
    S/N: A_3, B_2, D_1

Table 7. Summary of Analytical Results

	Type of Analysis	Optimum Level of Significant Factors				
		A	B	C	D	E
Resistance	Regular	1	2	1	2	1
	Lower-is-Best S/N	2	2	1	2	—
Bond Strength	Regular	3	2	—	1	—
	Higher-is-Best S/N	3	2	—	1	—

5. Optimization and Estimation

Trade-Off Decisions:

1. Factor A: Choose A_2

The resistance of a circuit is a more crucial quality characteristic than the bond force. In addition, looking at the S/N Ratio values, when the bond strength is traded to A_2 (from A_3) a loss of 1.25 dB occurs (and 95.8 bonds). If the other option were taken, and A_2 was traded for A_3 in resistance analysis, a loss of 11.1 dB would be suffered and 2,055 Ω increase in resistance).

2. Factor D: Choose D_1

The % significance of D in resistance analysis is very low (1.52% in the S/N analysis. In bond-strength analysis, D is over 50% significant in both cases. The optimum D for bond strength must be chosen.

Process estimate (at optimized levels):

Resistance:

$$\hat{\mu} = \overline{A}_2 + \overline{B}_2 + \overline{C}_1 + \overline{D}_1 + \overline{E}_1 - 4\overline{T} = 0 \pm 83.1 \text{ ohms} \qquad (17.3)$$

$$\hat{\mu}(S/N) = \overline{A}_2 + \overline{B}_2 + \overline{C}_1 + \overline{D}_1 - 3\overline{T} = -14.2 \pm 4.3 \text{ dB} \qquad (17.4)$$

Bond Force:

$$\hat{\mu} = \overline{A}_2 + \overline{B}_2 + \overline{D}_1 - 2\overline{T} = 901.2 \pm 43.6 \text{ pounds} \qquad (17.5)$$

$$\hat{\mu}(S/N) = \overline{A}_2 + \overline{B}_2 + \overline{D}_1 - 2\overline{T} = 59.34 \pm 1.6 \text{ dB} \qquad (17.6)$$

6. Conclusion

There was a surprising result. The effect of different conductors had not been evaluated, so it was a valuable improvement to find out that the copper conductor is very superior to nickel in resistance and does not affect bond strength at all. Resistivities at optimum experimental conditions have been significantly lower than in the previous trials. The result of the polyurethane coating increasing bond strength was also noted with great interest.

This experiment served as a proving ground for usefulness of Taguchi Methods in R & D applications. Everyone involved with the project became an enthusiastic proponent of designed experimentation. The development engineer who designed this experiment is confident that the results represent an optimization of the crucial quality characteristics.

Q & A

Q. This case is easy to understand and would make a good textbook example. Don't you agree?

A. Yes, but it is better to use a larger orthogonal array so that more control factors may be assigned.

Q. What if there are no more control factors?

A. Even if there are no more factors, a larger array is more desirable. Another point is that there are no noise factors. The variability between repetitions is not very large, in the resistance data. A noise factor, such as deterioration might be considered.

Q. Was a confirmatory experiment performed?

A. No, but there were no surprises during the initial trial.

Q. There was a tremendous reduction in product development time and cost. Have other companies realized similar results?

A. Most of the case studies in the U.S. have been of the problem-solving type. I hope there will be more R&D type case studies. For example, Aerojet Ordnance in California used Taguchi Methods to generate a technical database.

Q. There is an analysis of mean for both bond strength and bond resistance. Are both necessary?

A. No. S/N Ratios for both smaller-the-better and larger-the-better incorporate mean and variability. We need only the S/N Ratio to analyze the results. However, it is alright to conduct an analysis on the mean to get a feel for what the mean will be under the optimum configuration obtained by S/N Ratio analysis.

18. Process Development of a Parallel Gap Bonder: Improvement of the Bonding of Ceramic Chip Resistors in Microwave Circuit Boards

Eric Schild and Tim Pishko
Texas Instruments, Inc.

The objective of this study was to develop one bonder process schedule that would provide acceptable pull strength for bonding chip resistors to microwave circuit boards. Excessively tight controls on material plating thickness demand a process with a consistent output. An L_{16} orthogonal array was used to investigate five control factors, three signal factors, and one noise factor. The success of this experiment was realized with the development of a schedule allowing less stringent controls on plating thickness, in addition to using the same bonding parameters for tin-to-gold and tin-to-copper bonding. Allowing a wider range of plating thickness should result in an annual savings of $10,000. The reduction sensitivity to operator and machine variation will increase bonding yield for an annual cost savings of $33,000.

1. Introduction

In the manufacturing or microwave circuit boards (MCBs) for the High Speed Anti-Radar Missile (HARM) program, one of the critical assembly operations is the bonding of ceramic chip resistors to copper circuit lines on the MCB face.

The procedure used for bonding the resistors involves two major steps. The first is the bonding of the tin-plated nickel leads to each end of the thin film ceramic resistors. The leads are 0.040 in. wide, 0.072 in. long and either 0.0005 or 0.001 in. thick. Two leads are attached to each resistor. The bond surface on the resistor is composed of plated gold over a layer of sputter deposited gold. The resistor bodies are 0.010 in. thick and 0.045 by 0.045 in. in size.

From the *Fourth Symposium on Taguchi Methods*™, pp. 722–743, Copyright © 1986, American Supplier Institute, Inc., Dearborn, Michigan.

The second half of the assembly procedure is the bonding of the resistors to the MCBs. The boards are made of copper, laminated onto a layer of a ceramic-filled polytetrafluoroethylene (PTFE) material. The copper is imaged and chemically etched to produce the desired circuit pattern (Figure 1).

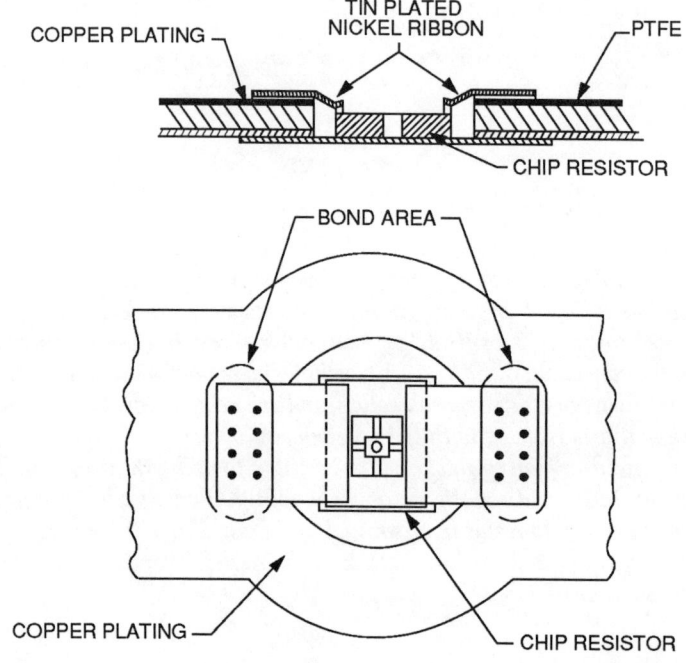

Figure 1. Ceramic Chip Resistor Bonded to Copper Circuit Line

2. Process Description

For both bonding operations, the same bond equipment is employed, this being a parallel gap bonder. This bonding technique utilizes two electrodes that are positioned side by side and separated by either an air or ceramic insulator. Fusing is produced between mating surfaces due to the joule heating that results from the passage of current from one electrode through the bond region to the second electrode. This technique is noted for its short bond times and precise control of bond energy. In this application, the heat generated by the bonder causes the tin plating to reflow and fuse with the substrate material, this being either gold or copper. Thus, the bond joint displays an appearance similar to that of a solder joint with the formation of a solder-like tin fillet.

For the primary bond process variables affecting the strength of the bond joint, it was decided that voltage, time (duration), and force must be strictly controlled to produce the desired results. Furthermore, bond-tip size and electrode gap spacing may be varied depending on the geometry of the surface being bonded. Other critical factors affecting the strength of the bond are machine variations, surface cleanliness, composition of surfaces being joined, and operator technique.

Stringent quality requirements have been defined for both the bonding of the leads to the resistors and the subsequent process of bonding the resistors to the circuit boards. The requirement for bonding the tin-plated nickel leads to the chip resistors are that the joint must withstand a lateral shear force of 10 oz. and also display the visual characteristics of a good-quality bond joint. These visual characteristics include visible bond impression, no evidence of lifted lead, no burn marks, and the presence of an acceptable tin fillet about the perimeter of the bonded leads. For the bonding of the lead to the copper etch, the same quality criteria apply. However, a quantitative requirement as to the strength of the copper/tin bond joint has not yet been formally defined.

From the bonding done to date, it was found that two unique bond schedules were needed to achieve the quality requirements. The factors that characterize each schedule are voltage, time, force, electrode type, and electrode spacing. The first schedule is used for bonding the tin-plated nickel leads to the gold-plated pads of the chip resistors. The second schedule is employed for bonding the tin-plated leads to the copper circuitry of the microwave circuit board. The reason for two schedules stemmed primarily from the differences in the materials and geometries of the components being bonded. In the case of the tin to gold-plated bonding operation, the smallness of the bond pads and the fragile nature of the chip resistors required that bond voltage be strictly controlled. Excessive force could lead to cracking of the ceramic substrate. Too high a voltage could cause the tin to flow excessively over the bonding area and onto the active area of the resistor, ultimately affecting resistor electrical properties. For bonding the tin-plated leads to the copper circuity, experience has shown that bond force and voltage again must be tightly controlled. Because of copper's tendency to readily form oxide, oxide removal prior to bonding was also found to be critical in attaining high-quality bond joints.

For both applications, it has been found, again from experience, that the thickness of the plating on the tin-plated ribbon is a critical variable.

Too thin of a plating thickness can prohibit the formation of a suitable bond joint unless excessive heat and force are employed, which greatly increases the risk of burns or damage to the substrate materials.

At the other extreme, too thick of a tin-plating can cause the tin to flow too freely, possibly contaminating adjacent areas of the circuitry or causing objectionable splatter of the tin-plating material.

Thus, a very tight process window has been defined for the thickness of the tin plating on the nickel lead material. Tight control of tin-plating thickness has resulted in improved yields for the bonding processes. Unfortunately, strict plating control has also proven to be a difficult task from an electroplating standpoint, resulting in increased plating costs and a decrease in the yields of plated lead materials.

3. Experimental Objectives

Several key objectives pertaining to the bonding process were evaluated. These objectives are as follows:

1. Develop a bond schedule that works successfully across a wider range of tin-plating thicknesses
2. Develop a bond schedule that is universal with respect to both the operator and the bond machine
3. Develop a schedule that works equally well for bonding tin to gold and for welding tin to copper
4. Define bonder parameters that would provide optimum bond strength and meet visual workmanship criteria
5. Determine the bonder process variables that have the greatest impact on bond strength
6. Develop an understanding of Taguchi Methods.

4. Quality Characteristics and Selection of Factors

As mentioned previously, the bond-joint quality is scrutinized both quantitatively and qualitatively via pull strength and visual appearance. In this experiment, both criteria were employed to judge bond quality. However, pull strength was the final indicator of schedule performance. The visual criteria were used for determining the levels of each factor to ensure that this characteristic would be satisfied across the entire experimental window.

Table 1 provides a listing of the factors and levels to be evaluated in this experiment. Note that these factors are categorized into the two main variable groups: Control and noise factors. The number of Taguchi levels chosen for the control factors were based on the linear nature of each factor with respect to pull strength.

Table 1. Factors and Levels

Control Factors	Levels			
Electrode Gap (EG)	0.001 in.		0.004 in.	
Electrode Size (ES)	0.004 x 0.008		0.008 x 0.015	
Duration (D)	10 millisec.		13 millisec.	
Voltage (V)	1.25 Volts		1.35 Volts	
Force (F)	575 grams		800 grams	
Signal Factors	Levels			
Plating Thickness (PT)	500 µin.	70 µin.	125 µin.	250 µin.
Bond Substrate (BS)	Gold		Copper	
Machine (M)	1		2	
Noise Factor	Levels			
Operator (O)	1		2	

5. EXPERIMENTAL DESIGN

After reviewing historic bond data, it was concluded that five one-factor interactions may exist. The interactions include: $EG \times D$, $ES \times D$, $EG \times V$, $ES \times F$, and $V \times D$. With this information, it was decided that in order to satisfy the required number of estimates (degrees of freedom), an L_{16} (2^{15}) orthogonal array was needed for the inner array. The outer array, on the other hand, was determined based on the four Signal-to-Noise (S/N) factors. An L_8 orthogonal array was selected.

The linear graph used for assigning the factors and interactions to the various columns of the L_{16} orthogonal array is illustrated in Figure 2. The final experimental design is given in Table 2.

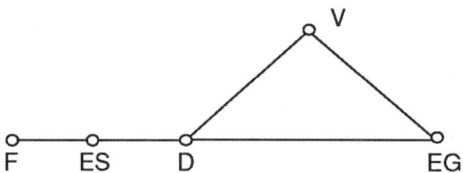

Figure 2. Linear Graph

The experiment was run using production equipment and materials. Specifically, the tin-plated nickel ribbon was taken directly from production supplies. The strap was then bonded on one of two Hughes MCW-550 bonders using ESQ-815-00 and ESQ-048-00 electrodes. The operators were two technicians from process engineering who had a combined experience base of 20 years on the bonder and comparable equipment. They were instructed to bond their straps to a either a clean, gold thin-film chip resistor or to a clean laminated copper-circuit board as directed by the experimental setup in Table 2. In order to prevent variation due to multiple bond impressions, the technicians were also asked to only make one weld hit per strap side.

Because of the difficulty of changing electrodes, the experiment was partially randomized on the electrode size factor. Furthermore, two repetitions were taken at each setup.

6. Analysis of Variance on the Signal-to-Noise Ratio

The actual pull-strength results are provided in the appendix. Before the analysis of variance (ANOVA) was run, the data was transformed into Taguchi's S/N Ratio using larger-the-better characteristics:

$$*S/N = -10 \log \left[\frac{1}{n} \sum_{i=1}^{n} \frac{1}{y_i^2} \right] \qquad (18.1)$$

*See Appendix to the Study, p. 279.

Table 2. Experimental Design

				INNER ARRAY												OUTER ARRAY							
															O	1	2	2	1	2	1	1	2
															M	1	2	2	1	1	2	2	1
			EG		ES		EG	V			F				BS	1	1	2	2	2	2	1	1
			×		×		×	×			×				PT	1	1	2	2	3	3	4	4
	EG	D	D	ES	e	D	e	V	V	D	F	e	e	e	ES								
1	1	1	1	1	1	1	1	1	1	1	1	1	1	1	1								
2	1	1	1	1	1	1	1	2	2	2	2	2	2	2	2								
3	1	1	1	2	2	2	2	1	1	1	1	2	2	2	2								
4	1	1	1	2	2	2	2	2	2	2	2	1	1	1	1								
5	1	2	2	1	1	2	2	1	1	2	2	1	1	2	2								
6	1	2	2	1	1	2	2	2	2	1	1	2	2	1	1								
7	1	2	2	2	2	1	1	1	1	2	2	2	2	1	1								
8	1	2	2	2	2	1	1	2	2	1	1	1	1	2	2								
9	2	1	2	1	2	1	2	1	2	1	2	1	2	1	2								
10	2	1	2	1	2	1	2	2	1	2	1	2	1	2	1								
11	2	1	2	2	1	2	1	1	2	1	2	2	1	2	1								
12	2	1	2	2	1	2	1	2	1	2	1	1	2	1	2								
13	2	2	1	1	2	2	1	1	2	2	1	1	2	2	1								
14	2	2	1	1	2	2	1	2	1	1	2	2	1	1	2								
15	2	2	1	2	1	1	2	1	2	2	1	2	1	1	2								
16	2	2	1	2	1	1	2	2	1	1	2	1	2	2	1								

The results are listed in Table 3.

Table 3. Calculated S/N Ratio

Treatment No.	S/N Ratio	Treatment No.	S/N Ratio
1	11.9576	9	7.2535
2	11.8558	10	12.0126
3	35.1423	11	40.7974
4	35.7907	12	35.1979
5	32.8510	13	11.9895
6	29.8817	14	25.5196
7	42.7841	15	25.4991
8	37.8277	16	22.9139

The ANOVA of the S/N Ratios is given in Table 4. Many of the main effects as well as the interaction effects were found to be insignificant at the 95% confidence level. Therefore, the sum of square terms of these effects were pooled with the error sum of square.

Table 4. Analysis of Variance Table

Source	df	S	V	S'	ρ(%)
EG	1	202.402	202.402	179.426	9.28346
D	(1)	96.3285	96.3285	—	—
ES	1	1099.44	1099.44	1076.47	55.6963
V	(1)	0.46428	0.46428	—	—
F	(1)	25.6480	25.6480	—	—
EG x D	1	209.796	209.796	186.820	9.66601
ES x D	1	352.177	352.177	329.201	17.0327
V x EG	(1)	19.1051	19.1051	—	—
V x D	(1)	0.68599	0.68599	—	—
F x ES	(1)	0.56976	0.56976	—	—
(e)	(5)	109.933	21.9867	—	—
e	11	252.735	22.9759	160.831	8.32139
T	15	2116.55	—	1932.75	—

7. Determination of the Optimal Condition

As indicated in the ANOVA table, electrode gap and electrode size and their interactions with duration are the most significant effects influencing the S/N Ratio. Of these effects, electrode size and its interaction with duration contribute over 70% of the total variation. To better understand their relationship with the S/N Ratio, the level means were calculated for each of the main and interaction effects and are provided in both a tabular and graphical format in Table 5 and Figures 3 and 4.

Table 5. S/N Level Means

Factor	Level	
Electrode Gap	29.7614	22.6479
Duration	23.7510	28.6583
Electrode Size	17.9152	34.4941
Voltage	26.0343	26.3750
Force	24.9385	27.4707

Interactions		
Duration x Electrode Gap		
	0.001	0.004
10	23.6866	23.8153
13	35.8361	21.4805
Duration x Electrode Size		
	4 x 8	8 x 15
10	10.7699	36.7320
13	25.0604	32.2562

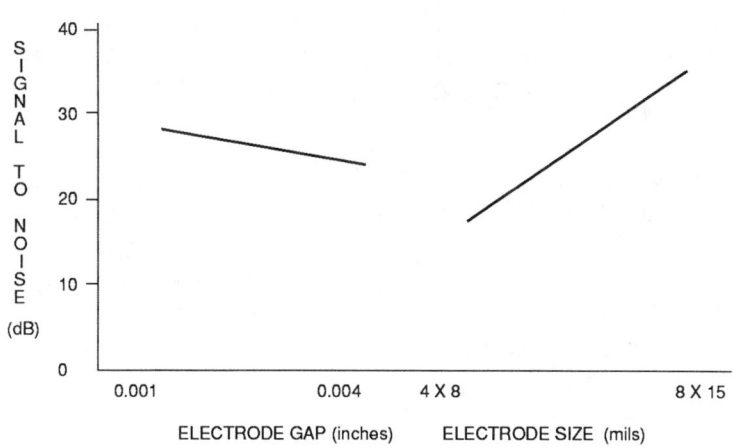

Figure 3. Response Graphs—S/N Level Means

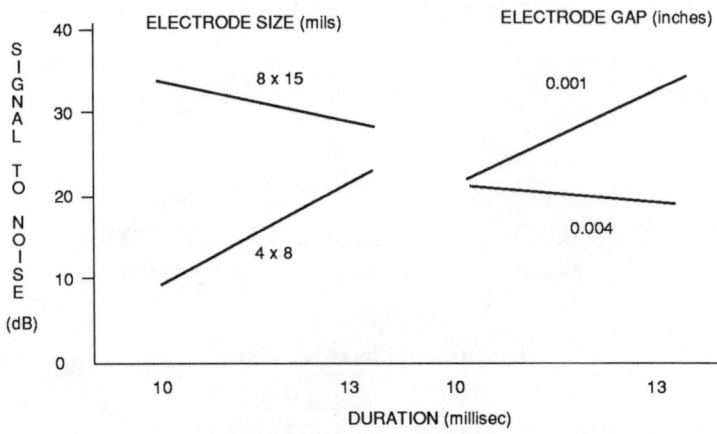

Figure 4. Response Graphs—Interactions

As becomes evident from the graphical displays of the significant effects, the best levels to select for these factors to maximize the S/N Ratio were EG_1, ES_2, and D_1. The selection of the low level of duration was based primarily on the $ES \times D$ interaction. Had we based it on the $EG \times D$ interaction, the high level of duration would have been chosen. Either case, though, would be satisfactory as long as the level of voltage were chosen correctly. Because of the effect of voltage and duration on solder flow and scorching, it is best not to run both factors at their high levels. Instead, it is better to run either $V_1 D_2$ or $V_2 D_1$. Hence, the optimum conditions as determined from this experiment are either $EG_1, ES_2 D_1 V_2$, or $EG_1 ES_2 D_2 V_1$.

8. Estimation and Confirmation

The true test of whether this experiment was successful in providing an optimum schedule that is robust against variation in ribbon-plating thickness, bonding media, machines, and operators is to compare it with the two existing bond schedules discussed in Section 2. Future work will include this comparison.

We can currently test the validity of this experiment to see whether or not the predicted optimum results can be generated in a follow-up experiment. The predicted mean S/N Ratio and its 95% confidence interval are given on the next page.

Predicted Range,

$$\hat{u} = \overline{T} + \overline{EG_1 D_1} + \overline{ES_2 D_1} - 2\overline{D_1} \quad (18.2)$$
$$= 26.20 + 23.6866 + 36.732 - 2(23.751)$$
$$= 39.12 \pm 5.9^*$$

$$* \text{ C. I.} = \pm \sqrt{\frac{F \times V_e}{n_e}} \quad F = F(.05, 1, 11) = 4.84, \quad (18.2)$$

$$n_e = \frac{16}{5} = 3.2$$

$$= \pm \sqrt{\frac{4.84 \times 22.979}{3.2}}$$

$$= \pm 5.9$$

Follow-up experiment:

$$n = 79, \, x = 293.1 \text{ gms}, \, s = 169.8 \text{ gms}, \, S/N = 43.3946 \text{ dB}$$

As can be seen, the S/N Ratio generated from the follow-up experiment does fall within the predicted limits of 39.12 ± 5.9 for the optimum conditions (EG_1, ES_2, D_1). Had they not fallen within the predicted range, the experimental results would be suspect in leading to the conclusion that other factors may be significant.

9. CONCLUSION

The major intent of this experiment was to develop a schedule that would allow for less stringent controls on plating thickness. This, as a result, would lessen the cost and increase the yield of producing tin-plated nickel strap. In this experiment, a schedule has been developed that accomplishes this objective and also allows the same bonding parameters to be used for tin-to-gold and tin-to-copper bonding. Moreover, the schedule is also robust against machine and operator variations.

Allowing a wider range of plating thicknesses to be used should reduce plating costs by $10,000 per year. Furthermore, by reducing the effect of operator and machine variation, the resistor-bonding yields should increase. These increases should result in cost saving of $33,000.

In this experiment, a question still looms as to whether it was feasible to create a schedule for both tin-to-gold and tin- to-copper bonding. It is thought that the properties of each bonding substrate may elicit different effects from the control factors. After observing the pull-strength data given in the appendix, it is evident that a significant difference exists between the levels of this factor. A simple comparison of means (t test at 95% confidence level) verified this conclusion. This indicates that bonding cases are different. However, can the tin-to-copper bonding be improved by choosing a different operating window?

Further work will attempt to address the differences between these two bonding conditions. The experimentation will focus on determining whether the operating window for tin-to-gold bonding is coincident with tin-to-copper bonding. The characteristics that will define these windows will be visual appearances and pull strength.

Appendix to the Study

Pull Strength—Raw Data

Treatment No.	1		2		3		4		5		6		7		8	
1	135	115	195	170	50	1	10	30	15	20	55	80	155	120	110	105
2	65	155	155	130	25	5	35	50	95	1	140	105	280	370	95	205
3	210	445	395	335	25	25	70	110	30	75	220	375	445	460	300	185
4	530	370	65	300	70	50	438	385	50	75	20	65	320	370	465	390
5	95	70	160	100	30	40	40	50	25	35	35	25	390	230	120	80
6	115	65	325	230	115	110	35	10	50	15	175	475	395	305	70	205
7	185	375	315	280	175	130	380	135	80	70	100	85	350	405	365	325
8	410	210	555	485	80	75	550	460	60	110	25	60	365	390	520	485
9	75	80	125	185	70	10	50	1	1	1	145	105	195	295	165	85
10	235	110	260	130	120	110	30	50	35	1	30	20	305	245	70	105
11	500	325	240	130	110	70	220	140	85	40	140	195	315	390	440	220
12	580	510	280	330	60	110	145	125	85	120	20	25	360	360	400	505
13	100	145	220	230	70	70	10	1	50	75	65	55	270	285	100	105
14	200	115	215	145	5	25	40	35	60	30	415	245	340	320	95	85
15	685	330	260	330	15	5	115	95	85	80	135	140	355	275	330	395
16	310	460	440	480	5	30	95	105	100	110	65	5	365	270	325	375

$$\eta = -10 \log \frac{1}{n} \left(\sum_{i=1}^{n} \frac{1}{y_i^2} \right) \tag{18.4}$$

Run 1: $-10 \log \frac{1}{16} \left(\frac{1}{135^2} + \frac{1}{115^2} + \frac{1}{195^2} + \frac{1}{170^2} + \frac{1}{50^2} + \frac{1}{1^2} + \frac{1}{10^2} + \frac{1}{30^2} + \right.$
$\left. + \frac{1}{15^2} + \frac{1}{20^2} + \frac{1}{55^2} + \frac{1}{80^2} + \frac{1}{155^2} + \frac{1}{120^2} + \frac{1}{110^2} + \frac{1}{105^2} \right)$

$= 11.95$

Q & A

Q. There are five interactions assigned in this L_{16} orthogonal array. Is this good or bad?

A. People in the United States have a tendency to include interactions. Dr. Genichi Taguchi states that it is not a good experiment if interactions show up to be significant. We should try to avoid interactions.

Q. What would you do in this case to minimize interactions?

A. Sliding the levels is one of the approaches. For example, interaction ESxD is significant. Factor ES is electrode size, and factor D is duration. A larger electrode gives more energy to the system. A longer duration also gives more energy. A smaller electrode with shorter duration might have less energy input. A larger electrode with a longer duration might have much more energy input. These two conditions might result in a worse result. This is due to an interaction between electrode size and time.

Sliding levels set the levels of a factor depending on the levels of another factor. When a larger electrode is used, we set the range of duration shorter; in the case of a smaller electrode, a longer duration is used. In this way, we can minimize interactions.

Q. The characteristic measured is pull strength. In a pull test, it may happen that the lead breaks and we get no data on pull force. In other words, there is no information. What could be done in this case?

A. This does not mean there is no information. When the pull force is greater than the strength of the lead, this gives us useful information; it tells us that the pull force is very large.

Q. Then how is data assigned in these cells so that data analysis is possible?

A. A certain number can be assigned for data analysis. Or in the case of the S/N Ratio, use a number that is three decibels larger than the largest S/N Ratio calculated in the experimental runs.

PART 4:
ELECTRICAL—PRODUCT

19. Improvement of the Design of a Power Supply Circuit

Joe Conticchio
ITT Avionics

The main objective of this exercise was to find the applicability of Taguchi Methods to power supply circuit design (by simulation). The secondary objective was to minimize the effect of voltage spike (10 KV) on critical nodes of a high-power supply circuit. Eleven design parameters were selected as controllable factors and assigned to an L_{12} array. The effects of eight design parameters were compounded and assigned as a three-level noise factor to the outer array. As a result of the 36 simulation runs, the successful reduction of voltage spike by a factor of 10 times was achieved. The use of Taguchi Methods in conjunction with computer simulation is a valuable asset for circuit designers.

1. Introduction

Among the more powerful benefits of the Taguchi technique is its ability to provide a scientific basis for which optimization experiments should be conducted. Significant parameters are varied in a pattern as dictated by orthogonal arrays. In the case of large multi-level parameters, the number of experiments is minimized by this experiment layout method. By a careful statistical analysis of the produced data, parameters that provide stability over large production schedules could be identified and optimized. Interactive effects between two parameters are easily identified in this type of analysis. These methods are very effective in those cases where performance-characteristic calculations are difficult, and the effect on any one, or several, of the components (parameters) on

284   PART 4: ELECTRICAL—PRODUCT

that characteristic is normally obtained through experimentation. The Taguchi techniques effectively structure these experiments. From this perspective, Taguchi Methods can be used together with other optimization methods to optimize an electronic circuit design.

2. Objective of the Experiment

To test and practice the Taguchi design of experiment approach in circuit-design optimization, an exercise case was selected, with the support of Avionics management team, from ASPJ high-voltage power supply.

To proceed with this exercise, a circuit from ASPJ high-voltage power supply that frequently failed was selected. Since there was no clear reason as to the cause of failure, the brainstorming group assumed that voltage spikes at certain nodes of the circuit probably caused the failure (Figure 1). Under this assumption, quality characteristics were selected with the objective of minimizing the effect of voltage spikes at nodes 22, 24, 7, and 4 of the circuits, including design parameter tolerance effects.

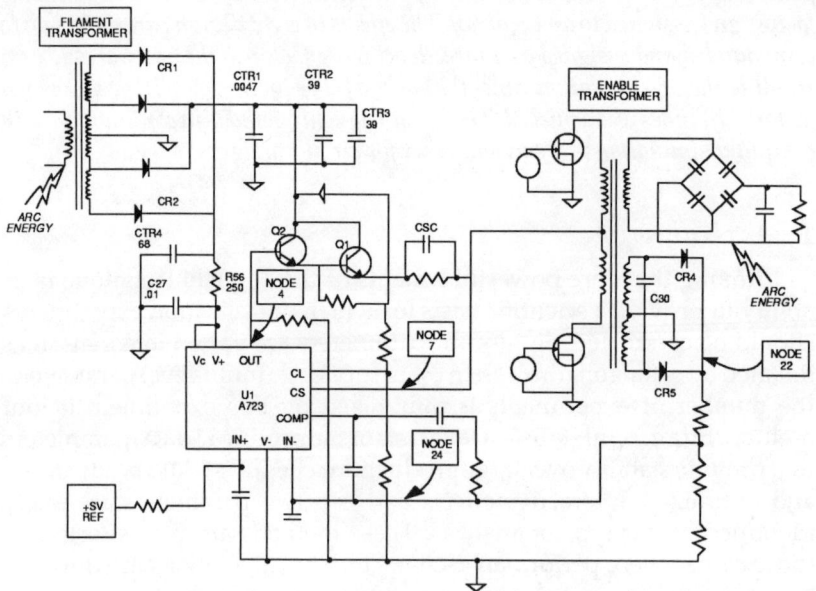

Figure 1. Circuit

In order to avoid the high cost of actual experimentation, computer simulation of circuit behavior against voltage spikes was used.

3. Brainstorming to Select Factors and Levels

This experiment was chosen as a test case since the simulation ability for this circuit already existed. The design optimization objective was defined to minimize the effect of voltage spikes at circuit location nodes 24, 22, 7 and 4 (Figure 1). The factors shown in Table 1 were selected as important design parameters as they were felt to have an effect on the reduction of these spikes at the selected nodes.

It was felt that during the manufacturing stage of the circuit the tolerances of the design parameters also had an effect on the voltage spikes. These tolerances were included as noise factors (uncontrollable factors) due to the difficulty in controlling them.

Table 1. Factors and Levels

Controllable Factors		Component Value		(Noise) Tolerance
		Level 1	Level 2	
A_1.	CTRW-1,2,9,10	Present	New	± 20%
A_2.	CTRW-3,4,11–14	Present	New	± 20%
A_3.	CTRW-5,6	Present	New	± 20%
A_4.	CTRW-7,8	Present	New	± 20%
B.	Q2	Present	New	Not Siginficant
C.	Q1 FT	Present	New	+100, − 50%
D.	el	Present	New	—
E.	Q2 FT	Present	New	Not Significant
F.	CSC	Present	New	± 5%
G.	C30	Present	New	Not Significant
H.	CR4,5	Present	New	Not Significant
I.	CR1, 2	Present	New	± 20%
J.	CW -1-4	Present	New	± 20%
K.	Q1	Present	New	Not Significant

Since factors A_1, A_2, A_3, and A_4 have to change their levels as a group, these factors' combined effect was taken as the behavior of factor A. The brainstorming group then decided to investigate the effect of 11 controllable factors for robustness against voltage spikes, including eight tolerance effects as noise factors.

Execution of the above objectives took the following form:
- Set up/verify the existing computer simulation.
- Choose controllable factors (components).
- Lay out the experiment using orthogonal arrays.
- Run the simulation experiments.
- Perform statistical analysis of the resulting data.

Since 11 factors, each with two levels, were selected as controllable factors, an $L_{12}(2^{11})$ orthogonal array was found to be the most efficient for obtaining the main effect of these factors (Table 2). The tolerances of eight design parameters were selected as noise factors. Since the objective was to reduce the cumulative effects of these tolerances, their effects were compounded to create one three-level noise factor (Table 2).

Table 2. Experimental Layout ($L_{12} \times F_3$)

Exp. No.	Controllable Factors											QA Simulation at Nodes 24, 22, 7 & 4 Compounded Noise factors		
	A	B	C	D	E	F	G	H	I	J	K	N1	N2	N3
1	1	1	1	1	1	1	1	1	1	1	1	0	0	0
2	1	1	1	1	1	2	2	2	2	2	2	0	0	0
3	1	1	2	2	2	1	1	1	2	2	2	0	0	0
4	1	2	1	2	2	1	2	2	1	1	2	0	0	0
5	1	2	2	1	2	2	1	2	1	2	1	0	0	0
6	1	2	2	2	1	2	2	1	2	1	1	0	0	0
7	2	1	2	2	1	1	2	2	1	2	1	0	0	0
8	2	1	2	1	2	2	2	1	1	1	2	0	0	0
9	2	1	1	2	2	2	1	2	2	1	1	0	0	0
10	2	2	2	1	1	1	1	2	2	1	2	0	0	0
11	2	2	1	2	1	2	1	1	1	2	2	0	0	0
12	2	2	1	1	2	1	2	1	2	2	1	0	0	0

4. Data Analysis

The simulation was modified to improve its correspondence to hardware and to increase its efficiency. A newly modeled filament transformer was added, and more complete component models for transistors and electrolytic capacitors were included to satisfy the former goal. To achieve the latter, the initial condition option of SPICE was invoked to reduce the running time of one simulation by a factor of approximately 200:1.

Twelve experiments were performed, each at three different noise conditions, wherein the voltage levels at the uA723 ports were monitored in the presence of an arc simulation. The arc was introduced by injecting a 10 KV positive-going pulse with a 5 nsec. rise time to the high-voltage side of both the enable and filament transformers. At no time was any voltage at the uA723 observed to be at a dangerous level. Nevertheless, the assumption that if the observed voltage spike could be minimized the device would be a more reliable circuit was still thought to be a sound assumption, and the effort continued.

The results of simulation for each quality characteristic (nodes 24, 22, 7, and 4) are shown in Table 3.

As can be seen from Table 3, the effect of voltage spike on nodes 22 and 7 was more dramatic than on nodes 22 and 4. For the sake of simplicity in this paper, only the analysis of nodes 22 and 7 will be discussed.

Since the objective was to minimize voltage spikes at these nodes, Taguchi's Signal-to-Noise (S/N) Ratio for smaller-the-better characteristics was used.

$$\text{S/N for smaller-the-better (dB)} = -10 \log \frac{1}{n} \sum_{i=1}^{n} y_i^2 \qquad (19.1)$$

where $\frac{1}{n} \sum_{i=1}^{n} y_i^2 = \frac{1}{n}\left(y_1^2 + y_2^2 + y_3^2 + \ldots + y_n^2\right)$

Analysis of variance tables (Table 4) and factorial effects (Table 5) for nodes 22 and 7 are shown following.

From Table 4 it can be seen that most significant factors for node 7 were factors J, I, F, and A. Factors B, D, E, G, H, and K, which were not considered as highly significant, could provide some improvement on the quality characteristics. Factor C did not prove to be significant at all. For node 22, factors J and C were the only factors found to be significant.

Table 3. Experimental Results

Exp. No.	Controllable Factors											Spike Voltage Amplitude At Node 24			Spike Voltage Amplitude At Node 22			Spike Voltage Amplitude At Node 7			Spike Voltage Amplitude At Node 4		
	A	B	C	D	E	F	G	H	I	J	K	N_1	N_2	N_3	N_1	N_2	N_3	N_1	N_2	N_3	N_1	N_2	N_3
1	1	1	1	1	1	1	1	1	1	1	1	0.60	1.60	1.00	9.0	45.0	12.8	8.5	10.5	9.0	-1.2	3.0	-1.3
2	1	1	1	1	1	2	2	2	2	2	2	0.08	0.07	0.06	3.0	3.2	3.0	4.5	5.7	4.7	-0.6	-1.0	-0.6
3	1	1	2	2	2	1	1	1	2	2	2	0.06	0.10	0.14	3.0	3.2	4.1	4.5	5.9	7.0	-0.6	-1.0	-1.0
4	1	2	1	2	2	1	2	2	1	1	2	0.60	1.80	1.00	9.0	45.0	12.8	8.5	10.5	8.7	-1.5	3.2	-1.4
5	1	2	2	1	2	2	1	2	1	2	1	0.06	0.08	0.135	3.0	3.2	4.7	4.6	5.7	7.2	-0.75	-1.1	-0.9
6	1	2	2	2	1	2	2	1	2	1	1	0.60	0.80	1.00	9.0	11.0	13.0	11.5	13.5	14.0	-1.2	-1.7	-1.3
7	2	1	2	2	1	1	2	2	1	2	1	0.06	0.08	0.11	3.0	3.0	3.7	4.5	5.4	6.7	-1.2	-1.0	-0.85
8	2	1	2	1	2	2	2	1	1	1	2	0.55	0.50	0.90	9.5	10.0	12.0	12.0	13.5	13.4	-1.2	-1.8	-1.4
9	2	1	1	2	2	2	1	2	2	1	1	0.60	0.50	1.70	9.0	10.0	50.0	11.0	12.5	67.0	-1.3	-1.6	6.2
10	2	2	2	1	1	1	1	2	2	1	2	0.55	0.70	0.90	8.5	10.0	11.8	8.5	18.5	8.5	-1.3	-1.8	-1.5
11	2	2	1	2	1	2	1	1	1	2	2	0.06	0.08	0.11	3.0	3.1	3.8	4.5	4.8	6.5	-0.6	-1.2	-0.8
12	2	2	1	1	2	1	2	1	2	2	1	0.08	0.08	0.07	3.4	3.0	3.2	5.6	5.2	5.5	-0.8	-1.0	-0.75

Table 4. Pooled ANOVA Tables for Nodes 7 and 22

S/N Smaller-the-Better
Node 7

Source	df	S	V	S'	ρ %
A	1	17.972	17.972	17.784	5.81
B	1	7.656	7.656	7.468	2.44
D	1	9.453	9.453	9.265	3.03
E	1	11.711	11.711	11.523	3.77
F	1	17.766	17.766	17.578	5.75
G	1	10.806	10.806	10.618	3.47
H	1	7.043	7.043	6.855	2.24
I	1	17.422	17.422	17.234	5.63
J	1	195.315	195.315	195.127	63.79
K	1	10.558	10.558	10.370	3.39
(e)	1	0.188	0.188	2.068	0.68
Total	11	305.890	27.808		

S/N Smaller-the-Better
Node 22

Source	df	S	V	S'	ρ %
A	1	7.536	7.536	1.519	0.21
C	1	45.548	45.548	39.531	5.44
D	1	8.358	8.358	2.341	0.32
E	1	9.726	9.726	3.709	0.51
G	1	9.725	9.725	3.708	0.51
J	1	615.545	615.545	609.528	83.90
(e)	5	30.085	6.017	66.187	9.11
Total	11	726.523	66.048		

Table 5. Summary of Level Averages
(Nodes 22 and 7 Voltage Spike)

Factor Level		Node 22 Voltage Spike		Node 7 Voltage Spike	
		Percent Contribution	Level Average (dB)	Percent Contribution	Level Average (dB)
A	1	0.2	−18.40	5.8	−17.54
	2		−16.82		−20.10
B	1	—		2.4	−19.68
	2				−18.08
C	1	5.4	−19.56	—	
	2		−15.66		
D	1	0.3	−16.78	3.0	−17.89
	2		−18.44		−19.87
E	1	0.5	−16.71	3.8	−17.89
	2		−18.52		−19.87
F	1	—		5.7	−17.66
	2				−20.90
G	1	0.5	−18.51	3.4	−19.83
	2		−16.71		−17.93
H	1	—		2.2	−18.11
	2				−19.64
I	1	—		5.6	−17.67
	2				−20.08
J	1	83.9	−24.77	63.8	−22.91
	2		−10.45		−14.84
K	1	—		3.4	−19.82
	2				−17.94

A summary table of factorial behaviors on the quality characteristics (node 24, 22, 7 and 4) can be found in Table 6.

5. Optimization and Confirmation

The average results and level of significance of all four nodes are shown in Table 6.

Table 6. Summary of Results (Nodes 24, 22, 7, 4)

Optimum Levels of Factors and Percent Contribution for Smaller-the-Better S/N Analysis

Quality Characteristics	Factors										
	A	B	C	D	E	F	G	H	I	J	K
Voltage Spike at Node 24	0.3 / 2		0.1 / 2			0.1 / 2	0.2 / 2			97.3 / 2	
Voltage Spike at Node 22	0.2 / 2		5.4 / 2	0.3 / 1	0.5 / 1		0.5 / 2			23.9 / 2	
Voltage Spike at Node 7	5.8 / 1	2.4 / 2		3.0 / 1	3.8 / 1	5.7 / 1	3.4 / 2	2.2 / 1	5.6 / 1	63.8 / 2	3.4 / 2
Voltage Spike at Node 4		/ 2	2.8					2.0 / 1		69.3 / 2	

As shown in Table 6, factor J proved to be the most significant and clear-cut factor, with no conflicts. As expected, it was a major contributor to the amplitude of the voltage spike at nodes 24, 22, and 7. Additionally, it was a major factor in the control of the variation at all nodes. In the role of fighting the interactive effects of tolerances, it was a minor factor in making nodes 22 and 4 more immune to tolerance variations. In light of the above, level 2 of factor J was assigned as optimum. Other clear-cut significant factors that reduced the effect of voltage spikes on all or some of the nodes were factors C and K (Table 6). All other factors' optimum levels were selected based on statistical analysis, engineering expertise, and cost trade-offs.

The Avionics engineering team came up with three feasible conditions:

	A	B	C	D	E	F	G	H	I	J	K
1.	1	2	2	1	1	2	2	1	2	2	1
2.	2	1	2	1	1	1	2	1	2	2	1
3.	2	1	2	1	1	1	1	1	1	2	1

The results of all three combinations, both calculated and simulated, showed vast improvements over the original conditions. The estimated calculations for this case, however, were deceiving. Some estimates for nodes 24 and 22 predicted negative voltages in response to a positive polarity transient. This is clearly incorrect. This prediction often occurs when the goal of the exercise is for minimizing results. This failure to recognize nonlinearities about zero does not invalidate the results.

Instead of using calculations to predict the new voltage levels, confirmation experiments were run for each of the three combinations. Figure 2 is a graphic presentation of these results. The N_1 condition (tolerance of factors) is compounded to obtain lower voltage spike response. N_3 condition (tolerance of factors) is compounded to obtain the higher voltage spike effect (creating a "worst case" scenario).

The voltage levels at all four nodes are consistently higher with the original circuit component values, as compared to each of the three new combinations. When viewed on this large scale, it does not appear that any one of the three new combinations has any great advantage over the others.

Figure 3, which is an expanded view of the area of interest, should provide an easier method for evaluating the three combinations. At all four nodes, the combination that yields the lowest voltage levels also is that combination (plot 3) that has the fewest changes from the original circuit values.

The results suggest that the following changes should be implemented:

1. The interwinding capacitance of the enable transformer should be minimized. The mechanism is obvious; by minimizing the capacitance, the coupling medium for the arc energy is minimized.
2. A device with similar gain but a higher bandwidth should be selected for Q_1. Apparently the effect is a more effective high-frequency buffer, which seems to quench some of the harmful arc energy.
3. The interwinding capacitance of the filament transformer should be increased by a factor of 2. The effect is a coupling of the arc energy into capacitance CRT1,2,3,4 and through R56 into C27. This represents a dangerous scenario, whereby the coupled energy could damage devices that have not previously shown a propensity to fail. Although the computer simulation did not show appreciable voltage levels at U1's V+ or Vc inputs, this

change is not recommended without a full analysis of the destination of the dissipated arc energy.

All other factors should retain their original characteristics.

6. Conclusion

The resulting combination of factors yielded a circuit which, in the simulation world, has an improved immunity to externally applied arc energy. The ramifications of the resulting changes vary in scope. Specifying a device for Q1 with a larger gain bandwidth is a relatively simple change. Specifying an interwinding capacitance on the enable transformer is a long and drawn-out process, requiring specification changes, engineering samples, and possibly a multiple-bid process. Finally, additional high-voltage capacitors could be added externally to the filament transformer to increase its effective interwinding capacitance. However, considering the limited production totals for this circuit, a question of practicality must be discussed before any action is taken toward these ends.

For this information to be useful, designers of future regulator circuits with a similar architecture should have at least considered the effects of interwinding capacitances and methods by which to harmlessly quench harmful arc energy. This of course assumes that all attempts have been made to avoid the occurrence of the unwanted arc.

The results obtained seemed to validate the effectiveness of Taguchi Methods. It can be concluded that use of Taguchi Methods, along with other optimization methods under the guidance of sound engineering experience, would produce quick, powerful, and cost-effective solutions to circuit design optimizations.

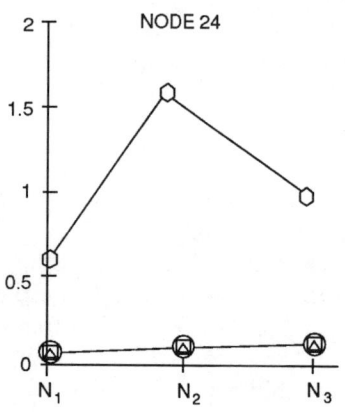
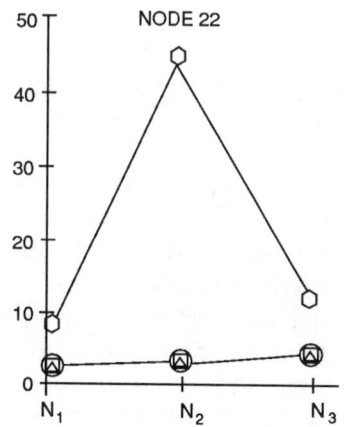
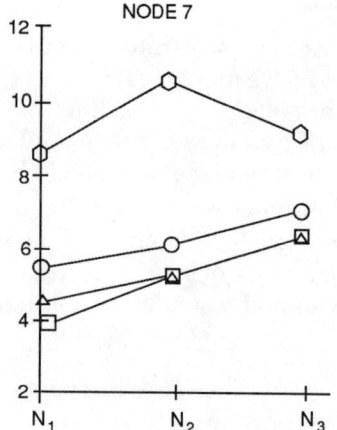
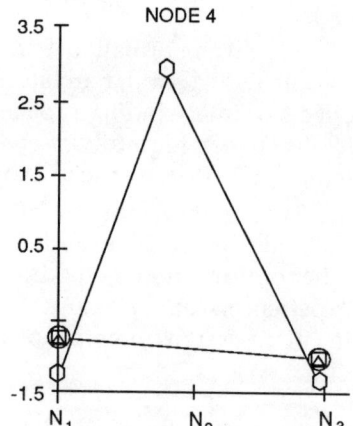

PLOT 1 FACTOR LEVELS (O): $A_1, B_2, C_2, E_1, F_2, G_2, H_1, I_2, J_2, K_1$
PLOT 2 FACTOR LEVELS (□): $A_2, B_1, C_2, E_1, F_1, G_2, H_1, I_2, J_2, K_1$
PLOT 3 FACTOR LEVELS (△): $A_2, B_1, C_2, E_1, F_1, G_1, H_1, I_1, J_2, K_1$
PLOT 4 (O): ALL ORIGINAL LEVELS

Figure 2. Voltage Spike Amplitudes Under Original and Newly Defined Conditions

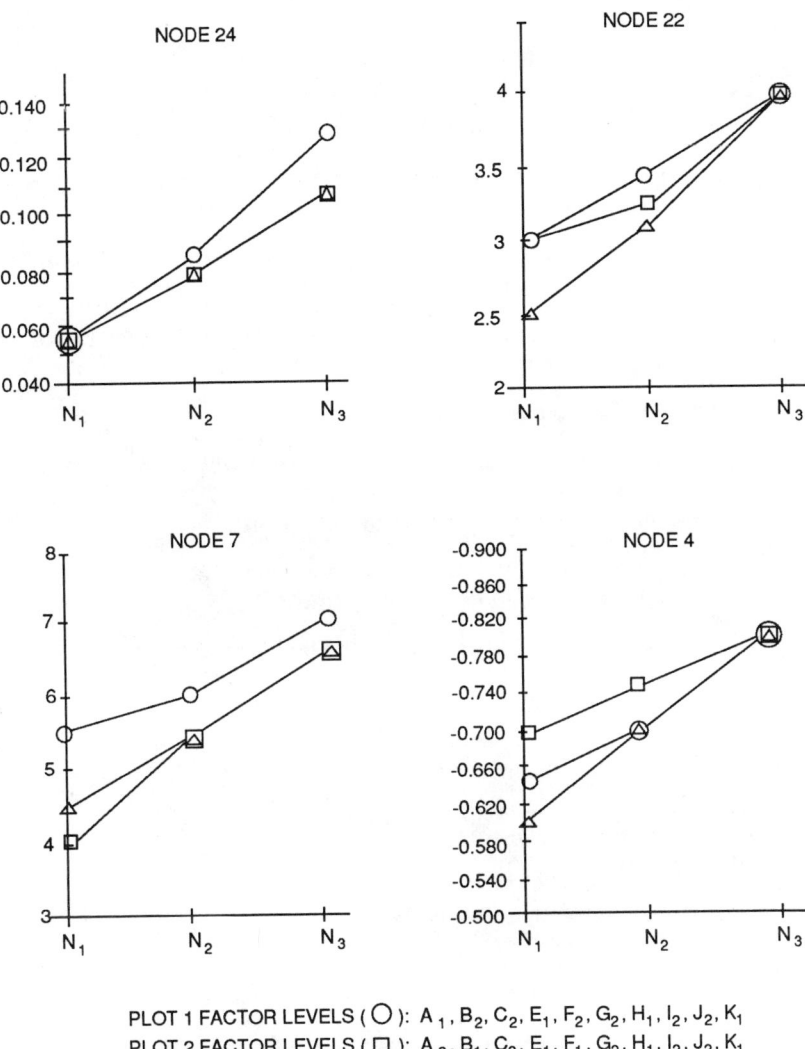

Figure 3. Expanded View, Voltage Spike Amplitudes Under Newly Defined Conditions

Q & A

Q. There are eight noise factors. How are the levels of noise factors set?

A. There are guidelines for setting the levels of noise factors to simulate actual noise conditions.

Q. For a three-level noise factor, can the nominal value be taken as the middle level and $\pm 3\sigma$ for the highest and lowest levels?

A. No. That would greatly exaggerate the effect of the noise factor. In some cases, a more realistic simulation is desired.

Q. Is there another explanation?

A. In a normal distribution, the probability of being out of $\pm 3\sigma$ limits is 0.3%. If all noise factors are set at those levels, it is too extreme. It does not effectively simulate actual variation.

Q. Does this mean that the first and third level of a noise factor should be somewhere between the nominal and $\pm 3\sigma$?

A. Yes. For a three-level noise factor, the levels to use are:

    1st level: (nominal) -1.22σ
    2nd level: (nominal)
    3rd level: (nominal) $+1.22\sigma$

Q. How about a two-level noise factor?

A. The levels are:

    1st level: (nominal) $+\sigma$
    2nd level: (nominal) $-\sigma$

Q. Is there a case where $\pm 3\sigma$ is used for noise factor levels?

A. Yes, this is done when we want to enhance the effect of a noise factor.

Q. Is compounding a recommended strategy for dealing with noise? How are noise factors compounded?

A. For each noise factor, we can calculate which noise factor gives a higher output value and which level gives a lower output value from the model. We then combine the levels of all noise factors, to producing one compounded lower level. Do the same for the higher output values.

Q. There are four outputs—four sets of Signal-to-Noise Ratios. It might be complicated to select the best conditions since there may be a conflict between the values to different outputs. In the response table of Nodes 22 and 7 for example, A_2 is better for Node 22 but A_1 is better for Node 7. Fortunately for factors D, E, G, and H, all of the better levels are in a consistent direction. How do we make such a decision?

A. It depends on which ouput characteristic is more important. It also depends on how much gain would be achieved for each characteristic.

Q. What do you mean by gain?

A. Gain is the difference in Signal-to-Noise Ratios.

For example, in the example we discussed, by selecting A_1 the gain is 1.5 dB for characteristic one, but by selecting A_2 the gain is 5 decibels for chracteristic two. It is obvious that here, A_2 is better.

Q. Is there any simple way to do this?

A. Yes. When there are four sets of S/N Ratios, calculate the total of the four S/N Ratios for each run of the L_{12}. Then make a response table and compare the gain for the different levels.

20. AN EXPERIMENT TO MINIMIZE VARIATION IN POT CORE TRANSFORMER PROCESSING

Gerard Pfaff
ITT Electron Technology

This paper addresses a transformer processing problem involving inductance changes. Due to inductance falling out of calculated ranges, much time and expense was involved in an attempt to rectify the problem. In this L_{16} experiment, it was determined that adusting the level settings of seven of these factors, average inductance can be reduced 90%. Annual losses attributed to this product were reduced to 28% per power-supply model.

1. INTRODUCTION

ITT Electron Technology is a division of ITT's Defense Group employing approximately 350 people. Basic product lines include traveling wave tubes, low- and high-voltage power supplies, power supplies, klystrons, power tubes, and integrated subsystems.

2. OBJECTIVE OF THE EXPERIMENT

The objective of this study is to minimize variation of inductance from transformer to transformer after processing. The inductance should be within calculated limits. A ferrite pot core transformer (see Figure 1) was the subject of the experiment.

From the *Fifth Symposium on Taguchi Methods*™, pp. 425–438, Copyright © 1987, American Supplier Institute, Inc., Dearborn, Michigan.

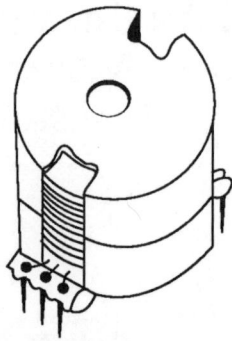

Figure 1. Pot Core Transformer

Manufacturing specifications are determined by the following equation:
where:

$$L = N^2 \frac{A_L}{1 \times 10^6} \qquad (20.1)$$

L = Millihenries
N = Number of primary turns
A_L = Inductance factor from core manufacturer's data sheets (specified with a tolerance)

Initial out-of-tolerance inductance indicates incorrect number of primary turns or incorrect core material. Large drops in inductance after processing indicate separated or cracked cores. This results in high magnetizing currents and flatter hysteresis loops. The present distribution of transformer inductance is shown in Figure 2, where 8.2% of the products are below the lower specification limit.

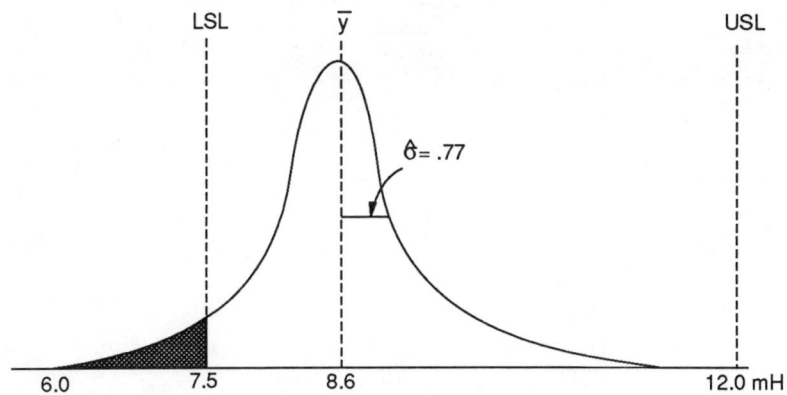

Figure 2. Present PS6501 Auxiliary Distribution Curve

3. Factors and Experimental Layout

The brainstorming group consisted of representatives from quality, product design, and manufacturing. A total of 12 people attended the brainstorming session, which lasted two hours. The transformer process-flow diagram, with factors and measurement steps, is shown in Figure 3. The group originally discussed 14 possible factors. The total was reduced to nine controllable and two noise factors, as shown in Table 1.

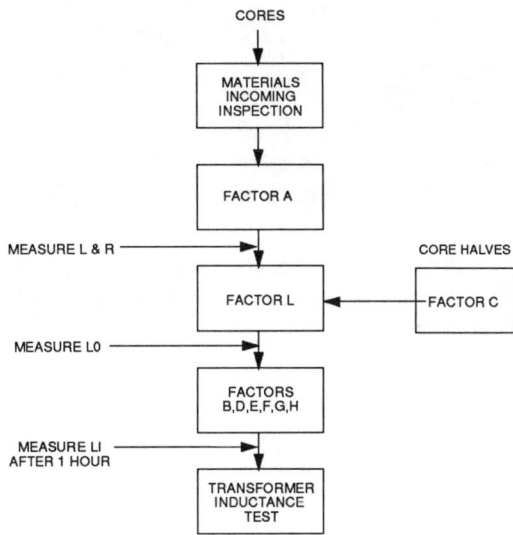

Figure 3. Transformer Process Flow Diagram

Table 1. Transformer Experiment Factors

Factors	1	2	3	4	5	6	7	8
A	Level 1	Level 2						
B	Level 1	Level 2						
C	Level 1	Level 2						
D	Level 1	Level 2						
E	Level 1	Level 2						
F	Level 1	Level 2						
G	Level 1	Level 2						
H	Level 1	Level 2						
L	Level 1	Level 2	Level 3	Level 4	Level 5	Level 6	Level 7	Level 8

From Table 1, it was decided to select two orthogonal arrays, one for controllable factors and another for noise factors. An L_{16} orthogonal array was modified by using a linear graph, (see Figure 4), and multi-level arrangement to yield an L_{16} ($8^1 \times 2^8$). A standard L_4 (2^3) orthogonal array was selected for the noise factors.

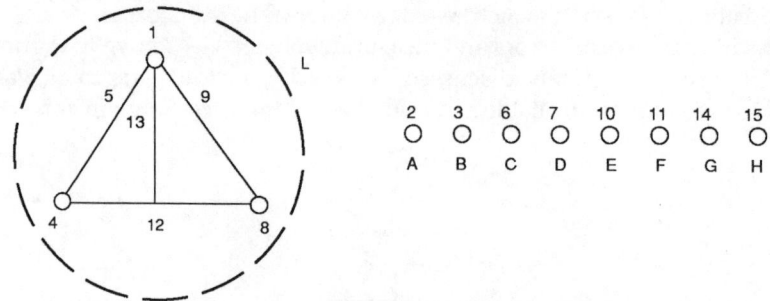

Figure 4. Experiment Linear Graph

Since available production time for the experiment was minimal, it was decided to process two transformers per experiment. The experiment layout is shown in Table 2.

Table 2. Transformer Experiment Orthogonal Array

									N	1	2	2	1
									Y	1	2	1	2
									X	1	1	2	2
									EXP	1	2	3	4
Array	L	A	B	C	D	E	F	G	H	\multicolumn{4}{c}{Data}	T	S/N*

Array	L	A	B	C	D	E	F	G	H	Data				T	S/N*
1	1	1	1	1	1	1	1	1	1	9.44	10.21	9.54	9.73	38.92	29.08
2	2	1	1	1	1	2	2	2	2	9.07	9.68	8.82	8.84	36.41	11.42
3	3	1	1	2	2	1	1	2	2	8.41	7.23	8.87	8.17	32.68	21.42
4	4	1	1	2	2	2	2	1	1	10.20	10.48	10.62	11.08	42.38	29.20
5	1	2	2	2	2	2	2	2	2	9.56	8.39	8.85	7.87	34.67	21.64
6	2	2	2	2	2	1	1	1	1	9.08	9.18	9.30	8.94	36.50	35.59
7	3	2	2	1	1	2	2	1	1	9.30	8.11	9.43	9.04	35.88	23.55
8	4	2	2	1	1	1	1	2	2	9.72	9.83	9.92	9.85	39.32	41.40
9	5	1	2	1	2	1	2	1	2	9.10	8.88	9.43	10.08	37.49	25.07
10	6	1	2	1	2	2	1	2	1	9.63	9.77	9.90	9.73	39.03	38.82
11	7	1	2	2	1	1	2	2	1	9.94	9.17	10.40	9.15	38.66	23.96
12	8	1	2	2	1	2	1	1	2	9.63	7.85	9.52	7.87	34.87	18.87
13	5	1	2	2	1	2	1	2	1	10.11	8.52	9.84	7.83	36.30	18.46
14	6	2	1	2	1	1	2	1	2	9.89	10.65	10.19	10.71	41.44	28.49
15	7	2	1	1	2	2	1	1	2	10.20	9.87	10.87	10.73	41.67	27.00
16	8	2	1	1	2	1	2	2	1	8.72	8.94	9.14	8.91	35.71	34.24

* S/N Ratio Nominal-the-Best equations on the following page.

4. Analysis of Experimental Results

A regular analysis was conducted using inner and outer orthogonal array concepts. This analysis identifies the most significant factors and interactions between noise and control factors. The following equation is the basis for variation calculations:

$$S_T = \sum_{i=1}^{n} y_i^2 - CF \qquad (20.2)$$

Nominal-the-best S/N Ratio analysis was also done. This type of analysis is more sensitive than the regular analysis, because (among other advantages) it provides robustness against all sources of noise, not necessarily only the controlled noise factors.

S/N Ratio Nominal-the-Best Equations for Table 2.

$$\eta = 10 \log \frac{1}{n}\left(\frac{S_m - V_e}{V_e}\right) \quad (20.3)$$

$$S_m = \frac{T^2}{n} \quad (20.4)$$

$$V_e = \frac{\sum_{i=1}^{n'}(y_i - \overline{y})^2}{n-1} \quad (20.5)$$

For Run 1:

$$S_m = \frac{(9.44 + 10.21 + 9.54 + 9.73)^2}{4} = 378.70$$

$$V_e = \frac{(9.44 - 9.73)^2 + (10.21 - 9.73)^2 + (9.54 - 9.73)^2 + (9.73 - 9.73)^2}{4-1}$$

$$= 0.117$$

$$\eta = 10 \log \frac{1}{4}\left[\frac{[378.70 - 0.117]}{0.117}\right]$$

$$= 29.08 \text{ dB}$$

5. OPTIMIZATION AND ESTIMATION

Optimum levels were determined from the response graphs and Table 3. A trade-off between interaction with noise factors, main effects, and S/N Ratio was considered to determine how a confirmation experiment should be conducted. The S/N Ratio determines the best factor levels for robustness against noise factors. The higher the S/N Ratio, the more robust the level setting is to noise.

Regular analysis determined that the best factor levels were L_2, B_1, C_1, D_1, E_1, and F_2. Factor G had a conflict between interactions with noise. Level G_1 is optimum for robustness against noise factor Y; G_2 is optimum for robustness against noise factor X.

S/N Ratio analysis identified levels $L_2, L_4, L_6, B_2, C_1, D_2, F_1, G_2, H_1$, and A_2 as best. Factor levels of L, B, D, and F were in conflict between regular analysis and S/N Ratio analysis. This conflict is not unusual, since S/N Ratio analysis considers variability of the quality characteristic due to all sources of noise, not just the noise factors controlled in the experiment. A confirmation experiment (see Table 4) was designed to identify the optimum setting for the conflicting factors.

Optimum factor levels, as a result of the confirmation experiment, were L_4, B_1, C_1, E_1, F_2, and G_1. Levels D_1, A_2, and H_1 were selected for production and cost reasons.

The process average equation for each combination of noise factors is:

$$\hat{\mu} = \overline{YL} + \overline{YB} + \overline{YC} + \overline{YE} + \overline{YF} + \overline{YG} + \overline{XD} + \overline{XG} - \overline{G} - 5\overline{Y} - \overline{X} \qquad (20.6)$$

Table 3. Summary Table

		Regular Analysis					S/N
		Interaction with Noise Factor				Main Effect	
		Y		X			
		1	2	1	2		$-10 \log \eta$
L	1	9.35	9.05	—	—	9.20	6.11
	2	9.06	9.16	—	—	9.11	12.13
	3	9.00	8.14	—	—	8.57	3.86
	4	10.12	10.31	—	—	10.21	15.21
	5	9.62	8.83	—	—	9.22	2.47
	6	9.90	10.21	—	—	10.06	13.61
	7	10.35	9.73	—	—	10.04	5.45
	8	9.25	8.39	—	—	8.82	7.69
B	1	9.62	9.47	—	—	9.55	—
	2	9.54	8.98	—	—	9.26	—
C	1	9.51	9.51	—	—	9.51	11.25
	2	9.65	8.94	—	—	9.30	5.38
D	1	—	—	9.44	9.92	—	6.90
	2	—	—	9.23	9.53	—	9.72
E	1	9.44	9.35	—	—	—	10.48
	2	9.72	9.10	—	—	—	6.14
F	1	9.62	9.08	—	—	—	9.44
	2	9.54	9.37	—	—	—	7.18
G	1	9.73	9.59	9.51	9.82	9.66	—
	2	9.43	8.87	9.17	9.13	9.15	—
H	1	—	—	—	—	—	9.60
	2	—	—	—	—	—	7.02
A	1	—	—	—	—	—	—
	2	—	—	—	—	—	—

Table 4. Confirmation Experiment

Exp. No.	L	C	E	D	H	A	B	F	G
1	4	1	1	2	1	2	1	2	1
2	6	1	1	2	1	2	1	2	1
3	2	1	1	2	1	2	1	2	1
4	Best	1	1	2	1	2	2	1	2

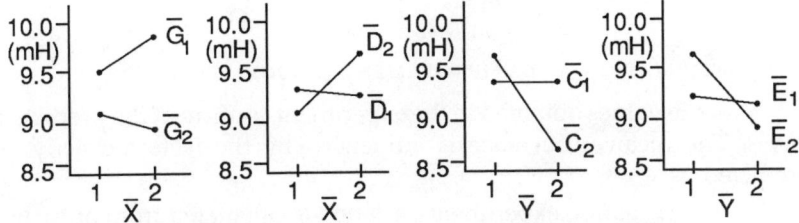

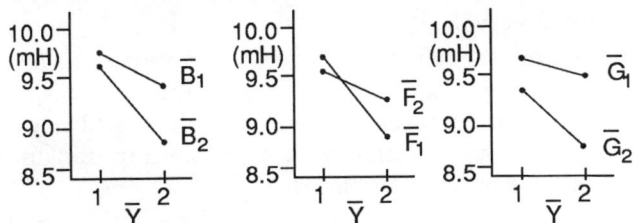

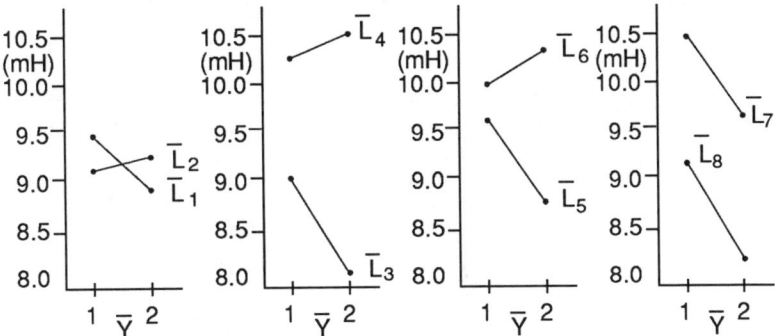

Figure 5. Response Graphs

The inductance results at optimum levels for each combination of noise factors is:

$\hat{\mu}_{x_1 y_1} = 10.01 \text{ mH}$

$\hat{\mu}_{x_1 y_2} = 11.40 \text{ mH}$

$\hat{\mu}_{x_2 y_1} = 10.17 \text{ mH}$

$\hat{\mu}_{x_2 y_2} = 11.56 \text{ mH}$

6. Confirmation and Improvement in Quality

Average values obtained in the experiment confirm at the predicted levels. The mean inductance is influenced by the factors exactly as predicted.

The confirmation experiment variation is calculated from only two samples, therefore more data should be obtained to determine the actual inductance distribution. The variation exhibited in the experiment falls within the range predicted in the analysis, although at the upper limit of the confidence interval.

Implementing the new factor levels will improve the capability of the process. A comparison of transformer inductance distributions is shown in Figure 6. Engineer and assembler time will not be wasted questioning out-of-specification transformers. Scrap transformers and production delays will be eliminated.

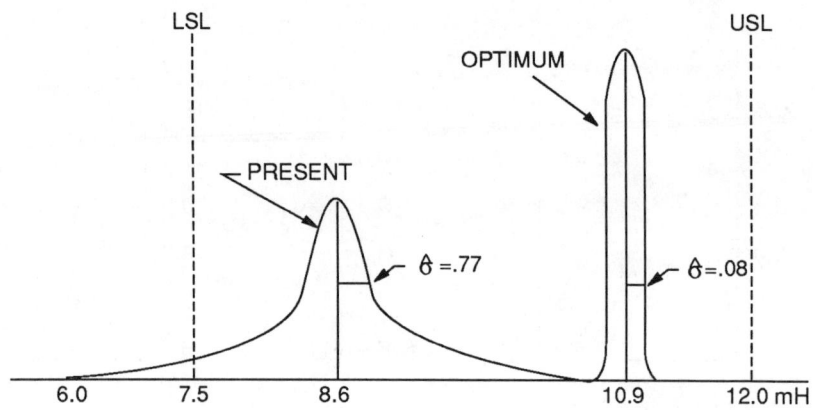

Figure 6. Comparison of Transformer Inductance Distribution

Savings, when calculated by the conventional method, are calculated to be about 28% annually. This calculation considers yearly production volume, rejection percentage, cost of scrap, and engineering and assembly time.

If costing information, specification limits, and target value are valid, savings calculated by the Quality Loss Function (QLF) will be reflected in real life. In this case, the annual savings calculated by the QLF are 30.60%.

After a more extensive confirmation/production run, the mean can be adjusted to the target value. This will increase savings due to minimizing loss due to quality to 99.67% annually (when the quality loss after optimization is compared to the quality loss before optimization).

Q & A

Q. In this experiment, many interactions are calculated. Isn't it true that interactions should not be assigned as a rule?

A. The interactions that should not be assigned are the interactions between control factors. When there are strong interactions between control factors, the main effects of control factors have poor reproducibility; therefore, they are less valuable or less useful. In this experiment, the experimenter took the interactions between control factors and noise factors. By studying these types of interactions, we can find control factor conditions that result in robust design.

Q. It is tedious to calculate interactions. Can the interactions be calculated if software is available to the experimenter?

A. Using direct product design, the conditions for stability are found from these interactions. This method of design was used in the early development of Taguchi Methods. This was the precursor of Dr. Genichi Taguchi's development of the S/N Ratio.

Now, instead of calculating interactions between control factors and noise factors, S/N Ratios are used to find stable conditions. When a control factor has a strong interaction between noise factors, there is a significant difference in S/N Ratios. Then we simply select the level with the higher S/N Ratio. In this way, analysis becomes very simple and efficient.

Q. Are two different analysis methods used for the same purpose?

A. Yes. But now the analysis of the S/N Ratio is generally used. After the stable condition is determined, the mean will then be adjusted.

Using the S/N Ratio is better. Suppose:

Control Factor: A
Noise Factor: N

	N_1	N_2
A_1	8, 12	13, 17
A_2	5, 20	18, 7

Data A_1 becomes better if the S/N Ratio is used. But AxN leads to the conclusions that A_2 is better.

Q. Control factor L has eight levels. How is it prepared?

A. This is one of a multi-level arrangement from 2-level orthogonal arrays. It is explained in *System of Experimental Design* by Dr. Taguchi. To explain briefly, a triangle and a vertical line between a vertex and a bottom line in a linear graph are selected. Using the columns of the three vertices, find eight combination of 1s and 2s horizontally and name each combination from 1 to 8 respectively. Then these seven columns are collapsed to form a single column with 7 degrees of freedom.

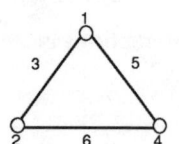
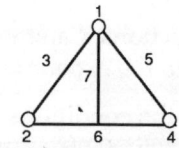

Column	Level
111	1
112	2
121	3
122	4
211	5
212	6
221	7
222	8

21. SABRE (EMD) DISK-DRIVE THERMAL PERFORMANCE IMPROVEMENT

Neal F. Gunderson
Magnetic Peripherals, Inc.

This case study demonstrates how thermal-head offset pattern and amplitude variability was virtually eliminated in Control Data's 9720X EMD (Eight Inch Disk Module Drive) 368 megabyte disk memory by the use of Taguchi Methods. The objective was to find a new design, new process, or tighter tolerances that would remove the sources of variability or give a design insensitive to these sources. Ten factors were investigated using an L_{16} orthogonal array. Analysis showed that sleeve shape reduced sensitivity to the distortion source. Implementation of the optimized design resulted in an increase yield from 40 to 80% up to 96 to 100%. Distribution outliers were eliminated and $\pm 3\,\sigma$ limits for worst head offset were reduced by almost two-thirds.

1. INTRODUCTION

It has been only six years since Japanese design-engineering philosophy and techniques have been revealed to small groups of American engineers. Through the writings and seminars of Dr. Genichi Taguchi, the U.S. has the opportunity to look beyond the popularized view of the Japanese manufacturing success story and examine the methods that have created a wide range of low-cost, high-quality products in both traditional and high-technology fields. Much of the source of this success is due to the design process and experimental techniques developed by Dr. Taguchi to maintain product specifications at their target value by reducing the sensitivity of the design to production and environmental variability.

From the *Fourth Symposium on Taguchi Methods*™, pp. 468–500, Copyright © 1988, American Supplier Institute, Inc., Dearborn, Michigan.

This report shows how thermal-head offset pattern and amplitude variability was virtually eliminated in Control Data's 9720X Sabre (EMD-8 in. disk module drive) 368 megabyte disk memory by the use of Dr. Taguchi's design methodology. Implementation of the optimum design resulted in almost 100% factory yields by reduction of the worst thermal-head offset 3σ limits by two-thirds and by elimination of normal distribution outliers (see Figures 1 and 2). This work was done without the help of statistical specialists by a design and manufacturing team that included two engineers with 80 hours of specialized training in Taguchi Methods. Finally, conclusions are drawn about the advantages and difficulties of this design technique.

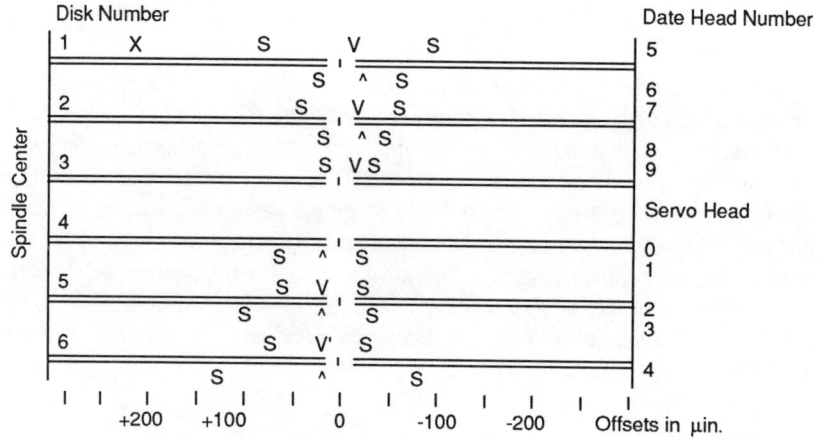

Figure 1. Original EMD Thermal Head Offset

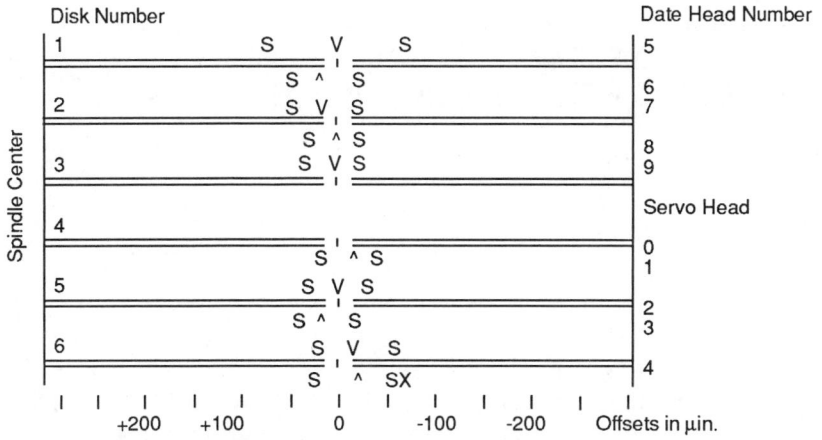

Figure 2. EMD Thermal Head Offset after Implementation of Optimum Design from Taguchi Experiment

2. The EMD Thermal Problem

For a high-performance disk drive with track widths of 1,100 to 760 microinches (900 and 1300 track per inch respectively) to read without errors over the operating temperature range (50° to 115°F) requires that the data heads stay within plus or minus 160 to 110 μin., respectively, of their original position relative to the servo head. Achieving this target requires substantial analysis and design creativity during the early system-design stages. The Sabre came off the drawing board meeting this stringent requirement with what appeared to be plenty of margin. But very early in preproduction, the head offset patterns started showing extreme amplitude and pattern variability. Only expensive testing and reworking of problem drives prevented this problem from getting to customers.

When the Sabre started showing thermal-head pattern and amplitude variability that produced read errors within the operating temperature range, both production and design engineering initiated a search for the failure mode. This is not a simple problem, for there are a number of different components of thermal-head offset (i.e., start-up and external-temperature-induced offset and hysteresis offset from inelastic expansion) that must be measured in all three dimensions (normal to data cylinder, tangent to data cylinder, and vertical to cylinder center) for each head with microinch accuracy. The sources of thermal-head offset range from system-level problems like read-write component off-track performance to mechanical distortions in individual components. For the Sabre, the problem type was isolated quickly. The head offset was induced by external temperature change and the offset was normal to the track. This problem was found to follow the actuator-block assembly. Figure 3 shows a top cutaway view of the Sabre module with rotary actuator assembly pinpointed. Figure 4 has the three main parts of this assembly highlighted, Figures 5 and 6 are an isometric and a cross-section view of the problem actuator-block assembly, respectively. This is one of the key assemblies of the module, because it is the point of force input through the voice coil for moving the actuator and the primary reference point for locating the heads. The cutaway view shows its key parts and the predominant adhesive-bonded interface between the aluminum block and the stainless-steel sleeve holding the bearings. Holographic analysis of this assembly showed this bonded interface as a likely cause of the distortion problem.

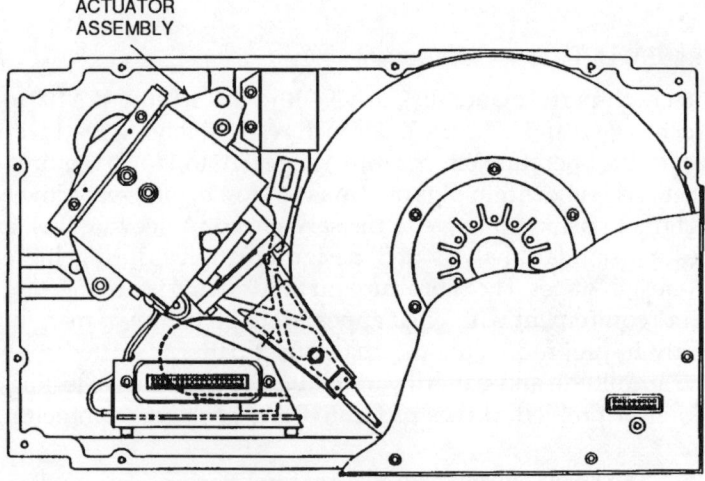

Figure 3. Cutaway View of EMD Module

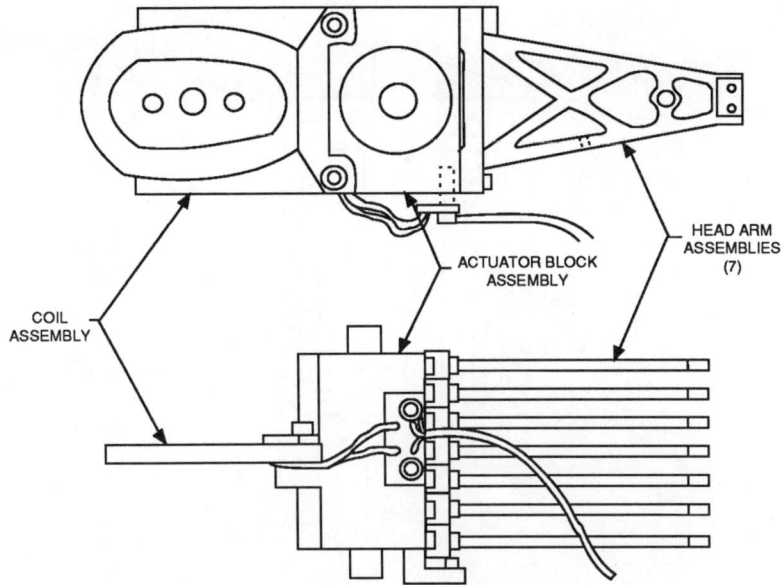

Figure 4. EMD Actuator Assembly

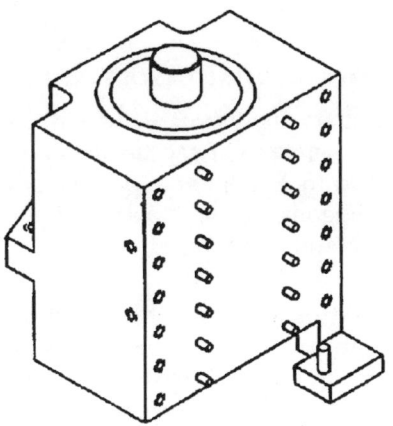

Figure 5. EMD Actuator Block Assembly

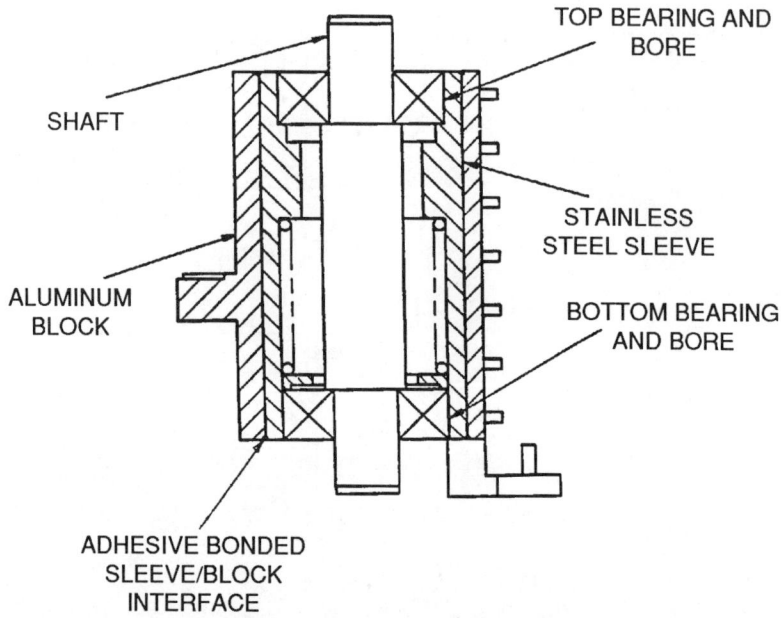

Figure 6. EMD Actuator Block Cross-Section

3. Factors and Experimental Layout

After this preliminary analysis, it was decided to use Dr. Taguchi's techniques. Taking advantage of the flexibility inherent in his techniques, it was decided to combine the parameter and tolerance steps together into one orthogonal array, so both design process changes and tightened tolerances could be analyzed as means of reducing performance variability.

The first step in setting up the array was to determine which factors and levels should be included. It was necessary to get the widest range of input possible to ensure that all the critical factors were included. After brainstorming with design and manufacturing engineering, visits were made to the two vendors involved in this assembly. This was to obtain their input into the selection of factors by discussion and observation of their processes. Table 1 shows the final list of design, tolerance, and process factors and factor interactions studied. Only those design factors that could be inexpensively reworked into standard production parts were used.

Table 1. EMD I Design of Experiments Factor Breakdown

1. Design Factors (Column Number of Orthogonal Array)
    A. Sleeve shape (1-2-3)
    B. Adhesive-bonded and heat-shrunk sleeve/block interface (4-8-12)
    C. Current or spring bottom bearing loading (5)

2. Tolerance Factors
    A. Sleeve/block diametrical tolerance (4-8-12)
    B. Block top and bottom taper (6)
    C. Bottom bearing/bore cleareance (10)
    D. Top bearing/bore clearance (11)

3. Process Factors
    A. Stress relieving of final assembly (7)
    B. Adhesive application method (9)
    C. Adhesive cure time (14)

4. Factor Interaction
    A. Bottom bearing loading/bottom bearing clearance (5x10)

5. Error
    A. Primary error (shows due to random variation) (13)

Table 2 shows the base L_{16} orthogonal array that was selected. It allows the testing of 15 two-level factors or two-way factor interactions with 16 experiments. The 15 columns are for the selected design factors or interactions, with the ones and twos representing the levels. The balanced arrangement allows the mathematically independent calculation of the effect of each factor. The 16 rows are used to determine which factor levels go into each test. In this case, they determined the types and tolerances of the piece parts and the assembly process for each block.

Table 2. L_{16} Orthogonal Array

Test #	\multicolumn{15}{c}{Design Factors}	Noise Factors
	1	2	3	4	5	6	7	8	9	10	11	12	13	14	15	$x_1 \ldots x_{10}$
1	1	1	1	1	1	1	1	1	1	1	1	1	1	1	1	$1_1 \ldots 1_{10}$
2	1	1	1	1	1	1	1	2	2	2	2	2	2	2	2	$2_1 \ldots 2_{10}$
3	1	1	1	2	2	2	2	1	1	1	1	2	2	2	2	$3_1 \ldots 3_{10}$
4	1	1	1	2	2	2	2	2	2	2	2	1	1	1	1	$4_1 \ldots 4_{10}$
5	1	2	2	1	1	2	2	1	1	2	2	1	1	2	2	$5_1 \ldots 5_{10}$
6	1	2	2	1	1	2	2	2	2	1	1	2	2	1	1	$6_1 \ldots 6_{10}$
7	1	2	2	2	2	1	1	1	1	2	2	2	2	1	1	$7_1 \ldots 7_{10}$
8	1	2	2	2	2	1	1	2	2	1	1	1	1	2	2	$8_1 \ldots 8_{10}$
9	2	1	2	1	2	1	2	1	2	1	2	1	2	1	2	$9_1 \ldots 9_{10}$
10	2	1	2	1	2	1	2	2	1	2	1	2	1	2	1	$10_1 \ldots 10_{10}$
11	2	1	2	2	1	2	1	1	2	1	2	2	1	2	1	$11_1 \ldots 11_{10}$
12	2	1	2	2	1	2	1	2	1	2	1	1	2	1	2	$12_1 \ldots 12_{10}$
13	2	2	1	1	2	2	1	1	2	2	1	1	2	2	1	$13_1 \ldots 13_{10}$
14	2	2	1	1	2	2	1	2	1	1	2	2	1	1	2	$14_1 \ldots 14_{10}$
15	2	2	1	2	1	1	2	1	2	2	1	2	1	1	2	$15_1 \ldots 15_{10}$
16	2	2	1	2	1	1	2	2	1	1	2	1	2	2	1	$16_1 \ldots 16_{10}$

Two-level orthogonal arrays are desirable since they allow the measurement of interactions, which cannot be accomplished with one-factor-at-a-time testing. Another advantage is that even though many mechanical design/process options are two-level, the columns can easily be modified for those factors that have three, four, or more levels. The modified orthogonal array used for the testing is shown in Table 3. Notice the combining of columns (1, 2, and 3) and (4, 8, and 12) to allow the testing of the four- and three-level factors 1 and 2. Figure 7 shows the four sleeve shapes used for factor 1. The noise factor used for this testing was the 10 individual thermal-head offsets measured for each test actuator-block assembly.

The 16 test actuator blocks were assembled by the key vendor using standard production processes and people. A design engineer was present to ensure that no extraneous variables entered into the experiment. This was especially important, since for practical reasons even the assembly of the test blocks could not be randomized. Deviations from statistically pure methods is accepted by Dr. Taguchi as a necessary price to pay to enable these methods to be used as a commonplace engineering tool. The lack of randomization also prevented obtaining meaningful

Table 3. EMD Designed Experiment

	1	2	3	4	5	6	7	8	9	10	11
	Sleeve Shape	Sleeve/Act. Tolerance-Top End	Bottom Bearing Loading	Act. Block Taper Top to Bottom	Stress Relieve Final Assembly	Adhesive Appl. Method	Bottom Bearing/Bore Clearance	Top Bearing Bore Clearance	Primary Error	Cure Time	5 × 10 Interaction
	1. Current 2. Middle 3. Top/Bottom Relieved 4. Side Relieved	1. Min. 2. Max. 3. Shrink Fit	1. Current 2. Side Load	1. Min. 2. Max.	1. None 2. Yes	1. Current 2. New	1. Min. 2. Max.	1. Min. 2. Max.		1. Current 2. 5 Minutes	
Column #	1-2-3	4-8-12	5	6	7	9	10	11	13	14	15
Test #											
1	1	1	1	1	1	1	1	1	1	1	1
2	1	2	1	1	1	1	2	2	2	2	2
3	1	2	2	2	2	2	1	1	1	1	2
4	1	3	2	2	2	1	2	2	2	2	1
5	2	1	1	2	2	2	2	2	1	1	2
6	2	2	1	2	2	1	1	1	2	2	1
7	2	2	2	1	1	2	2	2	1	1	1
8	2	3	2	1	1	1	1	1	2	2	2
9	3	1	2	1	2	2	1	2	2	1	2
10	3	2	2	1	2	1	2	1	1	2	1
11	3	2	1	2	1	2	1	2	2	1	1
12	3	3	1	2	1	1 (none)	2	1	1	2	2
13	4	1	2	2	1	2	2	1	1	2	1
14	4	2	1	1	2	1	1	2	2	1	1
15	4	2	1	1	2	2	2	1	2	1	2
16	4	3	1	1	2	1 (none)	1	2	1	2	1

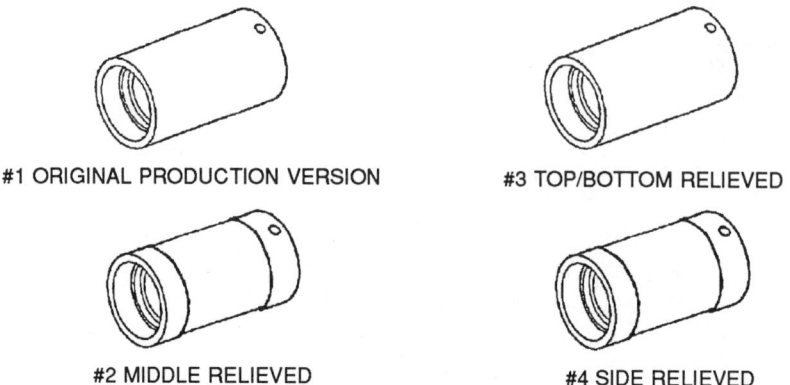

Figure 7. Sleeve Shapes for Factor 1 EMD Designed Experiment

statistical data from replications. The absence of replication had little practical impact on the results of the experiment (aside from greatly simplifying and speeding up of the testing), since orthogonal arrays have replications built in. In this designed experiment, any level of a factor is in from four to eight of the test blocks.

4. Test Procedures

The 16 test blocks were each built into one of two test modules and then given a series of automated Bode and frequency response tests to measure resonance peak amplitude and frequency. This was critical, for no change that reduced these margins could be accepted. The thin film heads used in the Sabre have high Signal-to-Noise (S/N) Ratios and are excellent displacement transducers. The thermal-head offset measurements obtained from the 10 thin film heads were made using a standard Sabre production module and electronics, except for a special read/write card for the internal design thermal test monitor. The test drives were soaked at 50°F until thermally stabilized. Immediately after start-up the test cylinders were written. After the internal module temperature had stabilized, start-up head offsets were measured, then the ambient temperature was raised to 122°F. Thermal-head offsets were measured. The ambient temperature was returned to 50°F and a hysteresis offset measurement was made to check for inelastic behavior.

5. Analysis of Variance

The resulting test data was entered into a database and secondary calculations (liner regress tilt, etc.) were done. Using the ANOVA™ software, the 15 types of analysis of variance (ANOVA) listed in Table 4 were run.

Table 4. Type of Analysis of Variance Used

- Worse head offset
- Worse head timing offset
- Worse head vector (timing/offset) offset
- Signal-to-Noise individual head offset (variability from target: zero offset)
- Signal-to-Noise vector offset
- Linear regression offset tilt
- Linear regression timing tilt
- First resonance amplitude
- First resonance frequency
- Second resonance amplitude
- Second resonance frequency
- Accumulation analysis (number of heads in each offset range: 0–24 microinches, etc.)
- Timing hysteresis
- Offset hysteresis
- Start-up offset

This large number of analyses was run both to completely explore the design space and to aid in the discovery of optimum methods for future work. ANOVA determines whether the sum of squares of the results of each factor are statistically significant when compared to the error factor. The F-test is used to determine the degree of significance of the factor and error variance ratios. Significance at 95% or 99% shows that the difference caused by the factor is real 95 or 99 out of 100 times and is not the result of natural variability in the data. Percent contribution of each factor is also calculated, because factors with a large contribution, even though statistically insignificant, can have a large impact on the problem.

As with the previous thermal test results, no problems were found in the hysteresis or start-up offset measurements, and none of the design factors were significant compared to the error factor. All the remaining

ANOVA techniques for thermal-head offset showed some of the design factors to be significant. Table 5 (also see Table A) contains the ANOVA results calculated from the amplitude of the normal to the track offset of the worse head from each test block. Five of the factors (5, 6, 11, 15, and 17) were insignificant, and they were pooled with the error factor (13) to form the test error variance. There were two significant factors (1 and 7), with the sleeve shape having the largest percent contribution. Taking the average offset for each shape showed that shapes 3 (top/bottom relieved) and 4 (side relieved) had the lowest amplitude offset. The other significant factor was stress relieving, with the current process (none) producing the lowest amplitude.

Table 5. Analysis of Variance for Worse Head Normal to the Track Offset

Source	Degree of Freedom	Sum of Squares	Variance	Percent Contribution
Sleeve Shape	3	3174.19	1058.06	33.69
Sleeve/Block Tolerance	3 (pooled)	(786.69)	(262.23)	—
Bottom Bearing Loading	1 (pooled)	(264.06)	(264.06)	—
Actuator Block Taper	1 (pooled)	(333.06)	(333.06)	—
Stress Relieving	1	1040.06	1040.06	10.99
Adhesive Application Method	1	742.56	742.56	7.12
Bottom Bearing/ Bore Clearance	1 (pooled)	715.56	715.56	6.77
Adhesive Cure Time	1	451.56	451.56	3.34
5 x 10 Interaction	1 (pooled)	(85.56)	(85.56)	—
Error pooled	(8)	1561.00	195.12	—
Total	15	7684.94	512.33	—

These results were confirmed by the other ANOVA methods. A_{11} found the sleeve shape to be significant, with the same shapes giving the best performance, while the current sleeve was always the worst. Figure 8 (also see Table B) shows the results of the accumulation analysis for this factor. This factor had a significant effect on the variability. When process factors were significant, the current process gave the best results. Except for stress relieving and offset tangent to the track, here stress relieving was beneficial. It is possible the orientation of blocks during stress relieving resulted in this directional effect. A_{11} tolerance factors were found to be insignificant, allowing a number of them to be loosened. The interaction of bottom bearing loading (factor 3) and the tolerance of the bottom bearing bore (factor 7) was significant for tilt and first amplitude resonance. The optimum combinations were the same and the interaction effect is shown in Figure 9 for the first resonance amplitude.

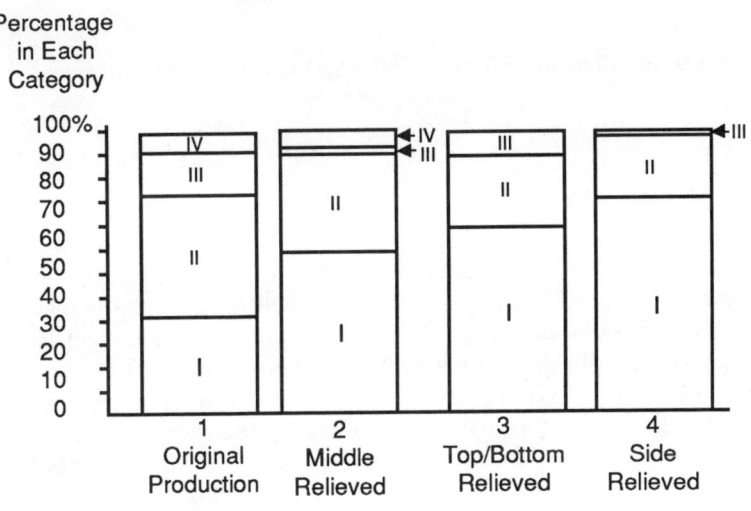

Category I: Heads 0–24 μin. off track
II: Heads 25–49 μin. off track
III: Heads 50–74 μin. off track
IV: Heads 75–100 μin. off track

Figure 8. Accumulation Analysis for Sleeve Shape

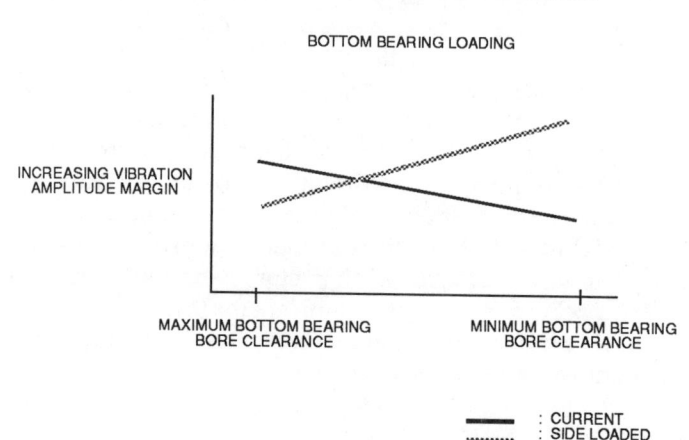

Figure 9. Interaction of Bottom Bearing Loading and Clearance for First Resonance Amplitude

6. Confirmation Testing

The surprising result of this designed experiment was that all of the normal-to-the-track head offsets were within an acceptable range. All of the test blocks would have passed the factory test. This was the result of a significant process factor being included only at its optimal level. Factor 2 compared an adhesive-bonded interface between the sleeve and the aluminum block at two tolerance levels to a heat-shrunk interface. The ANOVA showed that the heat-shrunk and the bonded interface gave the same performance. But the adhesive was applied very lightly for both of the tolerance levels when the original 12 adhesive bonded blocks were made by one assembler. Follow-up investigation found wide ranges of adhesive application under actual production conditions.

Dr. Taguchi always recommends confirmation testing of the optimum configuration. This was first done with small designed experiments and the building of small numbers of blocks for design-engineering testing. The effect of light and heavy bonding (easiest method to do consistently) on the original, top/bottom, and side-relieved sleeve shapes were first investigated. The heat-shrunk interface was not included due to vendor-assembly yield problems uncovered during the first experiment. Heavy bonding and the original sleeve shape gave for the first time a consistent offset pattern. Unfortunately, the offset amplitude was unacceptable for the top and bottom heads (see Figure A). The side-relieved was only slightly better, with the top/bottom-relieved having 9 out of 10 well within specifications (see Figure B). The outlier had one head at the specification limit due to the difficulty of ensuring that no adhesive got between the relieved ends of the sleeve and the aluminum block.

The vendor was informed of our plans to implement the top/bottom-relieved sleeve with a bonded interface. With the investigation of automated-adhesive application tooling still in process, this was clearly an inferior solution. Due to intimate vendor involvement in the experiment, they developed and proposed an inexpensive high-yield method of producing the heat-shrunk interface with minimum tooling.

7. IMPLEMENTATION AND IMPROVEMENT IN QUALITY

With the end-relieved sleeve showing little sensitivity to variability from the interface and the heat-shrink interface's elimination of the source of adhesive-thickness variability, a 50-piece pilot run was ordered without further testing. This production run achieved 100% yields, with almost a two-thirds reduction in the worse head offset 3σ limits. Figure 10 shows the results for the 50 heat-shrunk top/bottom-relieved sleeves, while Figure 11 has the distributions for 89 of the first production version (this factory test uses a smaller temperature range than the 50 to 115°F test shown in Figures 1 and 2).

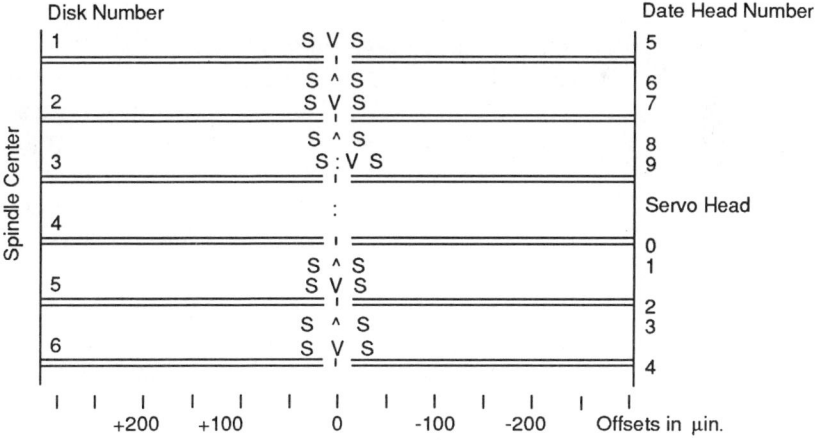

V = Average Head Offset for 50 Modules
S = 3σ Limits for 50 Modules

Figure 10. Results for First Production Run of the Heat-Shrunk Top/Bottom-Relieved Sleeve

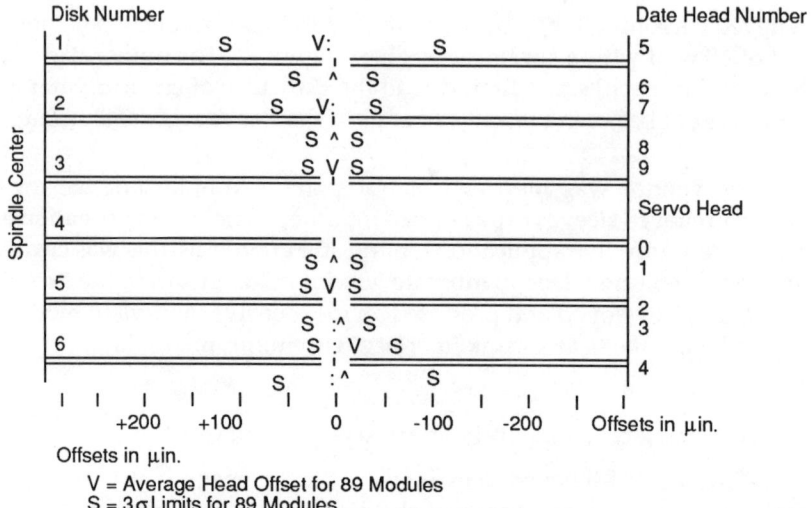

Figure 11. Results for Original Production Design

8. CONCLUSIONS

- Application of Taguchi Methods resulted in the discovery of a design that was robust to noise-induced variability. Tight distributions around the target value were achieved without increasing the cost of the product.
- These methods proved to be a good model of the effects of production variability, since high yields were obtained on the first and subsequent production runs. In contrast, significant results found by one-factor-at-a-time thermal testing have often had poor reproducibility in production.
- The solution path can be biased by careful selection of design factors. For this case, this resulted in an optimal design that could be reworked into existing parts.
- ANOVA ranks factors according to their significance and percent contribution and finds their optimum level. Often the discovery of insignificant factors is as important as the finding of significant factors.
- A solution was found quickly without having to resort to open-ended basic research for the cause mechanism and then possible major redesign to eliminate it.

- Taguchi Methods can be flexibly applied by engineers with only 40 to 80 hours of specialized training.
- The test strategy is disciplined and forces design engineers to become totally immersed in the production process to ensure all significant factors are included.
- Its major defects are: extensive time and effort (often by vendors or production personnel) for preparation of test samples; no intermediary results are available until the end of the testing; the recommended optimum design is often not built, which necessitates the running of confirmation experiments; and it is difficult to communicate the significance of the results to others not trained in designed experiment techniques. Taguchi, G. and Wu, Y. (1980).

REFERENCES

Bryce, Dr. G. R., and D. R. Collette, (1984). "Statistically Designed Experiments for Process Optimization." *Microelectronic Manufacturing and Testing*, pp. 25–28, October 1984.

Burgam, P. M. "Design of Experiments — The Taguchi Way." *Manufacturing Engineering*, pp. 44–47, May 1985.

Hunter, J. S. "Statistical Design Applied to Product Design." *Journal of Quality Technology* 17, pp. 210–221, 1985.

Kackar, R. N. "Off-Line Quality Control. Parameter Design, and the Taguchi Method." *Journal of Quality Technology* 17, pp. 176–188, 1985.

Phadke, M. S. "Quality Engineering Using Design of Experiments." 1982 Section on Statistical Education Proceedings of the American Statistical Association, pp. 11–20.

Sullivan, L. P. "Reducing Variability: A New Approach to Quality." *Quality Progress*, pp. 15–21, July 1984.

Symposia Proceedings, 1st and 2nd Supplier Symposium on Taguchi Methods, American Supplier Institute, Inc., Dearborn, Michigan, 1984.

Taguchi, G. and Y. Wu. *Introduction to Off-Line Quality Control*. Central Japan Quality Control Association, 1980.

Wu, Y. "Off-Line Quality Control: Japanese Quality Engineering." American Supplier Institute, Inc., Dearborn, Michigan, 1982.

Wu, Y. *Quality Engineering: Product and Process Design Optimization*, American Supplier Institute, Inc., Dearborn, Michigan, 1984.

Appendix to the Study

Table A. Worse Normal to Track Offset Test Results

Test Number	Offset in μin.
1	46.0000
2	92.0000
3	71.0000
4	99.0000
5	85.0000
6	81.0000
7	29.0000
8	68.0000
9	35.0000
10	58.0000
11	41.0000
12	52.0000
13	47.0000
14	24.0000
15	55.0000
16	44.0000

Table B. Percentage of Heads in Offset Categories for Accumulation Analysis

	Category*			
Test #	I	II	III	IV
1	70.000	30.000	0.000	0.000
2	20.000	30.000	40.000	10.000
3	20.000	70.000	10.000	0.000
4	30.000	40.000	10.000	20.000
5	40.000	50.000	0.000	10.000
6	50.000	40.000	0.000	10.000
7	90.000	10.000	0.000	0.000
8	50.000	40.000	10.000	0.000
9	80.000	20.000	0.000	0.000
10	50.000	30.000	20.000	0.000
11	80.000	20.000	0.000	0.000
12	60.000	30.000	10.000	0.000
13	90.000	10.000	0.000	0.000
14	100.000	0.000	0.000	0.000
15	50.000	40.000	10.000	0.000
16	60.000	40.000	0.000	0.000

* **NOTE:** Category I: Heads 0-24 μin. off track
II: Heads 25-49 μin. off track
III: Heads 50-74 μin. off track

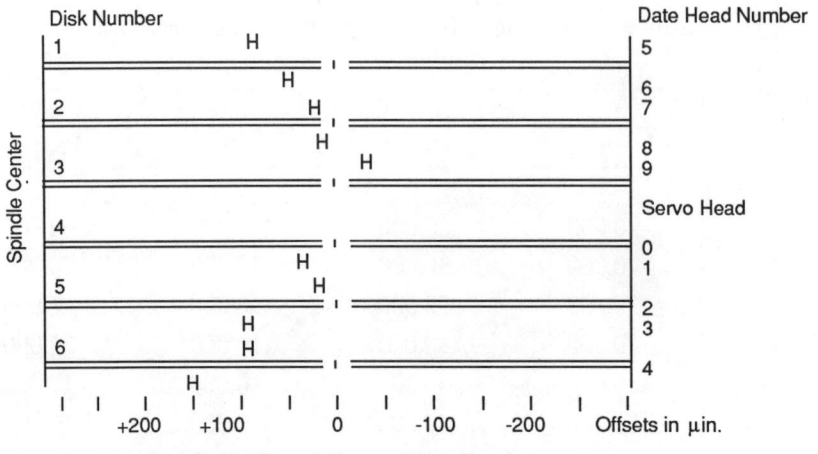

Figure A. Second EMD Design of Experiments

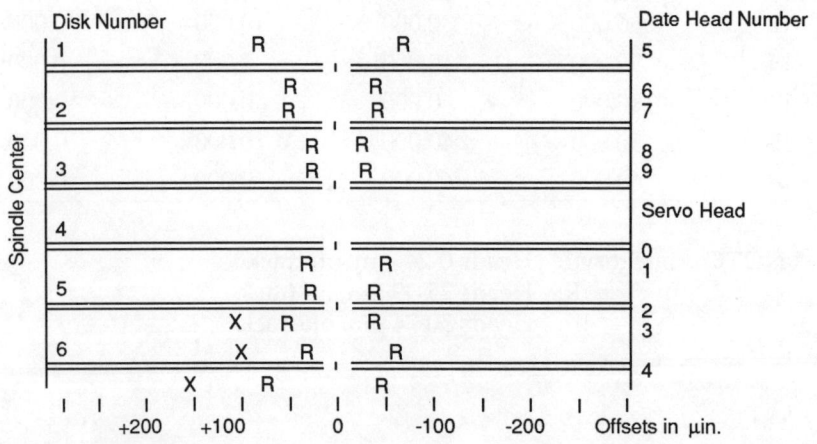

Figure B. Confirmation Run for End-Relieved Sleeves/Heavy Bonding

Q & A

Q. What was your impression of this experiment?

A. The author has excellent engineering insight. A successful Quality Engineering experiment is the result of a marriage between *"han-yo gijutsu"* and *"ko-yu gijutsu"* which in Japanese means "universal technologies" and "specialized field technology", respectively. I believe *ko-yo gijutso* contributes 80%, and *han-yo gijutsu* 20%, to the success of an experiment.

Ko-yo gijutsu (specialized field technology) includes:

1. Understanding the principles of the system's function
2. Selection of characteristics (what to measure)
3. Selection of controllable factors and their levels
4. Determination of noise factor(s)
5. Treatment of noise factor(s)
6. Defining the S/N Ratio for a dynamic case.

Han-yo gijutsu (universal technology) includes:

1. Orthogonal arrays
2. Data-analysis techniques such as:
   - Response table
   - Decomposition of total sum of squares to various compnents (linear, quadratic, cubic)
   - Interpretation of analysis
3. Techniques to modify orthogonal arrays
4. S/N Ratios
5. Strategies for parameter design and Tolerance design
6. Recognition of dynamic characteristics.

This author has a good understanding of *ko-yu gijutsu*, in his field of engineering. However, there are some points I'd like to make about this experiment.

Q. The layout for this experiment is an L_{16} ($4^1 \times 3^1 \times 2^8$) orthogonal array for controllable factors. Where are the noise factors?

A. Actually, temperature and disk-to-disk variation are the noise factors in this experiment. This is evident from the characteristic measured:

y = Offset of head reading (drift) due to temperature change

This experimenter is interested in reducing the impact of the noise factor, temperature. He is aware that temperature has a critical impact on the offset of the head readings. The recognition and inclusion of temperature is a sound experimental strategy.

Q. What about the S/N Ratio used in the analysis? The author uses:

$$S/N = -10 \log\left[m^2 + \sigma^2\right] \tag{21.1}$$

Where m signifies the mean.

A. The idea of this S/N Ratio is essentially the same as:

$$S/N = -10 \log \frac{1}{n} \sum_{i=1}^{n} (y_i - \text{Target})^2 \tag{21.2}$$

This S/N Ratio is used only when no method exists for adjusting the mean of the characteristic measured. In most nominal-the-best cases we do not use this S/N Ratio, because it is rare that the mean value cannot be adjusted.

However, when the characteristic is the drift due to noises during the usage of the product, such as y, two questions arise:
1. Can we find (consider) a design parameter to adjust the mean of the drift, or look for such a parameter from a design point of view?
2. Can we add a compensation loop in the system? (Although this tends to increase cost.)

It seems the answer is no to both questions in this case. When the objective is to reduce the mean and standard deviation of drift, S/N Ratio (1) makes sense.

Otherwise, the S/N Ratio should be:

$$S/N = -10 \log V_e, \quad V_e = \sigma^2 \tag{21.3}$$

Then, we maximize the S/N Ratio and adjust the mean to the target value using an adjustment factor(s). This S/N Ratio is used when y is nominal-the-best and takes positive and negative values, or the standard deviation is independent of the mean. In this case, we look

for a condition to minimally achieve a consistent drift.
There is one more potential problem when using S/N Ratio (2) for a nominal-the-best case. Interactions may exist. For example:

	Mean	Standard Deviation
A_1:	+11	5
A_2:	+3	5
B_1:	+18	5
B_2:	-4	5

S/N Ratio (2) will lead to A_2B_2 as the optimum. However, A_2B_2 probably will result in:
Mean = (3 – 7) + (– 4– 7) +7 = –8 Standard Deviation = 5
So:
Good + Good = Bad
This is just a hypothetical example; it did not happen in this case. But one should be aware of this. Often, problems occur because of interactions. With regard to interactions, Dr. Taguchi's philosophy is to:
- Treat interaction as noise.
- Select a good characteristic to avoid severe interactions.
- Select the appropriate S/N Ratio.
- Use dynamic characteristics.

Q. What about selecting a characteristic other than y = drift?

A. The author conducted analyses evaluating several characteristics. This is a good strategy. One of the most important objective of Quality Engineering is to look for a good characteristic to measure that accurately reflects the intent of the product or process.
Taguchi's philosophy states:
- Any function is a transformation of energy from one form to another.
- Reducing variability of energy transformation is the primary concern.
- The energy output should be non-negative.
- The standard deviation tends to increase as the mean increases for a characteristic relating to energy.
- The energy level should be adjusted via a signal factor. In the case of nominal-the-best analysis, the signal factor is called an adjustment factor. In the case of dynamic analysis, adjustability is treated as a dynamic characteristic, and the adjustment factor becomes a signal factor. (See the Flex case study on adjustability.)

Therefore, it is always better to select a characteristic that is "energy-related" and non-negative so that the standard deviation tends to increase as the mean increases at a similar quality level.

The S/N Ratio becomes:

$$S/N = 10 \log \frac{\frac{1}{n}(S_m - V_e)}{V_e} \approx 10 \log\left(\frac{m^2}{\sigma^2}\right) \qquad (21.4)$$

This is the most important strategy of *ko-yu gijutsu*. Sometimes measurement feasibility becomes a problem, i.e., there is an excellent characteristic to measure but measurement is infeasible, incapable, or too expensive. Then, "measurement engineering" becomes more important as technology advances.

22. COLD-START NOISE REDUCTION FOR HYDRAULIC ROLLER TAPPETS

Joseph Vihtelic and Robert Roos
Hy-Lift Division, SPX Corp.

An experiment using Taguchi parameter design resulted in a 96% reduction of cold-start noise in a 5.2 litre V-8 gasoline engine. This relates to an average cost savings of $16.70 per engine when applied to the Taguchi Quality Loss Function. The experiment tested fourteen 2-level factors, two 3-level factors, one 2-level noise factor, and two interactions. A modified L_{32} orthogonal array was used. Four major factors were found to be significant. As a result of this study, tappet noise was reduced by 75%, and estimated annual savings of $4,900,000 were achieved.

1. INTRODUCTION: THE COLD START NOISE PROBLEM

Imagine yourself behind the wheel of your brand new automobile. It is a rather brisk spring morning, and the air temperature is slightly below freezing. You turn the key to start the engine, and as soon as the engine turns over you are greeted by the loud "rap-rap-rap" of the valves slamming shut against the valve seats. As this continues for about three minutes you think of the money you wasted on this piece of junk, you vow never to buy another automobile from that company, and you think about the inconvenience of taking the car back to the dealer to be fixed. It is these losses — the cost of repair or replacement, the cost of customer dissatisfaction, and the cost of lost business — that Dr. Genichi Taguchi is referring to in his Quality Loss Function (QLF) analysis. These are the losses we are trying to reduce through this experiment.

This noise at startup is typically called "lifter noise" or "morning sickness." It occurs because approximately four of the hydraulic cam followers, or lifters, are on the nose of the cam when the engine shuts

---

From the *Sixth Symposium on Taguchi Methods*™, pp. 473–488, Copyright © 1988, American Supplier Institute, Inc., Dearborn, Michigan.

down. They then collapse over time from the force of the valve spring. Until these lifters can reprime themselves with engine oil the valve shuts prematurely, with excessive velocity causing the "lifter noise." Figure 1 shows the arrangement of the valve-train components. Normally, the lifter will reprime itself almost immediately. However, in this particular lifter application this has been a problem. This is why we, as the lifter supplier, have undertaken this program to eliminate the noise.

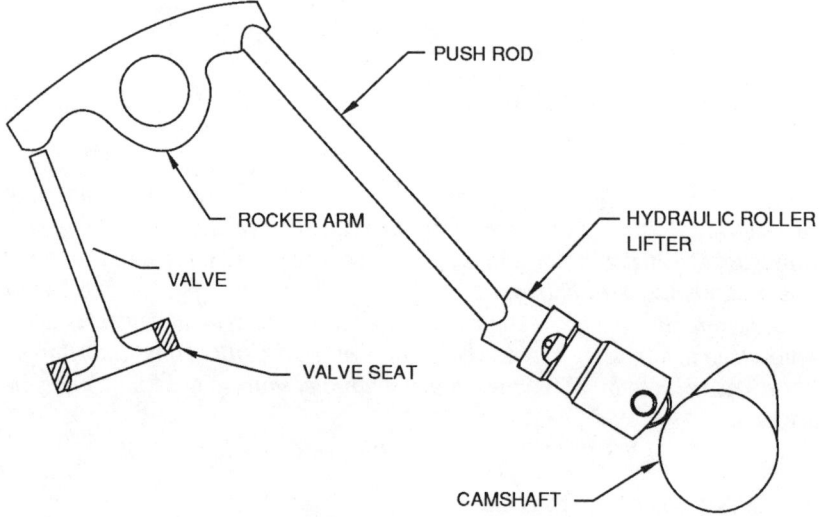

Figure 1. Valve Train Components

2. OBJECTIVE OF THE EXPERIMENT

The objective of this test is to identify design parameters that reduce lifter noise and make the lifter more robust against temperature and dry lash. At 70°F and at nominal dry lash there is typically no noise at start-up, but as temperature decreases or dry lash increases, the frequency and the time of lifter noise increases. Dry lash is defined as the difference between the collapsed and operating position of (see Figures 2 and 3) the lifter as measured at the valve tip. The ultimate goal of this test is to have no noise at –10°F and maximum dry lash.

Cold Start Noise Reduction for Hydraulic Roller Tappets

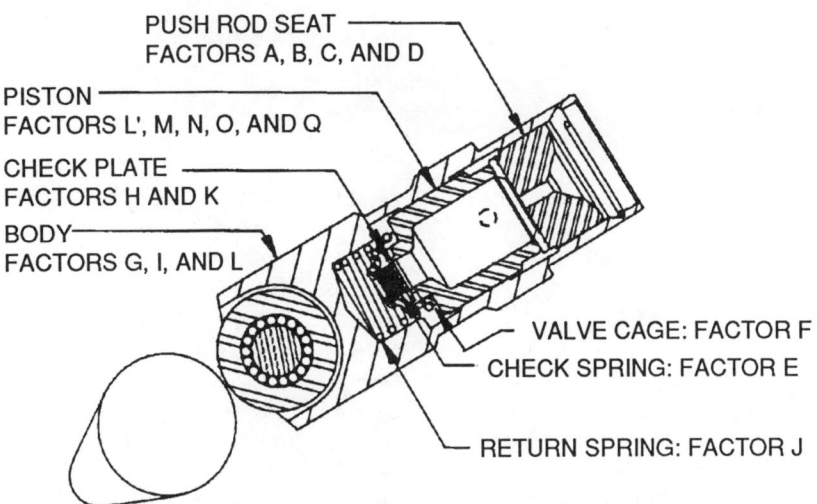

Figure 2. Hydraulic Roller Tappet Components
(operating position on base circle of cam)

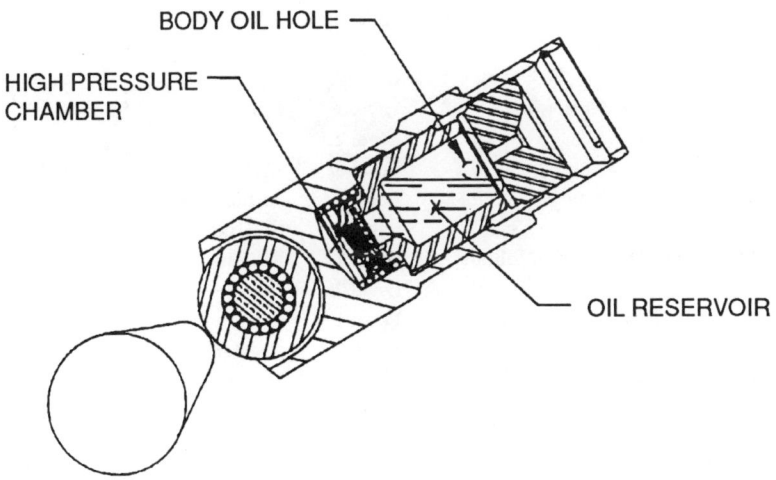

Figure 3. Features of Hydraulic Roller Tappet
(collapsed position on nose of cam)

Table 1. Factor List with Level Descriptions

Control Factor	Factors Description	Levels		Philosophy
A	PRS Clearance	Level 1:	0.001	I, II, III
		Level 2:	0.003	
B	PRS Drill Point	Level 1:	No	I
		Level 2:	Yes	
C	PRS Groove	Level 1:	1 Groove	I, II
		Level 2:	2 Grooves	
		Level 3:	4 Grooves	
		Level 4:	1 Narrow	
D	PRS Relief Diameter	Level 1:	Yes	II
		Level 2:	No	
E	Check-spring Rate	Level 1:	Existing	III, IV
		Level 2:	Lower	
F	Check-plate Travel	Level 1:	Existing	III
		Level 2:	Lower	
G	Leakdown Land Length	Level 1:	Existing	IV
		Level 2:	Longer	
H	Check-plate Thickness	Level 1:	0.028 in.	III, IV
		Level 2:	0.046 in.	
I	Body Oil Hole	Level 1:	0.094 in.	I, II
		Level 2:	0.062 in.	
J	Return Spring Rate	Level 1:	4 lb.	III
		Level 2:	8 lb.	
		Level 3:	12 lb.	
K	Check Plate Micro Finish	Level 1	As Stamped	III
		Level 2:	Ground	
L	High Pressure Volume	Level 1:	Existing	I
		Level 2:	Lessor	
L'	Piston Volume	Level 1:	Existing	I
		Level 2:	Greater	
M	Piston Face Angle	Level 1:	15°	IV
		Level 2:	25°	
		Level 3:	0°	
N	Wheelabrate	Level 1:	Yes	III
		Level 2:	No	
O	Piston Face Finish	Level 1:	Existing	III
		Level 2:	Rougher	

Control Factor	Factors Description	Levels		Philosophy
P	Test Engine No.	Level 1:	No. 1	I, II, III, IV
		Level 2:	No. 2	
		Level 3:	No. 3	
		Level 4:	No. 4	
Q	Piston Face Width	Level 1:	<0.015 in.	III
		Level 1:	>0.025 in.	

Noise Factor				
Noise	Leakdown	Level 1:	<15 sec.	
		Level 2:	>30 sec.	

Interactions
 E x F
 L x L'

3. THE FACTORS AND EXPERIMENTAL LAYOUT

After several meetings, with input from both the engine manufacturer and Hy-Lift, it was decided to test 18 control factors, one noise factor, and two interactions. The factors and levels are tabulated in Table 1.

All of the factors fall into at least one of four basic philosophies for reduction of noise. The first philosophy is that the tappet cannot rely on getting engine oil for some time after startup. Under this philosophy the lifter must maintain enough oil in its reservoir to operate the tappet until fresh oil arrives (see Figure 3). The factors using this philosophy have attempted to increase the reservoir volume, decrease the volume of oil required, and restrict oil from leaving the tappet during shut down.

The second philosophy is that the lifter does require engine oil to operate properly. The factors using this philosophy attempted to remove any restrictions between the oil gallery and the tappet reservoir. This philosophy was effective in previous testing, reducing the time-to-quiet of dry tappets in room-temperature, cold-start testing.

The third philosophy was to maintain proper check-valve operation. The check valve in the tappet allows oil to travel from the reservoir to the high-pressure chamber, but not vice versa. One hypothesis speculated that the cold-start noise was a result of the check valve not opening properly and not allowing oil from the reservoir to enter the high-pressure chamber (see Figure 3). Previous tests have shown this philosophy to be important in warm-engine noise.

The last group of factors were those that gave some improvements in the processing of the part. It was expected that these factors would not have a negative effect on cold-start performance, but that testing would be required before implementation.

Figure 2 shows the tappet components that were altered for each of the factors.

The factors are arranged in a multi-level L_{32} orthogonal array[1] (see Table 2). As shown in the L_{32} linear graph, Figure 4, the three- and four-level control factors, $C, J, M,$ and P, were developed by combining three two-level columns. To complete the array, the three unassigned columns were designated as error and pooled with e_1 error in the analysis. A single factor, leakdown, was included in the experiment as noise. This factor, which has no association with the noise problem, is critical to the overall function and reliability of the valve train. Any solution to lifter noise reduction must be able to perform equally well across all ranges of leakdown.

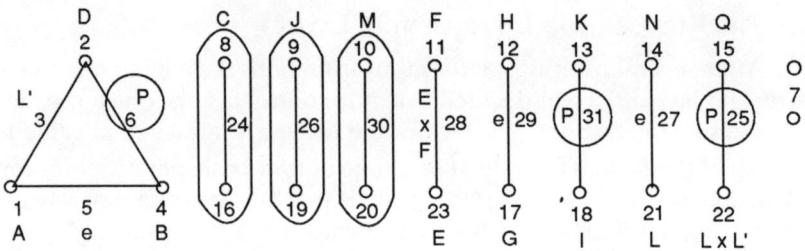

Figure 4. Linear Graph for Assigning Control Factors to an L_{32} Array

4. THE EXPERIMENT

The actual cold starting tqok place inside a refrigerated trailer at –10°F. Four engines were used in the testing. Each engine was mounted on a portable trailer that could easily be moved from the build-up area to the cold trailer.

Before each cold start, the engine was warmed up to operating oil temperature and then allowed to soak for a minimum of six hours until the oil temperature reached –10°F. This cycle would simulate actual worst-case field conditions. After each warm-up cycle was complete, the crankshaft was rotated until the #1 exhaust valve was on the nose of the camshaft. Field reports had indicated that this is where the noise is most likely to occur. Also, before each test the engine was placed on a 6° angle to simulate the installed position in the vehicle.

Table 2. $L_{32}(2^{31})$ Orthogonal Array

NOISE FACTOR
LEAKDOWN
1
2

Exp. No.	A 1	D 2	L' 3	B 4	e 5	P 6	O 7	C 8	J 9	M 10	F 11	H 12	K 13	N 14	Q 15	C 16	G 17	I 18	J 19	M 20	L 21	L 22	E 23	C 24	P 25	J 26	e 27	F 28	e 29	M 30	P 31
1	1	1	1	1	1	1	1	1	1	1	1	1	1	1	1	1	1	1	1	1	1	1	1	1	1	1	1	1	1	1	1
2	1	1	1	1	1	2	1	1	1	1	1	1	1	1	1	2	2	2	2	2	2	2	2	2	2	2	2	2	2	2	2
3	1	1	1	1	1	1	1	2	2	2	2	2	2	2	2	1	1	1	1	1	1	1	1	2	2	2	2	2	2	2	2
4	1	1	1	1	1	2	1	2	2	2	2	2	2	2	2	2	2	2	2	2	2	2	2	1	1	1	1	1	1	1	1
5	1	1	1	2	2	4	2	1	1	1	1	2	2	2	2	1	1	1	1	2	2	2	2	1	1	1	1	2	2	2	2
6	1	1	1	2	2	4	2	1	1	1	1	2	2	2	2	2	2	2	2	1	1	1	1	2	2	2	2	1	1	1	1
7	1	1	1	2	2	3	2	2	2	2	2	1	1	1	1	1	1	1	1	2	2	2	2	2	2	2	2	1	1	1	1
8	1	1	1	2	2	3	2	2	2	2	2	1	1	1	1	2	2	2	2	1	1	1	1	1	1	1	1	2	2	2	2
9	1	2	2	1	1	4	2	1	1	2	2	1	1	2	2	1	1	2	2	1	1	2	2	1	1	2	2	1	1	2	2
10	1	2	2	1	1	4	2	1	1	2	2	1	1	2	2	2	2	1	1	2	2	1	1	2	2	1	1	2	2	1	1
11	1	2	2	1	1	3	2	2	2	1	1	2	2	1	1	1	1	2	2	1	1	2	2	2	2	1	1	2	2	1	1
12	1	2	2	1	1	3	2	2	2	1	1	2	2	1	1	2	2	1	1	2	2	1	1	1	1	2	2	1	1	2	2
13	1	2	2	2	2	1	1	1	1	2	2	2	2	1	1	1	1	2	2	2	2	1	1	1	1	2	2	2	2	1	1
14	1	2	2	2	2	2	1	1	1	2	2	2	2	1	1	2	2	1	1	1	1	2	2	2	2	1	1	1	1	2	2
15	1	2	2	2	2	1	1	2	2	1	1	1	1	2	2	1	1	2	2	2	2	1	1	2	2	1	1	1	1	2	2
16	1	2	2	2	2	2	1	2	2	1	1	1	1	2	2	2	2	1	1	1	1	2	2	1	1	2	2	2	2	1	1
17	2	1	2	1	2	1	1	1	2	1	2	1	2	1	2	1	2	1	2	1	2	1	2	1	2	1	2	1	2	1	2
18	2	1	2	1	2	2	1	1	2	1	2	1	2	1	2	2	1	2	1	2	1	2	1	2	1	2	1	2	1	2	1
19	2	1	2	1	2	1	1	2	1	2	1	2	1	2	1	1	2	1	2	1	2	1	2	2	1	2	1	2	1	2	1
20	2	1	2	1	2	2	1	2	1	2	1	2	1	2	1	2	1	2	1	2	1	2	1	1	2	1	2	1	2	1	2
21	2	1	2	2	1	4	2	1	2	1	2	2	1	2	1	1	2	1	2	2	1	2	1	1	2	1	2	2	1	2	1
22	2	1	2	2	1	3	2	1	2	1	2	2	1	2	1	2	1	2	1	1	2	1	2	2	1	2	1	1	2	1	2
23	2	1	2	2	1	4	2	2	1	2	1	1	2	1	2	1	2	1	2	2	1	2	1	2	1	2	1	1	2	1	2
24	2	1	2	2	1	3	2	2	1	2	1	1	2	1	2	2	1	2	1	1	2	1	2	1	2	1	2	2	1	2	1
25	2	2	1	1	2	4	2	1	2	2	1	1	2	2	1	1	2	2	1	1	2	2	1	1	2	2	1	1	2	2	1
26	2	2	1	1	2	3	2	1	2	2	1	1	2	2	1	2	1	1	2	2	1	1	2	2	1	1	2	2	1	1	2
27	2	2	1	1	2	4	2	2	1	1	2	2	1	1	2	1	2	2	1	1	2	2	1	2	1	1	2	2	1	1	2
28	2	2	1	1	2	3	2	2	1	1	2	2	1	1	2	2	1	1	2	2	1	1	2	1	2	2	1	1	2	2	1
29	2	2	1	2	1	1	1	1	2	2	1	2	1	1	2	1	2	2	1	2	1	1	2	1	2	2	1	2	1	1	2
30	2	2	1	2	1	2	1	1	2	2	1	2	1	1	2	2	1	1	2	1	2	2	1	2	1	1	2	1	2	2	1
31	2	2	1	2	1	1	1	2	1	1	2	1	2	2	1	1	2	2	1	2	1	1	2	2	1	1	2	1	2	2	1
32	2	2	1	2	1	2	1	2	1	1	2	1	2	2	1	2	1	1	2	2	1	2	1	1	2	2	1	2	1	1	2

After each engine had cooled to –10°F, the engine was started. The length of time of the lifter noise was measured for three different noise conditions. These conditions were called "rap," "tick," and "hash." The same evaluators were used for all tests to ensure consistency. "Rap" is defined as very loud valve-train noise where nearly all cylinders are noisy. "Tick" is defined as noticeable valve-train noise from one to four lifters (typically, those on the nose of the camshaft during cool-down). Hash is defined as very slight noise that is not noticeable above normal engine operating noise, but is noticeable upon close inspection. Oil pressure was also recorded when all cylinders became quiet. Each experiment was done twice to strengthen the experimental results.

Because of dilution of the engine oil from the fuel and the assembly oil used in the lifters, the oil was changed after every eight cold starts. An oil sample was collected after every two cold starts to determine the change in viscosity. A linear regression was then done to determine the effect of viscosity on time to quiet.

5. Response Analysis and Analysis of Variance

A total of 132 cold-start tests were performed, 32 combinations of control factors by two levels of noise with two repetitions for each level. The results presented in this report are for statistical analysis of the intermediate noise condition "tic." With minor exceptions, these results are consistent with significant effects found at both noise conditions.

The data was evaluated in terms of Signal-to-Noise (S/N) smaller-the-better and raw data for the time-to-quiet to meet the experimental objective to reduce lifter noise. Analysis of variance (ANOVA) results for S/N (see Table 3) identifies three control factors as significant. Factor Q, piston face width, had the largest effect, accounting for 34.84% of the variation in S/N levels. Factor J, return spring rate, and factor H, check-plate thickness, accounted for 18.32% and 6.23% of the variation, respectively. Figure 5, a graph of level averages for the three significant control factors, shows the strength of level changes. Piston facewidth exhibited an average change of 15 dB at two-level settings. Return spring rate experienced an average change of 16 dB over three level settings.

Analysis of the decomposition of return spring rate effects into linear and nonlinear components indicated that the effect was predominantly linear. The quadratic component of this factor accounted for less than .4% of the total effect and thus was not considered for further analysis.

ANOVA results for the raw data (see Table 4), identifies six significant control factors. Factor Q, piston face width, had an effect larger than

Table 3. ANOVA Table Results of Data for Signal-to-Noise Smaller-the-Better

Source	df	S	V	S'	ρ%
A	1	25	25°		
D	1	112	112°		
L'	1	80	80°		
B	1	2	2°		
ERR	3	538	179°		
P	3	250	83°		
O	1	80	80°		
F	1	39	39°		
H	1	345	345	285	6.23
K	1	24	24		
N	1	16	16°		
Q	1	1654	1654	1594	34.84
G	1	23	23°		
I	1	12	12°		
L	1	16	16°		
L'x L	1	19	19°		
E	1	5	5°		
C	3	240	80°		
J	2	958	479°	838	18.32
E x F	1	14	14°		
M	2	15	8°		
e_1	2	108	54°		
e_2	0	0			
(e)	27	1618	60	1858	40.61
TOTAL	31	4575	148		

° indicates pooled w/error

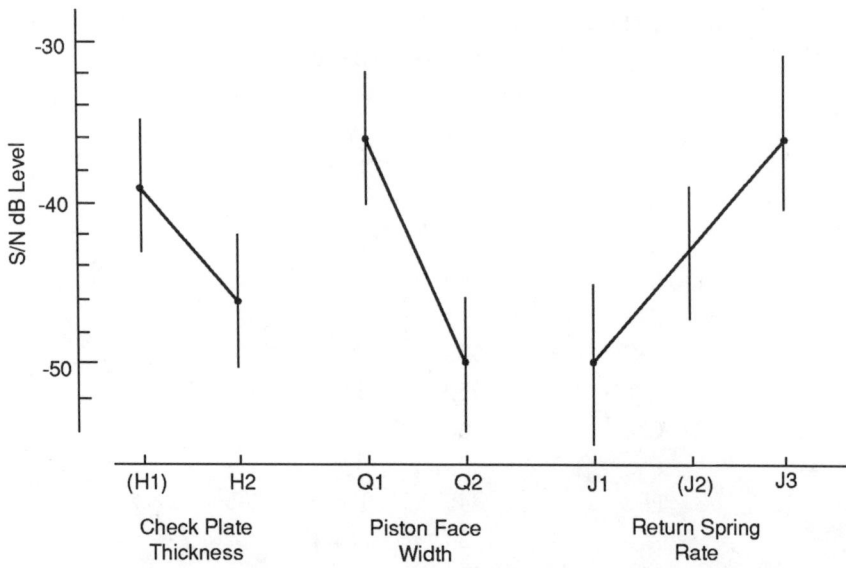

Figure 5. Graph of Signal-to-Noise averages with 95% confidence intervals. Parenthesis indicate existing levels.

all other control factors combined, accounting for 33.53% of the total variation in time to quiet. Factor J, return spring rate, and factor C, push rod seat (PRS) groove, were significant at the 99% confidence level, accounting for 13.56% and 6.92% of the variation, respectively. Factor P, test engine, was also significant at the 99% level. This factor was included in the control array as opposed to the outer noise array in an effort to economize or reduce the number of individual experiments, yet still provide information on the random effect of engine-to-engine differences. The results found the effect of engines to be minor as compared to other factors, as such we were able to discount engine effects without seriously jeopardizing the conclusion for other main effects. Factor F, check-plate travel and factor H, check-plate thickness, were significant at the 95% confidence level. The optimal level for check plate thickness for raw data agreed with the optimal level for S/N. The effect for check-plate travel was very small, less than 1.5% contribution.

Figure 6 is a graph of level averages for raw data for three major significant control factors. As shown, piston face width yielded an average improvement of 248 sec. for time-to-quiet. Return spring rate exhibited average reductions of time-to-quiet of 226 sec. from level one

Table 4. ANOVA Results of Raw Data for Time-to-Quiet

Source	df	S	V	S'	ρ%
A	1	8401	8401°		
D	1	67942	67942°		
L'	1	7954	7954°		
B	1	4790	4790°		
ERR	3	222403	74134°		
P	3	23082	76941	176076	3.03
O	1	70641	70641°		
F	1	104253	104253°	88004	1.48
H	1	112160	112160	93911	1.62
K	1	3905	3905°		
N	1	43108	41308°		
Q	1	1967880	1967880	1949631	33.53
G	1	13142	13142°		
I	1	11877	11877°		
L	1	856	856°		
L' x L	1	39445	39445°		
E	1	48633	48633°		
C	3	457251	152417	402504	6.92
J	2	824797	412399	788299	13.56
E x F	1	52448	52448°		
M	2	7534	3767°		
NOISE	1	43919	43919°		
e_1	33	636630	19292°		
e_2	64	833248	13020°		
(e)	116	2116876	18249	2317615	39.86
TOTAL	127	5814009	45780		

° indicates pooled w/error

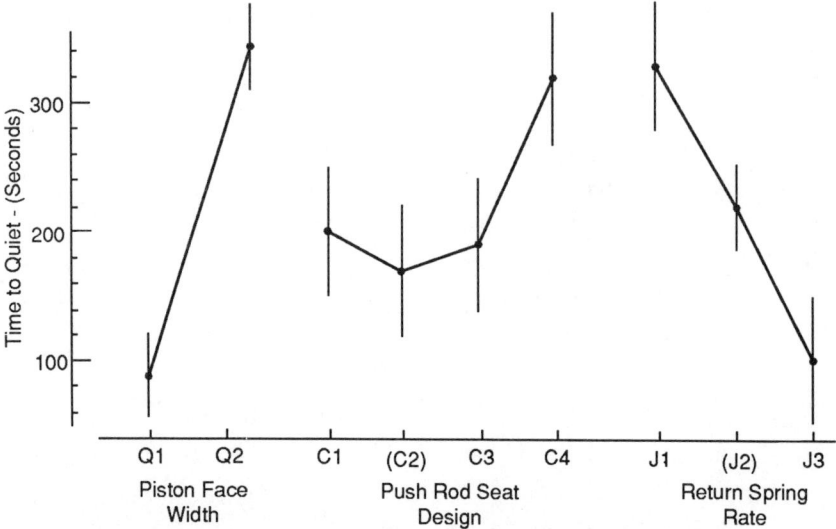

Figure 6. Graph of Raw Data Time-to-Quiet Level Averages with 95% Confidence Intervals (parenthesis indicate existing levels)

to level three. The figure shows that PRS groove-design levels one through three resulted in nearly the same average time-to-quiet, with no significant differences at 95% confidence levels. For reasons relating to the analysis of "rap" and "hash" noise conditions, level three was chosen as optimal.

Results of linear regression on time-to-quiet versus oil viscosity indicated no relation. This data supports and strengthens the above findings on main effect by indicating no confounding of oil viscosity effects occurred during the experiment. Results of regression analysis on time-to-quiet versus oil pressure indicated a small yet significant relationship. As oil pressures increased, time-to-quiet was reduced. This is an important finding for the engine designers; however, because engine oil pressure was treated as noise it does not change the results for main effects.

A number of confirmation tests were conducted following the experiment to evaluate the influence of the main effects. The maximum time of "tic" in these tests was 6 sec., which fell within the projected confidence intervals. Cold-start noise was not eliminated but was significantly reduced.

6. Loss Function Analysis

In consideration of the results for both S/N smaller-the-better and raw data for time-to-quiet, the factors and levels used to evaluate optimal design were:

1. Factor C — PRS groove, level three: four grooves
2. Factor H — check plate thickness, level one: .028 in.
3. Factor J — return spring rate, level three: 12 lb.
4. Factor Q — piston face width, level one: less than .015 in.

The S/N value for the existing design equals – 44 dB. The S/N estimates for the optimal design equals – 20 dB. The resulting effect of the optimal design yields a 24 dB gain.

The existing (cost-of-quality) loss due to cold-start lifter noise is $16.75 per engine. Using the formula below for estimating quality improvement, the new loss per engine is $.07.

At 1988 production rates, the estimated annual cost savings will be $4,904,802. This represents a 99.6% improvement over the existing design.

$$\frac{\text{Loss Existing}}{\text{Loss New}} = 10^{\frac{\text{dB (gain)}}{10}} \tag{22.1}$$

7. Summary and Conclusions

Based on data from 132 experimental trials, we were able to identify four major control factors for reducing lifter noise. One factor, checkplate width, remained unchanged from existing design and production specifications. Two factors, piston face width and return spring rate, involved retargeting nominal design specifications. And one factor, PRS groove, required a completely new design configuration. These four factors accounted for 61.2% of the variation in S/N levels and 55.7% of the variation in time-to-quiet. Recommendations for these changes are being implemented for the 1989 model year. Based on current engine production rates, annual savings should exceed $4,900,000.

Detailed data analysis revealed that check-valve function, preliminary philosophy III, was the most influential subsystem that we have the capability to control. Although we did not achieve complete elimination of cold-start lifter noise, we were successful in reducing time-to-quiet by 75%. The positive results of this study are encouraging new effects to design follow-up experiments, to explore new design proposals, and to further examine alternate levels of significant factors. Overall, Taguchi Methods provided a direct, timely, and cost-effective solution for reducing lifter noise.

Acknowledgments

This experiment was conducted through the diligent services of many Hy-Lift personnel. A special thanks is in order for those who helped turn wrenches in daily preparation of test engines, and those who actually conducted the testing.

Mark Bush, Sales Manager
Dan Hecksel, Dyno Technician
Gale Rager, Dyno Technician
Morrie Dadd, Marketing and Engineering Manager (Retired)
Dan Westhoff, Product Engineer

References

Taguchi G., and S. Konishi, *Orthogonal Arrays and Linear Graphs*, American Supplier Institute, Dearborn, Michigan, 1987, p. 7.

Wu Y., and W. H. Moore, *Quality Engineering Product and Process Design Optimization*, American Supplier Institute, Dearborn, Michigan, 1986.

Q & A

Q. This is a product design case using an L_{32} orthogonal array with multi-levels. Any comments?

A. It involves a mixture of 2-, 3-, and 4-level factors.

Q. How does one modify a 2-level series orthogonal array to assign 3- and 4-level factors?

A. For a 4-level factor, the multi-level arrangement technique is used by deleting three specific columns according to a linear graph and creating a 4-level column. For a 3-level column, create a 4-level column of the four levels created by multi-level arrangement and then use dummy treatment to create a 3-level column.

Q. Factor J, return spring rate, and factor M, piston face angle, are both continuous variables. Instead of dummy-treating one of the four levels, isn't it better to include one more level?

A. If it does not cost too much you may include an additional level.

Q. There are fourteen 2-level factors, two 3-level factors, two 4-level factors, and two interactions between 2-level factors; the total degrees of freedom is 26. The degrees of freedom of an L_{32} orthogonal array is 31. Therefore, the degrees of freedom for the error must be $31 - 26 = 5$. But in Table 2, the ANOVA for the Signal-to-Noise (S/N) Ratio, two degrees of freedom are shown under e_1.

Where are the additional three degrees of freedom?

A. They are hidden in ERR, which probably signifies the error.

Q. I can see only three columns that are not assigned, so the error degrees of freedom are three. Where do the remaining degrees of freedom come from?

A. There are two dummy-treated columns. In each dummy-treated level, there is one degree of freedom for the error.

Q. Why was the raw data used in the analysis of time-to-quiet?

A. It would be better to use S/N Ratio.

Q. Is it all right to just analyze the mean, since when the mean is reduced, variablity is reduced?

A. This is true in most cases, but there are also cases when the means are equal but variability is different, so we should always use the S/N Ratio.

APPENDIX: KEY DATES

1924	Dr. Genichi Taguchi born on January 1 in Tokamichi, Niigata-ken, Japan.
1942	Attended Kiryu Technical College; studied textile engineering.
1942–45	Joined the Imperial Japanese Navy; served in the Astronomical Dept. of the Navigation Institute.
1947–48	Employed by the Ministry of Public Health and Welfare.
1947–49	Served as a consultant to Morinaga Seika.
1948–50	Employed by the Institute of Statistical Mathematics, Ministry of Education.
1950–62	Employed by the Electrical Communications (ECL) Laboratory, Nippon Telephone and Telegraph Co. Taught experimental design to ECL engineers; consulted with industry.
1951	Wrote *Experimental Design and Life Test Analysis* (book is out of print and considered out of date by Dr. Taguchi).
1954–55	Served as visiting professor, Indian Statistical Institute; met R.A. Fisher; conducted 20 experimental-design applications in Indian industry.
1956–57	Wrote first edition of *Design of Experiments* (*Jikken Keikakuho*), in which he introduced the use of orthogonal arrays and analysis of categorical data.
1960	Awarded Deming Prize. Met Dr. W. Edwards Deming at international statistics conference.
1962	Wrote second edition of *Design of Experiments*, in which he introduced the application of the Signal-to-Noise Ratio to industrial research. Served as visiting research

	associate, Princeton University; interested in ideas of Dr. John Tukey, including the "jackknife" method, although not specifically for Quality Engineering. Awarded PhD in science degree by Kyusha University.
1963–64	Asked to be professor at Aoyama Gakuin University (the College of Science and Engineering was then under construction).
1964–82	Employed as professor, Aoyama Gakuin University; consultant to industry.
1976	Wrote third edition of *Design of Experiments*, in which he changed the mathematical base of his methodology from statistics to the quadratic system.
1982	Retired from Aoyama Gakuin; became advisor at the Japanese Standards Association.
1983	Named executive director of the American Supplier Institute, Inc.
1986	Awarded the Willard F. Rockwell Medal by the International Technology Institute.
1989	Received the Ranjuhosho Award, presented by the Emperor of Japan for outstanding contributions to Japanese economics and industry.
	Elected to the World Level of the Hall of Fame for Engineering, Science and Technology.

Glossary A: Key Terms

Additivity A concept relating to the independence of factors. The effect of additive factors occurs in the same direction (i.e., they do not interact).

Analysis of variance (ANOVA) Analysis of the impacts of variances caused by factors. ANOVA is performed after the decomposition of the total sum of squares.

Classified attribute The type of quality characteristic that is divided into discrete classes rather than being measured on a continuous scale.

Compounding of noise factors A strategy for reducing the number of experimental runs by combining noise factors into a single ouput for experimentation.

Confirmation experiment A follow-up experiment run under the conditions defined as optimum by a previous experiment. The confirmation experiment is intended to verify the experimental predictions.

Confounding A condition in which experimental information on variables cannot be separated. The information becomes confused with other information.

Consumer loss A term used to describe the cost incurred by a consumer due to a lack of quality in the function of a product or process. The consumer tolerance is related to consumer loss.

Consumer tolerance (LD 50) An expression for the limit at which 50% of customers view a product as not functioning. The consumer tolerance is related to consumer loss.

Control factor A product or process parameter whose values can be selected and controlled by the design or manufacturing engineer.

Cost-reduction factor A factor that has a weak effect on both variability and the mean. The selected level of such a factor is based on such considerations as lower cost and higher productivity.

Data analysis The process performed to determine the best factor levels for reducing variability and adjusting the average response toward the target value.

Decomposition of variation The decomposition of collected data into the sources of variation.

Degrees of freedom The number of independent squares associated with a given factor (usually the number of factor levels minus one).

Distribution A way of describing the output of a common-cause system of variation, in which individual values are not predictable but in which the outcomes as a group form a pattern that can be described in terms of its location, spread, and shape. Location is commonly expressed by the terms of the mean or median and spread is commonly expressed in terms of the standard deviation or the range of a sample. Shape involves many characteristics, such as symmetry and peakedness. These are often summarized by using the name of a common distribution, such as the normal, binomial, or Poisson.

Dummy treatment A method used to modify an orthogonal array to accommodate a factor with fewer levels.

Dynamic characteristic A characteristic that expresses the adjustability of the output of a system or subsystem.

Error sum of squares The total of the sums of squares that are considered as residual.

Expected value of a variance The mean of an infinite number of variances estimated from collected data.

Factor A parameter or variable that may impact product or process performance.

Factorial effect The effect of a factor or an interaction or both.

Fractional factorial layout An experimental design that consists of a fraction of all factor-level combinations.

Go/no-go specification The traditional U.S. approach to quality, which states that a part, component, or assembly that lies between specified upper and lower specifications meets quality standards.

Indicative factor A factor that has a technical meaning but has nothing to do with the selection of the best level.

Infeasible run estimate A procedure whereby a Signal-to-Noise Ratio can be estimated when an experimental run cannot be conducted for any reason in an experiment.

Inner array A layout or orthogonal array for the control factors selected for experimentation or simulation.

Interaction A condition in which the impact of a factor or factors upon a quality characteristic changes depending on the level of another factor (i.e., the interdependent effect of two or more factors).

Larger-the-better characteristic The type of performance parameter that gives improved performance as the value of the parameter increases (e.g., tensile strength, roundness, flatness, etc.) This type of characteristic belongs to the category of quality characteristics that has infinity as the ideal value and has no negative value.

Line A line represents the column placement for the interaction between the factors located at the two nodes of a linear graph.

Linear graph A graphical representation of numbered lines and dots that have a one-to-one correspondence to the columns of a related orthogonal array. Each linear graph is associated with one orthogonal array. However, a given orthogonal array can have several linear graphs. Linear graphs facilitate the assignment of factors to specific columns in the orthogonal array when information concerning interaction assignment or orthogonal array modification is desired.

Linearity A measure of the straightness of a response plot. Also the extent to which a measuring instrument's response is proportional to the measured quantity.

Loss to society Loss to society is defined by Dr. Genichi Taguchi as a quality loss in terms of time and money incurred by the consumer, the third party, and the manufacturer when a product deviates from the intended target function.

Manufacturing tolerance The assessment of the tolerance prior to shipping. The manufacturing tolerance is usually tighter than the consumer tolerance.

Mean The average value of some variable.

Mean data analysis An analysis performed to determine the mean values of experimental or simulation runs. Also called mean effects analysis.

Mean square deviation (MSD) A measure of variability around the mean or target value.

Mean square error variance The variance considered as the error.

Mean sum of squares The sum of squares per unit degree of freedom.

Measurement accuracy The difference between the average result of a measurement with a particular instrument and the true value of the quantity being measured.

Measurement error The difference between the actual and measured value of measured quantity.

Measurement precision The extent to which a repeated measurement gives the same result. Variations may arise from the inherent capabilities of the instrument, from changes in operating condition, etc. Also see repeatability and reproducibility.

Node A point (i.e., dot) in a linear graph that represents a column or factor.

Noise Any uncontrollable factor that causes product quality to vary. There are three types of noise: 1. Noise due to external causes (e.g., temperature, humidity, operator, vibration, etc.), 2. Noise due to internal causes (e.g., wear, deterioration, etc.), 3. Noise due to part-to-part or product-to-product variation.

Nominal-the-best The type of performance characteristic parameter that has an attainable target or nominal value (e.g., length, voltage, etc.).

Number of units The total of the square of the coefficients in a linear equation. It is used to calculate the sum of squares.

Off-line quality control Activities that use design of experiments or simulation to optimize product and process designs. These activities include system design, parameter design, and tolerance design.

On-line quality control Activities that occur at the manufacturing phase and include the use of the Quality Loss Function to determine the optimum inspection interval, control limits, etc. On-line quality control is used to maintain the optimization gained through off-line quality control.

Orthogonal array A matrix of numbers arranged in rows and columns in such a way that each pair of columns are orthogonal to each other. When used in an experiment, each row represents the state of the factors in a given experiment. Each column represents a specific factor or condition that can be changed from experiment to experiment. The array is called orthogonal because the effects of the various factors in the experimental results can be separated from each other.

Outer array A layout or orthogonal array for the noise factors selected for experimentation.

Parameter design The second of three design stages. During parameter design, the nominal values of critical dimensions and characteristics are established to optimize performance at low cost.

Percent contribution The pure sum of squares divided by the total sum of squares to express the impact of a factorial effect.

Pooled error variance The error variance calculated by pooling the smaller factorial effects.

Preliminary experiment An experiment conducted with only noise factors to determine direction and tendencies of the effect of these noise factors. The results of the preliminary experiment are used to compound noise factors.

Pure (net) error sum of squares The sum of squares after adding the error terms originally included in the regular sums of squares of factorial effects.

Pure (net) sum of squares The sum of squares of a factorial effect after subtracting the error portion.

Quality The loss imparted by a product to society from the time the product is shipped.

Quality characteristic A characteristic of a product or process that defines product or process quality. The quality characteristic measures the degree of conformance to some known standard.

Quality Function Deployment (QFD) A term used to describe the process by which customer feedback is analyzed and results are incorporated into product design. The QFD process is often referred to as determining the "voice of the customer."

Quality Loss Function (QLF) A parabolic approximation of the quality loss that occurs when a quality characteristic deviates from its best or target value. The QLF is expressed in monetary units: The cost of deviating from the target increases quadratically the further it moves from the target. The formula used to compute the QLF depends on the type of quality characteristic being used.

Repeatability The variation in repeated measurements of a particular object with a particular instrument by a single operator.

Reproducibility The state whereby the conclusions drawn from small-scale laboratory experiments will be valid under actual manufacturing and usage conditions (i.e., consistent and desirable).

Response factor The output of a system or the result of a performance.

Robustness The condition used to describe a product or process design that functions with limited variability in spite of diverse and changing environmental conditions, wear, or, component-to-component variation. A product or process is robust when it has limited or reduced functional variation even in the presence of noise.

Sensitivity analysis Analysis performed to determine the mean values of experimental runs used when the means are widely dispersed.

Signal factor A factor used to adjust the output.

Signal-to-Noise (S/N) Ratio Any of a group of special equations that are used in experimental design to find the optimum factor-level settings that will create a robust product or process. The S/N Ratio originated in the communications field, in which it represented the power of the signal over the power of the noise. In Taguchi Methods usage, it represents the ratio of the mean (signal) to the standard deviation (noise). The formula used to compute the S/N Ratio depends on the type of quality characteristic being used.

Signal-to-Noise (S/N) Ratio analysis Analysis performed to determine the factor levels required to reduce variability and achieve the ideal function of a characteristic.

Smaller-the-better The type of performance characteristic parameter that has zero as the best value (e.g., wear, deterioration, etc.). This type of characteristic belongs to the category of quality characteristic that has zero as the best value and has no negative value.

Standard deviation A measure of the spread of the process output or the spread of a sampling statistic from the process (e.g., of subgroup averages). Standard deviation is denoted by the Greek letter σ (sigma).

System design The first of three design stages. During system design, scientific and engineering knowledge is applied to produce a functional prototype design. This prototype is used to define the initial settings of a product or process design characteristic.

Tolerance design The third of three design stages. Tolerance design is applied only if the design is not acceptable at its optimum level following parameter design. During tolerance design, more costly materials or processes with tighter tolerances are considered.

Triangular table A table containing all the information needed to locate main effects and two factor interactions. A triangular table is used for linear graph modification and the assignment of interactions.

Variability The property of exhibiting variation (i.e., changes or differences).

Variance The mean square deviation (MSD) from the mean. The sum of squares divided by the degrees of freedom.

Variation The inevitable differences among individual outputs of a process.

Variation of a factor Same as the sum of squares of a factorial effect.

Glossary B: Key Symbols

Symbol	Definition
dB	Decibel. Unit to measure the effect of noise—10 times the logarithm of a value.
f	Degrees of freedom.
k	Number of levels of the signal factor.
M	Level value of the signal factor.
r	Effective divisor (also called the number of effective replication).
S_T	Total variation (sum of squares).
$S_\beta = V_\beta$	Variation of linear effect (equals variance).
V_e	Error variation (equals variance).
α	Ratio of intervals of signal factors.
β	Linear coefficient from raw data.
η	Signal-to-Noise Ratio.

INDEX

A

Additivity 38, 115, 147, 211, 217, 257
Adjustment,
    of the mean 71
    of the slope 71
    sensitivity of 72
Amplitude variability 312, 313
Analysis,
    accumulation 15, 18, 27, 128, 129, 132, 237, 323, 329
    additional 90
    analytic 177, 178
    circuit design 146
    data 287
    dynamic 60
    for response time 211
    for the first test 220
    for the second test 224
    holographic 314
    Loss Function 347
    multivariable 239, 240, 246
    nominal-the-best 23, 233
    of experimental results 137, 261, 303
    of the hot-forming process 102
    of the mean (see Analysis, regular)
    ordinary (see Analysis, regular)
    QLF 242
    raw data (see Analysis, regular)
    regression 346
    regular 22, 28, 37, 80, 90, 100, 101, 114, 233, 266
    response 44, 250, 342
    S/N Ratio 19, 28, 38, 45, 48, 91, 98, 287
    time-to-quiet 303, 305
Analysis of variance (see ANOVA)
Analytical methods 175
ANOVA 35, 47, 130, 168, 187, 193, 274, 321, 322, 342
    accumulation analysis 18
    average 222, 226
    for axial temp. difference 185, 189
    for surface defects 47, 48
    hot-stamp design 130
    of the mean 46
    photoreceptor defects 242

    pull-off force 80, 155
    push-out force 122
    regular analysis 22, 80
    S/N Ratio 21, 50, 52, 66, 82, 154, 186, 250, 272, 274, 289, 343
    sensitivity analysis 84, 251
    summarizing data 52
    variability 221
ANSYS program 180
Area ratio 191, 193, 197
Assembly-effort 132

B

Bar graphs 241
Beryllium-Copper Pin Contact 219
Beta 71, 72
Beta valve (see Beta)
Black box 206
Bond,
    electrical resistance of 259, 265
    process variables 269
    strength of 269
Bonding,
    strength 259, 261
    of ceramic chip resistors 267
Brainstorming 15, 32, 41, 42, 54, 59, 128, 136, 236, 248, 260, 285, 301
Braking,
    equipment 191
    types of 181, 191, 198

C

Capability,
    first time 31, 37
    of the process 308
Cause of variation 256
Cause-and-effect diagram 32, 33, 59, 75, 76, 128, 163
Characteristics, (see also, Quality characteristics)
    classified attributes 27
    dynamic 71, 147, 237, 333
    larger-the-better 105, 125, 147
    multi-quality 241
    nominal-the-best 18
    non-dynamic 71

optimization of the 114
smaller-the-better 28, 147
substitutional 28
static (see Characteristics, non-
    dynamic)
visual 269
Classified integers 246
Coding 26, 27
Coding scheme (see Coding)
Column assignment 43
Columns,
    dummy treated 349
    four-level 348
    three-level 348
Combination design 232, 245
Command,
    standard 205
    trivial 205
Comparison,
    before and after the experiment 25
    between reference and optimum
        S/N 99
    of prediction and actual results 170
    of optimal and current condition 196
Competitive position 159, 172
Compounding 90, 173, 174, 198, 286, 296
Computer simulation 285 (see also
    Simulation)
Conditions,
    actual load 204
    actual production 169
    best 36
    boundary and initial 180
    current 115, 116
    existing 171
    optimum 116, 118, 171
    recommended 96
    reference 96, 101
Confidence,
    band 158, 159, 170
    intervals 68, 116, 227, 228, 276
Confirmation, 145, 214, 255, 276, 291, 308
    experiment 24, 28, 37, 67, 70, 87, 102,
        118, 128, 158, 160, 215, 266, 292,
        305, 308, 324, 327, 330
    run (see Confirmation, experiment)
Confounding 49, 159, 164
Continuous improvement 159
Contribution,
    of significant factors 225
    to total variation 225

Control charting 171
Control factors, (see also, Factors,
    Controllable)
    layout of 110
    three-level 174
Controlling system 58
Cost reduction 26
Cost relationship 15
Costs,
    consumer 72
    scrap/rework 26, 38, 68, 309
    of customer dissatisfaction 355
    of lost business 335
    of manufacturing 296
    of quality 346
    of the experiment 89
    plating 277
    producer 172
    to society 172
Countable classified numbers 246
Cp 119
Cpk 235, 245, 255, 257
Cross-functional team 127
Customer satisfaction 136

D

Data,
    classified attribute 14, 18, 27, 90, 147
    for pull-off force 80
    for pull strength 278
    from the confirmation runs 24
    variable 18, 27
    0, 1 90
Decibels 257
Decomposition,
    into linear and non-linear compo-
        nents 342
    into linear and quadratic effects 120
Defect sum 52
Defects 136, 232, 239, 244, 246
Degrees of freedom 46, 170, 185, 187, 309,
    349
    additional three 348
    for error 160, 348
    for the factor 16
Design,
    direct product 309
    experimental 271
    multivariate 160, 169
    product 348

optimal 196
robust 309
sensitivity of the 311
Design of Experiments 37, 38, 54
Design selection 128
DISBK system 184
Disk drive 313
Distribution,
    heat-flux 191
    linear 192
    normal 296
    optimized 242
    transformer inductance 308
Drift 338
Dummy treatment 104, 348

E

Effects,
    average 65, 167
    exponential 197
    interactive 171, 283
    linear and quadratic 155, 160
    pure 167
    of factors 85
    of significant factors 35, 82
    of the mean 105
    of production variability 326
    random 344
    tolerance 274
Electrical circuit design 284
EMD,
    actuator assembly 313
    module 313
Emission control harness 73
Energy,
    of the process 18
    too much 15, 28, 146
    too little 15, 28, 146
    variability of 28
Energy transfer 95
Engineering 38
Engineer,
    product design 234
    design 318
Engineer's knowledge 216
Engineer's time 102
Error sum of squares 185, 274
Error variance ratio 321
Error,
    contribution of 191

estimate of 42, 54, 167
experimental 92, 225
pooled 47, 48
repetition 225
rounding 65
Estimated sample average 228
Estimation 23, 115, 239, 265, 276, 305
Experiment,
    conduct of 171
    cold starting 340
    design of 38
    follow-up 277
    fire-fighting type 37
    full factorial 208
    full production 238
    laboratory 238
    layout of 78, 94
    one-factor-at-a-time 87, 174, 217
    off-line 215
    response time 203
    utilizing an orthogonal array 38
    three level 232
Experimental,
    layout 16, 33, 128, 236, 248, 260, 301, 316, 339
    results 207
Experimentation,
    agricultural 54, 55
    ease of 42
    industrial 55
    multivariate 165
    one-factor-at-a-time 161
Extrusion 57

F

Factor effects 69, 65, 170, 213
Factor level averages 264
Factor levels, 108, 128, 136, 163, 285
    optimum 96, 157, 214
    selection of 15, 128, 157
Factorial effects (see Factor effects)
Factor interaction 317
Factors 33, 128, 219, 223, 236, 248, 260, 301, 316, 339
    allocation of 110
    affecting variation 18, 21, 23, 89 (see also Factors, significant)
    affecting the mean (see Factors, significant to the mean)
    control (see Factors, controllable)

control and noise 15, 76, 92
controllable 15, 16, 60, 92, 118, 139, 157, 181, 207, 271, 285, 286
environmental 89, 158
error 187
experimental 237
hardware related 208
hidden 159, 170
inside 77
insignificant to the S/N 235
noise 15, 55, 61, 76, 93, 105, 125, 136, 182, 271, 285, 286, 338
outside 76, 77
process 89, 317, 323
selection of 270
signal 60, 147, 226, 227, 271
significant 137
significant to the S/N 257, 233
significant to the mean 18, 23, 233, 257
software related 208
test 94, 96
that affect adhesion 27
that affect plating thickness 225
that affect shrinkage 162
that can adjust energy 147
to reduce variation (see Factors, affecting variation)
to shift the mean (see Factors, significant to the mean)
tolerance 317, 303
two-level 323
three- and four-level 348
whose levels are difficult to change 233
Failure mode 28, 313
Finite difference Solution 180
Fisher, R.A. 54
Fisher test (see F-test)
F ratio method 188
F-test 160, 167, 321
Full-factorial 109

G

Gain,
in variation reduction 229, 296
to society 172
Gold-plating thickness 220
Gold usage 229
Governing equations 178, 179

Graphs, (see Response graphs)

H

Han-yo gijutsu 331
Hot-stamping operation 127
Heat-flux 180, 182
Histograms 25

I

Idle column method 110, 120, 125
Implementation 325
Improvement, 131
after the study 118
in strip-force 256
by optimum production methods 98
in pull-out performance 98
in quality (see Quality improvement)
Infinity 29
Inner array 89, 182
Instrument panels 41
Interaction, 21, 34, 98, 100, 146, 323
between control factors 309
between loading and clearance 324
between electrode and time 94
between tubing preheating and material type 82
between two factors 349
duration x electrode gap 275
duration x electrode size 275
one-factor 271
with noise factors 90, 151, 309
Interactions, 36, 147, 280, 338
between control and noise factors 90, 151, 309
between inside and outside factors (see Interactions, between control and noise factors)
confounded 173
Dr. Taguchi's philosophy 333
even distribution of 216
factor 220
measurement of 318
one-factor 271
potential 33
Interwinding capacitance 293

K

ko-yu gijutsu 331, 334

L

Layout sheets 238
Level of significance 297
Levels,
    best 48
    control factor 44, 62, 208
    of factors 33, 76
    optimal 291
    significance 124
Lifter noise 335
Linear graphs, 209, 220, 272, 302, 309, 340
Linearity 57
Linear regression 342, 346
Linear relationship 58
Logarithmic,
    additivity 240
    function 211, 257
    scale 216
Loss, 133
    manufacturing 256
    per engine 349
    to the customer, 234
    to the supplier 234
Loss Function (see Quality Loss Function)

M

Macro-modeling 206, 207
Mean 101
Mean squares 47
Mean sum of squares 167
Means widely dispersed 233
Measurement,
    cost of 28
    feasibility of 28
    of tubing O.D. 62
    of response time 205
Micro-modeling 206
Microwave circuit boards 267
Model,
    analytical 197
    mathematical 197
    physical 177
    simulation 197
    three-dimensional heat transfer 197
    three-dimensional stress analysis 197
Modification 245
Monotonic 211
Multi-level arrangement 309, 340, 348
Multi-level technique (see Multi-level arrangement)

N

Nested factor experiment 125
Noise factors, (see also, Factors, noise)
    enhance the effect of a 296
    two-level 94, 296
    three-level 296
Noise,
    cold start 335, 339, 340
    domain 211
    valve train 342
Nominal-the-best,
    strategy for 27
Non-negative continuous variable 29
Nonlinearities 292

O

Objective function 211
Objective,
    of optimization 211
    of the experiment 14, 57, 108, 205, 235, 284, 299, 336
    of the study 107, 176, 295
    of using Taguchi Methods 177
Objectives,
    engineering 38
    of the development program 38
    of the experiment 41
Omega transformation 131
Operating window 278
Optimization, 33, 170, 214, 239, 255, 265, 271, 305
    approaches to 206
    circuit design 284
    for multiple characteristics 241
    hot-stamp design 130
Optimum condition 102, 255
Order,
    of convenience 211
    of experiments 54
Orthogonal array,
    L_4 (2^3) 302
    L_8 (2^5) 129, 132, 183, 260, 271
    L_9 78, 157, 160
    L_{12} (2^{11}) 42, 43, 54, 61, 174
    L_{16} (2^{15}) 33, 34, 94, 104, 164, 165, 173, 271

L_{16} ($8^1 \times 2^8$) 302
L_{16} ($4^1 \times 3^1 \times 2^8$) 332
L_{18} ($2^1 \times 3^7$) 16, 104, 136, 137, 160, 174, 183, 198, 209, 210, 216
L_{27} (3^{13}) 216, 249
L_{32} 340, 341, 348
L_{36} 198, 216
   modify 348
   three-level 104, 125
   role of the 38
Orthogonal arrays,
   larger 232, 266
   to prove interactions insignificant 217
   two-level 309
   Taguchi's use of 82
Orthogonality 210
Orthogonal nesting 110, 120, 121
Outer array 16, 89, 105, 183

P

Parallel-gap bonder 268
Parameter space 215
Parameters,
   disk-pad 177
   multi-level 283
   process 237, 239
   product design 237, 239
   that influence response time 206
   tool design 237, 239
Parts acceptance 131
Percent contribution 67, 167, 185, 188, 291, 321
Percent shrinkage 162
Performance gain 195
pH 233
Photoreceptor 235, 336
Pilot run 325
Plating,
   thickness 227
   time 233
Pooling 160
Post-extrusion shrinkage 162, 171
Pot-core transformer 299, 300
Pre-experiment 174
Prediction,
   formula for 170
   of the S/N Ratio 67, 170
   accuracy of 101
Principal function 28

Process average,
   adjusting the 227
   equation 240, 305
Process flow diagram 301
Process,
   cleaning 227
   control 131
   extrusion 58
   for producing GOP 32
   for outer covering 41
   heat-staking 13
   hot-forming 91
   sheet molded compound 37
   wave soldering 135, 147
   window 270
Product,
   development cycle 54
   development time 266
   plastic 54
Product/process development 233
Production run 325
Pseudo-factor method 124
Pull-off force 155
Push-out force 107, 108
Pull-strength 278

Q

Quadratic loss function 211
Quality,
   evaluation of 68
   visual 237
Quality characteristics, 42, 44, 60, 107, 108, 161, 236, 259, 270
   brainstorming to improve 216
   performance 240
   poor 90, 146
   multiple 239, 241
   other 233
   selection of 14, 232
   types of 146
Quality Engineering 256
Quality improvement 25, 27, 229, 242, 256, 308, 325, 347
Quality Loss Function 26, 42, 68, 70, 102, 133, 170, 172, 197, 309, 335
QLF (see Quality Loss Function)

R

Random order 220, 233
Random samples 164

Randomization 54, 55, 233, 272, 318
Ratio,
    of the mean squared to the variance 71
    of the slope squared to the variance 71
Reduction,
    in mean shrinkage 165
    of scrap/rework 27
Reliability 39, 136
Repetitions 47, 261, 272, 342
Replications 320
Reproducibility 125, 309, 326
Response graphs, 251, 305, 307, 313
    EEC holes 143, 144
    for control bridges 142
    for control holes 142
    interaction 276
    of significant effects 168, 169
    on average 226
    push-out force 112
    regular analysis 82
    S/N and Sensitivity 84
    S/N Ratio 51, 154, 157, 185, 275, 344
    time-to-quiet 345
    travel distance 112
    variation (gold-plating) 225
    voltage spike amplitude 293, 294
Response time,
    mean 211, 214
    standard 214
    reduction in 215
Response table,
    A x B interaction 99
    holes and bridges 140
    regular analysis 21
    S/N Ratio 98
Rework 235
Robust 39, 160
Roller tappet 337
Rotor 189

S

Sample size 25
Savings,
    additional 37
    annual 26, 37, 70, 117, 119, 234, 257, 309, 347
    financial 229
    per piece 70

    total 26
    yearly (see Savings, annual)
Sensitivity 72, 158
Shrinkage 164, 173
Signal-to-Noise Ratio, 39, 79, 105, 167, 193, 194
    difference in 309
    dynamic 62, 71
    equations for 71
    for bond strength 263
    for evaluation of EEC holes 137
    for pull-out loads 101
    for resistance 262
    larger-the-better 97, 155, 262, 272
    level mean 271
    maximize the 147, 322
    mean of 186
    nominal-the-best 71, 220, 250, 303, 304, 333
    plots 194
    predicted mean 276
    smaller-the-better 15, 49, 132, 165, 184, 246, 287, 342
Significant effects 99
Simplifying assumptions 206
Simulation, 198, 216, 287
    analytical 184
    results of 188
    results for each characteristic 281
Sliding levels 104, 280
Slope 72
Solder bridges and holes 136, 146
Speedometer Cable Casing 161
Stability 39
Statistical Quality Control 38
Statistical specialists 312
Strip force problem 247
Sum of squares, 47, 274, 321
    for the factor 167
    for the S/N ratio 185
Summary sheets 164
Supplier 335

T

Taguchi Methods,
    an efficient research method 38
    an iterative process 176
    benefits of 77
    in R & D applications 266

Technology,
    specialized 321
    universal 321
Technological understanding 28
Temperature differences 187
Test,
    heat-soak 162
    one-factor-at-a-time 326
    procedures 94, 96, 320
    samples, 327
    settings 223
    strategy 327
Thermal head-offset 312
Thermoplastic assembly 73
Thickness taper 181
Three sigma limits 296
Trade-off decisions,
    bond strength 265
    cost 291
Training 127
Travel distance 107
Tubing outer diameter 57, 58
Total,
    for a factor level 166
    for the experiment 168
    number of data points 168

U

Unassigned columns 342
Uncontrollable forces 146
UNIX operating system 204, 215

V

Vacuum harness 57
Vacuum valve 107
Valve train 336
Variability,
    between repetitions 266
    change in level 45
    of the pull-force 152
    of the process 45
    piece-to-piece 227
    sample-to-sample 232
    within sample 232
Variables,
    controllable 220 (see also Factors, controllable)
    continuous 55, 147, 348
    dependent 44

    extraneous 318
    independent 43
    significant 50
    statistically significant 220
Variance, 185
    estimate of 167, 187
    experimental 168
    within levels of variables 46
Variation ratio 185, 187
Variation,
    between repetitions 232
    in adhesive force 248
    of inductance 299
    of the error 188
    of response time 201
    pure 185, 187
VAX II-780 204
Vendor involvement 325
Visual appearance 270, 278
Voltage spike 284

W

Wave soldering 135
Weight, distribution 133
Weighted values 44
Wire-stripping machine 248
Worse-case,
    field conditions 340
    scenario 292

Y

Yield, 258, 270
    first run 136
    of tin-plated nickel strap 277